THE EDUCATION OF FREE MEN

THE EDUCATION
OF FREE MEN

AN ESSAY

TOWARD A PHILOSOPHY OF EDUCATION

FOR AMERICANS

BY

HORACE M. KALLEN

OF THE NEW SCHOOL FOR SOCIAL RESEARCH

FARRAR, STRAUS AND COMPANY · NEW YORK

370.1
K 125

Manufactured in the U. S. A. by
J. J. Little & Ives Company, New York

For

ROSE HAAS ALSCHULER
Whose Work with Young Children
Has Helped Develop at Its Foundations
The Art of Educating Free Men

CONTENTS

BY WAY OF PREFACE:—
WHAT IS FREEDOM AND WHAT ARE
THE SCHOOLS DOING ABOUT IT?

This book is a report of progress in an inquiry into the philosophy of education on which I have been engaged, now, more than a score of years.

Of course, every philosophy is, in one way or another, a philosophy of education. Even solipsistic systems are not produced as soliloquies but as communications. They would be neither expounded in classrooms nor printed in books unless they had been designed to persuade or convince others that what they say about the nature and workings of the universe, about our place in the scheme of it, and about our present role and ultimate destiny is accurate and reliable. Philosophers, like men of other vocations, assume in themselves an ability to teach, and in others a capacity to learn, that which man and nature truly are, what they are good for, and how these things may be surely known. The discipline which the philosophic profession calls "theory of knowledge" undertakes diversely to make those assumptions explicit. A philosophy of education but focuses philosophic appraisal on the sciences and arts of communication as these are involved in teaching and learning. It inquires into the goods of life that men strive to attain, the evils they labor to avoid or overcome; the faith, and the works with the tools, materials and methods resulting, by which the strivings and labors succeed or fail; how the old pass them on to the young; and how time and circumstance preserve or alter them.

Naturally, every such philosophy is itself an event at a time and in a place. It expresses some living man's responses to the culture in which he grew up and to the alternatives of belief and action that its religious, political, and technological economy confront him with. This economy may be as primitive as that of an Australian blackfellow or as sophisticated as a Boston Brahmin's. Primitive or otherwise, it will embody much remembrance of things past, all sorts of present problems and shapings of future hopes. The fulfillment or failure of the last may depend, perhaps wholly, on the transmission of the past unaltered, or on its transformation, by present thought through present action. A philosopher of education appraises the dynamic bearing of these options with respect to the past on the work of bringing the young to the maturity their culture defines for them.

For different societies, and different societies in different ages, employ different standards of maturity, composing of them personality-images into whose likeness they endeavor by education to shape their young. In every culture, the task of education is to realize the ideal of manhood it cherishes, its ideal and no other. Our own place and time has come to take the *Free Man* for its ideal and has drawn his lineaments from our faith in work and peace and our preoccupation with science and industry. Education in the modern world, especially the American area of the modern world, must needs be the education of free men.

Of course, the ideal of the free man and his freedom as the goal of education is, at least in phrase, no news in the world. Certainly it is no news among philosophers, for whom some concept named freedom is a vocational perennial. It is the novelty of our day's concept, its scope and consequences, that make the news. The crisis of our times, and the crisis of our education insofar as that is acute and not chronic, is the momentous option which modernity imposes between alternative meanings of the freedom of the free man. Treading with unsure feet a narrow ledge between the abyss of fatality and the precipices of fortune, with only his own wisdom and skill to preserve him from the foreordinations of the one and the uncertainties of the other, man has a choice to make between the alternative meanings of freedom that can well work out as a choice between mastery and drift, progress and stagnation, abundance and scarcity, even survival and extinction.

The meanings of freedom are many and diverse. They can be composed into two types. One conforms the multitude and variety of mankind into a simple, homogeneous human nature with an undifferentiated character and single destiny. It makes men indifferently interchangeable with one another and conformed in their true, indistinguishable equality to "the laws of nature and of nature's God." Their liberty is this conformation; all else is bondage. Another meaning of this type discriminates the multitude and variety of human beings into a hierarchical fixed order of caste and class, each determined by its God-given nature to a given status and degree in a progression of "thrones, dominations and principalities" from an ineffable high priest such as a pope or grand lama or emperor or king or other absolute monarch, through all the lower ranks and grades to the slave or serf decreed by God to be only "a tool with life in it." The freedom of each caste or class and of each individual composing it then resides in its un-questioning acceptance of its status and degree, its loyal submission and faithful service to the ranks above it, its unwavering warfare upon everything that would rebel against the established hier-archical order and disrupt its eternal and universal dispensation of faith and morals. For freedom is this order only, and unfreedom is whatever break in this order takes a man from the place where by nature he belongs and puts him in a place where by nature he does not belong, corrupting the fitness of things, confusing "the ends of life, the purposes of the state, and the order of goods," intruding satanic pride and rebellion into the universal and eternal harmony of creation.

The philosophers of antiquity who sought whatever freedom was, in their view, possible for man, found it in the conformation of his personal being to nature and nature's God-like rule. They were the Stoics and Epicureans of the disillusioned Hellenistic civiliza-tions. Their wisdom was tantamount to equating freedom with willing submission to the law of a nature or the authority of a ruler from which there could be no escape. Their freedom was resignation to the ineluctable compulsion. Early Christian philoso-phers reinterpreted this conception. As they regarded the human creature, he was by himself incapable of achieving the virtue of conformation which the pagan sages announced to be freedom. By nature he was corrupt with original sin which destined him to death. Salvation from this destiny could come to him only as miracle, as an ineffable free act of grace from the providence of a just yet merciful God. The precondition of the miracle of grace is an act of faith in defiance of reason, faith in the revelation of God's will to man, faith in the virgin birth, the death on the cross, and the resurrection from this death of God's only begotten son, whose crucifixion is vicarious atonement for man's original sin, and whose faithful are by their belief in that atonement saved from the doom which the sin imposes. The faith, Tertullian implied, was a saving faith precisely because it was a belief in the impossible in nature and the absurd in reason. It worked as an act of submission and obedience of impotent man to the revealed will of omnipotent God. Thus, if for the pagan sages, man is free by living according to nature and refusing to live according to man, he is free for the early Christian fathers by obeying God's commandments and disregarding the statutes of men: indeed, as ages later, rationalizers of the sacerdotal interest phrased it, "rebellion to tyrants could be obedience to God." For that matter, natural necessity as well as divine liberty could be and was invoked against social hierarchy and personal rule.

That such conceptions of freedom involved the assumption and use by both the pagan sages and the Christian fathers of an idea of freedom entirely at variance with the freedom they proposed as man's salvation is another story. The employment of this other idea of freedom sustained a paradox until the Democratic Revolution. It is a paradox shared also by the philosophers who succeeded the early church fathers as teachers of freedom to man, those who spoke amid the social economies that preceded the Democratic Revolution. They were the scholastics and the later rationalizers of priestly or royal pretensions. They made freedom the same as acquiescence in hierarchy, and hierarchy the same as the sacerdotal or secular embodiment of the good order of the universe and the will of God. They argued that no man could live according to nature and in obedience to God unless he lived where providence had placed him and devoutly kept intact the relations of the rank into which he was born with the ranks above and the ranks below. To know his place and keep it was his freedom, nor could he have any other.

Such, then, are the types into which freedom as conformity and submission divides. In one variety or another they survive the Democratic Revolution and are employed also by this day's hierarchical organizations of power. When such organizations make use of terms like "democracy," "progress," "liberalism," "free enterprise," "free conscience," they use them with meanings consistent only with the type of freedom they embody, preach, and support. When they affirm freedom of thought and expression, freedom of faith and worship, freedom from want and from fear, they give these freedoms meanings which conform them to the submission, obedience and hierarchy that is the substance of freedom to them. But the powers that so designate the substance of freedom are not themselves subject to its requirements. Being law-givers and not law-takers, their *de facto* freedom is of another kind. It is the kind that necessitarians and authoritarians in fact acknowledge whenever they suggest that man can do otherwise than he is doing, whenever they present alternatives of belief and action. It is the authentic and original liberty without which the liberty of submission and obedience cannot make sense.

Throughout history there have always been a few men privileged to exercise this initiating freedom, who have employed it to harness the equally authentic initiatives of the multitudes of other men to conformations with the doctrines and disciplines of their own preference; to identify their preferences with the laws of nature and the providence of God; and to claim that they were the privileged souls selected by nature and called by God to share with them the labors of government and creation. Their own freedom was thus freedom to rule, while the freedom of the multitudes was freedom to be ruled.

The Democratic Revolution turned on the recognition that the God-given freedom to rule is intrinsic and unalienable in all men, not in a privileged few only; that not the few, but all men are empowered by nature and called by God to share in the universal labor of government and creation. Only self-rule, hence, can be valid rule for democrats, and the claims of any society, religious or secular, to govern men are allowable only if they are expressions of self-government; the justification of its rule can be nothing else than the service it renders in sustaining and enlarging the equal rights of different human beings diversely to live and to grow in liberty and happiness.

The education of free men becomes thus the art of establishing these affirmations of the Democratic Revolution as a fighting faith and a habit of life and work. Its assignment is to incarnate the "American Idea" as the doctrine and discipline of the daily life. The man who perhaps first specifically designated the affirmations as the "American Idea" was probably the abolitionist, Theodore Parker. "There is," he told the Boston anti-slavery convention on May 29, 1850, "there is what I call the American idea . . . This idea demands, as the proximate organization thereof, a democracy —that is, a government of all the people, by all the people, for all the people; of course a government on the principles of eternal

justice, the unchanging laws of God; for shortness' sake, I will call
it the idea of Freedom." The earliest efficacious expression of this
idea was the American Declaration of Independence, which had
rung the trumpet call to equal liberty heard round the world. The
latest expression is the Universal Declaration of Human Rights
adopted by the Assembly of the United Nations Organization. Between the earliest and the latest the history of mankind takes form
on the gradient of an heroic unceasing sacrificial struggle for the
freedom and fellowship of different people *as* different, against the
tyranny of man over man in all forms of the human enterprise,
everywhere in the world. The ideal which directs and shapes the
struggle has received diverse expressions. All envision a world-wide
free society of free men liberated from want and fear, free to think,
to believe, to assemble, to speak and hear, to write and read, to produce or create or discover, and to exchange the fruits of their
thoughts and labors without let or hindrance, on equal terms. In
the undertaking of such a world, the task of liberal education has
been, and continues to be, overcoming the isolations of spirit and
flesh which tradition sustains; generating, by means of the arts and
sciences of free communication, mutuality of respect, understanding and sympathy among the different cultures of our civilization;
initiating such a habit of team play with the different that every
people, every culture, every individual of every people and culture,
experiences a greater fulfillment in freedom than by struggling on
alone. In a word, liberal education liberates by releasing the energies
of men through a union of the different on equal terms; liberal
education is thus hyphenation, and hyphenation is the art of dynamic civilization.

Unfortunately or fortunately, the answer to the question, *What
is liberal education?* is not completed with this. A school's acculturation of its pupils in the diversities of human life and thought
is not sufficient. It must needs impart also the matter and method
of division and of conflict as well as of co-operative union. Every
life, even the poorest and weakest, consists of the urges of many
passions, the requirements of many needs that work it into multitudinous relationships in the organization of ever more numerous
interests. A personality is the pattern which these relationships and
interests compose; its dynamic is their hyphenation, its life-story
is their orchestration. They may work in him as dissonance and

discord as well as harmonious union. Almost daily he finds his freedom engaged by a struggle between alternatives of action and passion that he would prefer to hold together in free concord on equal terms. And sometimes they become irreconcilable. If one is to go untrammeled, the other must be suppressed, if one is to be nourished and to develop, the other must be starved, perhaps perish. *Either, or* they demand of him, *choose!* In this situation, the hyphen expresses hierarchy instead of equality, separation instead of union, discord instead of harmony. When religions, cultures, industries or sovereign states find themselves in this situation, choice involves war. Inevitably, the education of free men must envisage the contingency of choices thus occurring and their bearing on equal liberty, alike in the ordinary affairs of the daily life, in personal crises, and in the crises of peoples and cultures.

Inasmuch as the Democratic Revolution established the faith that authentic liberty is inward to the nature of all men, our own time's actual as well as symbolic incarnation of this liberty is not one or another species of "élite" but the workingman free at last to learn the sciences and arts of living and by their means to recreate his existence from that of a freed man destroying his shackles, to that of a free man seeking the good life.

But the workingman is a workingman not by nature but by circumstance. The multitudes must work in order to live. Hence, our time has joined freedom with work as a right, and its ideal free man is the man of the multitudes who works. From the day he was born to the day he dies, this man will experience the urgency of labor toward liberty. His enduring task will be to deepen and enrich the liberty intrinsic to his original nature by patterning it in habits of thought and action which together make up an art of living. His biography will need to be the same thing as his education. His learning will need to be his living, his living will by nature be his learning. This is what his membership in a free, self-governing society of free men requires for the nourishment and growth of his freedom.

But no sooner is he entered in a school, than he learns that it erects a wall of separation between learning and living. His school instructs him that learning is not life but only preparation for life, that scholastic liberty is submission and obedience to pedagogic authority. At the same time it indoctrinates him in the precept that the liberty which is the American Idea consists in the practice of self-rule and self-service by men in the communion of a common enterprise. Needing and seeking the form of his own fulfillment in freedom, the contradiction which the school child thus experiences between doctrine and discipline, profession and practice, is enhanced by what he is taught of history. He soon comes to realize how arbitrary and unequal were the liberties monopolized by the privileged and authoritarian élite of the predemocratic past, and with what sadism such monopolies are guarded today in lands without democracy. Outside of the school, in the climate of opinion generated and sustained by science, democracy and the industrial arts, where today's workers, farmers, engineers, businessmen, manufacturers, traders and scientists live and move and have their being, the growing school child also encounters older types of certified personality. He notes the gentleman, the priest and the warrior, and he learns of their excellence from the literature of the past and the reverence and emulation they receive from the present. He comes to know them as the figures of freedom exalted from of old and approved and accepted as standards of human dignity and worth for today. The originals of some, he is instructed, are drawn from the records of the ancient Hebrews, of others from the Greeks or Romans or the mediaeval Europeans. Each has its singularity of authoritarian freedom. He notes also that alongside the tax-supported public school of his city or town, free to all its children, there is the segregated parochial school, isolating the children of the Roman Catholic culture from those of a different religious persuasion, and indoctrinating them in the liberty of submission and obedience essential to the upkeep of a sacerdotal hierarchy. He reads in addition of the similar segregation and isolation of the children of Soviet officials and functionaries in schools exclusively established for that purpose. He comes to know that in the countries of Europe and Asia and Africa and South America, there have been the Nazi and there remain, alongside the priestly organizations of priestly power, the communist, the fascist, the falangist educational establishments, all nullifying hyphenation and orchestration, all isolating instead of uniting, all imposing—each, of course, in its own way— authority as freedom, indoctrination as education; and by this method, making of the life-out-of-school and the school-life of the youth in their charge one continuous and consistent experience.

On the other hand, his own school, the free, tax-supported public school dedicated to education in the principles and practices of authentic freedom, at most only aspires to this mutual suffusion of learning and living, and achieves it rarely. His country's educational establishment is the most comprehensive, the most extensive, the most costly to the nation and least costly to the pupil in the entire world. Its given task is to confirm the nation's youth in freedom as faith and as works. Yet it has still not succeeded in freeing itself, on any level—whether the grade school or the university—from the rule and method of authority and in effecting a discipline of freedom in teaching and learning. This, although it has given rise to a science of education which provides a reliable ground for such a discipline, although it has available the records of a number of successful experiments in such a discipline, providing examples to emulate and improve upon. The essential attitude in school government persists. Frank Jewell expounded it in 1866 and it continues hardly modified to this day. "The teacher's authority as absolute," Jewell then wrote, "must be imperative rather than deliberative or demonstrative. His requirements and decisions, in whatever form presented, whether that of request, demand, or mandate, must be unargued. What he resolves upon and pronounces law, should be simply and steadily insisted upon as right *per se,* and should be fully and promptly accepted by the pupil as right, on the ground that the teacher, as such, is governor." The labors of the nation's great educational reformers, the Bronson Alcotts, the Francis Parkers, the Horace Manns, have somewhat mollified the imperative of this prescription. They have not, however, transvalued the judgment of right it expresses. Even John Dewey's pervasive influence has not succeeded in really upsetting that. The very position which a teacher occupies in the fixed hierarchy of a school system tends to preserve and enforce the pedagogic role of "governor" in the classroom. For the system entangles the teachers in a complicated network of rules and regulations that designate status, prescribe tasks, rates of progress, modes of communication with her superiors, to whose orders and inspections she is subject. This tends to make it her interest to please her principal, her supervisors, her assistant superintendents, her superintendent and her school board, rather than to enable her pupils eagerly and happily to learn whatever she is supposed to teach. It is not often that pleasing the higher-ups and learning by pupils become one and the same thing. The consequence is that the nation's schools are so pitted by inefficiencies and other bureaucratic evils, so distorted by pressures from all sorts of extra-mural interests that their educational achievement becomes a remarkable victory over unnecessary yet to the teacher inevitable handicaps. Their basic inadequacy resides, however, in the fact that the democracy they are designed to serve is served by an organization of doctrine and discipline which nullifies the democratic principle they are charged to communicate, to confirm and to extend. Throughout every level of the nation's school system we observe a class-war between teacher and pupil. High school and college are so organized and administered as to keep their students, most of whom are quite ready for self-rule and social responsibility, in a state of supervised infantile irresponsibility. In the esteem of most communities, the vocation of teaching is segregative, it deprives the teacher of the full civic liberties that other occupations enjoy, it imposes on her a strict habit of life and speech and taste, a superlative respectability, which should be an example to the youth in her charge. Yet precisely because of these requirements the common image of the teacher is the comic, impractical, sexless *schoolmarm*.

Again, the nation's faith in democracy's need of educated citizens is such that it makes the college education in the arts and sciences available to practically everyone who wants it and is able to benefit by it; the college population of the United States is the greatest in the world and is likely to become greater. Yet here, again, democratic doctrine and collegiate discipline look in opposite directions. What can the course of study of the college classroom provide if the mores continue it mainly as the price college students pay for the amenities of "college life"? Academic actuality tends to defeat academic intention. Traditionally, the liberal education is the education befitting the free man; under democracy it becomes the education which heightens and extends the arts of freedom for free society. But the free man of tradition was the member of a privileged élite in an unfree society. He was a gentleman of leisure, an embodiment of "culture and refinement" living his life in sport, literature and the arts, or perhaps the "learned professions" of law, religion, or medicine. He could be "disciplined"—that is, if he liked—in the trivium and quadrivium and the humanities as in horsemanship, fencing or tennis. But what provides the discipline

of a free man in a free society who must earn his living before he
can live his life? who soon or late, therefore, studies to be a chemist
or an engineer, or a merchant or an accountant, a plumber or a
carpenter, or a teacher or an archaeologist or a garbage collector?
How shall his education relate earning his living to living his life
so that his freedom is enhanced and not diminished? To earn his
living, he must work by day, producing goods and services for others
to consume. To live his life, he has the leisure of the night, when
he consumes the goods and services others produce. His day life
is the exercise of his vocation; his night life is his experience of
culture, as the table, sport, music, the theatre, the church, literature, the graphic and the plastic arts are presumed to constitute
culture. What must the education of the free man needs provide,
to bring back to fruitful union the day life and night life, production and consumption, vocation and culture which the economy of
our industrial civilization continues to put asunder?

Such are the inquiries into education to which this book addresses
itself, in the context of the situations that have rendered the problem of the education of free men the most imperative of our age.
Pursuing my research, I have had inestimable light and leading
from the observations and judgments of more than a generation of
students at the New School, from students of occasion at Ohio
State University and the Claremont Graduate School of Claremont
College in California. My debt to colleagues, particularly to Alvin
Johnson and John Dewey and Sidney Hook, stands out on every
theme, mostly so, perhaps, where my judgments depart from theirs;
I cannot sufficiently signalize what I owe to them. Or what I owe to
my wife Rachel Kallen, for her patient endurance the long while
this book was being written, her wise comments drawn from a long
experience as mother, and as teacher and principal of a progressive
private school, and of her help with the manuscript and proofs. To
all, my best thanks.

Some of the matter included in this book has been printed before,
either in articles or as pamphlets. All of that, however, has been
revised or entirely rewritten in the light of the changed and changing terms of the problems of education for freedom and freedom for
education.

HORACE M. KALLEN

The New School for Social Research
September 10, 1949

ACKNOWLEDGMENTS

The author wishes to thank the following publishers and copyright owners for permission to quote from their publications:

The Christian Century, for excerpts from "Spoiling a Good Case," 1940.

Harcourt, Brace and Company, Inc. for excerpts from *The Autobiography of Lincoln Steffens,* 1931; Carl Sandburg, *The People, Yes,* 1936.

Harvard University Press, for excerpts from Edward Thorndike, *Man and His Works,* 1943.

Alfred A. Knopf, Inc. for excerpts from William Healy, *The Individual Delinquent.*

Dr. John K. Norton for excerpts from a study released by the Institute of Church and State.

Dr. Howard E. Wilson of the Carnegie Endowment for International Peace, for excerpts from his address on "The University and Its World Responsibilities."

In reply to the request to the publishers of *A Manual of Christian Doctrine,* for permission to quote from it, the Director of that concern, the La Salle Bureau, wrote as follows:

> It seems to me that *for this date and for the United States* the author of "The Education of Free Men" Horace M. Kallen would do better to consult the recently published, A CATHECHISM OF CHRISTIAN DOCTRINE, No. 3., St. Anthony Guild Press, Paterson, N. J. Lesson 19, Question 243-248, Copyright 1949.

The italics are the author's.

The *Manual* has the imprimatur of Archbishop Dougherty; it has gone through scores of editions: it has not been officially withdrawn. The new catechism differs from it in content—at least so far as concerns Questions 243-248—by teaching the sacerdotal rule of the relations of church and state with much greater reserve. It leaves a great deal unsaid. But what is kept in neither contradicts nor nullifies what has been left out, nor does it in any sense modify the sacerdotal claims to special privilege and support. What the rewritings do suggest, together with the reluctance of Catholic publishers to have their publications quoted, is a certain anxiety over the fact that the authentic Catholic demands on state support are receiving widespread public attention.

Book I

THE SCHOOL AS INSTITUTION

Chapter One

"CRISIS"

During more than a generation our times have been felt, also educationally, as times that try men's souls. Educators' sense of crisis began in the Great Depression. It has since deepened and broadened. Neither World War II nor its consequent struggles for peace have diminished the scope or diffused the drive of this monitory mood. Flowing from the experiences and studies of teachers, and of teachers of teachers, it spread to administrators, thence to local and regional school boards, to the power-holders in colleges and universities, to state authorities and federal agencies, until at last it moved the presidency itself.

Each group, as it became aware of the mood's urgency, took, in its domain, one or another measure of appeasement. Plants were enlarged and improved; curricula were changed; vocational training was made a prime concern of the federal government; requirements of teacher education were stiffened; schools were multiplied; in older academic establishments new institutional units were set up while elsewhere new colleges were founded to serve new educational aims. Adult education was made into a major educational interest.

Up to December 7, 1941, the number of Americans engaged in one or another form of study kept steadily mounting. World War II was an interlude which obstructed the trend but diminished neither it nor the sense of crisis. War necessities but for the time diverted the nation's energies and resources. When the shooting stopped, education became an even more momentous concern of the public interest. The war had simply re-enforced the feeling of crisis with the facts of physical deterioration. Plants had been left in disrepair. Teachers had turned from teaching to occupations they believed to be more relevant, knew to be better paid and felt to be more respected. But at the end of the war, government enabled every soldier who had earned an education and wanted one, to become a student. At all levels of the educational establishment enrollments mounted. Since 1945 the number of students in colleges and universities has almost doubled,

3

and the ratios in high and elementary schools correspond. Yet teachers, buildings, school equipment, dormitories have sharply diminished.

In view of the trend, the President had appointed, in the summer of 1946, a Commission on Higher Education to "re-examine our system of higher education in terms of its objectives, methods and facilities; and in the light of the social role it has to play." The Commission looked to about twice the present number of students in colleges and universities by 1960. The National Council on Education had come independently to a similar conclusion. The doubling of numbers would bring with it, of course, a corresponding increase of enrollment in elementary and high schools. To repair the damages of deterioration, to render plant and personnel adequate to need, would cost immense sums which no private purse could produce. The education, now not of youth only, but of the entire American people, while remaining as it must, a prime responsibility of the community and of the state, would also need to become a first charge among the other obligations of the federal government. The whole nation would need to redress the educational balance so long uneven because some states were too poor to provide adequate education for their numerous youth, while others, with too few young, were rich beyond their generous needs. The whole nation should have to see to it that no state shall penalize itself and the entire American people by providing less than equal educational opportunity to those of their children whose skins were black or yellow, or whose religions were different from the dominant one, or whose parents were not native-born or not rich enough to afford them the schooling that could nourish and enlarge their powers, or who were discriminated against merely because they were women. As government must conserve and liberate, *for* the general welfare, the nation's natural resources, so the more must it conserve and develop, *as* the general welfare, the nation's human resources. In talent, in power, in intelligence, young America, the experience and studies of World War II have shown, comes at least twice as far as the pundits of education assumed and the schools admitted. Moreover, in what concerns the installations of the educational establishment, the American people were both able and desirous of meeting the bill.[1] The material needs could be served, with assurance and ease. The paramount urgency was not in these, nor would supplying them relieve it.

The paramount urgency was in the thrust of conflict over the *why* and *what* and *how* of the nation's schools, conflict that is always chronic and every so often is made acute. All the parties to the conflict were apparently agreed that the aim of education must be the freedom of men. But their views of the nature and conditions of freedom, of its methods and instruments could hardly be reconciled.

Of the embattled sects, one claims an ancient lineage which looks back to the very beginning of the debate over education in ancient Hellas. Its "free man" is a man with a "liberal" education. He has been disciplined to the "liberal arts," indoctrinated in universal and eternal principles of being and doing which "the humanities" exemplify and which certain philosophies promulgate. His education consists in a conformation to this discipline and doctrine, and his freedom is submission to their rule. Other sects repeat this idea of freedom in other ways. But all of them tend to assume that the present but repeats the past and the future brings nothing new that education need bother with. There is, they assert, a "Great Tradition." This tradition is a continuum, through which the eternal and universal comes to expression. Its unity gives whatever significance may accrue to the less noble interests which preoccupy less noble sects; in education the issue of the moment, thus, must be the issue of forever. What else, then, can the theme of education be but this unaltering and inalterable heritage, man's Great Tradition beside which the vulgar differentiations that in fact constitute both tradition and history can be only illusions and irrelevancies that tradition exposes and explains away?

The companions of this faith had long held the nation's educational establishment in fief. They were its aristocracy, and the prestige of their doctrine and discipline throughout the American school system seemed overruling and unchallengeable. Practically up to World War I, innovations in any curriculum, additions such as the sciences, natural or social, manual arts, the commercial dis-

---

[1] Cf. Report No. 21, National Opinion Research Center, University of Denver.

ciplines, agriculture, pedagogy, engineering, were made timidly, apologetically. However important they might have become in the orders of doing and having, in the order of prestige, pupils, teachers and parents long took them for studies and attainments of the second class. Nevertheless, they so increased and multiplied, that in the economy of the nation's schools the aristocracy of the educational establishment found itself shifted from the center to the periphery of studious concern. For many years its spokesmen continued complacent, hardly aware of their dislocation. But in due course, the import of the event was brought to the nation's attention by philosophic utterance. Its actual dynamic was defined, and its ideal implications were clarified.

This new philosophy envisaged education in terms of democracy and democracy in terms of the ways that free human beings in fact live and work together. Instead of deducing life and labor from doctrines and rules, this philosophy explained how doctrines and rules were devised to enhance life and enfranchise the worker. It showed how freedom and friendship are, both as philologic fact and social history, growths of a common root. Since the free man is an independent man, a man self-directing and sovereign, he is a man whose thinking and judging and doing, whose choosing and deciding, do not follow from the coercions of authority and are not held subject to another's will. His relations with the other grow from their equal liberty. The two are friends and not fiends when in their living and working together each feels "free and easy" in the presence of the other, each promotes the welfare of the other, each enhances the other's safety, happiness and growth. Both vary and change within. Both know how to take the changes of fate and the chances of fortune from the world not made for them, with their independence unweakened and self-rule unshaken. Democratic society is thus the society of friends. Democratic law is the organization, and democratic government the facilitation, of that equal liberty.

Education, this new philosophy then urged, if it is to be the education of free men in a free society, must be less concerned with merely transmitting and repeating the past, and more with appraising and changing it toward ever greater freedom and friendship of people, whatever their origins, status, faith, sex or occupation. Education must knock away the traditional wall between "preparation for life" and the actualities of living. The purely artificial and dangerous boundaries between learning and living must be abolished, the inevitable give and take between school and society must be relieved of obstructions; communication between them must be made open, continuous, and free. Education so conceived and implemented is able to mobilize the body's powers and its biological development as an ally and not a foe of the growth of the mind. Instead of laboring to coerce evolutionary plasticity into some final rigidity, education will aim to conserve and to nourish this power to learn, that is, to change and grow, to the day a man dies.

With the publication in 1916 of John Dewey's *Education and Democracy,* that in the American school which had been, for the most part, automatic adaptation, became conscious aim. A "progressive education" movement undertook to realize words in works. Its fortunes between the world wars are of record, and I shall have more to say about them later. Now it is relevant to record that the movement, self-recruited from parents and teachers and teachers of teachers, expressed the reaction of these volunteers to the chronic crisis in American education. By making it conscious they tended to render the crisis acute.

Whether by itself the movement could have brought the issue to its currently intense stage is far from sure. Other forces contributed, and their role may have been more critical. These arose in the Roman Catholic establishment. Between the two world wars the theory and practice of Roman Catholic education, especially as conducted by the Jesuits, came into the foreground of discussion. The hierarchy of that cultus was figuring more and more as an active power in the national economy, and forcefully pushing its claim to prerogatives in the American educational enterprise. It brought unexpected but welcome allies to the non-Catholic soldiers of traditionalism. The latter were now enabled to join Thomas Aquinas to Aristotle and to Plato in their insistence that authoritarianism in the schools prepares men for freedom in the world. They might also have added Stalin, Hitler and Mussolini, but they denied themselves.

The activities of those prophets of liberty, however, their uses of doctrines and disciplines which should conform children growing up into undeviating believers of their respective faiths, contributed to the deepening of the educational crisis. Protestant clergy urged

that it could be assuaged if the nation's schools allowed for religious education by each of the many denominations, and Catholic
authorities confirmed their argument. But the struggle, in effect
aspiring to restore to Protestant ecclesiastical interest the privileges
it had once held in education and to secure assent to the always
reaffirmed Roman Catholic pretensions to exclusive possession of
such privileges, only sharpened the crisis, bringing the issue at last
to the Supreme Court of the nation. Articles on the rights and
wrongs of education for freedom appeared in the public prints in
legions; books came from the press in battalions; radio addresses
roared in cataracts.

And all the time the global conflicts worsened. At home and
abroad apparent friends of freedom revealed themselves as actual
foes. More central than ever, as one directive for the national economy, became the American Idea that being a citizen is not less a
vocation for every man than being a machinist or a carpenter or a
mason or a doctor or a farmer or a clergyman or a plumber are
vocations for any man. The feeling spread that unless the people
of the land have studied out and have learned the *know-how* of
dealing with the common, everchanging problems of the nation, the
commonwealth of free men cannot be safe, nor can a world of such
commonwealths be attained.

Since men are not born with this *know-how,* it is the American
Idea that education can and must provide it. The more diversified,
industrial, richer and powerful grows a nation's inner structure,
the greater becomes its need of an educated citizenry. The more
numerous, varied and complex the nation's contacts with the rest
of the world, the more imperative it is that all its people shall
understand the *how* and *what* and *why* of these contacts. In the
new times which the expression "atomic age" connotes, adequate
education is the first and last insurance of the nation's continuing
to grow as a free society. More than ever before in mankind's history, knowledge is power. More than ever before in this history, the
greatest danger to the peace and liberty of the world is the monopoly of this power by a privileged few. As never before, the first
line of defense of the freedom and safety of the peoples of the
earth is the widest possible distribution of the power which is
knowledge.

The channels of this power, the argument continues, are all the arts, fine as well as industrial, which apply the sciences of man and nature to the liberation of life everywhere. The doctors, the doctrines and the disciplines of the Great Tradition were after all singular events of specific moments of the tradition. On the record, the many centuries during which the schools rehearsed and adored them were neither wiser nor more virtuous than the few generations which prefer Newton or Einstein to Aristotle, Jefferson to Plato, John Dewey to Thomas Aquinas. In most respects those older times were far more wicked and far less understanding. No élite could have been more completely disciplined in the classics and in Plato than the German élite of the past hundred years. And what did they find in Plato if not that education must employ "noble falsehoods," lies royal and audacious, that must work, first, through indoctrination in doctrines according to which the wicked are never happy, the good never miserable, the gods never wicked, the foreigner never the equal or superior of the native; and again, through a discipline of toil, pain and conflict aimed to create steadfastness in the face of the sufferings and fears, the pleasures and enchantments to which the doctrines at the same time deny any reality. To insure him against corruption no citizen should be permitted to travel before the age of forty or ever to look upon stage imitation of artisans or of any other beings whom Plato classifies as "inferiors." If a citizen spoke irreverently of the gods his punishment would begin with imprisonment and end with execution. Totalitarian countries have known how to profit by the Platonic instruction.

When the spirit of man reverts to this or to some other utterance of authoritarian reassurance, it does so at times when the tempo of living has been speeded up, when the structure of society is loosening and reshaping, when its members evince the feeling that their existence is precarious and their survival doubtful. In such times men and women compensate for the insecure mobility of the actual by imagining an ideal order at once coherent, unmoving, certain and safe. They call this creature of their imagination "reality" and the events of their experience "appearance." And they compose of this "reality" the doctrine and discipline of their salvation. So it was with Plato. So it is with his imitators and emulators of the twentieth century.

A certain irony attends the recurring situation, and has attended

it from those days in Athens when teaching changed from an un-
critical customary activity, in which every member of the community shared, into a special vocation of paid professionals, who
got a bad name for it. Those were the days of Pericles and Sophocles and Socrates and Aristophanes and the Sophists. As soon as
education, because of the activities of the Sophists, was recognized
as an independent variable with an identity of its own, it was made
an object of controversy. Theories were devised about its powers,
methods and uses, many of which Plato attacks, one of which he
champions. The debate's social result seems to have been as dramatic as M. Jourdain's discovery that he had been talking prose
all his life.

Readers of Aristophanes and of Plato will recall that the sore
point was less the fact that the Sophists were professionals teaching
for pay, than that they had introduced a new *method,* a method
which opposed cross-examination and dialectic to simple assent and
dissent, and argumentation to simple repetition. By general consent
Socrates was the champion user of this new method. Plato presents
him as the infallible victor in practically every debate; Aristophanes, as the master of the new learning which undermines the
authority of the old order to the point where a son may beat his
father, shouting: "Am I not as freeborn as you!" The scene occurs
in *The Clouds,* and the Chorus chants a comment upon that
father,

> Too late he'll curse the Sophist School
> That taught his son to cheat by rule
> And turned the modest life of youth
> In the vile art of torturing truth;
> A modern logic much in use
> Invented for the law's abuse,
> A subtle knack of spying flaws
> To cast in doubt the clearest cause
> Whereby, in honesty's despite
> The wrong side triumphs o'er the right.

In their libel on the Sophists, Aristophanes and Plato were attacking the force which the vested interest of their caste and station
most feared. The arts of oratory and argumentation and the dialectic underlying had become the most potent weapons in the
arsenal of Athenian democracy. But weapons, as is well known,
serve impartially all combatants, and it was the achievement of

Plato and Aristotle to apply the ratiocinative instrument to the vindication of birth, privilege and status. They added dialectic to the older Aristophanic curriculum of "virtue." Virtue, in their conception, is the vocation of the "free man" or citizen. Dialectic, devised as a tool of inquiry, deliberation and judgment, became now the preferred engine of indoctrination and regimentation, the equivalent of reason, and a major "liberal art."

Later ages, in acute phases of crisis, turned from dialectic to revelation, and still later ones back again from revelation to dialectic. Until the growth of the sciences brought in an entirely different understanding of the organs and tools of knowledge, of their nature, their workings and their consequences, education rang the changes on dialectic and revelation.

Since then, every change in the configurations of free society appears to have pressed the weight of interest toward extending, improving and varying these innovations. The transvaluation goes on slowly and in fact is not so extensive as is commonly believed, especially in the nation's schools. There, the resistances due to natural inertia came in the course of time to be justified as well as re-enforced by traditionalism at last awake to its insecurity. Upon the basic philosophies of traditionalist and progressive, changes are being rung. Essentialist and scholastic, humanist and vocationalist, joined their voices to the debate. Theorists complained of "scientism." Instead of "liberal education" they argued about "general education." From the definition of the goals and tools of education, and the construction of curricula thereby implied, controversy spread to the nature of teaching and the role of the teacher, the nature of learning and the relation of teaching to learning. Then it was carried to issues of the status of teachers and pupils in the school as an organized society, and of the meaning of the school, as experience of a social order, for the works and ways of a free society. Each such issue added its heat to the idea of crisis. Controversalists not of one sect alone, endeavoring to envisage the nation's entire educational establishment and the forces at play in it, reported a disorderly multiplicity of organizations, deplored the absence of a common aim. If they were the aficionados of a certain philosophy of life, a certain conception of the nature and destiny of man, they offered their philosophy as the end and means of unification. If they referred to freedom, they argued that it should be ever a means and never an end, apparently unaware that they thus demoted freedom to serfdom. That what seemed to them disorder might be to others the mobile, yet orderly association of the free, was not dreamt of in their philosophies; nor did their faith imply that what they called aimlessness could, on examination instead of by deduction, turn out to be the diversifications which ensue where freedom is the aim. A free society of free men is a society diverse and diversifying in its faiths, its occupations, its arts, its sciences, its government, its entire political and cultural economy. In so far as it is a society of friends, it is an orderly society. This holds whether the society is a church, a bank, a factory, a laboratory, a legislature or a school.

Although, in point of fact, the nation's schools are far more traditionalist, authoritarian, and hierarchical than traditionalism is willing to concede, they have moved forward. Nor, during the forty years' growth since the turn of the century, is their progress alone the effect of new events calling for new adjustments. The schools have advanced notably, also as a result of expert scientific inquiry—psychological, political, economic, managerial, and the like—into every component of the educational enterprise; and in the direction of ever clearer understanding of freedom as an aim and of the uses of freedom as a means to freedom.

Hence, for our democracy, the chronic crisis in the schools is not so acute as those who have sharpened it would like to believe. However piecemeal, however lumberingly, the nation's educational establishment *is* making progress toward democratization within and toward fruitful relations to democracy as a way of life, without. Teachers and administrators have available, as never before, a body of reliable knowledge, gained and tested by the methods of scientific inquiry, concerning human beings as learners and as teachers, and how the two may work together in growing friendship. Checking this knowledge by its consequences in application goes on continually, an experiment here, a program there, in regions of the country as diverse as California and Iowa, New York and Illinois, Tennessee and Michigan. It is true that the democratic way which has room for such untraditional procedures has even more room for their traditional and newer opposites, with all the powers of prestige and the forces of inertia that support them. In free society progress toward any goal, including the goal of growth in freedom, must be, in the nature of things, local, piece-meal, clumsy and slow.

But the time comes when the men and women diversely engaged in any undertaking, if they have freely discussed with one another their purpose, their ways of working and the results they work out, find themselves in an agreement which is neither the result of a vote taken nor a compromise arranged. It is a consensus that has grown from the competitive co-operation and co-operative competition whereof free discussion consists. The process which consensus consummates is such that no participant is coerced, and each has the same liberty as the others to enter his own theory and practice in the many-way flow of ideas. The history of education in the United States—the sharp conflicts of parties and principles not-withstanding—records also movement toward a consensus of this sort. The very citadels of traditionalism are known to make use of such untraditional findings as modern psychology and other natural sciences; while institutions on the very frontiers of educational enterprise find plenty of use for the approved disciplines of the tradition. The latter does move toward modern liberty. Progressives do evince a filial care for the past.

Those who argue that such unions of the diverse are disorderly, confused and illogical are often able to prove it logically. But relationships which hold together the freely joined parts of such wholes have a tensile strength and a flexibility beside which the strictly logical and purely rational unions turn out to be weak and brittle. If such confluences of the diverse move clumsily, not all at once nor equally fast, perhaps these traits are unalienable to the democratic way, and the price of its lasting stability. Certainly this appears to be the situation with the nation's schools, from kindergarten to university. Varied in size and quality as they are, they do somehow spontaneously form a system, part voluntarily interrelated with part, and the whole evincing the conflicts, the tensions, the paradoxes—often more obviously than the team play—which are common to unions of the diverse. True, educational practice rarely realizes educational principle; true, there are sharp, perhaps, inescapable, struggles between teachers and administrators, pupils and teachers; true, there are caste distinctions between teachers, and school systems often negate in performance the freedom they affirm in precept. But it is also true that there are units in the establishment which do exemplify the discipline, even as they teach the doctrine, of democratic freedom. And because this freedom is the nation's professed goal and guide, the works and ways of these units tend, on the record, to pervade and to alter all in education which is not consonant with them. Without planning, they realize a plan. Whatever be the resistances and countermovements, the units are, in any secular perspective, liberalizing "liberal education," humanizing the "humanities," and restoring culture to vocation.

We turn now to an inspection of the nation's schools as an institution intended to achieve the education of free men in a free society, and to an interpretation of its faith and works, of their failures and successes, and of the philosophy upon which they are postulated.

Chapter Two

THAT EDUCATION HAS BECOME BIG BUSINESS

It is a truism of the modern world that free men must be educated men, and that a free society is a society of educated men. Although a consequence of the Democratic Revolution everywhere in the world, the truism is one of the first articles of the American faith, and one of the most dynamic in the works and ways of the American people. In the United States education has become big business, with a structure and function no less institutional than those of the religious establishments. The Union of Soviet Socialist Republics of Russia is said to spend 7.5 per cent of the national income on education; the present government of the United Kingdom is said to be planning an expenditure of 3 per cent; the United States is spending only 1.5 per cent. But in flat sums of dollars and cents, this 1.5 per cent may be exceeding the total of all of Europe. However critics may appraise the nation's educational establishment, it is, taken on the whole and in the long run, the most extensive, the most varied, the most deeply founded and the most flexible in the Western world, and its economy is an expanding economy.

The American people are the pioneers in tax-supported, free public education, from the kindergarten to the university and beyond. True, their achievement is very uneven, as uneven as the development of the several states which compose the Federal Union. In one state, a school may be an ancient log cabin put together any which way, with planks across tree stumps for seats, boxes and barrels for desks, an inadequate not too healthy girl for the teacher of youths from five to eighteen years of age. In another state a school may be a complex structure whose form, arrangements and furnishings have been expressly designed to serve and to enhance the activities of teaching and learning; the teachers may be persons who have spent long years in studying how to teach as well as what to teach.

Between such extremes the educational establishments of the different states can be arranged in an order of excellence and cost. The two are usually but not necessarily members of one another.

The differences from state to state will go with differences in economic development, in folkways, mores, social and occupational diversification, community leadership and organization. These differences form culture-complexes characteristic of the locality and region. They produce an atmosphere, a climate of opinion, a spirit, and they exert an imponderable but definite and practically irresistible pressure upon the organization, the labors and goals of the educational plant. The more industrialized, the more urban the community, the more specialized will be its school buildings; the less will its furnishings and other equipment resemble those in common use in homes and public places. The educational plant in which youth is being prepared for life will impress an innocent bystander as being an environment very, very different from the home, the workshop, the places in which youth does live and grow.

Such specialization of the educational plant appears to vary, on all levels, with the size and industrialization of the communities whose schools they are. To begin with school architecture: Its point of departure is the Gothic building or the colonial meeting house of the religious sects whose functionaries served as teachers when education was a monopoly of the churches. Gothic or Georgian exteriors keep being reproduced even when interiors are functionally correct. That they should crop up in private establishments with denominational backgrounds is not surprising. Universities such as Princeton, Chicago, Yale, Duke (which houses females behind Georgian and males behind Gothic façades), Harvard, employ such traditional if otherwise irrelevant exteriors. But they are used for façades also of public establishments such as the College of the City of New York, of many public high schools and the like. School architecture which suits outer form to the function and use of the building is still rare. It is, however, definitely on the way. Essentially, in any urban public school system, at the base of form is the function of routing large numbers of the human young from one room to another in the course of a long, long day, divided into short periods of movement and longer periods of restlessness called study or recitation. Layout, interiors, lighting and equipment are conformed to these activities. Even in progressive schools will be found contraptions which are like nothing else in this world or the world to come. For example chair-desks, with seats presumably suited to the occupant's body, and tables to its materials and hands, the whole a movable unit not easy for a child to move. Add to these implements the needful blackboards, the textbooks, the maps, the geometric models and the other instruments of instruction. Then imagine this well-furnished schoolroom alongside any room in the home where a child lives its life. The former no more resembles the latter than does a floor in the factory where the child's father might be earning his living.

This specialization of plant and equipment is no small factor in the high cost of modern education. Indeed, it is greater than the cost of the corresponding specialization in the vocation of teaching. But that these have a necessary connection with the prevailing convention regarding the function and uses of teaching is not established. As an institution, the nation's school system possesses an individuality of its own, and a pattern of growth singular to itself. Its existence seems to consist in a process of inwardly regulated diversification and reordering. Alike as a material economy and a cultural organization it achieves a corporate character, a group-personality of its own, and tends toward always greater self-sufficiency and self-rule. The process is swiftest and most comprehensive in free societies such as date from the Democratic Revolution. Only, however, during the last fifty years, did the inner diversifications and their compounding develop mass and momentum. This heightening appears to have been concurrent with the new industrial levels attained by the national economy, the lift in the standard of living and the resurgent concern over the democratic idea. In cities, indeed, the new schools often suggested definite analogies with manufacturing plants operating by means of highly specialized machinery for the purpose of producing a particular sort of commodity. This appearance did not, however, make so deep an impression as the school system's trend toward independence and self-rule. The prominence of the latter was a consequence of certain widespread attitudes, social and political, which distinguish the modern from the unmodern mind.

What are these attitudes? How did they come to be? How do they differ from those of the unmodern mind? The latter are by no means of the past. They have lost little of their power. They appraised education in the light of the philosophy of life which gave these attitudes their articulate expression. Education, in this philosophy, could not be an institution existing and entitled to exist as "by inherent and unalienable right"; it had to be a hand-maiden, an accessory after the fact of other, master institutions to whom it must minister. The teacher, in this philosophy, is not first, last and always a teacher, whose entire vocation is to teach; the teacher is first and best a priest, a lawyer, a physician, a soldier, with whom teaching could be only a secondary and tangent interest. The school, in this philosophy, can be but a pendant to the church, the shop, the field, the battlefield. But it held shop, field and battlefield to be incidental and church paramount. For was not every pupil an immortal soul born in the sin whose wages is death, by nature given over unto wickedness, and requiring for its eternal salvation to be indoctrinated in grace, and disciplined into virtue? Shaped by this attitude education could not educate save as it corrects. Its task was to remold a child's corrupt original nature on earth so that it might grow up and grow old and die in order to live happily ever after it is dead, in heaven; if it failed to learn or the educator failed to teach, it could but live miserably ever after in hell. To spare the rod, hence, would be to spoil the child. The instruction of youth could not but be the charge of the church, nor the school but the church's instrument.

Because of this philosophical faith and the ways and works which it grounded and rationalized, all schooling had to be churchly indoctrination, and most of our schools and colleges began their careers as denominational establishments, whose aim was to circumvent "the one chief project of that old deluder, Satan." [1] The secularization of school and college is the consequence of a still unended bitter struggle with acute and chronic phases. Toward the middle of the eighteenth century, the intellectuals of the Western world had come to agree that mankind was certainly not born corrupt; that if human nature was not necessarily good, neither was it necessarily evil. They had come to see that values and facts could alike be learned without tears; that in view of how men learn, it was folly to seek to beat sin out or virtue in. John Locke, the philosopher of the second English revolution, gave this new appraisal of human nature its first telling statement. But it was that child of original sin and predestination, Calvinist-bred Franco-Swiss Jean Jacques Rousseau, who made it conscious, dramatic and persuasive.

---

[1] Enactment of the General Court of Massachusetts, 1647.

Not only his *Émile,* but all his expression, underlined his assurance that the dogma of man's inborn wickedness is a false dogma and that education has more to do with goodness and wickedness than has nativity. Let schools and teachers, he urged, cease to constrain and starve a child's spontaneous impulses; instead of damming them up, let them devise ways and means for their orderly free play! Let them put kindness in the place of harshness, and motivate learning by the hope of satisfactions and rewards instead of the fear of hungers and penalties.

From this seed has grown the new educational lore which makes up the theory and practice of education in our time. There is little in current psychologies of teaching and learning, in current philosophies of human relations, which is unimplied by the insights of Rousseau and the programs of Pestalozzi and Froebel. From these pioneers of the Enlightenment to our own pioneers of the democratic way in education, John Dewey and Edward Thorndike, the line is straight.

The line is straight, but not whole. The faith and works of Rousseau and his immediate followers little affected the faith, the form or the functions of the educational establishments which those innovations accused and challenged. The schools continued on their traditional anti-scientific and pre-industrial courses. Set to the requirements of a lapsing mediaeval society, they had no interest in the instruction—to say nothing of the education—of the plain people about whose freedom and happiness Rousseau was concerned. To discipline and indoctrinate them for an Otherworld was enough. The care of the school and the university remained to train the priest, the physician and the lawyer. Until the Democratic Revolution, Western education was essentially vocational education. The so-called liberal arts merely provided a common method for the three "intellectual"—that is, mostly verbal—occupations. The education of the clergy was designed to make them bankers of the deposit of faith, specialists in the mobilization of the supernatural toward the salvation of souls. The education of the physicians was designed to make them specialists in the manipulation of the natural toward the salvation of bodies. The education of the lawyers was designed to make them specialists in the manipulation of men and their laws toward the salvation of interests or "rights." There were no schools for the education of knights or men at arms. These served apprenticeships of which literacy was by no means an indispensable part. If they could wage war and make love, to the tunes of a music appropriate to these arts, they had all the knowledge and skill they needed. Craftsmen, artisans, traders who must needs record recipes, seek or give credit, keep accounts, might require the arts of reading and writing and reckoning in order to practice their trades successfully; but their occupations were ignoble, and the skills they called for unworthy of men wellborn, and in no way learned professions or liberal arts. They could have no place in the curricula of the schools. Father could teach son, master apprentice, on the job, and not so many jobs called for the arts of reckoning or letters. Until the Renaissance peer and peasant lived in equal contentment with illiteracy, the first because literacy was a token of servility, the second, because it was beyond his servile station in life. Not till the Renaissance did literacy and letters really begin to be valued as a possession essential to the wellborn man. In the course of time "scholar" rivaled, then, on occasion, took precedence over "soldier." It was during the Renaissance that the phrase "gentleman and scholar" became a part of English speech. It was during the Renaissance that literary knowledge and rhetorical skill were added to the gentleman's equipment, that schools and universities first supplemented, then displaced, divinity with the "humanities." The feeling for literacy as a necessary attribute of the commoner came only with the Protestant Reformation and remained long confined to Protestant enclaves. It was engendered when the Bible was put in the place of the church as the seat of religious authority, so that literacy was made, also for the laymen, an indispensable medium of unmediated and unmediable faith.

In Rousseau's day, however, the laymen were not many who could read and interpret the Bible for themselves. The invidious distinctions of the social order which schooling justified and confirmed had been somewhat blurred, but little weakened. Rousseau denounced them well, if not wisely, in his famous essays on the degradation of human nature by the arts and the sciences, and on the artificial inequalities between men which these establish and sustain. However one may think of his total critique, it was seminal. Among its ongoing consequences is a series of revaluations of the relation of education to the men and women who work with their hands as well as those who work with their tongues. The new place which the Democratic Revolution gave to education in the life and labor of the people provides the gradient for the consequences. Jefferson's thinking no less than Franklin's, Condorcet's even more than Jefferson's, are events in the development.

For on the whole and in the long run, democratic communities worked and fought to enact the principles that these philosophers of free societies thought out. The task of equalizing educational opportunity for all the people is long and arduous. Although every Protestant was to have access to the Bible, not so many were enabled to read it, even in New England, as might be imagined. Secondary and collegiate schooling remained long the unchallenged —although scarcely endured—privileges of birth and wealth. Jefferson, for example, was convinced beyond all doubt of the interdependence of democracy and education,[2] but his practical program for the multitudes did not go beyond a three years' course at public cost. After that, parents were to pay, except those poor ones whose children had "genius." Of these there was to be a progressive selection by examination. The chosen were to be carried at "public expense" through school and college: ". . . The object is to bring into action that mass of talents which lies buried in poverty in every country, for want of the means of development, and thus give

---

[2] "In every government on earth is some trace of human weakness, some germ of corruption and degeneracy, which cunning will discover and weakness insensibly open, cultivate, and improve. Every government degenerates when trusted to the rulers of the people alone. The people themselves, therefore, are its only safe depositaries. And to render even them safe, their minds must be improved to a certain degree. This indeed is not all that is necesssary, though it be essentially necessary. An amendment to our Constitution must have come in aid of public education. The influence over our government must be shared among all the people. If every individual which composes their mass participates of the ultimate authority, the government will be safe; because the corrupting the whole mass will exceed any private resources of wealth; and public ones cannot be provided but by levies on the people."
(Notes on Virginia, Ford, iii, 252)
"I know no safe depository of the ultimate powers of society but the people themselves; and if we think them not enlightened enough to exercise their control with a wholesome discretion, the remedy is not to take it from them, but to inform discretion by education. This is the true corrective of abuses of political power."
(To W. C. Jarvis, September 1820)

activity to a mass of mind, which in proportion to our population, shall be the double or treble of what it is in most countries." [3] In his Sixth Annual Message to the Congress, Jefferson suggested a constitutional amendment to enable the establishment of a national university and its financing with "an endowment of lands." The Congress did not follow the suggestion, and in his last years Jefferson devoted himself to the establishment, against the opposition of "the priests of the different religious sects," of his University of Virginia, to be "based on the illimitable freedom of the human mind . . . not afraid to follow the truth wherever it may lead, nor to tolerate any error so long as reason is left free to combat it." [4]

The idea that free public secondary and collegiate education might be as necessary and desirable for all the people as the elementary kind Jefferson undertook to provide for, was slow in developing. Yet it was implicit in his basic insight that knowledge is power, that freedom depends on equal distribution of this power, that free society rests therefore upon its individual members thus made free. As the economy of the nation began to take on its prevailingly industrial forms, the Jeffersonian insight was exalted into a fighting faith of the Jacksonian era. The mechanics and farmers of the period demanded cultural parity with the bankers and lawyers, the clergy and physicians. They argued that the limitation of educational opportunity to a privileged group was a violation of the democratic principle. Organized in unions, in mechanics' societies or granges, they became in their several states a potent influence for the establishment of a system of free, tax-supported public education. The intellectuals of the time backed the contentions of the workers with ideas deriving from Jefferson and Rousseau and from the scientific conception of the natural parity of different human beings.

Workmen and wordmen had a not too willing ally in the various religious denominations. The latter were numerous and diverse. Almost every variety of the Protestant derivation may be said to have begun its career in the Catholic mood and attitude. That is, each claimed to be the unique and exclusive keeper of God's word to man, and the custodian of the one and only way to salvation. Each said to the others: "We alone have the true doc-

---

[3] To M. Correa, 1817.
[4] To Mr. Roscoe, 1820.

trine and discipline of Christ. Therefore you have not. Learn ours, or acknowledge yourselves worthy only to be cut off and shut out from the communion of the saved, and cast into eternal damnation." Their early history was a bitter sectarian warfare. The stronger ones held out, the weaker made exodus toward the retreating frontier where they could satisfy God's will according to their own infallible doctrines and disciplines. As the country grew more populous, the number and variety of the denominations also grew. The half-dozen became sixty or seventy. If the non-Christian are counted, there are now many hundreds, and the world being what it is, their increase and multiplication will know no stoppage. Willy nilly, they must needs live alongside each other as neighbors. If their life together were not to be an hourly battle, they had to attain an attitude of mutual toleration. That is, they might neither love nor respect one another, but they had to endure and suffer one another. Such toleration is, of course, repugnant to the democratic insight. In that insight difference, otherness, is not the same as wrong and evil; the unlike is equally good and right *as* unlike and *because* unlike. The free man's role, in free society, is to understand and to respect the unlike, to achieve a sympathetic realization of what he is and how he works, and to arrange ways of co-operation, to liquidate moods of sufferance. This change, under the reshaping vectors of the democratic idea, came slowly and unevenly upon the denominations. It is today noticeable, not only in the form of the Federal Council of the Churches of Christ, but in the existence of an interfaith movement and of a conference of Christians and Jews. Long before it came to the surface, however, the less denominationally partisan among the people and politicians decided that the most effective way to keep the schools free from the warfare of the sects was to secularize them. They knew that not only interdenominational peace, but also the intent of the First Amendment and the separation of church and state required such secularization. And secularization developed and spread, though always against the resistance of the variegated churchly interest which has never relaxed its efforts to indenture the schools to its support.[5] During the Jacksonian era, moreover, the Protes-

---

[5] This ranges from ecclesiastical pressure upon state legislatures to appropriate public funds for the transportation of children to predominantly religious schools—mainly the parochial schools of the Roman

tant interest found cause for alarm in the extensive Catholic immigration of the time. The immigrants would need to be decatholicized and a secular education would be safer for the nation, many Protestants urged, than popery.

The traditional agonist of the generation-long struggle for free public education wisely organized and competently administered was Horace Mann. A lawyer and something of a stuffed shirt, but with a genuine passion for the education of the people, Mann felt the inadequacy of the nation's educational establishment as not many have felt it since. He took official charge of bringing it to some sort of sufficiency, at least in his native Massachusetts. He studied the organization and management of schooling in other parts of the world, particularly in Prussia. Like Matthew Arnold he took home thence an articulate conception of an educational order. At the time, all the subjects of the Russian czar were serfs and most of the subjects of the multitude of German princes and princelings were not far from serfdom. By contrast American society was free society. The few million black slaves did not present a worse condition than the many million white serfs of the European continent—and serfs and slaves received their legal liberation at about the same time.

Abolitionism and free public education were growths of an identical soil. They developed concurrently, fed by the same political and moral passion. Although Massachusetts succeeded Virginia as the matrix of doctrine and inspiration, practical achievements in the establishment of democratic schooling was the work of the independent farmers of the Northwest. The men of Michigan made theirs the first of the states to implement a program ranging from elementary school to university. A plan had been ready in 1817, while Jefferson was still active. The common school was set up a year after his death, the University opened a few years later. In another decade, Michigan had schools to train the blind, the

---

Catholic denomination—the purchase of textbooks, release of school time for religious education, and the like. Illinois, Indiana, Louisiana, Massachusetts, Maryland, Michigan, Mississippi have passed one or another such law; the courts of Delaware, Kentucky, Oklahoma, New York, South Dakota, Washington and Wisconsin have held such laws unconstitutional. New York overruled the courts, in 1938, by an amendment to the State Constitution.

deaf, the crippled and the mentally deficient. By 1855 a program of vocational training was launched, and in 1870 women were admitted as students in the University of Michigan.

It was Michigan, not Virginia, that implemented and improved upon the Jeffersonian vision. Also other western states are of the heroic pioneers in the epic of the American school, which owes far more than schoolmen are aware to the spirit of the frontier. That spirit transfigured the knowledge which the easterner took west with him, and brought to action the program of free public education envisioned by Jefferson, enriched and implemented by Horace Mann. Of course free public education became, and continues to be, a major political issue. From 1830 to 1850 it stood as such in local and nationwide political discussion. Its champions were farmers, mechanics, intellectuals, men of science, and all convinced democrats, men and women on the firing line of social change, with frontier minds. Its opponents were all who had a vested interest in the educational status quo—the clergy, the beneficiaries of private institutions, the employers of labor and the wealthy taxpayers. Some argued that education would be as dangerous to children of the "lower classes" as liberty to a black slave. Others argued that free public education would degrade standards and, by its poor requirements for the poor, level the schools and academies of the rich downward, or eliminate them by competition. Still others, sure that the place of woman is the home, and woman's work that of a domestic to her family, urged that she might be improved by "accomplishments" but spoiled by education. At the frontier a woman was as good as her man, and often, significantly better—she had to be. But in "the settlements," in the cities of the east, the idea was nurtured that a woman with any pretensions to education could be only a bluestocking, while a woman with any pretensions to political equality could be only indecent. Anti-feminism and anti-education went together.

The rallying point for all the opponents of free public education was, however, the idea of its cost. Too many taxes! This cry is coeval with the American school system. It is strident today. That the American people spend about $56.00 per person for liquor, $22.00 per person for tobacco, and $20.00 per person for cosmetics, is mere small change beside the less than $18.00 per child they spend for elementary and high schools. The first item of public cost which gets cut in a depression, the first which is squeezed in a crisis is the school system. So recent is its establishment, so imponderable and still unfamiliar are its relations to free society, that custom combines with parsimony to keep its service to the growth of free men at a minimum.

Nevertheless, this service has been an expanding service. Between 1830 and 1900 or thereabouts, the struggle to set up a free, tax-supported system of public education was waged with uneven success, in every state of the Union. The first differences between education in America and education in European countries could hardly be said to favor the American establishment. But when, toward the turn of the century, there came that positive upswing in the nation's consumption, that lift of the national standard of living toward abundance, it brought also a heightened momentum in the building of the school systems of the states. Education as such ceased to be a debatable issue. It took the place in the American faith which Jefferson had designated for it. The American people came to take it for granted that every state, every community, would maintain a public school system free and open to all.

The now familiar tale of growth began to tell itself. Concern spread from the local community to state and federal governments. Teaching began to be looked upon as a permanent vocation for men, and as peculiarly adapted to the powers of women. Horace Mann's normal school at Bridgewater and the pioneer institution at Terre Haute, Indiana, were challenged and emulated by similar establishments everywhere in the land. Wages and salaries for teachers went higher. States found it needful and desirable to equalize local inequities in school resources. Educational journals came to birth, increased and multiplied. Old Dr. Winship's *Journal of Education,* issued from his fane on Beacon Hill in Boston, now has a thousand alternatives, endlessly specialized. McGuffey's readers have been replaced by multitudes of competitors. Societies to study, promote and watch over education, like the Herbart Society, the public education associations, the sodalities of teachers, the associations of teachers and parents, craft and administrative groupings among teachers—invidiously based like the principals', the high-school teachers', the trades-unions of teachers, and the like—took form and established vested interests. The over-all National Education Association was set up. Under the stimulus of the

s arts first supplemented, then grew way beyond the
mechanics' institutes of earlier days. The instruction of defectives
and delinquents was developed into vocational specialties. The
school building as the shelter and instrument of a specific occupation began to receive the special attention of architects, and the
schoolbook, and all the other accessories to teaching and learning,
became the peculiar care of publishers and manufacturers. Businessmen found considerable profit in making and selling the old
tools of schooling, and in devising and multiplying new ones.

By the end of World War I the American public school had
grown into a national institution with an expanding economy.
Education had ceased to be thought of as an accessory to church,
state, industry, and merely their instrument. Americans came to
believe in it as an end in itself, an institutional peer of church and
state, of the army, the navy, the corporation, the factory; as taking
its equal if not superior place beside these structures. The nation's
educational establishment came to be regarded as one more
precious and singular mode of human association whose life and
growth are patterned by the quality of its own autonomous élan,
seeking the attainment of its own characteristic excellence.

Growing into a self-ruling institution, the educational establishment grew, also in the diverse schools and systems which compose
it, a free spirit, a soul of their own, with wants and works and ways
singular to themselves, no longer harnessed to other institutions, to
be their draft-animals or servants. The system, which the interplay
of the nation's schools grounds and sustains, now struggles for life
and enlargement among the other institutions which environ it
as their peer. Indeed, some among its priests and prophets have
come to claim that education, instead of being a society's agent or
tool, should be its principal and rule, shaping and guiding the
common life. As against Aristotle's observation that "what contributes most to the permanence of constitutions is the adaptation
of education to the form of government," they would so interpret
the Constitution as to adapt the form of government to education.
If a society is to be a free society of free men, they argue, not government, nor the church, nor business should decide the task or

fix the function, the structure and costs of the educational establishment; the establishment must determine these things for itself. Unless it may do so, unless it may define and appraise for itself its relation to other institutional interests, it cannot be education for a democratic society. That is, the educator must be free to seek and to tell the truth about these interests and to decide for himself the form and methods of his seeking and telling.

This is a far from welcome view of the rights and duties of education, even among educators. The bodies of knowledge most accessible, most readily transmissible, are the traditional residue of past generations. The curriculum, how to teach it and why it is taught, are an inheritance, for the most part an inheritance repeated without renewal, and not a creation. The ideas and their ordering are taken ready-made, and the steps of their communication are counted and measured from the top. Their succession is governed by what tradition has decided the last step should be, not by what in nature the first step must be. Very largely they are conformed to the convention that the formal climax of schooling should be either the baccalaureate which crowns "liberal education," or the degree in ministry, medicine or the law. Secondary and elementary education were graded in steps mounting to these peaks. What the professors were teaching, in the colleges and the professional schools, governed what high and elementary school teachers must impart in the grammar and high schools.

Because of this the soul of the free public school system had to be, from its birth, a divided soul, a split personality with conflict at its heart. Custom and tradition gave it a curriculum determined to indoctrinate gentlemen in the liberal arts, and to discipline a residue of them in the learned professions. At the same time, the aspirations and needs of the plain people, whose efforts had brought the educational establishment to birth, looked toward a consummation in schooling which should release and satisfy their powers relevantly, to the actualities of their life and labor. Since "liberal education" was the seal of the gentleman's schooling, and indoctrination in "the liberal arts" the gentleman's trademark, Americans were disposed to demand equal access to the liberal arts for all their children. If the gentlemen were the Joneses, the American school was going to enable every American to keep up with

the Joneses; as a free man in a free society he would be as good as
his betters, and would endeavor to make himself better.

On the other hand there were the insights, the knowledges, the
skills, that accumulated outside the academic disciplines. There
were the natural sciences. There were the social sciences. There
were the agricultural and mechanical arts. There were the fine arts.
There were the arts of the manufacturer and the businessman.
These arts and sciences had become the powers with which men
worked for their livings, and it had been ever doubtful if, outside
the academic enclaves, many lived their lives in the "liberal arts."

The competition of the "practical" with the "liberal" arts for a
place in the schools makes one of the most ironic chapters in the
history of education. The arguments of Thomas Henry Huxley and
Herbert Spencer on behalf of the sciences in the curriculum are
now classics of that competition. The protestations of academic
beneficiaries of "liberal education" against the unceasing attrition
and displacement of their "humanities" and "liberal arts" by the
arts and sciences more genuinely relevant to the life and aspirations
of the people, are equally unceasing, and become ever more strident. The educational establishment has not grown into the institution it is by the multiplication of unaltered old subject matter
and the repetition of old methods. Its size and power rest upon the
continuous addition of new subject matters and the invention of
new methods.

Nevertheless, the "colleges of liberal arts" are still the Joneses of
the academic scene, and the schools of agriculture, engineering,
business administration, commerce, and the like, the academic
plebeians. This remains the case even though elementary and high-
school curricula got diversified, old subjects displaced, new ones
added, and values transposed. For a time the word for such changes
was "enrichment." Secondary schools began to be thought of not as
"preparatory" but as "terminal." Public schooling turned, broadly
throughout the nation, into an emulative enterprise; for communities also, it became a matter of keeping up with the Joneses. No
sooner would a prosperous suburb or a well-to-do county build a
central high school or devise a more desirable school policy than
neighboring communities near and far would take the attitude:
"We mustn't do worse, we must try to do better than those educational Joneses!"

Thus the drive which sustains and alters fashions also affects the building and conduct of schools. Between World War I and World War II it worked with a notable potency. The Herbart Society renamed itself the Society for the Study of Education. Building became a form of conspicuous consumption, with constructions ever more spectacular, complicated, skyscraperish, even when functionally bettered. There was a genuine contagion from Big Business and the factory system. Somehow economy was assimilated to size, administration to hierarchy, and competency to centralization. Bigness of plant, numbers of children and concentrated control of program and procedure came to be assumed as marks of educational progress. More and more women and men turned to teaching for a career, especially women. Complaints were heard that the schools were being overpopulated by women teachers, with too many not mature enough emotionally nor trained vocationally to carry the personal and professional responsibilities intrinsic to the teacher-pupil relation. They flocked to the normal schools and the teachers' colleges. The normal schools and teachers' colleges multiplied requirements and raised the costs of teacher education, without in fact bettering the teachers' equipment. They did, however, bring about certain moral and technical modifications in the conception of the teachers' function.

A somewhat new breed of teachers of teachers, new brands of psychology and the new organization of industry were the paramount modifying forces. Schooling came once more to concern itself, some thought, exclusively with what William James had called "the bitch-goddess, Success." Toward the close of the twenties, it began to look as if the national system would vindicate Aristotle after all, but with education adapted to serve the constitution of business, not of government. The idea of education as the way of freedom became recessive, the idea of education as the way to privilege, wealth and station became dominant. It worked on the traditional private boarding schools and colleges as well as on the public systems. It gave rise, on their fringe, to an ever-extending series of "educational" enterprises. One was "university extension," offering women shut out from the fanes sacred to the male, glimpses of the higher learning suited to their weaker powers. Another was the night schools for the foreigners and the unlettered; another was the correspondence school—there are some four hundred of them today, conducted at a profit, training some six hundred thousand pupils for any career from the civil service, radio, writing, the motion picture, the stage, music, accounting, police work and whatever else a customer may desire. Social settlements multiplied clubs and classes. Trades-unions, emulating the Workers' Education Association in England, launched enterprises in workers' education. Managements of Christian and Hebrew associations, in view of the hungers of their patrons and clients for vocational, intellectual and athletic studies, found themselves under the necessity of allowing the religious interest to become marginal. The New School for Social Research, organized in 1919, gave adult education a new turn with a new meaning. Before the decade ended an association for adult education was set up.

While these new arrangements for learning and teaching were coming to birth, the traditional ones neither diminished nor weakened. On the contrary, the private denominational schools, the Roman Catholic parochial schools, the snobbish secular private schools, the ostensibly military schools, grew concurrently. Shortly after World War I parents and teachers, disturbed by the theory and practice of education in both the costly private and free public schools, formed the Progressive Education Association, and with the educational philosophy of John Dewey as their fighting faith, organized experimental schools as different in size, endowment, power and influence as New York's City and Country and Lincoln schools.

A visitor to the United States just before World War II, looking at the nation's schools, would get the impression of a somewhat cubistic composition. The public school system would present a dominant ground plan, repeated about 130 times, with extreme variations, in state after state, in country as against city, in the urban north as against the agricultural south, and ranging from kindergarten to college and professional school. Athwart this basic design, our observer would see the denominational and secular private schools, the parochial establishment ruled by the Roman Catholic authorities, the ways and works of all directed toward "accomplishments" for girls, the traditional doctrines and disciplines for boys. Less tangential, more concurrent with public education, the non-collegiate and the private vocational schools, the schools for the special needs of our children and youth, the labor schools and the schools for adults would come under his eye.

Finally, spotting the scene like tourbillons or foci of fission, he would take note of the progressive schools and of the public school units of experiment in progressive education. Inquiring into the school population—children, youth and adults—our visitor would be told that in 1928 the nation counted 31,000,000 children of school ages—that is from five to seventeen years old; that of these some 25,200,000 were enrolled in the schools and about 20,700,000 were in attendance; that close to 4,000,000 of those in attendance were pupils in 29,930 high schools; that these millions were being taught by about 1,011,000 teachers of whom some 800,000 were women. Between 1928 and the present day, the visitor would be told, a depression and a world war had intervened, each with its characteristic impact on pupil and teacher, yet with no important modification of the total picture, save indeed to deepen the American faith in the powers and import of education. Depression and war made differences in school enrollment, in teacher attitude. Both brought the federal government into active partnership with local educational authorities alike in matters of instruction and of construction. Depression tended to increase the school population by a few millions; war, with its call for man-power in field and factory, its high wages, and occupational opportunities, drew millions of pupils and hundreds of thousands of teachers from the schools to other fields of activity; war facilitated the depreciation of the educational plant which had to go on without repairs. War arrested new building, so that by 1946 some five billions of dollars were said to be required for the rehabilitation of plant alone. Teachers were said to be nearly 400,000 fewer in number than before the war, far from so well trained, eager to find other and better paid occupations, and women more than ever outnumbering men. Although schools are overcrowded, pupils are fewer, and their numbers in the high schools and colleges are mounting again. There are some 6,000,000 in the high schools alone.

Non-public schools have, of course, changed correspondingly. But their variation from the 1928 measures are even less significant respecting the dominant trend and characteristic pattern. There were close to 80,000 teachers in the nearly 1800 private schools—the majority male—and about 205,000 pupils. From 650 to 700 of these schools were non-sectarian, with about 76,000 pupils, and some 1400 were parochial, with some 1,600,000 pupils. Even though the national expenditure for schooling is less than for liquor and tobacco, it still runs to upward of $15,000,000 a day, and close to $3,000,000,000 a year. In 1928, the national average cost per child per day—in terms of buildings, equipment, administration, teaching and the like—was 62¢; with a lowest annual per capita rate of $52.00 in Atlanta, Georgia, and a highest of $134.00 in Los Angeles, California. In 1946 the lowest per capita rate was $42.00, the highest, $203.00. Of these sums, the teachers' wages are not important parts. Factory workers, even farm hands, are better paid.

The elementary and secondary schools, our visitor will learn, are basic but not final. The nation's colleges and universities play a critical role in its educational economy. In 1928 they had an undergraduate population of, in round numbers, 600,000 men and 400,000 women and a graduate population of about 30,000 men and 20,000 women; their professional schools counted some 94,000 men but only 6000 women; in 1946, partly for causes originating in the war, partly because of trends in the population and in the nation's changing economy, there was not an institution of higher learning in America which did not claim to have too many students, too few teachers, too little money, and which was not seriously considering ways to federal aid for higher education. Yet, in 1928 the total income of colleges and universities from student fees alone had been upward of $180,000,000, their income from productive funds, $60,000,000; from gifts and benefactions, $190,000,-000; from contributions by states and cities, $116,000,000 and from the federal government, $18,000,000. By 1946 public contributions had been increased, income from productive funds had fallen off, student fees had been raised from 10 to 30 per cent. The total capital holdings—land, buildings, real estate and the like, amounted, in 1928 to about $41,000,000,000; college libraries, costing some $6,250,000,000, were custodians of close to 40,500,000 books; the value of college grounds was estimated at upward of $300,000,000,000 and of college buildings at about $1,020,000,000. They held endowments of $1,150,000,000 and other property with close to $103,000,000.

Such figures are astronomical. They are ineffably Big Business. There is no way of giving them concretion save by actually experiencing the possessions they compute and this is not within the scope of anybody's lifetime. The entire story suggests simply that with all the changes and chances befalling our educational establishment, American teachers are still numerous enough to make a small state or a mighty army; that American schools compose into an institution with a personnel and an economy potential of very great power and in fact strong enough, if it had the *know-how,* to modify the national being from the grass roots. It is in a strategic position to do so. The American people have faith in the school as a democratic institution. Every generation, since 1840, has given it more time out of its life. Then there were at most only 208 school days to a lifetime. In 1933 there were 1400. As we add night schools, schools of mechanical arts, vocational schools, schools for adults, the number of days increases. More and more the school becomes a locus for leisure as well as occupation, for the community of interests as well as the advantage of the individual. The nation's school economy continues to be an expanding economy. The nation's schools have been moved from the periphery toward the center of the American scene; the educational establishment is jostling and squeezing the others which together with it make up the national life. Of those some, like the churches, resent the change and jostle back; but to date most are acquiescent, some even pleased.

Yet the time is not far off when the American people may seriously question whether their schools give them what they pay for, in the form of free men. Support and backing from the secondary businesses which live within the school economy—from the textbook publishers, the school supply manufacturers, the architects and builders—will little avail before such questioning.

Already it has become a questioning that embraces in its challenge the ultimate meaning of education; its import for teachers, beyond the living, such as it is, which they earn in the school system; the hopes, the ambitions which the school fulfills or frustrates in the children whom it purports to educate, and in the parents who entrust their children to it.

Perhaps its merit follows rather from the faith upon which it lives and works than the achievement it presents. Perhaps the event that nearly everybody survives his education should be enough. For the direct operation of the classroom and the syllabus leaves an ambiguous trace. All too often *curriculum* is but the pedagogue's word for the run-around which the schools give the pupils. Unintended impacts seem often far more telling in imparting the direction and shaping the ways of experience for the young who pass through the schoolrooms. However, the record contains nothing to warrant a contention that some other institution, such as the church, can do better than the school in the education of free men. Indeed, the record does contain many things to warrant the contention that they have done and are doing worse; and would do still worse without the schools to measure by. But the tale of education, as of all else in democracy, does tell that it is good to be continuously vigilant, good to inspect the inside of the educational cup very carefully, to keep reconsidering what it is we mean by education for freedom, and to seek our meanings through observing and interpreting actualities of schooling instead of the exercise of a dialectic about a concept of the school.

Chapter Three

THE TEACHER: WOMAN INTO
SCHOOLMARM

As institutions go, the democratic educational establishment is a
recent and still precarious growth of our civilization. Its liberation
came so late that its independence and autonomy are still con-
tested. In order to grow without distortion and function without
servility, it has every need to vindicate beyond challenge the
equality and liberty of all the members of the teaching profession.
These—particularly the rank and file—are the natural target of all
those interests, institutional and private, religious, political and
economic, which never cease pressing the nation's schools toward
their special service. The teacher is at once the weakest and the
most important figure in the educational establishment and thus
the first and last point of attack upon the integrity of the educational enterprise.

Now teachers, even after they are conformed to their vocation,
are people. They are women and men, each an individual human
being with purposes and passions singular to herself, weaving the
years of her life into a personal biography to her unique and
ineffable. But after a time in the practice of the teacher's craft, their
diverse individualities become overlaid with characteristics acquired from their common occupation. They take on a generic
manner of being with definite stigmata. They become embodiments of a social type. Of course the complete dissolution of any
individual in the type is an occurrence so rare as to be unique;
but assimilation does as a rule go to a point where it is easier to
recognize a person as a schoolteacher than as a woman or man.

What, then, is the type, Teacher? The custom of the country
and the practices of authority maintain a distinction, both tacit
and overt, between this occupational category and other ways for
men and women to earn their livings. Statistically, the teacher is a
female; some satirists transpose statistical preponderance into cultural totality and make the teacher all feminine, regardless of sex.
However, the women do outnumber the men many times in the
entire profession, and in the elementary classrooms they count one
hundred to one. The type is female, and like the worker bee,

female with her femininity suppressed or absorbed. Her years are close to forty. She is unmarried. Not improbably she is without any kind of marital experience, allowed or illicit. All her identifying characteristics are embraced in the expression *Schoolmarm*.

One is likely to know the Schoolmarm, first of all, by her voice. However gentle and low it may be when she first takes a class, years of endeavoring to rule and instruct reluctant children develop in it a certain stridency of pitch, rhythm and accent. This quality has led some school administrators, with the traditional fatuousness of the tribe, to lay a good deal of stress on teacher-training in voice and speech. But the cause is not in the teacher. The stridency is an occupational acquirement, a consequence of the peculiar dynamics of teacher-pupil relations in classrooms with too many pupils. With the voice goes dress. There is, by and large, a certain Victorian uniformity in the way school authorities like schoolteachers to dress. All women teachers appear to be sensitive to the imposed dowdy correctness and all men teachers react to it. Dress is the easiest, because the most external, attribute of the Schoolmarm or pedagogue to alter—if a teacher has the wherewithal, and is truly struggling against schoolmarmization. Most do truly struggle. But if they stay in the school system, their battle is a losing battle. Vocational conformations first suppress, then harness up original disposition; spontaneous preference is exhausted in unwilling habit. Unconsciously, teachers exhibit a mode of dress almost as occupationally uniform as a clergyman's or a policeman's. With the Schoolmarm's dress and voice goes her manner with people. One gets an impression of a certain staccato thrust, like that of a top sergeant, a policeman, or other holder of delegated authority, but with not quite the assurance of those occupational types. Her deliverances are apt to be repetitive and dogmatic, her attitude assertive rather than inquiring. When she asks, she already knows the answers, so that her asking feels like a kind of telling. The exigencies of her practice of teaching atrophies her power of learning. Teachers of very young children and college instructors are more likely to be free from this manner than teachers of children at puberty or just before puberty.

During recent years the quality of voice and speech, the peculiarity of dress, of posture, of physical attitude and psychic pattern have been interpreted—especially in metropolitan school systems—

as a neurotic syndrome. Schoolmarm thus would name an occupational type as a neurotic personality. If this be the case—and the
idea is plausible enough—the personality traits are not original,
but effects of the social pressures which mold and give its pattern
to the occupation, teacher. Those, as they close in on the young
normal school or teachers' college graduate, shut her up and shut
her in. They demand of her a postural rigidity which shall be an
example to the pupils whom she orders to fold their hands and
sit up straight, so that she may be sure those idle hands will not
do the mischief the devil is sure to find for them. The actual
posture is today more or less a metaphor; but its spirit and intent
still pervade the classrooms. That vital looseness, that easy mobility
of mind and of body which are required in order to initiate the
young (or any age) into new knowledge, are forbidden to the
teacher. By the time she has conformed to type, they would make
her uncomfortable and insecure, natural flexibility would feel unnatural or improper. The community which employs her requires
her to impattern propriety and respectability.

Yet although the ideal teacher must be respectability incarnate,
she is not respected. The community does not accord to woman as
Schoolmarm parity of status with the minister or doctor or lawyer
or banker or politician, or even butcher or baker or candlestick
maker. Teacher holds a low place in the hierarchy of social
esteem. This judgment, which few teachers consciously acknowledge, is inward to the mores of Main Street and colors its attitude
toward the vocation of teaching. It soon becomes an emotional
dynamic in the making of the pedagogical mind and the formation
of the Schoolmarm personality. The nearest and most immediate
external molds are those shaped by a school's administrative control, a control analogous to that of top sergeants in armies or
foremen in factories. Those who exercise it—the principals, supervisors, superintendants, school boards and the like—are over-
whelmingly male. What the female teacher does, how she does it,
in her classroom and out, must follow directives channeled from
this hierarchical bureaucracy.

Consider her day's work. At the core are her five hours of teaching. During the early years of her service she must add to these the
hours of preparation. As she grows older in her work, these
diminish toward zero; her activities become automatic and repeti-

tive; if they do diversify, it is not from inner spontaneity but because of outer demand; the variation is merely laid on, not grown. Add to the hours of preparation and classwork, the hours of record keeping, report writing, paper and examination grading. Add to all these the hours of meetings and conferences and consultations with principals and other administrators, with parents and relatives. The reasons for much of the paper work is not intrinsic to the school system itself: the powers which demand it lie elsewhere, and are important in giving direction to educational policy. In due time it adds up into a bulky dossier for each pupil —a cumulus of tabulations which can tell a teacher everything about a pupil except what alone it is important for the teacher to know—the dynamic of learning personal to the pupil.

Every so often a teacher's tasks may be complicated by new requirements. A faddist with influence on the school board, a textbook vender, or a spokesman for some other special interest may succeed in forcing into the day's work something more, that does not belong with the program of the classroom. So far as they can, teachers' colleges eager to "experiment," social agencies doing good as a profession, endeavor to divert the teacher toward their own interests. They want the teacher to uncover for them new data or check new theories about the growing human nature in their charge. They want the teacher to visit pupils' homes, and take over other tasks of the family case-worker. Even when proper and valuable enough in themselves, such multiplications and extensions of the teacher's tasks distort her more and more from woman into Schoolmarm.

That educational authorities are aware of some of the consequences of the pedagogic vocation to the human person is attested by the imposition of a widespread urban administrative requirement known as *alertness*. In New York, for example, no teacher is paid her normal salary increase without "earning credit" for courses taken in some institution of more or less higher learning. Teachers enroll in thousands in evening sessions of various such institutions. When they enter a classroom as pupils most of them have been serving as teachers to classes numbering from 38 to 60 children, instructing each class during five consecutive hours, in subjects with which the children have only that concern which their teacher can compel. In addition, the seekers of "alertness credit" have spent several more hours writing up records, conferring with colleagues and superiors, dealing with refractory pupils, and what have you. They have barely had time enough to bolt the evening meal, before they are due at their classes as pupils, ready to demonstrate "alertness." Of course the demand is utopian. A visit to a motion picture, a dancing party or a bowling alley or an early bed will in these circumstances produce more meaningful alertness than any "course" in the world. The administrative remedy for schoolmarmism here only deepens the disease.

Nor is it mitigated by the various more or less compulsory memberships in local teachers' societies, or great federal organizations like the National Education Association, with schoolmen's politics and male-controlled executive and administrative structures. Women officers of such organizations make an impression of figureheads. One of their "sect" may on occasion be carefully screened for president; one or two may be taken into this or that board or committee. But representation and power in proportion to their numbers and abilities are not in evidence. The male-female ratio repeats itself also in the local associations—political, religious and philanthropic, as well as occupational—which social pressure forces teachers to join because they are teachers, earning their livings by pedagogy. To the invidious distinctions between male and female, moreover, accrue others as following from the differences of grade in the schools. A castelike order of rank and esteem appears to hold for elementary and high-school teachers. The distinctions of status and salary, which the two orders maintain, increase, it may seem, inversely as their professional responsibilities. Their hierarchical gradation rests on nothing essential to their tasks; it is an event in "the system," not an effect of the dynamics of teaching and learning. The "system" is primarily an administrative device. It rests upon the wide base of the elementary school and tapers to the college, where the glory of being called "professor" often is the sole compensation for the lack of every other comfort. The title, like a uniform, receives the highest lay and occupational respect. But the invidious rankings within the pyramid of the craft are secondary to rankings within another pyramid, with quite different functions. This is the administrative order itself—the pyramid of employers and managers over and against the pyramid of employees. While beyond all and over all, a Ptolemaic *primum mobile,* are the school boards and college trustees.

Under the rule of these diverse thrones, dominations and principalities, the Schoolmarm lives, moves and has her being. What she is, what she does or does not, how she got that way, is determined practically by these moral conditions of her employment: by the personnel of her school board; by the kind of men the administrators are who mediate between her and her board, and who often happily exploit her and tyrannize over her in the board's name. It happens not rarely that keeping a school up as a going concern, making other adjustments to the pressures in a community, leads to violating every principle managers and managed have learned regarding the works and ways of education. Very often an administrator may have to be all things to all men and not let his left hand know what his right hand is doing. Very often an educational establishment is too weak to implement and support educational ideals against non-educational pressures. The ideals continue to stand as mere professions learned in the teachers' colleges. On the job they are a way of talking which passes over into ways of doing only by accident; educational professions and educational practices may not live together. Schoolmarms have no illusions about their irreconcilability. Young women fresh from their training schools may bring to their posts a vision and a program which their experience on the job turns into an hypocritical pretense.[1] They learn, as they become hardened to the career of teaching, not to take the fine words of their college professors at their face value. The teachers' colleges, too, are under

---

[1] "The noblest wealth of a nation is not in its mines, its soil or its forests, but in the idealism, the affections and the energies of its teachers. When nations spend more for teaching than for fighting, the turning point in human affairs will have come and the world will move forward to the finer and richer things of life at a pace hitherto unknown." *The Journal of the National Education Association.* Vol. 20, January 1931. Celebrating its tenth anniversary, this journal cites the late Professor George Herbert Palmer of Harvard University on *The Ideal Teacher*— a person able to tell his pupils "look at Truth, not me," endowed with sympathetic imagination, knowledge and a nature able "to invigorate life through learning" and to find the rewards of teaching in teaching itself: "A trade aims primarily at personal gain; a profession at the exercise of powers beneficial to mankind." Teaching is not a trade, since "the real payment is the work itself."

the compulsions of a struggle to survive, a competitive pressure which has led to the overproduction of pedagogic lore, wherewith they must either persuade or compel the potential customer to buy what they have to sell. Currently custom has fallen off, customers are poor in spirit. Would-be teachers have a high scarcity value. But this is only a phase of the cultural weather. The normal schools and teachers' colleges must needs increase and multiply; they will continue to stake their prosperity on diversifying the modes, multiplying the tasks and prolonging the time of teacher-training. They will continue to compete with other institutions for jobs for their graduates. By the enormous mass of their pedagogic lore, bristling with new-coined technical terms—which amount in fact, to an occupational argot like law Latin, baseball English or jive talk, long ago christened Pedagese—and with columns of figures able to repeat obscurely and ceremonially, thus authoritatively, a truism as a discovery and a mistake as a revelation, they will continue to convert education from a craft into a science and to ready a living woman of mind and heart for conversion into a professional Schoolmarm.

The mere mass of that pedagogic learning endows it with authority. But there is something else. Everybody is aware of the feeling of hidden wisdom which the strange terms of the learned professions stir up. Law and medicine speak with authority not only because society really accords them authority for their works but also because it is imposed upon society by their words. The still unlearned profession of teaching gains a similar advantage from Pedagese. Education, like other institutions of national life, has its cycles. The demand for teachers expands and contracts; the disposition of young men and women to teaching as a career mounts and falls. When the Great Depression intensified competition for jobs because of the disemployment of teachers, a considerable proportion of the students in all institutions of collegiate rank were students in teachers' colleges and normal schools. After the declaration of World War II, the superior attractions of higher pay and greater personal liberty going with jobs in shop and factory, brought down the enrollment to a mere seven per cent. The number of male students reduced to a trickle and women became restive and defiiant.

But on the whole and in the long run, enrollment will go up.

In spite of the stuffing of bunk and hokum, in spite of the make-work ceremonialism which attend the teaching of teachers because of these schools, a science of education is emerging in support and improvement of the art. As time goes on, the teaching of teachers will be unstuffed; it will work itself down to fighting weight. The formal barriers to admission to the craft, like college degrees, the formal requirements for continuation in it, like "alertness credit," will be modified into channels of power and skill. For a time anyhow. At present they are little more than union cards and tickets of admission. A degree does not create a good teacher nor improve a bad one. The techniques of expression and communication by which a teacher awakens curiosity and arouses the learner to learn do not depend on the discourses heard in the teachers' colleges. They come, first and last, out of experiences of give and take between personalities. The best that textbooks, lectures and the like can do is to talk about such experiences; they cannot provide them. And without them, pedagogy is about as relevant to teaching as numerology to bookkeeping. Of course it will have its statistical successes and its own ever-elaborating, ever-diversifying dialectical interest. But as a means to consequential education it merits the skepticism which is the price of the knowledge that is power. For those who choose a career of teaching there is an imperative. Whatever may be set before them, they must never cease asking: *What is it? What is it good for? How do you know?* They must keep curiosity ever alert. They must always require that authority shall accept the tests and receive the confirmations of experience. Unless this happens, a reliable body of knowledge regarding education cannot form nor can a genuine science of teaching and learning develop. The doctrines of schools for teachers come from lecturers to teachers whose remoteness from the drama of classroom give-and-take is proverbial. When they are close to experience of this give-and-take, what they say tends to be confirmations of the past, not innovations breaking with the past, such as are reported in *A Primary Teacher Steps Out*.[2] If she is to hold her job, the primary teacher mustn't step out, much as she may want to. For, lacking test and confirmation, the ultimate control of ideas regarding the *what* and *how* of education will remain

---

[2] Miriam Kallen, *A Primary Teacher Steps Out* (Boston: Lothrop, Lee and Shepard Company, 1936).

where it is now, with administrative authority; instead of where
those ideas must be born and where they survive or perish—in
the classroom, with the classroom teacher.

As, however, the system works today, unchecked authoritarianism
is matter of course. Placed as she is, a teacher by herself is helpless
to effect the changes which experience has taught her can facilitate
and not obstruct learning. What she may or may not do is governed
by the school economy, by the temper and training of her superiors,
by the policy of the school board *en garde* over the taxpayers'
money. The propitious growth of the taxpayers' children is hardly
ever a first consideration in decisions on what to spend where.
Innovations, whether in a system's plant or process, rarely originate
within the system itself. Most systems are characterized by organizational rigidity and functional automatism which make them unfit
to make the modifications that life and experience suggest, on their
own initiative. A business must reorganize itself continuously or
be bested by its competitors. But education, public and private,
has no effective competitors. Whatever it unwillingly takes over
from experimental schools, psychological research or business enterprise, it reworks quickly into a self-repeating educational scholasticism which can dominate all curriculum-making.

The jungle of "tests," intelligence, aptitude, attitude, performance, Rohrsach, achievement, and what not else—each a monu-
ment to its inventor and called by his name—provides one example
of such scholasticism. Testing is a major device in the modern
handling of the school child from first grade through high school.
It rests upon certain assumptions concerning human nature and
its growth that exfoliate into what is known as educational psychology—that is, the theory and practice of applying these assumptions to the processes of teaching and learning. Since psychologies
are many, and often contradict each other, educational psychology
in practice usually liquidates assumptions in the techniques of
testing, which can be employed indifferently by the different communicants of all the different psychological sects. In this way learning, its range and limitations, may become an abstraction independent of what is learned; "method" becomes a discipline of teacher-
training cut off from matter. One hears of instruction in how to
swim regardless of medium, how to fly regardless of mechanism,
how to read a book regardless of the book, how to think regardless

of ideas, how to nourish oneself regardless of food, as by chewing gum. In experience, what one does and how one does it are confluent with the stuff one does it to. Every matter calls out its own manner, singular to itself. The two are not livingly separable. We write psychologies either by describing how particular people behave when they feel and act and think and then saying that everybody behaves that way, or by abstracting from that which particular people do, quantifying it, and formulating it into a conceptual system. But like an actuarial table, a statistical norm, or a ready-made garment, such a system, fitted for everybody, can exemplify nobody; every one of its uses must be a modification of it, falsifying its generality. Actually, it is either a working hypothesis or a scholastic abstraction taken far from the living event whence it sprang. In sum, teacher-training operates its own characteristic distortion of the human being toward the Schoolmarm. It has only lately begun to abandon the polarity between pedagogy as idea and teaching as experience.

And does not the same thing hold of the verbiage regarding administration and supervision which we call courses or "units" in those doings? Are not their actualities—apart from the face-to-face relations of superior and inferior constituting their operative reality —the techniques of bookkeeping peculiar to the school economy? If they seem closer to experience, is it not because, conceptual themselves, they are directed to concepts and not to men and women? because such techniques can be handled as a means which is its own end?

All in all, the import of most of the "units" and "credits" which a girl must "take" in order to be qualified as teacher resides in a systematic abstraction of *how* from *what* that derealizes both method and matter. What is communicated to her is not experience but discourse, a body of words about words about words, a body of knowledge removed from acquaintance with that which it is presumed to be knowledge about. All teaching is a teaching of something by somebody to somebody. All learning is a learning of something by somebody. The specific differences get generalized into different assumptions and the assumptions get built into different systems of educational psychology which are then put in the place of teaching and learning, as real events.

The conformation of the human personality into the occupational type begins with the indoctrination and disciplining of teacher-training; it finishes by means of the taboos and prescriptions which mold a teacher on the job into a Schoolmarm. Teachers are required to take oaths that lawyers, ministers, doctors, legislators, army men, plumbers, undertakers, policemen and firemen are exempt from. What evil force is there in the Schoolmarm that she should be required to swear twice a loyalty which other public employees need vow only once? Why are her ideas about God, freedom, immortality, sin, salvation a condition of her employment and not of others? Why are her political preferences, her personal life, her manners and her habits objects of a scrutiny the practitioners of other vocations would challenge as insufferable insolence? A woman—or a man—who chooses teaching as a career, chooses constriction of all personal rights and powers. She exposes herself to inquisition into all her ways. A teacher must be orthodox in all things, regardless of how heterodox the school board members allow themselves to be. The Bill of Rights is not the same for teachers as for other occupational categories.

Custom, it would seem, cannot endure *difference* in the teacher. Teachers must conform in every matter of faith and morals. In some places they may not with impunity believe in evolution. In others their hairdo—whether they wear it long or wear it short, wear it marcelled or heedless of the beautician—is a menace. They arouse anxiety if they use rouge or lipstick or cosmetics of any sort. To smoke in public, or at all, is manifest unfitness for their high vocation; to take a cocktail, deadly sin. If their skirts are no longer than is the fashion, if they are not worn six inches or less from the ground, the wearers are suspect: teachers' limbs—legs to their sisters with jobs other than teaching—should be invisible. It is improper that teachers should dance, wrong for them to have beaus. As for marriage—women, not teachers, may marry as they can or choose; but teachers—with no considerable exceptions, the custom of the country requires teachers to be celibate. That is, woman teachers. Not many can keep their jobs if they marry, or get one if they are already married. "Old maid" and "Schoolmarm" are almost interchangeable concepts. How this requirement works on the person and art of the teacher, how great is its role in distorting woman into Schoolmarm, a generation of psychological study has made clear. Mental hygienists think anything but highly of this requirement. It does not produce that state of the personality best suited for successful teaching. The optimal teacher-pupil relationship is more readily established by persons whose sexual life is normal. Many psychologists recommend that not celibacy, but marriage or its equivalent should be a condition, if not of entering, then of remaining in the teaching profession.

That this is not the case is due to many causes. One which gets less attention than it deserves is the fact that teaching used to be a monopoly of the clergy and in Catholic enclaves is still the charge of priests and nuns.[3] Society's traditional image of the teacher retains essentially clerical features, and the most compulsive of these is sacerdotal celibacy. Although the Protestant Reformation lifted this particular commandment from the men, the new man's world which ensued upon it developed little change in the attitude toward women. It cared little or not at all that women should be equal with men and equally free. To reconcile the ever-mounting divergences between sacerdotal profession and sacerdotal practice —the pre-Reformation craftsmen in divinity being no better than they had to be—both the Reformation and the Counter-Reformation projected a way of life—not thought—for such as would follow a religious vocation which came to be known as puritanical. The man of God was imaged anew as a synthesis of suppressions; the image was made into the very incarnation of respectability. Protestant communities—more particularly Calvinist ones—succeeded better in embodying and sustaining the type than Catholic ones. In both, the clergy retained power over education. With the

---

[3] Most teachers in parochial schools have some kind of sacerdotal occupation. They are priests, lay brothers and, in the very great majority, nuns. The latter, being members of religious sisterhoods, receive no pay for their work. They live in their nunneries isolated from contact with "the world," wear a specific identifying uniform, and follow the discipline of their respective orders. There are in the United States some two hundred and fifty-nine such orders into which girls in their teens are as a rule recruited. With the veil, they take vows of poverty, chastity and obedience, and receive new names, often male, to go with their new way of life. As teachers they repeat both the method and the matter of what they have been taught: all themes and thoughts are conformed to the doctrine and discipline of the Church and the order. Their inexpensive services enable the parochial schools to offer the lowest-cost schooling which the nation knows, with corresponding values in the comparative result.

march of time, but notably after the Democratic Revolution, the interests of men turned, from mortification in this world for the sake of salvation in an Otherworld, to life, liberty and the pursuit of happiness in this world; religion and the sacerdotal establishment ceased to be at the center and went shifting toward the periphery of men's concerns. That divine "mission to teach," by which the Catholic hierarchy especially rationalizes sacerdotal pretensions to the monopoly of education, lost its authoritativeness; clerical status ceased to be so privileged; a great liberty accrued, openly at least to the Protestant clergy. Ministers of today are much more like free citizens than their like of one hundred years ago.

The prescriptions and taboos which had impatterned their sacred occupations are not dead; some say, not even dying. They now give her shape to the Schoolmarm. The penance of respectability is today laid upon the teachers. It is their social heritage. It subjects them to pressures which, in the light of today's knowledge, lay a definite handicap on the power of the teacher to teach. They impede improvement in the arts of communication and obstruct genuine team play of teacher and pupils. The rationalizations wherewith they are condoned are as obvious and matter of course as they are false and hypocritical. Teachers, the argument runs, are custodians of the nation's human capital, the guardians of the nation's youth, the keepers of the nation's most precious treasure, the shapers of the nation's future. Society entrusts to the teachers the building of the character of the next generation. They must, hence, embody the perfections they prescribe. They must stand before their charges as the models that the latter's parents can not be expected to be, nor that the children freely seek to emulate. Unless teachers are paragons of respectability, they betray their trust. They cannot, hence, continue to be women merely. They must become Schoolmarms.

That this compulsion perforce creates in the teacher a conflict between her occupation and her natural self, that it creates in the community a conflict with its actual works and ways, needs no emphasis. Like the priesthood before it, the schoolmarmhood, in assuming the required respectability, risks and loses all natural respect. Teachers do not figure as heroes or saints of the Great Tradition. They figure as its absurdities and comics. *Pedagogue* is a Greek word. It denotes the Athenian household slave who daily led the free-born child of his owner to the Gymnasium, where he was able to observe and imitate the excellence of older and stronger free men. The word's peers, *Schoolmarm, Schoolmaster,* have acquired a somewhat wider meaning. None of the three, however, is exactly a term of praise. They are epithets of offense and belittlement. They classify those to whom they are applied as practitioners of a somehow slavish art, bound to certain slavish habits of life. Aristophanes' teachers are weaklings and charlatans. All the schoolmasters Shakespeare drew are drawn with scorn and laughter. The career of Edward Eggleston's Hoosier schoolmaster had nothing noble or free in it. Washington Irving's *Ichabod Crane* was neither a saint nor a hero. The schoolpeople at Dotheboys Hall in Dickens' *Nicholas Nickleby* are anything but brave and beautiful. Hughes, Meredith, Kipling, Samuel Butler, almost the entire procession of writers who delineate pedagogic types, delineate characters somehow submissive yet vain, gauche, pretentious, naively sly, yet impractical and easily fooled by their pupils. They are humorous characters, incapable of coping with the changes and chances of a free society, unfit to live anywhere but in the strange securities of the pedagogic scene, yet supposed to be preparing the reluctant next generation for life. Scorn of the teacher as a man of affairs is notorious. It is attested by the attacks on Woodrow Wilson when he was running for president—"a mere *professor*." It is attested by the outcries against the employment of teachers of youth on public business—"impractical professors," a "braintrust" unworthy of any trust for the conduct of the affairs for whose conduct they are said to be preparing the children of their detractors.

There is evidence of a change in the public attitude, a change which began after World War I and gathered momentum through the Great Depression, the New Deal and World War II. The play *Journey's End* gave warning of it. This is a war play in which an English boy comes down to the trenches fresh from school, barely trained for his tasks of officer. He is helped through hard emotional places by a charming, modest, soft-spoken captain who wins his confidence and affection. Talking of what each had done "before," the captain tells that he had been a schoolmaster. The boy cries out, "What, *you* a schoolmaster!" or words to that effect. The cry and the character signalize both the traditional attitude and the turn from it. How very startling that a schoolmaster could be a man

and a hero! For that which the climate of opinion holds for a schoolmaster contains nothing brave, adventurous, wise, practical, tactful
and thoughtful. The schoolmaster personality is one routinized by
its occupation of repeating year after year to identical grade after
grade the same lessons according to the same rules under the same
requirements; of repeating, not discovering, not inventing; of serving merely as the policeman of the past instead of the husbandman
of the future. And in the teacher, most conspicuously in the woman
teacher, social expectation creates, far more than in craftsmen of
other vocations, its own fulfillment. The words of a woman chosen
by the men controlling the National Education Association to be
its president and to represent its multitudinous woman membership
give us a stereotype of the pedagogic mentality. "Ignorance and
narcotics," declared the lady, "tend to standardize, weaken and
defeat people. Education fosters individuality, distinction and
achievement. Has there been in all history so colossal a standardiz-
ing process—such a vast demonstration of the sheep-like qualities
of the human race as in the spread of the tobacco habit? Can we
afford to spread, even among our children, a habit whose cost is
greater than the total cost of free public education; a habit surely
unworthy an age that has produced a Lindbergh?" [4]

Almost a generation has passed since this communication from a
president of the National Education Association was put in print,
and the world has changed ominously in the interval. But there is
small indication that the Schoolmarm psyche has changed. The
mood and matter of this utterance are still representative. Its
"puritanism," its tangency to the dynamic realities among which
schools must struggle and children grow, has been hardly mitigated.
Today's symbols may be different. Another concretion of the
Schoolmarm's delight may have replaced the "lone eagle" of yore;
the comic strip and the radio may be today's competitors with
yesterday's narcotics. But the insight, the judgment and the values
remain untouched. Women, in being translated into Schoolmarms,
are shut into papier-mâché towers, where they may envisage
neither themselves nor their pupils nor their labors as church,
government, industry, the arts act on them. The Schoolmarm is by
vocation a figure heedless of the dynamics of experience.

[4] E. Ruth Pyrtle in the *Journal of the National Education Association*,
April, 1930.

How much this is so is attested by recurrent complaints that teachers, unlike doctors and lawyers and ministers, lack professional esprit de corps and seem unable or unwilling to acquire a professional attitude toward their craft. The best schools for the training of teachers are doing their best to inoculate their pupils with such an attitude, but it does not take easily. Educators who aspire to make teaching a profession the peer of the other learned professions, know that the professional spirit must become general and pervasive before the body of teachers can exert any genuine influence either on the nation's schools or on trends in the nation's life.

Their aspiration strikes against certain social facts. A girl who becomes a teacher cannot, like a man, learn the craft with any expectation of making its practice her life-work. If she is normal, she looks forward to marrying and a family of her own, and marriage would, in most places, cut her off from teaching. To remain a teacher she must accept the emotional and practical consequences of the unmarried state, and this very few women can or should do willingly. It is the woman frustrated and left behind who contracts into the Schoolmarm. The process of contraction usually begins with the girl's first job. She is then twenty-one or twenty-two years old. She starts her work believing what the professors who "trained" her have told her about the power and mission of the teacher. She is enthusiastic, hopeful, ambitious. She is a trustee of society and she will give her all to her trust. But she soon finds that the system will not permit her to give her all to her trust. She discovers that there is an uncoverable distance between the school as a fact and teaching as an ideal; that faith is falsified by works, that practice nullifies profession. Experience crystallizes into disillusion. If she continues as a teacher, it is not because she wants to but because she has no acceptable alternative, marriage being the most natural and desirable. By the time she reaches twenty-six or twenty-seven, she suffers a sort of crisis. She begins to feel out of it. The mood of uncertainty, insecurity, unhappiness becomes dominant; her automatic compensations for it appear as that assertiveness of manner and stridency of voice which signalize the Schoolmarm. She may have a "nervous breakdown"; she may leave teaching for office work or even for a factory. She may carry on. If she does, the still viable new personality traits get set as fixed habits. Her conflict deepens, but she ceases to be aware of it. The new pattern of her existence continues until her thirtieth year with reasonable stability. She may develop ailments—headaches, "nervous stomach," a neuralgia of one kind or another—and these, too, she may incorporate into the routine of her life. But between thirty and thirty-five, signs appear of tiltings of that stability and toward her fortieth year they begin to call for considerate attention. That school authorities, mostly male, are irked by these phenomena goes without saying. In New York City there have been on occasion charges and countercharges. Resentment among classroom teachers when such observations receive notice is automatic and natural. But both they and their bosses would gain advantage by a thoughtful consideration alike of the psychosomatic processes and of the social conditions whose function they so largely are. Those conditions impose occupational hazards of which teachers are innocent victims. They start their work as young, warm, healthy, idealistic human beings. But the work, the working conditions, and the community's taboos and prescriptions for the worker dehumanize them into the soured, unhealthy, comical social type, the *Schoolmarm*.

The antidote to this dehumanization of woman into Schoolmarm has long been known and every time there is a crisis in the schools, comes in for public discussion. But the action it calls for would inconvenience administrators too much for them to take it willingly. Nor is it likely that the multitudes of teachers, to whose wellbeing this action is necessary, would be willing to take it. To date only militant minorities employed in city schools have made a stand for any part of it. One powerful deterrent seems to be purely the feeling of occupational caste. Most American teachers are the offspring of manual laborers, skilled and unskilled. For them, becoming a teacher is a rise in social rank. The custom of the country grades schoolmarming among the genteel occupations of women. Before the development of our public schools it had been the quite proper mode of making a living open to decayed gentlewomen. The aura of that past continues to gild the Schoolmarm's present. It gives the latter the feeling that she has risen a cut above her family, and for the most part she has been willing to pay the price for the rise in lower income and greater social restrictions, lag of mind, constriction of heart. For the most part the Schoolmarm prefers to count as a respectable but unrespected teacher to counting as a mistrusted but respected trades-unionist. Though an orchestration of teachers' occupational interests with those of the trades-union movement is one sure way toward professional autonomy and personal freedom and equality, teachers' unions are small in number and not highly regarded by the teachers. Yet, if the women who make up the overwhelming majority of America's teachers are to win for their craft the status of the learned professions, and for themselves parity with the males who are its masters, they must needs adapt union principles and union methods to the exigencies of their vocation. All the disabilities laid upon women as women, even in our free society, are heightened where women become teachers. Only as they take their liberation in their own hands have they any chance of achieving it. Only as they themselves undertake to free their being and vocation from the absurd bonds in which they are bound; only as they conquer for themselves in fact the freedom of speech and association which they are supposed to have in law; only as they compel the inward democratization of their craft, can they truly perfect it into a profession and protect themselves from dehumanization. Humanity and humanism in the teacher-pupil relation can be brought to efficacy only by the teacher herself. The salvation of the teacher's own humanity on which the relation depends can be only the work of the teacher herself. The powers that be will not give her these as a gift. She will have to conquer them. But she cannot conquer them if she stands alone. Her natural, her inevitable allies are all those able workers with head and hand who still struggle for the equal liberty of free men in a free society. In their union is her strength. Without them she remains the woman buried alive in the Schoolmarm.

Chapter Four

THE GROWING CHILD AS CLASSROOM PUPIL

There are many tokens by which a culture separates man from the beasts of the field and the birds of the air. One, however, that underlies them all, rarely gets attention. This one is man's relation to time. As compared with non-human species, Homo sapiens struggles for an existence which fuses without identifying all three "dimensions" of time. His mature experience is an experience of past, present and future as both mutually exclusive and mutually suffusive. He early distinguishes between *now, soon* and *then.* As he grows older the phases of his perception of duration grow larger, more variegated and more massive. His sense of time shows itself to be a sense of *lasting.* Animals, on the other hand, are said to experience for the most part an unlinked *now,* whose instancy hardly lapses into an immediate past or overflows into an immediate future. By comparison with man, animals live in eternity. Compared with the beasts, man lives in time. Of human experiences, alone the idiot's comes close to the eternal of the beastly consciousness. Time is far more complex than eternity. Time is potent where the latter is impotent. Time is becoming, at once continuity and innovation, while eternity is ineffable sameness without movement, without mutation.

The distance between eternity and time, between an instant present and a lasting one which by lapsing becomes past and by growing becomes future, is spanned by memory. Man lives in time and not in eternity because he remembers, and he remembers because he can learn. Ultimately, to learn and to remember are one and the same action. Our knowledge, our skills, all our arts and sciences are built upon this almost unique trait of our nature as humans. *What* we recall, *where, when* and *how* reveals whether we are wise or silly, whether we live abundantly or poorly, grow or fail. Where the dynamic of memory is mistaken or ignored or misunderstood, teaching may be the greatest of all barriers to learning; the schools, the teachers, the entire educational enterprise may serve only as an assault upon the learner, and he may appraise them as Macbeth appraised all life—a tale told by an idiot, full of sound and fury, signifying nothing.

Men of the twentieth century have, in some degree and not too willingly, recognized this contingency. To the extent that psychology has been worked over into a genuine knowing of the human psyche, it has become more and more a psychology of learning; learning has been envisaged as not merely an event in a schoolroom, managed by a teacher, but as the entire process of growing up and growing old, the inward stuff of every biography from conception to dissolution. Henry Adams signalized this new apprehension when he called his autobiography *The Education of Henry Adams*. In the understanding of our day, learning is an autonomous sequence which starts before birth and stops only at death; living is learning and learning is living.

It follows that only if the newborn child is born a learner, that is, with the capacity of retention, recall and projection, can it have a biography; or a nation of such psyches have a history. In the economy of any culture, hence, the critical place is the child's place. What happens to the child and how it happens determine whether the culture shall merely survive or shall grow, shall deteriorate only or shall perish. The school, with its doctrines and disciplines and teachers, is one mode of social control over this *how* and this *what*. When the child is taken, as custom and tradition almost everywhere take it, for the possession of its elders and the ward of the church or the state, it may be rightly called that which Franklin Roosevelt once called it—the nation's human capital; and teachers may be designated, as Franklin Roosevelt then designated them, the custodians of this human capital. Where the child is regarded as a capital possession, the teacher's task is first and last to make sure that the capital shall not be squandered but so invested as to bring its owners the greatest profit.

But the nature of the child vetoes this conception of its relation to the grown-ups. The psychophysical organism, even in the behaviors of helpless and dependent infancy, reveals the traits, not of a live chattel but of a free human being in the making. This making, which is its education, all too often takes the form of a gerontic struggle permanently to establish possession, to shut the child in and harness it up in a doctrine and discipline, in habits of submission and conformity, instead of releasing it to the hazardous liberties of self-rule and self-help in an open world of thoughts and things. Every newborn child, the experts tell us,[1] is a specific animal organism with an individuality as singular and indefeasible as the fingerprints which signalize its identity; even its identical twin, if it has one, embodies no repetition of, but diverges from that identity and sustains a uniqueness all its own.

However different each infant be from every other, all are equal in their dependence and helplessness. Without the care and guidance of mother or nurse all would equally perish. Care and guidance are activities whose tools, materials and forms alter from culture to culture, and within each culture from group to group according to religious, occupational, political, caste and other differences. The old ones undertake with varying skills and diverse successes to guard the infant from perishing and to ensure and direct its growing. Whatever be the singularities of folkways, mores and practical wisdom to which they shape its growing, the original force of all is each infant's animal drive. This appears to be an ambiguous quantum and unique pattern of vital energies organized in the forces and composing the gradient of a culture's being and growth. It is this organization that guidance and care orchestrate to the culture of the guides. The orchestration, as everybody knows who was ever a child, is not all harmony.

An observer of guidance and care will first see its forms and its tools, not the individuality upon which they work. The molding culture is what first strikes the attention. Only with time can the onlooker pass from the over-all American or Hindu or Arab or British or Russian or Swedish or French or Argentine skyline of a growing child's existence, toward the nearer ones of his region, his community or his family-group with its differentials of extraction, income, vocation, cultus and cultivation. Only at the very last can an inquirer's look, outside a laboratory, see into the personal singularity of the child's psychological springs. A long procession of travelers, reporting on American children, speak of them as creatures without discipline, rude to their elders, unrespectful of the stranger, self-centered and demanding. But they also note them as somehow more self-dependent and self-directive than their European peers, and as living more happily and more abundantly. Some

---

[1] See Arnold Gesell and Frances Ilg *Infant and Child in the Culture of Today; The Child from Five to Ten,* etc.

thereupon quote Plato; [2] and American schoolmasters sounding off
the perennial pedogogic alarums echo the quotation in anxious
choruses:

In a democratic country you will be told that liberty is its
noblest possession, which makes it the only fit place for a free
spirit to live in . . . the spirit of liberty is bound to go to all
lengths . . . It will make its way into the home until at last the
very animals catch the infection of anarchy. The parent falls into
the habit of behaving like the child; and the child like the
parent; the father is afraid of his sons, and they show no fear
or respect for their parents, in order to assert their freedom . . .
the schoolmaster timidly flatters his pupils and pupils make light
of their masters as well as their attendants. Generally speaking,
the young copy their elders, argue with them and will not do
as they are told; while the old, anxious not to be thought disagreeable tyrants, imitate the young and condescend to enter into
their jokes and amusements. The full measure of popular liberty
is reached when the slaves of both sexes are quite as free as the
owners who paid for them; and I have quite forgotten to mention
the spirit of equality in the mutual relations of men and
women . . . the very dogs behave as if the proverb, 'like mistress,
like maid' applied to them . . . the whole place is simply bursting
with the spirit of liberty.

The modern sciences of man do not, however, draw the same
consequences from Plato's animadversions that the modern Platonizers draw.[3] The Platonic appraisal of freedom as evil is a judgment of value, the expression of a bias, not the observation of an
event. If the Platonizers of education do not like the fact that the
"typical" American school child lives a freer being than his like
elsewhere in the world, so much the worse for the Platonizers. From
their prophet's day until our time they have been the power-holders
in the schools and the consequences of their role demonstrate not
only the illusions of their psychology and the hopeless cruelty of
their doctrine and discipline; they demonstrate also the vital relevance of the American way—even though the schools tend to de-
nature it—to the spontaneous impulses of the human young
toward self-rule and self-help. Into the larger atmosphere of institutional attitude and social appraisal which we idealize as Ameri-

---

[2] *Republic Book VIII*, 562, 563.
[3] See Roger J. Williams: *The Human Frontier*, (New York: 1946).

canism, the lesser ones of region, community, family, pour their confluent influences. The primacy of the family's is a truism.

Every newborn child entering a family circle possesses a definite but undirected and undeveloped equipment. This initial endowment is sometimes called "the wisdom of the body." It is a blind wisdom, a helpless, and for the time being a brainless wisdom, an adience [4] without aim that stirs in every limb and every organ, and stops only when it hits upon warmth, or food, or easement of any other kind. It seems the wisdom of an autonomous yet plastic automaton. Its action embodies neither manners nor morals. None of the elders' measures of good and bad or right and wrong as yet exist in it. These it learns and absorbs as channels for its cravings toward the stilling of its wants, the relieving of its pains and pangs, the help and comfort of the human touch. All its doings, in the brief hour or two that it stays awake, are but adiencies groping after those satisfactions and reliefs. Its attainments are discoveries, not predictions, and they must be experienced as unexpected ends before they can be employed as means to expectations.

The infant's method, hence, is the method of trial and error. Its instinctive urges are but working hypotheses, not inborn certainties. Its searchings and seekings go on without shame, without guilt, without any sense of *thine* and *mine*, and without any image of anticipated consequences. Learning, for it, is the bridging of *now* and *soon*, by projecting *then* into the dark beyond of time.

Its linkage and projection of its experiences reveal a beat and rhythm singular to itself. Every baby lives and grows by an inward organic time to which the clock-time of the grown-up's convenience may bring but dearth and opposition. Loud, sudden sound, sharp,

---

[4] So far as I know, Edwin Holt is the first to employ this term. He means by it a going toward anything in order "to get more of it." The organism, he says, is equipped "from an early period of its life with an overwhelming number of reflexes which go out to meet the stimulus, get more of it, repeat or reproduce the stimulation; which are in short adient." (p. 41). The opposite of this going toward is avoidance, which Holt calls "*abient*" response." He is, of course, here discussing behavior on a "simple" physiological level. On more complex levels *adience* may be said to compound into curiosity, love, hunger, friendship, and many other organizations of outgoing actions. See Edwin B. Holt, *Animal Drive and the Learning Process* (New York: Henry Holt and Company, 1931).

sudden light, will stop an adient infant in its tracks, will bring on the recoils we know as fear and rage. For that matter, any check of its adience, any hard barrier to its ongoing movements, may bring those on; and what the elders do about them may quickly dissipate them or establish them as habits.

Mother, and—more or less—father, are central here. Biologically, family life is a symbiosis of individuals whose focus is the fact that human infancy, with its helplessness and dependence, lasts a long time. Animals without infants do not form families; and among those with infants, the longer the infancy, the more continuous and stable the families. Only among men are there families purposely without children, and children without families. If the former are to be understood as social prolongations of the male-female relation outside the breeding function, the latter may be interpreted as a socially induced reduction of that function to the nine months of gestation. Both exalt marriage above motherhood. The first approves the childless wife. The second condemns the unmarried mother. But the first and second, like the family with children, receive their status from the prolongation of human infancy and the human young's many years' dependence upon adults for survival and growth.

Surrounded by people and the things people make and use, the child's responses to people are the most dynamic and important events in its experience. Its relations with them, like its relations with things, begin contingently and grow into inward connections. Impressions rain in upon it, mingle with the manifold variety of its adiencies of limbs and organs as those discharge their motor, their secretory and excretory impulsions, and all come out in awareness of craving and satisfaction, discomfort and relief, which flow together in the stream of the child's consciousness and make themselves evident as the multiform approaches and withdrawals composing its behavior. This confluence and mingling are not an adaptation to the environment. Infancy cannot by itself accomplish adaptation. Infancy learns adaptation only as it grows. While its inner adiencies carry it from the experience of spatiality to clear and distinct ideas of the dimensions of space in about a year, they take three years, more or less, to advance its awareness from the instancy of animal eternity to the durational stretch of human time. A year of propulsive explorations bring it selectively to fix a year of discovered gratifications; bring it intentionally to cling to *here,* *there; hither, yon; up, down, on, in* and *out; beside, before, be-* *hind.* But it requires a much longer period to establish a continuity of discrimination between these spatial relations; and it needs eighteen months to realize *now,* twenty-four to realize *soon;* and thirty-six to have any explicit awareness of present, past and future as both distinct and interfused. The infant is able to know itself as bigger before it can appreciate being older. It cannot distinguish between one and many until it is twenty-four months old, nor count to ten before sixty months, nor until then readily identify color or texture, nor have a sense of agency rather than of simple occurrence. Likewise its speech requires experimentation, search- ing and seeking, configuration and refinement.

Not until a child's fifth year have its trends crystallized into its ruling passion and the direction and the shape of its works and ways become prophetic of lasting goals. By then its infancy is over, its milk teeth are being replaced by its permanent molars. Both embryologists and philosophers as well as psychologists [5] suggest that the development of the living child, from conception to birth, from birth to its fifth year—and beyond, to the coming of puberty —is a tremendously foreshortened recapitulation of the life story of the race; that the development has a certain irresistibility, a certain intrinsic tempo and form, of which learning is an aspect; that it proceeds in alternations of activity and quiescence, like the explo- sions of a rocket; that each explosion of searching, seeking, reject- ing, avoiding and accepting is followed by a phase of consolidation and refinement, until action ensues again from the newer, more manifold and complex level of organization. The bursts and silences, the crests and troughs of the wave, reveal only a variable regularity. Development is, like the weather, an event made up of fluctuations. The most potent of all outer influences upon it continue to be the persons of the family.

What can these persons figure as, in the experience of a helpless infant? They embody, even more than they furnish, the hazards and happinesses of the infantile experience. Gargantuan powers, that the so small infant is helpless to resist, the family spontane-

---

[5] Cf. George Corner, *Ourselves Unborn;* Henri Bergson, *Creative Evo-* *lution;* Gessell and Ilg, *Infant and Child in the Culture of Today;* Edward Thorndike, *Man and His Works;* G. Stanley Hall, *Adolescence.*

ously treat it as a possession which must learn to suit their requirements and not they its. The simple mother, little contaminated by
the guesses of child-study circles, being bound to her infant by her
own endocrine processes projected outward in patterns provided by
the culture of her immediate group, will act like any female of the
species, in the nurture and protection of her babe. From the father
his child may evoke the reactions to a nuisance and a rival as well
as those ordained by his group's idea of paternity or by his own
idea of the child as a vehicle of fulfillment of his ungratified ambitions. To brothers and sisters a baby will figure first as an object
of curiosity, then as rival or nuisance or as both. All are likely to
dam up one or another of its spontaneous adiencies, to discourage,
check or control. From such occlusions the adient infantile energies
can flow back only to the infant's own organs and their inner
impulsions. Lacking the nipple, it may learn that the attention and
comfort it seeks comes from sucking its thumbs or handling its sex
organs; it may learn that elders bring what it likes when it cries
and vomits or is otherwise incontinent, commonly by wetting its
bed. It may stage a tantrum; refuse to eat; either cling or run away
when it shouldn't. It may be just "contrary." By its fifth year, it
may have developed arts of escaping inhibition and frustration at
the hands of the bigger and stronger by means of showing off,
hiding away or playing out roles of power and release through
impersonations which make up in make-believe for the insufficien-
cies of its actual living. In daydreams or in play a child may
pretend the strengths of adults or work out its revenges upon the
tyrannies of those strengths with laughter or with tears. Most of
its world will be two-faced to its seeing because most will both
withhold and grant, restrain and spur on. Mother, father, brothers
and sisters, however, will do so more than any. They are the overruling powers of the childish world, its providence of freedom, of
fulfillment, or of frustration. Once it has learned that their service
follows its expression, it automatically tries to bring them to service
by these means, the only ones at its command. From its beginning,
the infant's existence is a tug of war with an environment of
persons seeking to shape the infant to their convenience, and an
infant personality seeking to secure from the personal environment
the satisfactions its nature craves.

A sound psychology of learning would show how to make this

conflict over into co-operation. Such a psychology is available [6] but its employment is still only occasional and timid. The child which for the first time goes from home to school is rarely seen by the teacher as the psychosomatic personality that, between birth and schooltime, he has grown into and will grow out of. The living child is seen in the reflections of the persistent tradition. A social image, not an individual and scientific perception, supplies the directive for the attitude of teacher to pupil, and this image contains little of the nature of the child and much of the troubles of the grown-up. Those the image embodies and projects upon the child. Thus, during countless generations, the child was imaged as a small adult; its autonomous growth processes were accounted for as original sin, its instinctual urges as natural perversities. If gifted, and therefore different, it was doing the work of the devil; if dull, it was ridden by an incubus. Whatever the condition of the child, if it did not conform to the convenience of the adult, it was satisfying the lusts of the flesh, instead of performing the duties of the spirit. To educate it, hence, was to discipline it. And to discipline it was, significantly, to beat faith and obedience into it. Up to 1900, "spare the rod and spoil the child" was the first principle of pedagogy. The cane, the rattan, the ruler were prime agencies of doctrine and discipline. Their ancestor is the scourge which the Romans used to beat their slaves with. Discipline was conceived as the exercise of superior power in order to compel children to do what they couldn't like and wouldn't want to do. Discipline was liberating the spirit by mortifying the flesh. And present spokesmen for the tradition of discipline declare that "true freedom is identical with duty," that "it is discipline that makes the mind free." For, although there has been some relaxation since 1900, general pedagogic sentiment still looks upon fear of the teacher as the beginning of schoolroom wisdom and to depart from schoolroom evil as scholastic understanding. The unconscious image of the child as a vessel of natural depravity still rules the classroom, and grounds the suppressions and the inhibitions on which the teaching tasks are postulated. Rules and regulations impattern it; fear of punishment rather than interest in achievement motivate it. In spite of

---

[6] Thanks to the pioneer work of Edward Thorndike and his followers, of Kurt Lewin and Max Wertheimer, and of Sigmund Freud and the Freudians.

Rousseau and Froebel and Pestalozzi, in spite of Dewey and Thorn-dike, of Freud and Gesell and Lewin, the teacher still figures as the enemy of the pupil, and teaching as the antithesis of learning. Remembering, as the test of learning, is still a barren reproduction or an empty rehearsal rather than a fruitful use of the past.

True, Dewey and those other pioneers of insight into the nature of man-in-the-making have drawn their insights from schoolroom observation and experience. True, it is the need of the educator which, more than any other, has brought into being a realistic and relevant knowledge of the nature and growth of the mind. True, this new psychology has overlaid the old feelings and judg-ments with the disguise of a new vocabulary, and education is nowadays defined as "socialization," or as "acculturation." True, educators avail themselves of many devices, of which the intelli-gence tests were the first parents, whose invention and use the scientific study of learning and growing has suggested. True, in more than one industrial community, the hardships of the school become the child's refuge from the more unbearable hardships of his home. But, by and large, neither the insights, the gadgets nor the dialects of the psychologists have much affected the operational idea of the child or the prevailing teacher-pupil relation. Only the nursery school and the kindergarten may continue, in one form or another, the material arrangements and social relationships of the home from which the child is taken. But with the first grade, the school setting, with its economy and its demands, becomes ever less relevant to the effective needs of the growing child. The three R's as taught, are imposed drudgery where they could and should be accepted adventures. "Enriched" by specialists in curriculum-making though it be, the nationwide curriculum neither awakens nor sustains curiosity. Indeed, many curricula give the impression that they have been purposely designed to shut out anything that would thus affect the pupil. That which the school requires of the pupil and that which its needy growth requires coincide only by accident.

Mostly, the irrelevancy of the matter is interpreted as the sin or the deficiency of the child. His relation to his world of people, thoughts and things is far more a function of his development than his development a function of his environment. The latter, like his nourishment, serves directly but as a repressor or releaser, only indirectly as a transformer. He grows up and grows old as a stream flows. Whatever immediate turn it takes, its direction is always forward. So is a child's learning or development. Its course is a confluence of psychosomatic attitudes and energies, cutting for their flow the easiest, smoothest, shortest channel which the powers and patterns of the surrounding scene permits. In the language of the professionals, maturation underlies acculturation. Maturation grounds all the improvements in a child's powers of movement and performance, in its tonus and moods, its sense of self and sex, its relation to other children and grown-ups, its fantasies, imaginings and dreams, its recognition of *thine* and *mine,* and its attainment and use of the concurrent symbols, verbal and other, with which it expresses these events and situations. But the curricula are prepared with a minimum of consideration of the life-process with its order of interests and passions. They do, in fact, undertake to do what Mr. Mark van Doren deplores that they do not do—"store his memory . . . with things deserving to be there." The gradations of a syllabus in any subject are far more syllogistic than developmental. Except for mathematics, the subjects themselves are represented in symbols rather than presented in things and events. Geography, the sciences, the social sciences, history, as well as the three R's are taught verbally as modes of talking without any perception of what the stuffs and persons and events talked about are like, and without dynamic linking to the dominant drives and ruling passions of the child as it grows. The persons of these children, the learners, with the vital momentous options of their daily lives and long-run trends, hardly figure in our prevailing programs of instruction. For these programs they are not boys and girls with hopes and hungers, with fears, aggressions and curiosities, all loaded with pleasures and pains, struggling to live and to grow in a world they never made. For curriculum-makers, children are disembodied intelligences dedicated to acquiring and repeating the multiplication tables of the pedagogic disciplines. That they fail is the sin of the children; when they succeed, it is the virtue of the discipline.

Can any reasonable person wonder that, as repeated tests have shown, the nation's school children do not learn what they are taught, however much the schooltime of their lives is prolonged? Who, knowing the facts, is astonished that the learning they do acquire is a bootlegged learning they impart to one another; that it is about sex and begetting and death and power and God, about the duality of the elders' ethics and politics, about the worth and rightness of frustrating the elders' powers and nullifying their rules? Who, aware of the realities, can blame school children for preferring comics and soap-operas and movies to "readers" and musical classics and textbooks on this and that? Small wonder that "dyslexia" has become an important word in the Pedagese of pedagogues and that the land is spotted with "reading clinics" where the child is examined for everything except the irrelevancy of what he is expected to read. Not that wise teaching, heedful of the learners' wants and cravings, could not make it relevant. The much-deplored extra-curricular reading matter of youth is sufficient testimony. . . .

The total effect of the survival of the ancient image of the child in the ways and works of the contemporary school is a continuation of the traditional war between teacher and pupil. For the pupil, to whose innocent and outgoing kindergarten heart the teacher is at the outset a friend and helper, encounters in the teacher soon after entering the grades, a tyrannical taskmaster demanding the performance of empty and meaningless tasks. Hence it becomes first a matter of self-defense, then a matter of prestige and honor to fool and to frustrate the teacher. The truest, most ancient, most perennial, most classical of all the class-wars, is the classroom war between teacher and pupil. In the course of this war, teaching has become for the teacher a pedagogue's discipline designed to induce submission, compel obedience, and punish independence of mind as well as behavior. The attitude is already explicit in Plato who prescribes "noble lies" as molds and models for the growing personality to be shaped to. In reaction to it learning has become for the pupil a techinque of evasion and pretense designed to quiet the teacher without obeying his rule, and to maintain independence without incurring his punishment. In fact, most school children live a double life. One consists of the attitudes, behaviors, and expressions which the grown-up world of parents and teachers exacts. The young do not long remain deceived by the tartuffian "noble lies" of their elders. Their disillusion plays its part in the making of the other, deeper mode of their developmental becoming. That consists of the works and ways of the growing psyche finding its place among its peers in the "gang" with its codes and secrets, its collective "honor," its inner rivalries and emulations, its outer feuds, its alert and embattled aliency to the grown-up world.

The duality shows itself very early in the growing child's career as a classroom pupil.[7]

Since only rarely at any level of schooling, does the role of the teacher rise from that of master to that of leader, the class-war of teacher and pupil continues through college. The duality repeats itself, although its terms alter. If in the elementary school the growing child is required to comport himself like a grown man, in college the grown man is subjected to the regulations and policings of the growing child. College prolongs infancy.

---

[7] See George Madden Martin, *Emmy Lou: Her Book and Heart* for a moving exposition of this duality, as valid today as when it was written half a century ago.

Chapter Five

HIGH SCHOOL AND COLLEGE IN THE
SOCIAL PROLONGATION OF INFANCY

Until the industrial revolution, the human growth cycle and human culture were largely in harmony. Biological maturation was the unconscious common base of social adulthood, and love and begetting, birth and work and war and play, with the institutions which channeled them, had for their nuclei critical moments of the organism's development from the day it was born to the day it died. This is still the case with the overwhelming majority of the cultures of the world. But it is no longer the case in industrialized societies—the more industrialized, the less it is the case. Those societies—most notably our own, in America—carry the prolongation of infancy far beyond its biological termination. They have developed, and are extending, a social prolongation of infancy whose most signal instruments are the high school and the college. Broadly speaking, elementary education is completed about the time boys and girls reach puberty. But the organization and management of high school and college prolong the pre-pubertal dependence, its juvenility and social non-responsibility to the twenty-second or twenty-third year of life.

In the usage of our times "college man," "college girl," "collegiate," have acquired meanings which hold a significance for the pupil similar to the significance of "schoolmarm," "pedagogue," "professor," for the teacher. If to be a schoolmarm or schoolmaster is to be old before your time, to be repressed, sour, lean, impractical and maladjusted; if to be a professor is to be a figure with, in William James's words, "a starched shirt and spectacles . . . a stock of ideals," and to be despised as "a prig, a pedant and a parody," then to be collegiate is to embody a certain type of youthful gentleman able to live without working for a living, to have money in his pocket, to wear "collegiate" clothes, to use collegiate speech, to conduct himself carelessly, ungenerously, and with a false irresponsible lightness. Young people who work for their livings envy and emulate this gentlemanly type; a maid will favor a man she believes to be "collegiate"; she knows "he is going to be a good date." But college students themselves are by no means unanimous in approving the image: not so long ago sophomores at Barnard College in New York initiated freshmen into their undergraduate communion with the advice "Don't be collegiate." The presumption was that without this advice newcomers from the high schools would labor toward that higher excellence.

The forces which keep alive and potent this modern mutation of an ancient original are many and varied. Fundamental is the democratic ideal which underlies the struggle to equalize educational opportunity for all the nation's children, and to enable each to become as good as his betters and better. Harmonics to this dominant theme sound from other sources. One is the fact that industrial society is by and large a society of people who live longer than their forbears. Within half a century, the expectation of life has been raised from forty to forty-eight years. Our society tends more and more to become a society of old people, a society with a falling death rate and a descending birth rate, a society in which the secular trend joins to the other values of childhood and youth the value of scarcity. Here in our United States we counted, in 1790, 1000 children for every 780 adults; by 1900 the count had fallen to 1000 children for every 1580 adults; in 1920 it was 1000 for every 1890 adults; in 1930, it was 1000 for every 2000. Because of World War II, the proportion of births has somewhat risen; but experts on population-growth hold firmly to the proposition that the rise is an interlude of deviation in a generally undeviating trend. Children become fewer, and as their numbers decrease, the value of childhood and youth increases. They become increasingly objects of solicitous attention. Efforts multiply to know them, to understand them, to preserve them, to protect them. Agencies and bureaus, public and private, are created to serve "child welfare," to study and direct child life. These instrumentalities tend to alter existing folkways and mores, to develop new institutions and diversify or greatly extend existing ones; to bring on the enactment of new basic laws, such as the still unadopted Child Labor Amendment to the Constitution. Significantly, the resistance to this Amendment is strongest in those regions where children are most numerous, and in those religious establishments whose ideals are most traditional, fundamentalist and authoritarian.

But even in those enclaves of resistance there is now operative an appreciation of youth as youth for which other ages and other cultures provide no parallels—an appreciation signalized by the community's disposition toward "collegiate" works and ways. High school and college impart to the social prolongation of infancy a conspicuous singularity, for they divert the process from the development of the social readiness which is its natural terminus.

This consequence becomes clearer in light of the relation of youth to adulthood in other than democratic industrial societies or institutions. All over the world, social adulthood coincides more or less roughly with puberty, with physiological maturity—that is, with readiness to get and bear children, to found and maintain a family. Puberty is followed by initiation into the society of the grown-ups and admission to the responsibilities of adult life. Among primitives the only formal education a boy or girl receives is that inflicted on them at this critical moment of development. They are then most painfully initiated into the doctrine and discipline of the tribe. For three weeks or so the pubescent boy is cut off from the rest of his fellowship, shut in with his elders who beat him, torture him, scarify him, perhaps circumcise him or slit his urethra, while they divulge to him the incantations and rituals of his totemic tutelage. Some initiations not only hand on the tribal illusions; they also debunk. An Arunta boy in Australia will all his life have heard the terrible voice of Baimai or the Alchuringa and felt duly prostrated and awed. But at initiation the elders will show him the bull-roarer with which they produce the divine clamor, and instruct him in its making and use. Initiation completed, he is a full-fledged adult of the tribe, a warrior with the right to join in battle, a huntsman, a male with the right to take a female as he can, a peer of any champion with the right to challenge him; any champion, that is, but the old men of the tribe—their persons and authority are taboo.

The Western world transposes the primitive initiatory rite into the ceremonials of baptism, confirmation, and the like of its own religious establishments and confessions. The rituals are more symbolic, less painful to the neophyte, but they rest on the same fundamental assumptions: readiness for the responsibilities of adulthood in a nature perverse and corrupt with original sin, of which it must be cleansed before the readiness can be acknowledged by the elders and the responsibilities of maturity undertaken by the youth. The Catholic rite of confirmation is performed, roughly, at puberty. For little girls it appears as a sort of symbolic marriage in which, wearing veils and dressed in white, they become in spirit the brides of Christ; little boys appear accoutered as bridegrooms and may be said to be inducted into an avowed army of the Lord. Most Protestant churches call for a conviction of sin and an avowal of faith as a part of joining the church; many require that the initiate undergo baptism as the final cleansing which makes him an acceptable one who takes on himself the responsibility of the adult before his Maker. Fundamentalists in Judaism have long practiced a complex initiatory rite for boys. Each, of course, has been ceremonially circumcised on the eighth day after his birth, but he stays socially an infant until his thirteenth birthday. Then he goes before the congregation of the synagogue with his father and the latter publicly renounces all responsibility for him. Until that moment the guilt of the boy's sins, of omission and of commission, have fallen upon his father. From then on, the guilt is the boy's own. In another ceremony he becomes Bar Mitzvah, answerable in his person for observing the 613 commandments of the Judaistic code, entitled to count as one of the ten persons necessary for public worship, marriageable, admissible to the responsibilities of a family.

Before World War II there were still, in the simple primitive Polish and Austrian lands, correspondingly simple Jewish communities where boys were married at fifteen and girls even at thirteen. Marriages at puberty or soon after are indeed by no means uncommon in the more primitive communities of our South, and of very many European countries. Early marriage, even child marriage, many children, go with fundamentalist religion, Catholic or Protestant, everywhere in the world. For women—it is different for the male—it goes with wealth, even in democratic industrial societies; here the hillbilly and the *haute monde* join hands.

The practice is parallel when it comes to acknowledging readiness to work for a living. Child labor, for the benefit and under the supervision of the parents, is still common in agriculture; it used to be just as common in industry. There was a time when parents could dispose of the labor of their children at will. Nowadays most free societies require that a child shall have basic public education before becoming an earner. The requirement is a step in the social prolongation of infancy. The age at which permission is first given varies from ten to sixteen. Before World War II it averaged twelve in England, thirteen in the United States. And the average is being raised. To date, however, society recognizes that youth has come into its power of self-help and self-support at about the time it becomes able to get and to bear children. Pressure grows to postpone acknowledgment of the first power to an ever later date after the maturation of the second. The enormous increase in the enrollments in high schools and colleges, between the two world wars, is in part a response to the growing pressure. Modern society uses schooling as an alternative to working: it continues to add to the required number of schooldays and to put off to a later and later year the time when a boy or girl may entirely leave school.

The school, however, retains rules and requirements which are more relevant to the perceptions and convenience of the schoolmen than the needs and dispositions of their pupils. To those, content, method and organization are largely irrelevant, and being so, give the social prolongation of infancy, which they serve, a perverse turn.

For inwardly adolescence is more dynamic, more curious, more self-reliant, self-ruling and self-supporting, and yet self-doubting than the school permits. Benjamin Franklin was on his own at twelve, and hawking his own verses on the streets of Boston at thirteen. Thomas Jefferson became the head of his own family and the planner of his own career before he was thirteen; he was the companion of the governor of the Dominion and crony of his teachers before he was out of his teens. Blaise Pascal had devised his arithmetical machine at nineteen. Herbert Spencer worked as an engineer at seventeen. Horatio Nelson went to sea at thirteen and commanded a ship at fifteen. Montcalm and Wolfe were generals at sixteen. Lafayette was one at nineteen. Every war calls attention to youths, volunteers and draftees alike, who start at scratch and emerge before they are twenty-five as captains and majors and colonels, with all the responsibilities these grades import.

The same holds for artists and men of science, in their several domains. They are seriously about their business in their teens. Galileo was seventeen when he determined the law of the pendulum by taking his pulse while watching the lamps swing from the roof of the Duomo in Florence. Edison, Einstein, Leibnitz, Darwin and Spinoza came into their vocations before they were twenty.

Of course, social ripening more nearly coincided with psychosomatic maturation in the societies where these notables were growing up. But they were then, and remain now, representative as well as notable, and embody a truth about youth that the present prolongation of infancy ignores and the schools which are its instruments suppress.

Yet not only the contemporary church, also the military establishment plays close to this truth. Eighteen is the conventional age for volunteering as well as for conscription. There are places and there were times when it was sixteen, and sixteen already manifests an urge toward military enterprise. Yet a citizen must be from three to seven years older than eighteen for civic responsibility; he is held to be adult enough to fight and die for his country long before he is permitted to vote for its legislators and rulers. Society postpones admission to political maturity long beyond admission to religious, industrial and military maturity. Age, holding power, will share it only with its like.

And for the most part the power-holding sex is the male sex. Women are still far from participating on equal terms with men in the enterprises of the common life. In so far as they do, they also are subjected to the social prolongation of infancy. If, in the domains which the mores keep peculiarly woman's, social and psychosomatic adulthood are nearer together, a social prolongation of infancy is manifest nevertheless. Thus the "age of consent" is variously set between the tenth or eleventh and eighteenth year. The more complex and industrialized the culture, the later the age of consent. It is early in our deep South, later is such states as New York or Wisconsin. Rarely is it set before the onset of puberty, although in India, according to Katherine Mayo, girls are regarded as ripe for cohabitation at the age of eight. Child marriage is a somewhat different matter. But it is significant that the fashionable worlds of Europe and America present their daughters in the marriage mart at more nearly the age of biological readiness. Those presented are the "debutantes"; those between nubility and the year of presentation are "subdebs." The presentation is today's form of social initiation of the females of those enclaves.

By and large the religious, the industrial and the military establishments, together with leisure classes whose women must not work for a living and whose men, if they do work, work only for fun, tend, in their admission of youth to the activities if not the status of adulthood, to depart very little from the moment of developmental readiness, and to make for rough coincidence of social maturity with physiological maturity. On the other hand, the democratic faith, the changing ratio of youth to age in the population, the ever-increasing diversification of the "body of knowledge" and complication of the techniques of the industrial economy, tend to push social maturity to an ever later time than psychosomatic maturity. They tend to keep growing youth socially a child although its soul and body have ripened into the adulthood their natures presaged. And they accomplish this retardation for the most part through the schools and the colleges.

One may say it was the humanitarian textile manufacturer, Robert Owen, who started to employ the schools for this purpose. A self-made man and captain of industry who married the boss's daughter, Owen was deeply disturbed by the horrible consequences of child labor in the textile mills of his England. He voluntarily raised the age for employing children in his factory at New Lanark and provided a school where these thus scandalously disemployed infants, the scions of England's "industrious classes," could keep their hands uncontaminated from the work which the devil finds for idle hands to do. Hitherto, some of his protégés might have been exposed only to the enlightenment of a Sunday school. Now it was to be a school that kept every day in the week, and at the boss's expense. Private enterprise generally regarded such extravagances with horror; and the public, tax-supported school was slow and slight as it came to England, where it is still of retarded growth. But in the United States, where education was believed to be a guarantee and defense of democracy, the people themselves slowly, and with much labor, secured the establishment and insured the growth in each state of a free public school system, from kindergarten to university. Up to 1900 American schools multiplied steadily but not conspicuously. Then their increase took on a dramatic acceleration.[1] In 1900 only 72 per cent of the children of

---

[1] This expansion of the free tax-supported public school exercised a vitalizing influence on the nation's private, or as they call themselves to-

school age attended school; by 1940 the percentage was 85, and the number of days of attendance had been increased from 99 to 152. In 1900 the expenditure per pupil was $14.00 and the cost per capita of population was $3.00. By 1940, the expenditure per pupil had been raised to $92.00 and the cost per capita of population was $18.00. Teachers were receiving an average salary of about $325.00 in 1900; and $1,441.00 in 1940. The nation's total spending on free public education from kindergarten through high school had increased from the $215,000,000 in 1900 to the $2,344,000,000 of 1940. In the same period high-school population had risen from 696,000 to 7,113,000 while high-school graduates had multiplied from 95,000 to 1,228,000. In the colleges of liberal arts, the colleges for teachers, and the professional schools the 238,000 enrolled in 1900 increased during the same period to 1,493,000—somewhat more than seven times the increase of the total population. After 1940, the war reduced the total high-school and college population by about a million. However, the number of college students is expected to reach from 3,000,000 to 4,500,000 by 1960.

The numbers here cited, it must be remembered, represent the upshot of a process of selection and survival of which the father's occupation, the family's income, the size of the family, the place of habitation and the neighbors' standards of living are all determiners. The American people have the right to congratulate

---

day, "independent" establishments. Challenging the invidious distinctions which the schooling of the prosperous sustained and emphasized, it broke a monopoly, compelled emulation and competition which on the whole and in the long run, tend to improve curriculum, methods and administration. The impact of the growing public school system on the religious school, particularly the parochial school of the Roman Catholic establishment, was notably salutary. Confronted by the competition of the free public school, the managements of the parochial system were under the necessity of raising standards, expanding their curriculum, and improving their methods. Even though they pretend that they have not compromised their authoritarianism nor altered their doctrine and discipline, their educational establishment is the most modern and progressive in the Roman Catholic world. They count today some 79 per cent of the nation's 12,727 private schools; and indoctrinate, if they do not educate, 92 per cent of their 2,611,000 students. They owe all their superiority over Catholic schools elsewhere to the competitive standards set by the free public schools. That they dislike the competition and call the competitive schools "Public Enemy No. 1" is a testimony to their value.

themselves on the fact that more American children have had more schooling (and that all are eligible to any level of it that they can make), than the children of any society in the world. They may point with pride to the fact that they spend more for education and make more of it available to a greater proportion of the nation's youth than the whole of Europe, and perhaps of Asia and Africa too. Yet fewer country children are able to get to high school or college than city children; fewer children of large families than of small; fewer children whose parents work at blue-shirt, mechanical trades than those with parents who follow the white-collar clerical occupations. From 40 to 45 per cent of children of high-school age are not in high school; 60 per cent of those attending high school are not likely to graduate. Far less than half of the tenant farmer children get to school at all, and little more than one-quarter of the Negro children. Only about 15 per cent of our youth of college age get to college, and of those admitted a considerable number leave before graduation. According to an overall estimate 90 per cent of all the children born in any year will go as far as the sixth grade of an elementary school; 60 per cent will reach the second year of high school; 45 per cent will graduate from high school; 15 per cent will finish the sophomore class in college; 7 per cent will take their degrees.

Two explanations are usually given for this situation. One is the economics of schooling—its costs and a family's inability to continue a child even at a free tax-supported public school, after it has reached physiological adulthood. Those employ this explanation who look to an ever-greater contribution by the state to correct the imbalance due to the poverty of the citizen. Another is the conception of levels of fitness for high school and beyond—the idea of different and unchangeable natural endowments which intelligence and other tests establish and measure scientifically, so that schools and colleges operate by a kind of natural selection of the fit for "higher" education. Spokesmen for both interpretations of the facts, often equally liberal, and eager that the nation's children shall receive the most of the best, look upon the school as the unaltering institution and automatically assume that the young must fit the school. They make the school the measure of the young, not the young the measure of the school.

Now as measure, the school is a quantitative hierarchy. Its values are graded from above downward, and its values are dual. The peak is the college, and the status of a college depends first on its social desirability—on the costs and amenities of "college life"—and secondly, on its entrance examinations. The conditions of graduation are a secondary matter; almost anybody who has been admitted, can, if he wants to take the necessary trouble, pass out with a diploma certifying that he is one of "the company of educated men," whether he be one or not. In the admission policy of most colleges social eligibility and intellectual capacity weigh differentially, and it is not intellectual capacity that necessarily weighs the most. Wealth, station, extraction, faith, politics and connections regularly play preponderant roles. There is a traditional connection between these qualifications and the transmission of the well-known liberal arts in whose perfections colleges of liberal arts purport to discipline the prospective baccalaureus, so as to turn him out a gentleman and a scholar. The education of the gentleman is not so ancient a social enterprise as the education of the priest or soldier. Historically, the gentleman is a wellborn warrior whom the appearance of the modern state deprived of his vocation. He is a landed knight made jobless because there ceased to be a use for his services, and thus with "free" time on his hands. To fill the leisure that would otherwise become *tedium vitae* he takes up the clerkly occupations: he concerns himself with the humanities, with music, with dancing, with the skills of love and personal honor. Hence he continues to be trained in the arts of personal warfare, but as an accomplishment, not as a vocation.

Castiglione's *Book of the Courtier* draws us an early plan for the education of the gentleman. Whatever the latter does must be freely done; it must involve nothing that would degrade him to the level of a person gainfully employed; he must not work; he must only pass the time—doing things at once beautiful and useless and unprofitable. When the universities of Europe added to their mediaeval tasks of training men for the vocations of divinity, law and medicine, the training of gentlemen for the vocation of leisure, that is, no vocation at all, they had perforce to make of the "humanities" a separate doctrine and discipline. And this *regulum studiorum,* with varying fortunes and changing rationalizations, has been maintained up to this day. A convention established itself and was kept up till the turn of the century that becoming a cultivated man consists chiefly in learning the languages, the verbal arts and letters of the ancient Greeks and Romans, and that those are the alpha and omega of all that the mind of man has achieved or discovered since. The dogma was not unchallenged. It initiated the well-known "Battle of the Books" and gave rise to the unending war between the ancients and the moderns. To this day the ancient disciplines are widely held as the nobility of the classroom, while the Greek-letter fraternities and sororities impose themselves as the nobility of the campus, the one a mark of intellectual superiority, the other of social privilege.

This social privilege is likewise no novelty, but a transposition and prolongation of a mediaeval status which underlay frequent clashes between "town" and "gown," between the educational establishment and the neighboring community. For the mediaeval schools were practically sovereign. They had their own economy and their own laws (within the canon law) and they alone had jurisdiction over the always incipient priests, their students. The lay community had no rights the student needed to heed. He could not be tried and punished for any misconduct; he could only be reported, and then the academic authorities could judge him and punish him or not as they saw fit. In practice this meant that often, when not in the society of his peers, the student could misbehave with impunity. The relation of gown to town was frequently the relation of betters to inferiors—supercilious, antagonistic, predatory. The social life of the gownsman was the self-contained social life of a peculiar fellowship or gang. With only incidental modifications, the modern college continues the town-gown relationship. To Americans, certainly, "college man" is a privileged social category. And because of the aura of divinity that trails from the collegiate past, "college," "college life," "college education" are spoken of with a certain reverence. They imply an invidious distinction such as pertains to the priest's vocation or the gentleman's leisure.

In our lay-minded age, the more important of the two is the gentleman's leisure. Here in America the religious brotherhoods are replaced by the Greek-letter fraternities, which from their beginning set the standards and ordain the statutes of the social life of colleges. Phi Beta Kappa is the exception which proves this rule, for this "honor" fraternity, too, was by first intention a gentleman's drinking club, and later litters of the breed adhere to the bright delights of that first intention. Qualifications for brotherhood—or sisterhood—are now far more pecuniary than fashionable; but that people without money can hardly be people of fashion, and that people with money can always be promoted to the status of fashionables, is still a fact. This fact seems to be the gradient for the ways of fraternities and sororities. Deviations from the gradient occur where there are not enough rich to go round. Then a fraternity will make a virtue of literary or athletic distinction, or of "contacts." But Negroes, Jews, Catholics, no matter how wealthy, talented, skilled or advantageously connected, will be ineligible to brotherhood by fraternity rule. Desirables are selected, "rushed" and "pledged." During this period of courting, nothing is too good for the frater prospective. Once he has committed himself, he undergoes an initiation which may retain most of the sadistic features of primitive initiations. He also pays an initiation fee—which in some fraternities is only $50.00, in others $1,000.00. He is then taught the service and deference due to his elder brothers and upperclassmen; he is required to learn the Greek alphabet so that he may recognize the letters on fraternity pins and banners; if he has money only, he is required to learn correct manners, table and other; (such failures in correctness as drinking from his saucer, dunking, spilling gravy, reaching, are punished by fines which range from five cents to one dollar). Since his remaining an active frater is conditioned on his remaining in college, he is taught the evasive arts by which he can safely remain with least effort. The competition between fraternities for desirable new brothers being sharp and not too scrupulous, he is expected to keep an eye out for, and to make "contacts" with, eligibles even in high school. But though fraternities are rivals in these and in many other respects, they present a united Greek front against the barbarian *hoi polloi* who make up the majorities of the college population. Through their parties, proms, and the like, through the management of their "houses," and in the rivalries of undergraduate politics, fraternities bring their members into contact with realities of human nature and human relations which are alien to the classrooms. Their upward of 6,000 chapters and 200,000 members, more or less—holding millions in real property—compose the high place of college life. They sustain and guard the college "traditions" and the collegiate mores. These tend to perpetuate the fundamental conflicts between classroom and campus, the class-war between teacher and pupil.

Many years ago, the dean of a great American college which long bore strong resemblances to a country club for young gentlemen, identified undegraduate morality as "gang morality." He saw all college students in the likeness of a primitive tribe, and compared their local variations to those of clans within a tribe. He described them as ruled by a common code, confirming and restraining the castelike distinctions of rank, privilege and conduct between freshmen, sophomores, juniors and seniors; distinctions signalized by differences in totemic insignia, dress and other collegiate tokens of rank and right. This code regulates a sort of permanent duello with the faculty, and with the non-collegiate community—especially its policemen and other authorities. Within the unwritten constitution, cheating and cribbing regardless of honor systems are not dishonesties but a brave's triumphs over the enemy faculty. Stealing traffic and campus signs, disturbing the peace, behaving bumptiously toward authority and conducting oneself in a generally irresponsible manner toward the entire out-group or any member thereof, are aspects of the foreign relations of the in-group which contribute to the brave's distinction and importance. Sometimes faculty are included in the in-group. Then the collegiate's way becomes ambivalent, and must at one and the same time "put it over" on the faculty and stand victor over the out-group. The attitude may be carried even into graduate study which is supposed to be adult and responsible. An episode reported by Lincoln Steffens exemplifies the situation.

And yet Wundt had a philosophy, not only of facts; no, and not only of theories, either. He said that theories were only aids to experiment, which was the test. He taught and I learned from him the discipline, the caution, and the method of experimental procedure of modern science. But Wundt, in practice, had established facts, he thought, by this method, and he built upon them conclusions which formed a system of philosophy written into several volumes. With an ethics, too; it was all complete. Well we knew it. It was under attack at the time. Some fresh young men were challenging, with facts, experimentally determined data, some of the very foundations of Wundt's psychology, which in turn was the basis of Wundt's philosophy. We were working for the truth, of course, but also we were fighting, and when we got results which confirmed Wundt we were glad and when we got results that seemed to support the enemy. . . .

Some of us were looking over the laboratory records of an American student who had stood high with the Professor, and therefore, with us all. He had gone home, taken a professorship, and was holding high our colors. He became afterward one of the leading men in American science and education. His student papers were models of neatness, and as we looked we saw that they were a masterpiece of caution, wisdom, and mathematical labor. The records of his experiment showed that he got, at first, results which would have given aid and comfort to the enemy and confounded one of Wundt's most axiomatic premises. He must have suffered, that promising young student; it was his thesis for the degree of Doctor of Philosophy, which he needed for his career at home; he must have thought, as a psychologist, that Wundt might have been reluctant to crown a discovery which would require the old philosopher to recast his philosophy and rewrite the published volumes of his lifework. The budding psychologist solved the ethical problem before him by deciding to alter his results, and his papers showed how he did this, by changing the figures item by item, experiment by experiment, so as to make the curve of his averages come out for instead of against our school. After a few minutes of silent admiration of the mathematical feat performed on the papers before us, we buried sadly these remains of a great sacrifice to loyalty, to the school spirit, and to practical ethics.[2]

If such conduct gets any into trouble, the members will stand by each other with the absolute loyalty of gangster to gangster, practicing the honor that is among thieves, and a mark of every in-group.

Now the community gives a sort of assent to all of this. It expects and accepts social irresponsibility from the college personage. A college boy's "prank" is a working boy's "crime." Let a Western Union messenger boy steal a barber-pole and burn it, or a street-marker and pin it up on his wall, and he has committed a crime which may bring him a jail sentence. Let a college youth do the same thing, and boys will be boys, college men are naturally pranksters. In the eyes of the community, working for a living and social responsibility go together. The typical "collegiate" is not supposed to work for his living, nor to participate in the economy

---

[2] *The Autobiography of Lincoln Steffens*, Chap. XXI, pp. 150-51.

on which he depends. For the most part that is a hotel-economy whose goods and services his parents buy for him from his college. Although in his person and potencies a man grown, he is supplied with food, clothing, shelter, entertainment, medical services through labors other than his own. The assurance of these supplies stretches the dependencies of infancy far, far beyond the years that naturally require them. It also assimilates the college man to the gentleman of leisure of tradition, who, because others earn his living for him, is free to live his life as he will and lives it seeking the irresponsible pleasures and satisfactions already prefigured and defined during his actual infancy. These, however, the college man neither seeks nor finds in that which a college president once celebrated as "the serious purpose for which the colleges exist"—the course of study and the requirements of the classroom. He sees the latter as simply the disagreeable condition under which he is free to lead his irresponsible agreeable college life. Indeed, he must not excel in conforming to this condition. His code requires that he should distinguish himself from the "greasy grind" by making no more than a "gentleman's mark." He is most collegiate when he keeps just within the bounds beyond which lies expulsion from the college.

Need it be argued that the ways of the colleges set the standards of the nation's entire educational establishment? It is not merely that high schools are prevailingly geared to "preparation" for college. It is that college life is envisaged by youth as the good life, whose ways are the desirable ways. In so far as the high-school students develop a school and social life of their own, they are apt to do it in imitation and emulation of what they believe or know to be collegiate. Living at home, younger than the college men, no less adult physiologically, no less dependent economically, no less shut out from adult responsibility—socially, high-school students are equally confined by school and home to a social prolongation of infancy from which they seek to escape. Like college students they find some field for their suppressed interests and powers in athletics, fraternities and sororities. Like college students they develop necking, drinking, gambling and other "extra-curricular activities" into ceremonial acts channeling self-expression. Like college students they live by a code of class-war with teachers in school and elders out of school, and enjoy all the distinctions and amenities which their laws of war provide and permit. Their ways and works have made them a source of anxiety to parents and teachers. Many states have forbidden fraternities in the public high schools, and every year one or more joins the group enacting prohibitory statutes. Fraternity brothers graduated from high school within recent years have in consequence become anxious enough over the future of their fraternities to take trouble to reform them. They have organized an Interfraternity Congress, adopted a code that calls for the encouragement of scholarship, forbids the customary fraternity practices, prescribes co-operation between fraternities and school authorities, and the like.

The aim of high-school fraternities, spokesmen of this Congress declared, should be "good citizenship." Such also, responsible fraters with college degrees might add, should be the aim of college fraternities, and indeed, of the entire collegiate enterprise. But then would follow the question: What does this "good citizenship" consist of? Where and when and how is it to be learned? At what age is its practice to begin?

So far as concerns most high schools and colleges, "good citizenship" is to date a subject of classroom profession, not a mode of campus practice; it is a system of doctrines, not a program of co-operative self-discipline. High school and college are so organized and so administered that in practically all matters that relate to the political economy of the establishment, students are shut out from participation as infant and child are shut out. Their needs are served for them and not by them, and their vocation as students has little or no vital relations to the service of their needs. Kept thus in a state of social infancy, they serve themselves as best they may. Adolescence and youth call for a degree of social responsibility adequate to channel and to express the physiological adulthood of this period of development. The years from thirteen to twenty-five are the years that strive pre-eminently toward personal independence, toward self-help and self-rule. They are the years of adventurous initiative, of imaginative enterprise, of originality and generosity. On the record, it is during these years that leaders of men come to the first insights, convictions, techniques or expressions, of which later life is the continuous development and transformation. And the leaders of men are but plain men with abilities heightened and energies liberated and speeded. Adolescence and youth are the periods of crescent vitality and sustained spontaneous activity, nature's time for directly facing the perennial critical problems of civilized society. During depressions, wars, catastrophies and other crises, even youth at school confronts reality because its urgencies compel, the reluctance of parents and teachers notwithstanding.

But so long as the crises of existence remain only the chronic ones, the schools' curricula offer little beyond a verbal rehearsal of the past, whereas guidance is called for to understand and act on the present; curricula bespeak the habits and vested interests of the oldsters without any save accidental relevance to the feelings, the problems and needs of the youngsters. College professors and high-school teachers are not exactly men of the world with an experience of life such as underlay the *savoir-vivre* of their oft-quoted Socrates. These people are as a rule schoolmarms and schoolmasters whose entire existence, from their sixth year to their sixtieth has been spent in a world of schools. From six to twenty-six, the years of most eager and most abundant vitality, they have lived and moved and had their being in the school—the one social institution that instead of educating, more than any other shuts out and cuts off the free play of the passions and powers of men. Pedagogic attention is concentrated on the records of the past because the pedagogue's first task is to repeat those records to their pupils and to exact from their pupils repetitions of their own repetitions. Employing the past to illuminate the present, using it to create the future, seems to lie beyond pedagogic ambition. The name for the ambition is "scholarship," that is, the theory and practice of searching out, remembering and reproducing the past. Though educational establishments are supposed to prepare the next generations for the future, and teaching is supposed to serve as a pointing of the ways to the future, schools and colleges are in effect but repositories of the past, and the one future they cultivate is a continuous dealing with present signs and symbols, residues and vestiges, as instruments for reaching to the absent past.

Now except for such pupils as desire in their own lives to imitate, emulate and repeat, so far as repetition is here possible, the lives of these teachers, "scholarship" is an alien ambition. But every pedagogue is disposed to shape his pupil in his own image. The classroom separates those who can and will from those who can't or won't reflect that image. As a rule, even though they may be

made passionately relevant, the classroom's matter and manner
relate to the vital interests of the pupil only accidentally, contingently. What students do in fact learn has little to do with what
they are taught, nor are the subjects they pass examinations in and
get degrees for the subjects they have been educated in. The latter
are the stuffs learned in living the college life; the antagonisms of
town and gown, of fraternity and fraternity, and fraternity and
barbarian; athletics as business and more or less as sport; the decisions between alternatives of their various personal relations; the
bull sessions regarding love and fate and personality and freedom,
and the arrangements of works and ways in which they take form.
When students are about the real business of their lives, teachers
and professors figure as inimical outsiders. If such a one happened
on a bull session in which the young people were frankly and
freely talking their hearts out, his appearance would silence them
and their talk would shock him. Very rarely does a student feel that
he can share with a teacher that which he most deeply cares about,
and is really thinking on. Also the small minorities of adult-
minded youth—those that are stigmatized the campus "radicals"—
will react to even the most popular professor as a spiritual outsider.

This very widely diffused feeling that student and professor are
incommensurables is a consequence of the social prolongation of
infancy which our high schools and colleges implement. By and
large it sustains the tradition that the pupils exist for the schools;
that teaching is a progressive conformation of a socially undesirable
original nature, with its individuality and idiosyncrasies, into a
socially approved standard personality; that education is "for
citizenship," "for efficiency," "for service," "for success," for what
you will; that, as Aristotle declared, it is the chief agency of
government in the perpetuation of its constitution. In modern
democracy, however, the very idea of the state, of the Constitution,
of education, contradicts the tradition. Governments are tools and
servants, not masters; schools exist for the pupils! Teaching is a
progressive liberation of the pupil's original nature by means of
the arts and sciences into the fullness of its individuality; education is the development of the person and his powers as the team
play of a team mate in the free society of free men. The task which
accrues to the school, hence, is anything but traditional. Modern
democracy does not establish the school to teach a grammar of

assent, but to impart an art of inquiry and judgment. It permits and enables an increasing autonomy of its educational establishment and facilitates its development into an institution equal in right and status with the church, the law and business, so that it may freely judge and criticize as well as serve the society of its peers, where, like them, it is an organ and member. Since appraisal is trustworthy only as the appraiser searches out, knows and understands, rather than merely accepts and employs the standards by which he judges, democracy asks of its school that it shall be a learner as well as a teacher, that pupil and pedagogue shall be equal fellow-workers in a common enterprise. It is not often that a high school or a college satisfies this democratic requirement. For the most part they practice, through the organization of their government and the matter and methods of their instruction, the social prolongation of infancy.

Now as the American people become older in years, and the American economy becomes technologically more complex and diversified and productive, the nation's need for an ever more democratic education of its citizens becomes greater, not less. The attendance at high school and college must and will increase. Unless the management and curricula of these establishments are so altered as to put an end to the class-war between teacher and pupil, between classroom and campus and gown and town, the effect of the socially desirable postponement of gainful occupation by these millions of young Americans cannot fail to be as socially undesirable as it became in the totalitarian countries of Europe. As presently conducted, most high schools and colleges direct the vital powers of their charges toward the futilities of an artificially prolonged infancy. The reform of secondary and higher education must look to such a change of their government and program as will no longer separate learning from living; as will provide full play for the energies and passions of the nation's youth and enable them all at least to live and to act as responsibly and purposefully as the members of a football squad.

The complexities of industrial society and the changes in population which accompany it seem to make a progressively greater social prolongation of infancy inescapable. But the social prolongation of infancy accompanies a completed psychosomatic maturity. The ways and works of the typical high-school and college student are largely a consequence of the conflict between the social lag and the biological development. There is no more serious task before the schoolmen of our time than fitting the works and ways of the schools to the powers and needs of the pupils, thus humanizing rebellious social futility into free, self-ruling, co-operative personality.

Chapter Six

THE EDUCATIONAL ESTABLISHMENT IN THE ECONOMY OF "FREE ENTERPRISE"

Our school system, like those of the rest of the world, consists of two, perhaps three, societies whose interests, relationships and behaviors are expected to be pacific and harmonious but are in fact discordant and embattled. There is the society of the teachers and the society of the pupils; and the society of the administrators could well be considered a third. The divergences between teacher and pupil become more explicit and articulate as we pass from the elementary to the secondary school, from the secondary school to the institutions of higher learning; while the antagonisms between school boards, superintendents, supervisors and principals on the one hand, and the classroom teachers on the other, enclose and somewhat channel those of teacher and pupil on all levels. Although direction and management of schools largely turn on these antagonisms, little is said of them in the discussion of the principles and practice of education, its financing and its policies. These are postulated on "the serious purpose for which the schools exist," and it is assumed that their hierarchical ordering and management are the means most harmonious to the attainment of this purpose. That the educational establishment has become something of an independent and sovereign competitive institution, asserting equality with its elder brothers in the national being and constantly making claims on an ever greater share of the national income, is of record. Education, like war and salvation, has an immediate price but brings no immeditae profit. The schools do not constitute a self-supporting enterprise. With the church and the army, they are a charge upon the economy and its taxation.

This charge is frequently questioned by spokesmen for taxpayers with the largest incomes, and attempts recur to reduce or abolish it. But its vital necessity to the growth and survival of a free society of free men is one of the basic articles of democratic faith. The deposit of this faith—contained in documents from the Declaration of Independence to Franklin Roosevelt's message to the 77th Congress of the United States on the Four Freedoms—concerns what Jefferson called "the inherent and unalienable rights

87

of man." Unchanging in a world otherwise all change, a world thereby free from all infallibility, these rights and the documents announcing them are subject to the reinterpretations which changing times and situations require. Democracy establishes public, and encourages and protects every sort and condition of private, agencies of interpretation. Chief among the private ones are the arts and newspapers. Chief among the public ones are the courts and the schools. It is assumed that all so work as to keep the primary ideas of the free man in a free society alive and growing amid the new forces and events which have made a new interpretation desirable or necessary. Of the forces, contemporary opinion identifies the economic as the most compelling.

The schools are of necessity responsive to changes in economy, whether national or local. Economic changes affect plans, personnel and curriculum in immediately familiar ways. But they occur in the context of "a body of knowledge" inherited from the past and traditionally entrusted to the schools where the pupils must receive them intact. The claims of this body of knowledge are honorific; it holds a certain aristocratic precedence which even crisis in a school system has little affected. Within the last generation, however, it has been confronting the challenge and undergoing modification of another kind of knowledge which is designed for teachers, not pupils. This is "the science of education," established by educational research and taught in normal schools and teachers' colleges. Substantially, it is an employment of basic natural and social sciences such as statistics, chemistry, biology, psychology, sociology, and the like, in the analysis and interpretation of learning and teaching, and the creation thereby of new fields of theory and practice called "educational psychology," "educational sociology" and the like. Today, even church schools have recourse to the findings of the science of education. John Dewey and Edward Thorndike have been the great initiators of this peculiarly American enterprise. In many ways opposed to the pedagogic custodians of the traditional "body of knowledge," the protagonists of the science of education share with them a common ground in their resistance to the demands, which farmers, businessmen and manufacturers make upon the schools, for a youth trained to obedient service in their respective occupations. To the particularistic "vocational training" asked for by the special interests, they oppose a "general education" which may enable a full and varied "spiritual" life, a "cultural" attainment, not immediately bound up with the knowledges and skills which are required to get food, clothing and shelter, protection against disease and against enemies, entertainment and sport.

In spite of contemporary opinion to the contrary, that this conflict must have economic roots is not a foregone conclusion. The economic enterprise itself is not by any means intelligible on merely economic terms. No more than anything else is it an effect which is its own cause. Its motivation lies elsewhere than in the gaining of profits and the accumulation of wealth through making, buying, selling and monopolizing things. Rich men wear their wealth much as their wives and daughters and mistresses wear their furs and jewelry—as trophies and tokens of personal distinction, as signs of championship in a duel of skill and knowledge, as expressions of personal power. And they continue to invest their riches not because in effect they want to get richer—they know well enough they can't use it up here or take it with them there—but because they find wealth an apt weapon in their spontaneous struggle for power. Judge Gary of the Steel Trust advised students to get money because money is power. When their power becomes more or less uncontested, the rich tend to turn their wealth to other uses—such as philanthropic and cultural foundations, the endowment of schools and colleges, the collection of pictures and support of missionaries, museums and orchestras, even the housing of the United Nations. It is true that these uses are new ways to prestige, new modes of expressing power, but it is with business as with sport in most high schools and colleges. The economy of football or baseball or hockey, or even chess or debating, is developed for the sake of the interscholastic or intercollegiate contest; the contest is not devised for the sake of the economy. Some institutions do put the contest to profit-making uses, but these do not stand high in the respect of the community, even when they win championships.

Educational ideals and educational practices owe their nature and existence to the entire aggregation of impulses and energies which make a community. All feed and form the schools and the schools repeat their conflicts and concords in their own inner warfare between professions and practices. Democracy as a doctrine is widely at variance with democracy as an actual discipline. Often its concept and ideal serve, not as a description of events going on, but as a compensation for the undemocratic, even the anti-democratic, traits of democratic society as a going concern. Free enterprise, private initiative, as principles of social philosophy, may be employed by those who profess them in order to rationalize their opposites, and by those who desire and really believe in them in order to compensate in imagination for their scarcity in existence. It often happens that actually individualistic societies do not express the effective dynamic of their being by philosophies of individualism. The individuality of individuals is an indefeasible psychosomatic fact, and the various ways that individuals associate with each other suppress or liberate this individuality in the multitudes. In Jefferson's day, the social, political and religious order of Europe and America suppressed it. After his day it received considerable liberation in the Western world, and his expression of it has worked and continues to work all over the globe as an inspirer and releaser of the energies of men. But since his day, too, the economy of the globe has undergone transformations whose initiating centers are the most industrialized of the Western lands —conspicuously the United States, Great Britain and Germany.

Industrialization brought certain now familiar changes in the associative forms of the world's works and ways, and a shift of philosophic attention from the *terms* of the associative relationships of human individuals, to the *relations* of the terms. This shift signalizes the difference between Jefferson's world and Dewey's, and underlies the philosophic reinterpretations which Dewey makes of their common democratic faith. Beyond the Jeffersonian "old" individualism, Dewey set a "new" which would interpret the individual as a function of a changing society, instead of society as a changing function of an indefeasible individuality.

Both interpretations were reactions to very different situations which made problems, even tragic problems, of the freedom and happiness of the individual. Each was a mode of solving the problem, according to the nature of the trouble constituting it. Both were intended to serve the survival and growth of men's freedom and happiness; both were conceived as different means seeking similar consequences at different and continually differentiating times. Both Jefferson and Dewey, each in his own way, were concerned for the multitudes of plain people, every one different from every other, needing to live together. The failure, not in the schools only, to realize sufficiently this situation, has led among liberals to a certain conflict and confusion about the nature and purpose of free society, and about the tasks of its schools, whether as transmitters of culture, trainers for vocations or preparers for life. Critics of the schools, such as this day's leading light of a midwestern university, observe hence, not incorrectly, that they live by merely responding to pressures—pressures from business and industry, pressures from academic traditionalists, pressures from professional "scientists of education"—but serve no preponderant ideal.

There is a consensus that of all the pressures the most powerful is exerted by business and industry. Business and industry profess a true religion which they call free enterprise, and the public relations experts and the propagandists who are its home missionaries, as well as the presidents and vice-presidents of the National Association of Manufacturers and of other such brotherhoods of the faith who are its apostles, preach it diversely up and down in the land. Their preachment, however, neither describes the national economy nor offers a program for its reform. It impresses the innocent bystander rather as a demand that the government shall refrain from any and all forms of interference with the trend of business enterprise toward centralization and monopoly. This terminus is the polar opposite of free enterprise. Enterprise is free when all individuals are equally protected by law in their efforts, and equally assured by society of the opportunity to use their powers to do what they want to do, so far as doing so does not diminish the equal right of any. The criteria of free enterprise inhere in the range and diversities of self-possession, self-support and self-rule, of initiatives in faith and works among the multitudes of men, employing their knowledge and skill to act on their personal beliefs at their own risk. The economy of free enterprise is measured by the number and variety of businesses that constitute it. Such businesses may be personal undertakings; they may be partnerships or associations in which members figure equally as participating individuals, as associations whose rule is one man, one vote, not one share of stock, one vote. They may be associations of producers or associations of consumers, or both. They are incarnations of free enterprise when their form of organization and function excludes monopoly and assures equal liberty to all their members.

Small business and co-operative societies are generally held to be exemplifications of such free enterprise. But Big Business is attacking co-operative societies in both the legislatures and the courts of the nation, and of the sixteen million small businesses organized between the end of the last century and the present time, only two million survive. Their survivial is not specific, not personal. Most Americans who launch some sort of enterprise in which they hope to be their own masters and do their own work at their own risk do not try again after the failure through no fault of their own. But individuality is indefeasible and the hunger for self-help and self-support is inveterate. Every generation sees a new crop of such undertakings, and each year the abstract number remains in the vicinity of two million. Their plight has long had the attention of the Congress and of the executive branch of the government. The Senate's latest special committee on small business has turned in a report with fifty recommendations, among them the creation of a government department of small business, a revision of the tax laws so as to provide incentives to free enterprise, and of course, the prosecution of trusts and monopolies. The Small Business Committee of the House found that the Department of Justice had been lax in this matter, that by 1942 trusts had acquired control of more than half of the nation's industrial undertakings. The Senate Committee reported that monopoly had made itself stronger than the competitive system in every major industry. Mr. Thurman Arnold pointed out that monopoly was basic to the creation and operation of—so largely German-bred—cartels, with their secret understandings called "gentlemen's agreements," often tacitly supported by governments, with all the forms of restraint of trade these conspired to bring about: among them price-fixing, protective tariffs, wage-cutting and disemployment. On the record, enterprise is in fact anything but free. For the multitudes of farmers, workers and small businessmen, free enterprise is an illusion. The mechanisms of the market and the price system no longer so work as to preserve to each his marginal product. They have been replaced by the administrative decisions of the planned economies of trust and cartel.

These latter dominate the nation's business. Little that happens in it can happen save within fields of force which are consequences of the forms and functions of those establishments. Their form is hierarchical. Their structure repeats that of an army or an authoritarian church. There are specialists who contend that since 1900 the entire national economy has passed under the proprietary rule of some sixty families, more or less intermarried; and that some two thousand individuals, by their control of company stock, their interlocking directorates and the like, can tie up all the business of the country. Others showed that prior to 1940, one-tenth of America's families received 42 per cent of the national income, while one-fiftieth received 55 per cent of the nation's corporate dividends; that only one million or so Americans have incomes between $5000 and $75,000. Still others showed that the aggregate income of New York, Philadelphia, Detroit and Chicago, exceeded that of all American farmers put together. They added that although the standard of living of workers and farmers has risen during the past generation, it has not risen to the point where they can do any saving to speak of. The experts pointed out that, in 1936, 14 per cent received less than $500; 42 per cent less than $1000; 66 per cent less than $1500; that even with the year of grace abundant in 1929, only 1.6 per cent of the nation's total savings could be credited to 59 per cent of the families. Analysts of the state of the national economy during this fourth decade of the twentieth century declare that upward of one-quarter of the productive wealth is held by a couple of score "billion dollar clubs."

The cost of labor accounts for less than twenty-five per cent of the price of its product. According to the Federal Reserve Board one-third of the families of the United States receive less than $1000 yearly; almost one-half, less than $2000. While corporation profits have risen beyond their war-time high, real wages have fallen by nearly 20 per cent. An analysis, by the Bureau of Labor Standards, of the cost of living for a family of four with an annual wage of $2000, shows a monthly charge of $25.00 for rent, between $90.00 and $100.00 for food and clothing, $5.00 for health and medical care. This family paid no taxes and was unable to save anything. On the contrary, it went into debt for about $200 during the year. According to the Department of Agriculture, 20 per cent of the people receive 45 per cent of the cash income of the nation and put aside 82 per cent of the savings. Thus the bulk of American savings is due to the very small minority whose income exceeds their most extravagant spending. And those savings go back largely into corporate investment, as another stimulus to price-fixing, to the restraint of trade, to the purchase and storing of inventions which, if put into production might renew competition in their fields. Although an American maxim affirms that it takes three generations to pass from shirt sleeves to shirt sleeves; although a marriage between Bessie the sewing machine girl or Gwendolyn the show girl and the boss's son makes Hearsty headlines in the tabloid press, it remains the fact that marriages and remarriages tend to contain themselves within the boundaries of income, and the ways of life which income sustains. Although Americans do not stay stratified according to income as much as other folks, income marries income in America much as elsewhere. The concentration of wealth and power thus has social and cultural extension. It comes out as caste.

Now, to re-enforce this trend toward the arrest of the social and cultural mobility so long characteristic of the American scene is intrinsic to modern industrial technology. As the corporation with its administered economy drives out free enterprise, so the mechanized factory dispenses with the energies of men working. According to studies made at the Brookings Institute in Washington, the average output per man increased more than 25 per cent even during the great disemployment of the depression years 1929-1935. Little more than a decade ago it took 100,000 men to do the work that fewer than 15,000 do today. In the spinning of cotton thread 2 girls now do as much work as formerly 650 did. How the dial system has disemployed thousands of telephone operators and serves as a strike breaker is notorious. And so it goes wherever "labor-saving" devices are installed. The new vocations introduced by their production doubtfully compensate for the insecurities they set up in the hearts of men. On the farm the tractor displaces scores of farm hands. When the cotton picking machine will definitely enter into use, the entire economy of cotton-farming will be overturned. Machines threaten the livelihood of even the migratory agricultural workers—the fruit and berry and nut and vegetable pickers—of the truck farms of California. The small-scale tenant farmer who today makes up the bulk of the farm population—he who tills 70 per cent of the farms of Iowa, Illinois and Minnesota, more than 50 per cent of the entire Middle West, he who is the backbone of the South's share-cropper economy—is on the way to be displaced by corporately owned, machine-operated, great farms, orchards and truck-gardens, which form concurrently purchasing and selling combinations and screen their monopolistic essence by calling themselves co-operatives. With all this chronic and growing disemployment, there are hundreds of times as many unemployed dollars as men. And who knows what a range of disemployment rests potential in devices patented and kept in desuetude, or in an adequate constructive utilization of atomic energy?

That human beings without employment are first at a loss and then on the loose, are men and women without a base and without a direction and purpose for their lives is no news to those who have observed what happens to men and women, without distinction of age, during the depression phase of a business cycle. With all the injustice, the misery and heartache, the anger and the spiritual regression which signalize the mood of depressions, it is not really national dearth of "the necessities of life" which generates the mood. This day's outcry for "security" has another spring besides economic insecurity, and no degree of economic security is likely to still it. The machines that displace men produce more goods and better goods than all men working together could produce. An inch-sized cube of fissionable uranium could provide as many million kilowatts of electricity as three million pounds of coal. It could be burned in such a way as to produce more fuel than it consumes and make obsolete the degrading and hazardous occupation of coal mining. Every kilowatt hour could supply the electrical equivalent of the hourly labor of ten men. In an atomic age the merely economic meaning of the business cycle might disappear. In fact, the depression of 1930-1936 had comparatively little economic content, since even the multitudes of disemployed Americans had made available to them, and on the whole and in the long run received, a larger and better proportion of "the necessities of life" than fully-employed peasants and workers of China and India and Russia. In the light of that which—in the way of food, clothing, shelter, medical care and entertainment—was within the reach of the pioneers of the covered wagons whose enterprise built the land, even men and women today on relief enjoy an undreamed of economy of abundance. By comparison with early Americans and with contemporary non-Americans, the peoples of the United States have in fact established the third of Franklin Roosevelt's freedoms —freedom from want. History records nothing comparable to the general abundance that has come with the industrialization of the economy; [1] but neither does it produce many parallels to the mood of "insecurity," the demands for "security," the outcry for "full employment."

Now the idea of "full employment" is the projection of a technology that employs fewer and fewer men and is able to support more and more. Even at the height of war employment and selective service there were millions of both sexes who neither worked nor served. During 1935 one-sixth of the nation's youth on relief had never worked; and all those who had lately finished high school or college were unemployed. A great deal was heard about a new right, "the right to work," and government enterprises like the Civilian Conservation Corps or its various public works projects— from building roads and schools and post offices, to enabling teachers, actors, dancers, painters, sculptors and writers to practice their vocations—was a recognition of that "right." Many held that it would have been cheaper and simpler to pay them than employ them. And in terms of mere animal survival that money can measure, perhaps it would have. But the issue was not one of animal survival. The issue was one of the preservation of manhood. Saving in money would have meant bankruptcy in men, especially in young men. "Full employment" and "the right to work" are psychological necessities before they are economic ones. They are as indispensable to the rich as to the poor. The difference is that the rich can be self-employed, that they can live without working, and their employments can be those of the gentleman of leisure. The poor, on the other hand, cannot be self-employed. For their jobs they depend on others who pay them a wage for which they work without living; their employments are "gainful"; they are tasks of labor, not leisure.

And the tasks of industralized labor differ in another, profound way from those of leisure. Not only is the gentleman of leisure self-

---

[1] Chief Justice Vinson, in a report to the President when he was head of the Office of War Man Power and Reconversion, wrote: "We are in the happy predicament of having to learn how to live 50 per cent better than we have ever lived before."

employed. That which he is about, he is wholly about. Let him be an amateur of sport or art or athletics or cabinet-making or motoring or plumbing or tailoring or what you will. He carries through his entire project, from plan to product. His enterprise is a genuinely free enterprise. Labor, on the other hand, has undergone division. For example, shoemakers with the knowledge and skills to make a complete pair of shoes, have been displaced by shoe-factory operatives. The shoemaker's awl and needle and other tools, which are prolongations of the man, have been displaced by factory's stationary machinery of which the man is a prolongation, attached and detached like any other movable gadget. The art of turning a hide into a pair of shoes in a box, is broken up into, say, one hundred separate steps; each taken by a different man with a separate device at a separate place along the continuum of shoe machinery. Each can learn to repeat his special operation a thousand times a day. Easily and quickly. Each must suit his own action to those of the other operatives, and all must conform them to the terms and tempos of the machinery running on impersonal electric power. Together they produce daily an abundance of shoes such as a craftsman's lifetime could not suffice for. But no operative knows anything beyond his special operations. None has the shoemaker's knowledge of the whole act of making a pair of shoes, or of the wholeness of the pair he makes. Each is only a fraction of a shoemaker, one one-hundredth of a shoemaker. The whole shoemaker is the factory, and the factory is a regimented hierarchy in which, unless there is a trades-union, the operative has just about the same status and the same freedom as a private in an army. He is hired and fired as an inanimate gadget is attached and removed. He has no power over his own support. He feels deeply insecure.

With all the rising strength of trades-unions, all the factory legislation, all the social security enactments and all the devices for safeguarding the human wholeness of the industrial worker, the latter's feeling of insecurity mounts. His personality defends itself from the dehumanization of the machine and the coercions of management in a variety of ways. Some of these ways have long been under observation by industrial psychologists. They speak of withdrawals into reverie, of automatic slowdown and ca'canny on the job; of irritability; of sudden outbreaks of temper. Off the job the worker's Saturday night may become orgiastic: the entertainment he seeks, the music he chooses, the literature he reads, the movies he prefers, seem to be those that afford the maximum escape from the rhythms and action patterns in which his working day is enchanneled. They, not his occupation, are the enterprises in which he finds some modicum of the freedom his nature craves.

This situation has as yet received hardly any recognition from the school. For the school's structure and government by and large repeats that of the factory. Its pupils seek the same reliefs from its coercions that their parents seek from the factory's. Curricula, however, draw very little upon the actualities of the struggle for a life and a living, very largely upon tradition with its "classics" and correctnesses. The classroom either treats the realities as if they were not, or scorns and forbids them. The critics of the schools then deplore the intellectual laziness of their pupils, their spiritual dependence, the way they persist in their nest habits, their resort to tabloid clichés as substitutes for free inquiry and analytical thinking. As for the basic antithesis between the ideal of free enterprise and the actual structure of the national economy, as for the contradiction that the structure and management of the school almost everywhere oppose to the democratic instructions, if any, of the classroom—these do not enter into the consideration of today's critics of American education. Yet these are the critical conditions, and there is no telling to what degree they may be ignored with impunity.

To a large section of the population the problem of security is only economic. It is a problem of jobs. They believe, hence, that the first task of education is to prepare youth to fit into the economy as employees of a going concern. To the Middletowns of the land, the national status quo is good enough. Let the schools teach youth to prolong and to repeat it. Youth, living by its nest habits, feeling not too insecure, looks to a future that shall repeat the parental past, perhaps with more money, on a bigger scale, but repeat it. This youth takes its school and college traditionally, at ease in that Zion of irresponsible prolonged infancy; and then it moves out into the Babbit-warrens of whose ways and forms its education has been the monitor. Part of this group will take no thought whatsoever for the future. It will pass the time of its schooling without reflection, drifting from one day into the next day, doing the next pleasant thing, avoiding, so far as possible, the next unpleasant, in a truly infantile heedlessness, but no longer with the infant's compensating organic impulses toward maturity. These have been consummated, and any urge to grow now must come from without. On the record, the classroom provides hardly any; but strikes, minority tensions and military questions, animate students of this order to an automatic enlistment on the side of the dominant power which keeps and feeds them. The violence they then exercise may still seem frivolous, "college boy stuff," and in America for the most part has remained so. Let it, however, be made into the works that go with a justifying faith and with its rationalizations, and it may become revolutionary violence. Ducking a "red" in a campus lake may become lynching a Jeffersonian on a city street. Such mutations were critical events in Italy and in Germany and in Spain. They are by no means unknown in Russia, whether of the Czar or the Commisar. Thrown into jitters of insecurity by the failure of support for its nest habits, the youth of the schools of those lands readily enough converted their schoolboy violence into organized religious aggression against freedom and the responsibilities of free men in free society. The material and moral dependence on parental power of support in the private life was replaced by dependence on *Vozhd, Duce* or *Führer* in public affairs. Stalin, Mussolini and Hitler were able to make themselves surrogates for the father and substitutes for God. What the pope could only pretend to, they achieved, and their achievement exceeded Hirohito's inheritance. For all the faithful, the vision of life summed itself up in the Mussolini's rule: *credere, obedire, combattire*—to believe, to obey, to fight; the organization of living became the interlocking hierarchies of the economic, political and military monopolies in which Communist, Fascist and National Socialist societies consist. Although Hitler and Mussolini have died not inappropriate deaths, Stalin is still in his Kremlin and Franco in his Escorial; their diverse authoritarian systems continue to exercise fascination upon myriads of young minds wherever in the world authoritarian economy is accounted free enterprise, wherever its conduct enables or requires a social infancy too much longer than the biological one, and the schools are its ways and vehicles, themselves teaching liberty and practicing coercion.

Ineluctably, the question presents itself: Can the idea of a true free enterprise in a free society of free men, can democracy, exert a rival fascination? Can youth be brought to take freedom for a fighting faith? to believe in democracy? to obey its laws? to fight for its survival and growth? The answer to this question involves far more than the general passive acquiescence to the requirements of selective service in the United States or the passionate defense of their homeland by the peoples of Great Britain. It calls for something other than the credos taught in the classrooms and the liturgies and gestures repeated by rote and acquired by drill. This other is the conscious realization of the nature and history of the democratic idea, of its effects in the lives of men, of the feel of its workings as the personal discipline in interpersonal relations and in the folkways and mores of culture. With this realization must needs go a deep sense of the vigilance that is forever the price of liberty, and of the unending battle by which its survival and growth are daily secured. For the schools to awaken this sense, to bring to life this realization, is not possible without a prior conformation of practices to principles in their ways and works. This indispensable conformation requires that the structure and administration of the nation's educational establishment should altogether part company from the structure and administration of the nation's business enterprise. It requires such a reorganization of the schools as will bring teachers and pupils together as partners in the free enterprise of the education of free men, converting the teachers from masters to leaders, and the pupils from classroom subordinates to team mates. Education as free enterprise is the vocation of the school in democracies, and the school can answer its vocation only as it embodies the doctrine and discipline of democracy in its ways and works.

But can the school thus answer its vocation without endangering, at least for a long time, the support on which it depends? But again, can it survive at all as an autonomous institution of democratic society—as the institution on which democratic culture most relies—unless it accepts this hazard with courage and without illusion?

Book II

THE DEMOCRATIC FAITH AND ITS EDUCATIONAL ENTERPRISE

Chapter Seven

ON THE IDEA OF A FREE SOCIETY AND THE AMERICAN WAY

What, it is now proper to ask, is the idea of a free society that the school must exemplify and transmit? And what is its bearing on the American way?

The American answer to these questions obviously depends on who answers it. What people are, what they really believe, where they live, what they don't have and want, what they have and don't want, what sort of neighbors they are, exercise a preponderant influence upon the shape of the answer. A son of the sixty families cannot be expected to give an answer that a son of toil can freely repeat; nor a union lawyer to cause an echo in a corporation counsel. A gentleman from Alabama will not respond like a citizen from Maine; a sister of a Retail Clerks' Union as a Daughter of the American Revolution; a Methodist as a Catholic, a Unitarian as either. Nor will a farmer give the same answer as an industrial worker; a scion of the immigrants of Plymouth Rock as a descendant of the immigrants of Ellis Island; nor a Republican as a Democrat, nor as a Socialist, nor all three as a Communist. A Negro or an Indian could hardly give the same answer as even a poor white, nor an American of Chinese or Japanese ancestry as an American whose forbears came from Europe. And so on, without end. Even if the types of Americans accept such facts of record as different and differing schools of history will show a consensus on, the various types will give those facts a perspective, will set them in a frame of reference, will assign to them a cause and a meaning that are more expressive of the passions and prejudices of the assigning groups than of the nature of the facts themselves. The very speech in which they state and interpret the facts will vary according to the area of habitation, the local economy, the local history, the regional diction—its tone, accent and rhythm—in which the speakers live and move and have their being. The differences, say between Maine and Florida, Vermont and California, Louisiana and Rhode Island, Texas and Michigan, Virginia and Alaska, Illinois and Puerto Rico, New York and South Dakota, or for that matter, northern New York and southern New York—the differences of climate, topography, natural resources, ethnic origin, industrial development, municipal organization, school systems and the like, are present in differences of speech and song, diet and doctrines, work and play. These differences together constitute the being and doing of more than one hundred and forty million individual human beings unevenly distributed over the area of the earth's surface known as the United States of America, who are yet equally free men in a free society according to the American way.

But none was born that way. Each is that way because, in his struggle for a life and a living, he got that way; because his *now* is the present moment for the process of his whole life before, the present effect of which his past is somehow the present cause. *Present cause* for the reason that his whole being must consist in his somehow keeping his past immediately present, keeping it somehow alive and at hand; *present cause* for the reason that his personal identity is made up of his living memory—memory as the habits and dispositions and skills of his body; memory as the recollection and disposition and associations of his mind. Let him lose his memory, and he has lost himself; let him forget his past, and he has no future before him. Like many men and women you read about in the papers every so often, who have had a physical blow or a mental shock, he would be without psychological, that is, personal, identity; he would, like a newborn babe, have to start naked to build one up. How would he build one up? By learning new habits, new skills, new ideas, new attitudes. In sum, by acquiring a memory.

Without memory, no personality and no biography; and by the same token, no social unity, no national character and national ideal, no history. And if no history, if no insight into the dynamic of the process of the national life, then no adequacy in controlling the present and shaping the future. In a very obvious sense there is no education which is not historical education. For no matter how passionately, how aggressively, education may be directed toward the future, it is so directed only as it makes the past available, and successfully directed only as it makes available the truth of the past.

But passions and prejudices complicate the intrinsic difficulties of the research after the truth of the past. As often as not, history is written and taught as a special plea on behalf of the claims of some particular tradition or interest to privileged consideration; while the plot of events themselves is the pattern of the competition and co-operation of that one with many others, some strong, some weak, and none with a superior claim. The dynamic of the plot is their struggle. And the meaning of America as a free society is the characteristic interpretation which the singularity of the struggle has received in the United States, and which very few openly reject as doctrine however much they labor to corrupt and destroy it as a discipline, as the way of life.

How, now, has this meaning taken shape? What the peoples of America were, how they lived, what they hoped for and what they feared before Columbus discovered our Western continent will hardly be included in this meaning. Indeed, our Indians were willfully and cruelly excluded, by white sentiment and government policy, until the investigation of the record of the relations with the American Indian led to the change of policy initiated in 1932. The 3,000,000 who were said to inhabit what is now the United States have been reduced to about 350,000. Their multitude of languages, their diverse social structures, economies, ways of thinking and living, have been reduced from powers and instruments of men alive into inert themes for the anthropologists' study. Whatever survives of them may or may not now be the sympathetic care of the Bureau of Indian Affairs. Before their ancestors passed, they did however contribute to the cultural heritage of the white man's skills and materials, words and images and ideas that enter into the concrete meaning of the American Idea.

The land from which the Indians were steadily driven during three hundred years was an empty land. Their original three million would not be noticed among today's one hundred forty million who have journeyed to it, they or their forbears, from the miscellany of Europe and the rest of the world, and do not yet fill it. To the north, to what is now called Quebec, and to Louisiana in the south, the French came, and from these centers spread west and north. The Spaniards set up their works and ways in Florida and California as well as in Mexico; the Dutch conspicuously in what is now New York; the Swedes first in Delaware, the British in New England, in the "old South" and in Pennsylvania; the Germans in Pennsylvania. All but the Germans came with the power of government behind them. Each waged war against all, and all practiced murderous aggression against the Indians. The Spaniards reduced the Indians to peonage and slavery, and their descendants in South America still so hold them. The English brought in the African Negro to be a similar tool with life in it. In this struggle of Europeans to possess the continent and exploit its native inhabitants, the British came out victorious. They overcame the Dutch; they conquered and expelled the French power; they made themselves masters of the French in Canada. Although they did not prevail against the French in Louisiana or the Spaniards in Florida, they became the dominant power on the continent of North America.

To many of the diverse peoples (English, Scotch, Welsh, Irish) and numerous sects (Congregational, Baptist, Episcopalian, Presbyterian, Methodist, Quaker, Romanist) of which the British were composed, their cultus was of primary consideration, with an importance almost as overruling as the Catholicism of the Spaniards was for the Spaniards. Their mutual aggressions were often even more religious than political. In many cases they regarded their congregations as theocracies and their structure and government as functions of their faith. That Roger Williams, the prophet of liberty of conscience, should be outlawed, that Quakers should be mutilated or tortured or killed, that every man and woman who held different beliefs regarding human nature and human destiny should be horribly penalized for those beliefs was long a matter of course to Massachusetts Puritans and their peers elsewhere on the continent. The "freedom to worship God" which they are said to have sought on New England's "stern and rockbound coast" was a freedom for themselves from others, not a freedom for others from themselves.

But the conditions of freedom and of life on the American continent were radically different from those of Europe. If one European sect or people there tried to escape the persecutions of another, they could only flee to a third, who might be even more intolerant. In America they could always find space in the wilderness, with even the Indian aborigine too far away to be considered a neighbor. Fronting upon the wilderness, with their backs turned upon the settlements, Europeans could have little time to cultivate intolerance for the glory of their particular gods. Sectarian differences receded in importance as the union of neighbor with neighbor was imposed by the common struggle against nature and the native. The way of life of the frontier called for a mutual toleration and respect, a neighborliness of which the settlements long would want more. On the frontier people could not well ask each other, *Are you a Calvinist? Are you a Quaker? Or Baptist? Or Congregationalist? Or Brownite? Or Methodist? Or Espiscopalian?* It had to be enough that they were men and women who did or did not possess strength or knowledge or skill to contribute to the safety and freedom of all together. Those, not sectarian privilege, had to be the first and last interest of a community.

For the same reason the relegation of sectarian privilege had to be accompanied by the desuetude of all habits, precedence and privilege based on birth, wealth, race, sex and the like. All over Europe, there was a hierarchy of difference between the gentleman and his man. The gentleman commanded, the man obeyed; the gentleman could live, as of right, without working; the man survived under duty and worked without living. The gentleman enjoyed leisure as a God-given right and liberty as a divinely granted privilege; his man suffered labor as a divinely imposed burden and servility as a God-ordained duty. The gentleman wore a sword as the symbol of his leisure and liberty; his man had no title to wear arms. We still do not speak of the common man of leisure, only the gentleman of leisure.

Now the Puritan spirit had a certain indictment of the gentleman of leisure and his privileges, which entered the Puritan theology and became a component of the education of children. As the New England primer puts it:

> When Adam delved and Eve span
> Who was the gentleman?
>
> When Adam delved and Eve span
> The devil was the gentleman.

Although to the people of the frontier the gentleman was no devil, he was—and this is far more important—no use. Of course he was endowed with all the innate excellences. He was noble and good by birth and did not, therefore, need to be by conduct. But when it comes to hunting game for food in the wilderness, to building a cabin or making a clearing, to sowing and tilling a field or curing a skin, what use is it to have had a noble lord for a grandfather and a wellborn lady for a grandmother? Under the conditions of the wilderness men *were* what they *did;* birth and station became impertinences; strength, skill and knowledge—*know-how,* we continue to say—became essentials; a person is not *born* good, he *makes* good.

So the frontier initiated that new direction of thought, that new way of life for human beings together, which we call the American way. *Make good* is an idiom of the American language. It implies a certain conception of human nature and human destiny; the idea that no man is born with a capital endowment of status and advantage on which life ever after pays him the interest accruing to that superior advantage; the idea that every man earns his way by the consequences of his action. The frontier established a new ground for men's judgment of each other's differences: to the Europeans' invariant hierarchies of birth, rank and station, it opposed the mobility and relevancy of function. On the frontier all sorts and conditions of men came together, each different from the others in his present being and, by necessary implication, in his past history. But that past history was, as such, an irrelevancy. It was not inquired into. Men were taken at their face value, and their records became matters of concern only as their ways and works hurt and hindered instead of helped the frontier community, the community which justified its togetherness by the event that each of its members, in living and working together with the others, felt himself better off than he would be alone. Everybody had to labor at a task, no matter what belted knights were in his ancestral line. In Europe no gentleman born could well soil his hands with work. In America Thomas Jefferson, gentleman born yet a growth of the frontier, could declare that his new trade of nail making—which he took up to recoup the losses he had suffered while absent from home in the service of his country—was as ennobling to him as a new title of nobility would be to a European.

The day came when the new way of life and its new ideal of human relations received expression as the articles of a fighting faith. That day was the birthday of Americanism as the idea of a free society. On that day the American Idea became an articulate, self-conscious ideal and program, a doctrine and discipline for the life of man. The day was July 4, 1776. The expression was the Declaration of Independence. The Declaration is the basic document in the bible of democracy.

Consider the affirmations of this document which experience of the frontier, more surely than the philosophic reflection of English libertarians and their French interpreters, made "self-evident" truths to their authors and signers; the affirmations for whose support they mutually pledged each other their lives, their fortunes and their sacred honor.

The Declaration affirms:

> That all men are created Equal, that they are endowed by their Creator with certain unalienable Rights, that among these are Life, Liberty and the pursuit of Happiness.
> That to secure these rights, Governments are instituted among men, deriving their just powers from the consent of the governed. That whenever any Form of Government becomes destructive of these ends, it is the Right of the People to alter or abolish it, and to institute new Government, laying its foundations on such principles and organizing its powers in such form, as to them shall seem most likely to effect their Safety and Happiness.

What, to begin with, could the signers have signed to, when they underwrote the proposition that all men are created equal? Did they mean by "equal" similarity and equivalence as of one penny to another—all so essentially repetitious of each other that any could be substituted for each—the same in size, weight, appearance and value, capable of the same work in the same way? This obviously is nonsense. Half the human world are women; far more than half are Negroes, Chinamen, Hindus, Mongols, and the like, who not only differ from peoples of European stock in appearance and culture, but also differ no less among each other. The European peoples, whether in Europe or in America, also were no less diverse: English and Scotch and Irish, Dutch and French and German and Swedish and Spanish; not to mention the varieties of Slavs, the Jews, the Turks and all the others. Add to the differences in language and culture, the momentous differences in cultus; Buddhist, Brahmin, Confucian, Taoist, Mohammedan, Judaist, Christian; and the sectarian diversification within each cultus; as Catholic and Protestant among the Christians; Roman, Greek, Uniate, and so on, among the Catholics; Episcopal, Calvinist, Congregational, Presbyterian, Baptist, Mennonite, Quaker, Unitarian and so on, among the Protestants. Add to the differences in cultus differences in birth, rank and station; the differences in occupation; the differences in possessions and income. Add the diversifications consequent on

these differences. Then consider the structure of society, the pattern
of life, the character of rule and government in state, church, economic establishment, educational institution, polite society. Everywhere people, if they had the power, were penalizing each other
for their differences, were either holding the different to bondage
and servility, because it was different, or altogether denying its
right to exist. Everywhere people were being penalized for their
sex, their color, their faith, their occupation, their poverty, singly
and together. A doctrine and discipline obtained, in all the diverse
communities of mankind, according to which some few were elected
by God to be the masters of the many; to be gentlemen of leisure
with life, liberty and the pursuit of happiness as their divine right,
whom the rest were created but to believe, to obey and to serve.

To all this the Declaration said, *No.* Female and male, Indian,
Negro and white, Irishman, Scotchman and Englishman, German
and Spaniard and Frenchman, Italian and Swede and Pole, Hindu
and Chinaman, butcher, baker and candlestick maker, workingman
and gentleman, rich man and poor man, Jew and Quaker and
Unitarian and Congregationalist and Presbyterian and Catholic—
they are all different from each other, and different as they are, all
equal to each other. "Equal," in the intent of the Declaration, is an
affirmation of the right to be different, of the parity of every human
being and every association of human beings according to their
kinds, in the rights of life, liberty and the pursuit of happiness.
These rights the Declaration selects to designate as "unalienable,"
that is, rights that can never be taken away from men; not therefore a grant or concession from above, nor the consequence of a
pact, but properties inborn, constitutive, elements of the essential
nature of man, without which he could not be man.[1] The authors

---

[1] This is how Abraham Lincoln read the meaning of the word "equal"
in the first of these "axioms of a free society" opening the Declaration of
Independence. "I think," he told his Springfield audience in June, 1857,
during his great debate with Douglas, "I think that the authors of that
notable instrument intended to include *all* men, but that they did not
intend to declare all men equal in all respects. They did not mean to
say all were equal in color, size, intellect, moral development or social
capacity. They define with tolerable distinctness in what respects they did
consider all men created equal—equal with 'certain inalienable rights
among which are life, liberty and the pursuit of happiness.' This they
said, and this they meant. They did not mean to assert the obvious un-

indeed had written "inherent and unalienable rights" but the Congress had dropped "inherent."

Then the Declaration designates the relation of government to these equal unalienable rights of different people. To secure these rights, it says, governments are instituted among men, and they derive their just powers from the consent of the governed. When this proposition was set down, however, government, everywhere in the world, whether political, ecclesiastical, economic, or cultural, was conducted on the dogma that it was established from above by God; that God had delegated some of his own supreme powers to the existing rulers of men, to the kings, the nobles and their ministers, to the popes, the bishops, the priests and their surrogates; that these all ruled by divine authority, and that their subjects were bound to obey and serve them by divine commandment; that they, the subjects, existed on earth for this purpose only, and not for life, liberty and the pursuit of happiness; that government would reason why, that its subjects had but to do and die.

This is the doctrine and discipline which authoritarian religions invoke, which the Fascists and the Nazis have so effectively resurrected and for whose imposition they plunged the world into its bloodiest war. This is the "dictatorship of the proletariat" which keeps the peoples of Russia prisoners of their government. This is the doctrine against which the Declaration enters its mighty *No* again. Government, it affirms, is made for men, not men for government. Government is a servant, not a master; it is made by men, not by God, and it is made by men in order to secure the unalienable rights with which God endowed men. It receives its powers—its *just* powers only—from its makers, who create those powers by their consent. Government, we say today, is a coming together of people who are different from each other in an association which they so design that each may live more abundantly, more freely and perhaps more happily than he is able to by himself alone. Government is a tool whose makers and users ever have the right to alter so as best to secure their unalienable rights, best to bring them "safety

---

truth that all were then actually enjoying that equality nor yet that they were about to confer it immediately upon them. In fact, they had no power to confer such a boon. They meant simply to declare the right, so that enforcement of it might follow as soon as circumstances should permit."

and happiness." The principle holds for every form of rule: religious, social, economic, and cultural, as well as political.

This then is the faith whose "axioms of a free society" were declared to "the opinion of mankind" on July 4, 1776; this the program that was initiated on that day. The struggle to make of it a faith that has become a fact, a program that has become an achievement, constitutes the dynamic inwardness of American history. In England, Dr. Richard Price wrote at the conclusion of the American Revolution: "Perhaps I do not go too far when I say that, next to the introduction of Christianity among mankind, the American revolution may prove the most important step in the progressive course of human improvement." Lincoln spoke of the Declaration as having given "liberty not alone to the people of this country, but hope to all the world for all future time." It initiated the Democratic Revolution for the entire world. In America this revolution began with the war for independence from Great Britain. Those who fought that war with sword and pen were not alone natives of the American scene like George Washington and Thomas Jefferson. They were Frenchmen like Lafayette, Englishmen like Tom Paine, Poles like Kosciusko and Pulaski, Germans like Closen and Steuben, Jews like Haym Solomon, Swedes like Fersen, Swiss like Albert Gallatin, West Indians like Alexander Hamilton. The union of such different men of different origins and cultures and faiths in the co-operative enterprise of the Democratic Revolution was a symbol and an omen for the union of American states which was its first fruit. It was the American Idea in action, in harmony with the "laws of nature and of nature's God." It consists of a One made up by the free coming together of unequal Many on equal terms and not of a One produced by the coercive conformation of the Many to some elect and privileged One. Thomas Jefferson recognized, and argued all his life, that uniformity, whether in bodies or in minds, is unnatural, and that no matter how cruelly men may seek to impose it on one another, they fail; "The minority," he pointed out in his First Inaugural, "possess their equal rights and to violate (them) would be oppression." The varieties in the structure and action of the human mind, as in those of the body, he wrote to James Fishback in 1809, "are the work of our Creator, against which it cannot be a religious duty to erect the standard of uniformity." Nine years later he wrote to Charles

Thomson: "If no varieties existed in the animal, vegetable or mineral creation, but all moved strictly uniform, catholic and orthodox, what a world of physical and moral monotony it would be . . . It is a singular anxiety which some people have that we should all think alike. Would the world be more beautiful were all our faces alike? Were our tempers and talents, our tastes, our forms, our wishes, aversions and pursuits cast exactly in the same mold?"

The American Idea was thus in its premise and its intent the idea of a One whose being consists in the co-operation of the unequal Many on equal terms; a federal union of many states; a religious congeries of many cults, a national civilization of many cultures. The unity is not a condition but a process, a spirit, an action going on; a *way* of life; it is always *e pluribus unum*. Its making is not the work of people of British descent alone, nor of white Europeans alone. The native Indian has his share in it; the African Negro, slave as he long was to the European who brought him in chains to these shores. It has been enriched and strengthened by the peoples of Asia and the islands of the Pacific. The miscellany of the world has gathered to its making, and there is today no stronger, freer or more prosperous nation on the face of the earth.

Of course the making never ends. Of course it is a struggle, marked by force and schemes and stratagems, and often by the shedding of blood. The shaping of life in America into the works and ways of the American Idea was and remains a slow and far from unarduous process in which the workers for the Idea were from the beginning opposed by the strength and cunning of vested interests to whose survival the Idea was the spiritual challenge and a material threat. The Constitution which was devised to perfect the Union and to secure the blessings of liberty to the generations was far from a perfect instrument for this end. A clause in the fourth article, for example, perpetuated slavery. It denied men the unalienable liberty which the Declaration affirmed and the Preamble of the Constitution named as the Constitution's purpose to secure.[2] "No Person," it said, "held to service or labour in one

---

[2] Lincoln held the terms of the Preamble to mean that no state could hold a right superseding the rights of man, and that the task of the Union, which made it overruling, was "to secure those rights." Concerning slavery, he said in 1859: "This is a world of compensation; and he who would be no slave must consent to have no slave. Those who deny

State shall, in Consequence of any law or Regulation thereon, be discharged from such Service or labour, but shall be delivered up on Claim of the Party to whom such service or Labour may be due." This article applies to white indentured servants as well as to black slaves. It guarantees property in human beings or in the labor of human beings. It has never been rescinded. It is still a part of the Constitution, but it has been made a part null and void by the adoption of the Thirteenth, Fourteenth, and Fifteenth Amendments. These, it is well to remember, did not come easily. They followed the terrible Civil War which was the climax of four score years of struggle to establish in the United States equal liberty for different people. It took more than a hundred and fifty years to enfranchise the women of the land. It took more than one hundred and thirty years to make the Senate directly responsible to the people. On the other hand, these changes of the Constitution were achieved because in the Fifth Article the Constitution provided for its own alteration, thus implementing the proposition of the Declaration of Independence that the people could change the form of government so as to hold adequate to their purpose the agencies with which they secure their "unalienable rights." And it is well always to keep in mind that the Constitution as a whole was voted only on condition that there would be added to it a Bill of Rights forbidding government to limit freedom of conscience, of speech, of press, of association, of defense and of person. In the language of Mr. Justice Brandeis these amendments confer "as against the government the right to be let alone—the most comprehensive of rights and the right most valued by civilized men."

Conspicuously also, the Bill of Rights finally and definitively established the separation of church and state. The acerbities of religion, whose mutual intolerances greatly disturbed Jefferson all his life, were mollified by the shaping influence of the American Idea. The sects, each at the outset, insisted that it alone had the truth and all others were purveyors of falsehood leading to damnation, and therefore, worthy to be cut off and shut out from equal liberty. They came first to a sort of literal toleration during which they suffered each other but neither appreciated nor co-operated with each other. From this they passed to an attitude of *live and let*

freedom to others deserve it not for themselves, and under a just God cannot long retain it."

live.[3] Today they make the effort to be good neighbors, to *live and help live*. The miscellany of Protestant denominations have formed the Federal Council of Churches of Christ in America. The members of this religious society cherishing their differences one from the other, are joined together for the sake of those differences, joined that each may live and grow more abundantly than it would standing alone. The doctrine and discipline of the Federal Council define a good neighbor policy for Christian churches. Only the Roman Catholic establishment stands aside and continues to push its pretensions to exclusive rule in the Christian world. But among the others, a competing miscellany has formed itself into a cooperative team, again *e pluribus unum*.

This *unum* made up by a plurality defines on all levels the process and form of democracy, the free society which, we may say, is the American religion. Democracy may indeed be described as a religion of religions, since in it and through it, different religions formerly at war with one another are reconciled without any diminution of difference and none penalizes any for being different. The entire life-story of the American nation is an exemplification of the struggles toward the confederation and union of the different, and is signalized by the union's victories. In the conquest of the continent and in the conversion of its wilds and waste into natural resources, and those into tools and goods for human use which is one of its consummations, all of the peoples of the globe have borne and bear a part. They have brought to the nation not only the energy of their bodies, the skills of their hands, but their speech, their cooking, their faiths, their arts and their letters. Irish, or Poles, or Magyars, or Japanese; Jews, or Italians, or Germans, or Swedes; Chinese or Dutchmen, Frenchmen or Czechs, they came bringing the fellowship of a common life and they added this as they could to the national being. Together with the peoples who had preceded them they built the American way into the might

---

[3] Goethe remarked while Jefferson was still alive: (*Zur Natur-und-Wissenschaftslehre*) "In New York there are ninety Christian sects each of which deals with God and the Savior according to its kind, without getting into trouble with any of the others. We must attain the same state in the study of nature, indeed, in any research whatsoever; it is unspeakable that anybody should prate of liberation and seek to keep the other fellow from thinking and speaking as is proper to him."

and abundance which is today the hope of the nation's friends and the despair of her enemies. The principle of the United Nations cannot be other, nor their program seek anything better, than this.

But as America's churches were divided by irreconcilable claims to infallible truth and exclusive sovereignty, her cultural communities were segregated, kept apart, inferior and servile because they were not like their native neighbors. Being different, immigrants were not appreciated for what they were, but condemned for what they were not. As a small, weak, out-group each ethnic and cultural society was judged a "minority" which must submit to the will and conform to the ways of the "majority" by a decision in whose making it was permitted no part, and whose intentions, far from realizing, contradicted, the American Idea. For a long time submission and conformation were the alpha and omega of "Americanization." It assumed that newcomers had, culturally, everything to take and nothing to give in exchange. It set a premium upon "assimilation." It set a stigma upon difference.

Difference *from what* was never made explicit nor could be. The *what* varied with the type that enjoyed prestige and power in the different regions of the land. "Leading citizens" spoke, looked, believed and acted in one way in New York, in another in Texas, in a third in Oregon, in a fourth in Alabama, and so on. The common denominator of all was only printed English, tabloid, boiler plate, and comic—and ready-made factory styled clothing. To these, later, the movie and the radio brought parallel additions. Yet all the time most of those who commanded "assimilation, assimilation!" made it impossible for the immigrant to liquidate his difference and lose himself in sameness with them, by refusing every contact with the newcomer because he was different. The effect was to cause the latter to feel that his group is inferior and unworthy and at the same time to throw him back on this group, generating within it tensions between parents and children, between the inherited folkway and what appeared to be the enviable American way.

Then, slowly, relationships changed, as among the churches. With each new community's naturalization in the American scene, Americanization as submission and conformity of the underprivileged Many to a privileged Some, gave way to Americanization as orchestration of the Many into One. The assumption that minorities, especially minorities of the different, have no rights which majorities must respect was recognized to be contrary to the American Idea of free society and subversive of the democratic way of life, which is the endeavor to maintain equal liberty for different individuals and associations of individuals, regardless of their station, size, occupation, wealth or power. The democratic way of life rejects alike the exploitation or enslavement of the different, or the "assimilation" of the different into the same. For the democratic way of life American society is open society; Americanization consists in naturalizing differences, in joining them to those already co-operating in the national enterprise, in enlarging, strengthening and enriching the national being by variation, not repetition. The American way is the way of orchestration. As in an orchestra, the different instruments, each with its own characteristic timbre and theme, contribute distinct and recognizable parts to the composition, so in the life and culture of a nation, the different regional, ethnic, occupational, religious and other communities compound their different activities to make up the national spirit. The national spirit is constituted by this union of the different. It is sustained, not by mutual exclusions, nor by the rule of one over others, but by their equality and by the free trade between these different equals in every good thing the community's life and culture produce.

This is the relation that the Constitution establishes between the states of the Union; this is the relation that develops between the regions within the states and the communities within the regions. It is because of this that the United Nations may be envisaged as the extension of the axioms of free society to all the peoples of the globe. In all directions there would obtain what Louis Adamic calls a two-way passage, a mutual give and take in equal liberty on equal terms. The result in America is a strength and a richness in the arts and sciences which nations of a more homogeneous strain and an imposed culture like Spain, for example, do not attain. The unprecedented cultural and ethnic diversity of the American people not only implements the national achievement in industry and agriculture, it underlies the innovations which America has brought to architecture, to music and to letters and the distinction that has come to the American people in painting and sculpture. Each ethnic and cultural community serves as a reservoir of some specific tradition and excellence which one or another of its sons may lift into the powers and perspectives of the larger national life, making it stronger and richer. The excellence may come from the kitchen, like the Chinese chow mein, the Jewish gefullte fish, the Italian spaghetti, the French wine. It may come from the field or the church or the barroom, like the Negro's spirituals and swing music; it may come from the vernacular press, like the novels of Abe Cahan and Sholem Asch; it may come from the vernacular theatre like the acting of Paul Muni or Sam Jaffe or Edward Robinson. But the more varied and numerous the sources, the greater the likelihood that it will come. From the action and reaction of the Puritan culture of New England, the French of Louisiana, the "Dutch" of Pennsylvania, the German and the Scandinavian of the Middle West, the Spanish and Indian of New Mexico and California, the Jewish of New York, the Negro of the South, in their cooking, their music, their folklore and folk arts, their more formal expression in words and images and dramas, flows the greater culture of the American nation. It flows of course, also, in the wider stream of the world's spiritual and material past, that provides the sustaining context of the American text which it is the task of the schools to transmit; but naturally its living springs are the many and various local forms of the life. It is a new different thing born of the orchestration and compenetration of this multitude and is at once an effect of liberty and a carrier of liberty as the Declaration intends liberty and the Constitution endeavors to secure liberty. Today this Cultural Pluralism has become a conscious goal for all the churches, not Christian only, with their interfaith movements and their federal councils; a content and a method for our schools, with their Springfield Plans, their committees and programs of intercultural education; a postulate of foreign policy in the State Department with its Division of Cultural Co-operation and its program of international free trade in things of the spirit as a means of developing sympathetic understanding and mutual appreciation and respect between the different nations, and the co-operative union of these differents as the United Nations. Herein is the basis for deciding what it is that American schools must needs teach in order that children in America may grow up into Americans.

Certainly that which makes a man an American is not the place where he was born. The epithet "foreign-born" as applied to American citizens in public life is an instrument of aggression, not loyalty; a stick to beat a dog with, employed in malice, prejudicially, out of motives that cannot easily bear the light of public discussion. Hearers and readers are intended to infer that an American who is not born in the United States is necessarily somehow less American than one who is. Nothing could be further from the truth. The native-born are as capable of un-American behavior, of subversion and of treason as any foreigner assigned to the task by a foreign government; they have shown themselves capable of bitter enmity to democracy, and of totalitarian faith and totalitarian works, Fascist, clericalist, Communist or cartelist. No, it is not where a man is born that makes him an American.

Neither is it how he speaks English or that he speaks English at all. The dialects one hears in Congress are as varied as the regions the representatives come from, as diverse in vocabulary, grammar, rhythm and oratorical forms. Nor is a man's Americanism in how a man dresses or what he eats, or what he works at or where he worships, or what he reads or where he plays. These are even more varied than the dialects. That which establishes a man as an American is first of all, a formal, legal fact—the fact that he is or is not a citizen of the United States; that if a native of voting age, he has not abandoned his national allegiance and sought another; that if naturalized, he has sworn to abandon every other allegiance for allegiance to the United States. This is the law's determination of an American. But in the only sense in which the determination can have meaning and value, it is legal, not vital. On the record, there are plenty of natives whose allegiance is a convenience or a pretense, or a screen for a continuous aggression against Americanism. On the record, there are plenty of naturalized citizens who have sworn falsely, who have sought citizenship even with the express intention of working against the liberty, the security and the welfare of the American people. That which beyond any doubt establishes a man as an American is his faith. He is truly an American who has a fighting faith in the doctrines of the Declaration of Independence, in the rule and discipline of the Constitution by which the doctrines may come to realization as the American way of life. A man in whom this faith is alive and at work but is not legally a citizen is more truly an American than a man who is legally a citizen and lacks this faith. Americanization consists in acquiring freely and freely implementing this faith. Americanization is the education of men in the American Idea. Often natives stand in need of it far more than the "foreign-born."

Chapter Eight

THE PLACE OF EDUCATION IN THE AMERICAN IDEA

The idea, which the Declaration of Independence expresses, of the free man in free society, serves in the history of the American people somewhat as a field of force acting upon men and interests of every sort and condition and drawing them, with unequal success, into the relationships whose dynamic lines are its energies. It was the directive for the struggle to establish sovereignty which the War of Independence from Great Britain initiated and the War of 1812 brought to a conclusion. Liberty,[1] as Barrett Wendell points out, was long thought of more in terms of this independence of the colonies from the mother country than the self-rule and self-support of the peoples of the colonies. Once independence became certain habit, the relations of the colonies—now each itself a sovereign and independent state—to one another, and the effect of this relation on personality and property became the issue of paramount concern. The idea of the free society of free men was now the catalyzer in the struggle over the status and function of the union of sovereign states which had taken the name United States of America. In this struggle state sovereignty was invoked against its modification by federal government. Somehow, in action, the abolition of slavery and the preservation of the Union became the two faces of an identical cause, however they might be distinguished in discourse. Repudiating nullification, Daniel Webster held out for "Liberty and Union, one and inseparable, now and forever." But this liberty could no longer be the arbitrary liberty of the sovereign state. It had to be the unalienable right of the sovereign individual, to secure which, governments are instituted among men. This phase of the struggle comes to its term with the Civil War and the adoption of the Thirteenth, Fourteenth and Fifteenth Amendments to the Constitution. The direction and form of the next phase are predominantly what we call democracy. Democracy is the local and general compenetration of personal liberty with the laws and the governmental organization that the

[1] Barrett Wendell, *Liberty, Union, and Democracy.*

word *Union* stands for. It is the body of rules, programs and procedures in the warfare of moral ideals by which government is shaped ever more into an instrument of the governed, and by which its powers are made ever more amenable to the consent of the governed. Its differentiae were the rewriting of the laws so that they affirmed that labor is not a commodity, nor the labor union a monopolistic conspiracy in restraint of trade. Its differentiae are amendments to the Constitution providing for the election of senators by the people, the income tax, votes for women, and the like.

Perhaps that neither the Declaration nor the Constitution has anything to say about education, whether as a personal right or a public instrument, is an ironic commentary on education as practiced when these pronouncements were composed. For in the vision of their authors, the idea of education is organic to the idea of democracy: the prophets of a free society of free men were sure beyond all doubt that the power of freedom is knowledge and skill, that the spring of knowledge is freedom, that neither can survive long without the other. "If a nation," Thomas Jefferson wrote in 1816 to Colonel Yancey, "expects to be ignorant and free in a state of civilization, it expects what never was and never shall be. The functionaries of every government have propensities to command at will the liberty and property of their constituents. There is no safe deposit for these but with the people themselves; nor can they be safe with them without information." It was an enduring aspiration of Jefferson's to establish a system of public education to be capped with a national university. His role in creating the University of Virginia he esteemed as on a par with his authorship of the Declaration of Independence and of the Virginia Bill of Religious Liberty: these three were the achievements he wanted engraved on his tombstone.

Jefferson's self-taught fellow-countryman and collaborator on the Declaration, Benjamin Franklin, concluded a generation before the independence of the British Colonies in America was even thought of, that the capacities of youth required such cultivation as would render them better citizens and managers and fit them "for any business, calling or profession except such wherein languages are required"; he made certain revolutionary proposals concerning the education of youth in his adopted country, Pennsylvania. Condorcet, a French friend and fellow-libertarian of both Franklin and Jefferson, reporting for his Committee on Public Instruction to the Revolution's National Legislative Assembly in April 1792, told his listeners that education is a natural right, a duty which society owes its members, the means by which free society actualizes and makes real "the political equality decreed by law." Although Jefferson's ideas of the content and method of the education of free men called for a much greater use of the traditional curriculum than Franklin's and Condorcet's, all three projected changes which would modify schooling as profoundly as the Democratic Revolution would modify government.

For if, until the Democratic Revolution, education had been the gentleman's privilege, after the revolution it became the laboring commoner's necessity. Freedom might be his inalienable right, but the security of this right lies in the knowledge which is power. For the gentleman of leisure, learning could be the acquisition of the otiose accomplishments; for the workingman free at last, it had to be the mastery of the sciences and the practical arts. Franklin knew this from the beginning. This American, of whom John Adams wrote that the French accorded a fame "more universal than that of Leibnitz or Newton, Frederick or Voltaire," had been on his own from boyhood. His Boston teachers regarded him as a dull pupil to whom they couldn't teach arithmetic and who showed an even greater resistance to Latin than his betters. Self-educated, he grew up in the realization of the import of *know-how* for a life and a livelihood and preferred the "useful" to the "ornamental." His learning had to be the natural function as well as a conscious purpose of his living, and he became in the process one of the merriest, clearest-headed, generally esteemed and widely loved wise men of his age, father of the Philadelphia Library, the American Philosophical Society and the University of Pennsylvania, the institution of higher learning remade from the Academy he founded.

It was not a university that Ben Franklin intended, when he published his *Proposal* in 1749, but an academy on unprecedented lines. He was concerned that young Pennsylvanians should know that "true merit" consists in "an inclination joined with an ability to serve mankind" which "ability is . . . to be acquired or greatly increased by true learning, and should indeed be the great aim and end of all learning." For "true learning" Franklin proposed reading the history of man, "the new universal history" that would give a connected idea of human affairs, as well as affairs limited to the nation only. Historical events, he said, would make real the problems of morality and the power of oratory, the advantages of constitutions and of liberty. The conflicts which history presents should be debated "in conversations and in writing" and out of the debate would develop an understanding of logic and a desire to master it. Logic, Franklin called "the art of reasoning to discover the truth, and of arguing to defend it, and to convince adversaries." Interest in language would arise similarly out of wanting to comprehend the great men whose lives and actions history records. But chiefly English should be taught, and only secondarily the foreign tongues, living or dead. English is to be learned through reading the best of the writers whose style is both clear and concise. The reading should be accompanied by writing, via exchanges of letters between the pupils and repetitions in their own words of what they have read. On a par with the history of man for these purposes would be the histories of nature; for the study of nature is not only material for discourse but serves all the practical arts. It calls for observation and experiment as well as reading, for the practice of "gardening, planting, inoculating, etc."; and for excursions to the "plantations of the best farmers." It calls for the study and understanding of the science of mechanics with its practical consequences in peace and war. The whole enterprise calls for a teaching staff whose relations with their pupils should be not schoolmasterly but friendly and fatherly.

Clearly it was no gentleman that Franklin planned to educate. The longer he lived abroad, the lower the gentleman fell in his esteem. When in 1782 he prepared an "information to those who would remove to America," he said that it is the farmers and mechanics who are made welcome. "The people," he wrote, "have a saying that God Almighty is himself a mechanic: . . . and he is respected and admired more for the variety, ingenuity, and ability of his handiworks than the antiquity of his family. They are pleased with the observation of a Negro, and frequently mention it, that Bocaroora (meaning the white men) make de black man workee, make de horse workee, make de ox workee, make eberyting workee; only de hog. He, de hog, he no workee; he eat, he drink, he walk about, he go to sleep when he please, he libb like

THE PLACE OF EDUCATION IN THE AMERICAN IDEA 125

a gentleman. According to these opinions of the Americans, one of them would think himself more obliged to a genealogist, who could prove for him that his ancestors and relations for ten generations had been ploughmen, smiths, carpenters, turners, weavers, tanners, or even shoemakers . . . than if he could only prove that they were gentlemen . . . living idly on the labor of others, were *fruges consumere nati,* and otherwise good for nothing, till by their death their estates, like the carcass of the Negro's gentleman-hog, comes to be cut up."

Poor Richard's plan for the education of youth took hold, but not as its author intended. Instead of one school the prejudices of its sponsors made it necessary to set up two. The English School which was first in Franklin's vision and affections was made secondary to a Latin School; nevertheless it did a more vital job of education while Franklin could look after it. But in 1757 he went to England on a mission for his country of Pennsylvania and during the next generation spent comparatively little time at home. The English School languished of maltreatment and neglect. Latin and Greek continued in their ancient precedence and the rest of the curriculum was aborted to serve the invidious distinctions they signalized. What precedent was there, the traditionalists demanded, for ever joining to a college "a school for teaching the vulgar tongue, and the sciences in that tongue." Back home to stay at last, with the infirmities of a man in his eighties weighing him down, Franklin, the last survivor of the original trustees, recalled their true intention with a memorandum to the authorities he entitled "Observations relative to the intentions of the original founders of the Academy." He took occasion therein to make some significant remarks about the springs of traditionalism. . . . "There is in mankind," he wrote, "an unaccountable prejudice in favor of ancient customs and habitudes which inclines to a continuance after the circumstances which formerly made them useful cease to exist. For example, when hair was elaborately curled, hats disarranged it. But instead of giving up hats, they were retained, but carried under the arm. I call Latin and Greek 'the chapeau bras' of modern literature."

Franklin had been long dead when the American Philosophical Society he founded offered a prize for "The best system of liberal education and literary instruction adapted to the genius of the government of the United States, comprehending also a plan for instituting and conducting public schools in this country on the principles of the most extensive utility."

Thomas Jefferson, third President of the United States and an early head of this Philosophical Society, had long pondered such a scheme. He had devised one for his "country" of Virginia, when he was its wartime governor, together with a revolutionary legislative program, designed to apply the principles of the Declaration in the practice of government. Before they could all be put through, he went to France to replace the aged Franklin. Writing in 1786 from Paris to his friend and teacher and fellow-committeeman, George Wythe, he urged that "by far the most important bill in our whole code [2] is that for the diffusion of knowledge among the people. No other sure foundation can be devised for the preservation of freedom and happiness . . . Preach, my dear Sir, a crusade against ignorance; establish and improve the law for educating the common people. Let our countrymen know . . . that the tax which will be paid for this purpose, is not more than the thousandth part of what will be paid to kings, priests and nobles, who will rise up among us if we leave the people in ignorance." Three years later, he wrote to Dr. Price in England. "Whenever the people are well-informed they can be trusted with their new government: . . . whenever things get so far wrong as to attract their notice, they may be relied on to set them to rights."

The bill was introduced into the Virginia Legislature in 1777. It was not accepted, even in principle, till after Jefferson was dead, and then, like the bill on religious liberty, grudgingly. It called for the division of counties into wards, the shaping of the wards into school districts, and the building of district schools. The first three classes were to be free; attendance at the later ones was to be paid for but the fees were to be small. The curriculum was to consist of the three R's with readings in Greek, Roman and American history, especially those events which concern freedom. After the district schools, "grammar" schools. Fees would continue to be small; there would be scholarships for the able but poor, and the best students would be eligible to free instruction at the

---

[2] The new code of laws which excluded entail and primogeniture, and established religious freedom and education. The other members of the Committee were Pendleton, Mason and Lee.

College of William and Mary, Jefferson's own alma mater. "Grammar" pupils would board at school. They would study English, geography and mathematics as well as Latin and Greek. The curriculum at William and Mary was to be reorganized. Theology would be dropped. Municipal common law, equity, commercial, marine and ecclesiastical law, ethics, the fine arts, natural philosophy, political economy and mathematics would partly displace and partly supplement the traditional content of liberal education. Also a state library was to be set up.

The event fell far short of the idea. Jefferson labored the rest of his life to implement his vision. As President he urged more than once upon the Congress the establishment of a national university "on a donation of public lands." Such a donation would have been consonant with an enactment by the Continental Congress of 1785 declaring that "schools and education should be forever encouraged," and allocating a lot in each township of the Northwest Territory "perpetually" for the use of schools and "for the purposes of religion." The adoption of the Bill of Rights, which clearly and distinctly effected the permanent separation of church and state, eliminated the subvention to religion; but actual and would-be beneficiaries of such subventions have never relaxed their pretensions to them.

Jefferson, of course, was foremost in the fight for religious liberty and the freeing of education from doctrinal bias and clerical control. Nearly one hundred years passed before the nation's educational establishment came, as a whole, anywhere near his vision, and within a far shorter period that of his Virginia had undergone a profound physical and moral deterioration. Jefferson's idea was that education in general would teach a man "to observe with intelligence and faithfulness all the social relations under which he will be placed." In his private affairs it would equip every citizen with the information he needs for the conduct of his own business; enable him to keep accounts, to measure, to write down and preserve his own ideas and contracts; to read, and nourish by reading, the growth of his abilities and virtues. As a citizen education would bring a man understanding of his duties to his neighbors and to his country and skill to discharge with competence the functions confided to him by either. He would also know his rights, how to exercise with order and justice those he retains, how to choose with discretion the fiduciary of those he delegates, and to notice their conduct with diligence, candor and judgment. In 1817 Jefferson wrote President Monroe that "we must make military instruction a part of collegiate education. We can never be safe till this is done." He was the first to suggest that military education should be a part of general education. As for the classics, they were to be taught in so far as they could serve the freedom and happiness of free men. Jefferson himself found in the ancient letters sustenance for his democratic faith and intellectual liberty. Toward the end of his life he esteemed them as an "innocent and elegant luxury." But he knew also that they could be and were employed as vehicles of reaction. In a letter to Dr. Joseph Priestley, January, 1800, he wrote of his education bill of "about 20 years ago; I drew a bill for our legislature, which proposed to lay off every county into hundreds or townships five or six miles square, in the center of each one of them was to be a free English School; the whole state was further laid off into ten districts, in each of which was to be a college for teaching the languages, geography, surveying and other useful things of that grade; and then a single university for the sciences. The Gothic idea that we are to look backward instead of forward for the improvement of the human mind, and to recur to the annals of our ancestors for what is most important in government, in religion, and in learning, is worthy of those bigots in religion and government by whom it has been recommended."

The establishment of "a university of the sciences" was the effort of Jefferson's closing years. The Congress had not agreed to a national university, but the idea of one as "a full and perpetual institution for all the useful sciences" endured. That Virginians went abroad to study, to Harvard or to the European universities, and came back indoctrinated against democracy, was a goad. The Academy in Albemarle County of which he had been made a trustee in 1814, was an opportunity. To make it over into the university of his beloved Virginia became "the hobby of (his) old age." Its principle, he wrote Destutt de Tracy in 1820, was to be "the illimitable freedom of the human mind to explore and to expose every subject susceptible to its contemplation." It was to be an institution where men "are not afraid to follow the truth wherever it may lead, nor to tolerate any error so long as reason is left free to combat it." It was to break with tradition in the matter of discipline and leave as much of it as possible to student self-government. Studies were to be elective instead of prescribed. Courses were to be offered in history, government, law, agriculture, medicine, military and naval science, political economy, physics and chemistry as well as the traditional ones. There was to be no instruction in theology. The faculty was to be the best that Europe and America could supply.

The University opened its doors in the spring of 1825, with Jefferson as its visitor and first rector. Writing of it to Ellen Coolidge toward the end of August of that year, the eighty-two-year-old head and founder said, "Our University goes well. We have passed the limit of 100 students some time since. As yet it has been a model of order and good behavior, having never yet had occasion for the exercise of a single act of authority. We treat them as men and gentlemen, under the guidance mainly of their own discretion. They so consider themselves and make it their pride to acquire that character for their institution. In short, we are as quiet on that head as the experience of six months only can justify. Our professors, too, continue to be what we wish them. . . ."

Within less than a year, Jefferson was dead. What character would American education have developed, if he, the shaper of the democracy of his country, had lived to shape its higher education, treating students "as men and gentlemen, under the guidance of their own discretion" both as to the conduct of life and the choice of studies? But Jefferson died. Others took up the cause of education as the sustenance of freedom. De Witt Clinton, Daniel Webster, Robert Owen and his son, Robert Dale Owen, Frances Wright, Horace Mann, Abraham Lincoln, each raised his voice on its behalf. The mechanics, newly organized in trades-unions, made equality of educational opportunity the first article of their program for "the elevation of the labouring portion of the community." But they did not think of the school as a self-governing community of free men. Teaching remained in their thought as an art of indoctrination by authority, learning a submission to discipline in the correct, the desirable ancient "liberal arts." It hardly occurred to any that learning naturally was a free and deliberate seeking of the new, consummated in a choice or decision between alternatives. Although in the course of time, tax-supported, secular, universal public education became a strand in the fabric of the national life—"to free governments the absolute necessity," Thaddeus Stevens told the Pennsylvania legislature in 1834—its matter and method continued traditional and authoritarian and successfully resisted the infiltration of the science of freedom until the turn of the century.

By that time the educational enterprise had acquired some of that independence and autonomy which the churchmen's interests fought to keep from it, and which gives its work the liberty it needs from interference by the state as well. Prophet and warrior of freedom that he was, Jefferson, so far as is now known, had no realization that there was any link between such a sovereign liberty for education and "the illimitable freedom of the human mind to explore and to expose every subject susceptible to its contemplation." The formulation of that insight was the contribution of his friend and fellow-libertarian in France, the Marquis de Condorcet. The two men had met when Jefferson was minister of his country in Paris. Both were frequent guests at Madame d'Houdetot's salon. Condorcet, by training and inclination a mathematician, by vocation an associate of Turgot's in his impossible labor to balance the monarchy's budget, had of course read the Declaration of Independence and other works of the "penman of the American Revolution." He knew intimately the writings of Thomas Paine, and he had himself made a signal contribution to the social sciences by applying, according to Arago for the first time, mathematics to politics. He devised, indeed, a new subject of study for citizens that he called "political arithmetic"—it has since become the gargantuan statistical elaboration of the social sciences. Long before Jefferson had arrived in France, Condorcet had decided that the Democratic Revolution was the most critical event of the age in the history of mankind. He published this view (de l'influence de la revolution d'Amerique sur l'Europe) the year Jefferson appeared in Paris, 1786.

It was Condorcet's idea that in spite of natural evil and the malice and corruption of men, mankind as a whole is and ever has been on the march to truth, and to freedom and equality as a consequence of its progressive attainment of truth. There are ten movements from the beginning to the end of the march, and Condorcet's own lifetime saw the end of the ninth and the beginning of the tenth. The ninth was born with the victory of the scientific spirit, for whose voice Condorcet chose Descartes. Its ruling faith was the abolition of the claims of the ruler over the ruled and the deceiver over the deceived. Of its spokesmen were Newton, Locke and Rousseau, and its mission was to expose error and make clear to man that there is no limit to the perfection he may attain. Its culmination were the two revolutions, the American, and the French, which completes the American and closes the history of the liberation of man. Now the tenth epoch is on its way. This is the epoch not of liberation struggled for but of liberty won. It is the epoch in which men equally free move freely and equally to ever greater peace, wellbeing, reasonableness and freedom, liberating slaves, stopping exploitation, universalizing education.

Condorcet's own share in the initiation of his tenth epoch was not inconsiderable. His sketch of the progress of the human spirit of which this epoch was the current climax was his last act of service to it, "composed," writes M. Buisson [3] "in complete disregard of self and misfortune, and containing no reference to the disastrous circumstances under which he wrote." For Condorcet wrote when he was in hiding, his life forfeit to the fanatic intolerance of the edict of revolutionists that had taken power in the Convention. He was guilty of being too reasonable, too just, too devout. He believed that the cool daylight of reason could be the savior of mankind: "Every society," he declared, "which is not enlightened by philosophers is deceived by charlatans." Being an enlightener, he was held too radical to be elected to the Legislative Assembly of 1789; the Convention proscribed him as too reactionary. When the Legislative Assembly dawdled over promulgating the Declaration of the Rights of Man and Citizen, he joined with another reasonable man, Sièyes, in an address to the people warning them of the danger to their liberties. The address did not add to his popularity nor did his judgment that Louis XVI, by running away, had broken his compact with the people, and that hence his abdication was called for and a Republic due. The interval between abdication and Republic, Condorcet, away from Paris on public business, filled with the composition of his famous *Memoires sur l'instruction publique*. Their date is usually given as 1790.

---

[3] Condorcet. Paris, Alcan, 1929.

Paris elected him as deputy to the Assembly when he returned. His platform, naturally, was Constitutionalist; he held that the law should be obeyed until it is changed. The Assembly made him its secretary; the Convention, which replaced it, elected him vice-president. All the while, he labored to change the law, to frame a constitution so democratic "that never would insurrection be necessary." By 1793 he was ready. With Thomas Paine, who had been voted a citizen of the French Republic, as one associate, he drafted that Girardist Constitution which the Convention rejected as impractical. Condorcet challenged the constitution that the Convention did adopt for failing to safeguard the liberties of the people. Thereupon his arrest was ordered. He fled and went into hiding. From his refuge he wrote the Convention a letter: "Quand la Convention n'est pas libre, ses lois n'obligent pas les citoyens." Thereupon he was condemned to death.

The sentence of death in no way shook Condorcet's faith in reason and progress or dampened his enthusiasm for the Revolution. The irrationality and injustice of his own proscription he interpreted as among those more or less inevitable contingencies of the general movement of mankind toward liberty and happiness. That he commended his daughter to the care of Thomas Jefferson, or, failing that, of Franklin's son-in-law, Bache, in case anything should happen to him, suggests that he fully expected something to happen; suggests that this aristocratic devotee of freedom, this mathematical philosopher of society with the countenance of a *mouton enragé* knew what risks he ran with his faith. After he was dead, perhaps by his own hand, the Convention unanimously voted to publish three thousand copies of the sketch of the history of the human spirit which was its author's testament of the faith to which he was a martyr. His foremost service to it, between 1791 and his death, was his plan to embody faith in fact which he submitted to the National Legislative Assembly on the twentieth and twenty-first of April, 1792. For this is the inwardness of the famous *Rapport sur l'organization générale de l'instruction publique*.

In many ways the Report summarizes and simplifies the *Memoires*. Condorcet looks upon education as "the cultivation of the physical, intellectual, and moral powers of the generations, contributing thus to that general and gradual perfection of mankind which is the final end of every social institution." He conceives of knowledge as the food and arms of the free society of free men, the equalizer and the protector of men's rights against privilege and every other invidious distinction; education, which is the discovery and distribution of knowledge, is thus both the road to truth, and truth's support. For truth and only truth is man's sole insurance against irresponsible and unjust power. Truth is the antagonist both of the power and the power-holders. The more nearly universal its distribution, the weaker must be the hope of privileged power to rule mankind; the more completely truth is known, the less need there is for rule of any kind. Truth is thus the *sine qua non* of free society, and "liberty would be in the greatest of dangers" if a government, any more than a church, had the smallest influence over the art of discovering and transmitting truth, and could fix a body of doctrine and impose a discipline. This art is peculiar to education. Hence power over education and educators would lead to an arrest of progress, fixation in ignorance. Ignorance is a form of poverty. It is the poverty of the spirit which makes a man a dependent on the alms, and a victim of the exactions, of the learned. He "who knows ordinary arithmetic, that he needs in daily life, is not dependent on the learned mathematician. The latter's talents can then be of the greatest use to him, without endangering his enjoyment of his rights." That he know what those are, that he know how to exercise and how to defend them is indispensable to both justice and liberty. Education, hence, must provide this knowledge for everybody. Where it is made a monopoly, it produces and supports an educated caste which tries to prevent the spread of education and holds back personal development and social progress. The discovery and dissemination of truth is made safe only as enlightenment is made general.

And what can serve such a diffusion of knowledge, if not a public school system, available without cost to all the people? Lacking such a system the people can hardly learn democracy and the rights and duties which democracy entails; a widespread improvement in the economy of people's lives cannot take place; women continue to be kept in servile subjection; the liquidation of "social institutions favorable to inequality" can be only violent. The sort of human being that education nurtures when it truly serves freedom is a person of sympathetic curiosity, enlightened, liberal, critical,

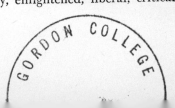

unprejudiced, undogmatic and progressive. The method by which
he is educated is the opposite of that of authority and conformation to authority. The latter may build up gentlemen, but freedom
calls for citizens, and the citizen must be a man of reason, habitu-
ated in the *libre examen,* the free inquiry into the nature and
causes of all things, even of the Bill of Rights of the Man and the
Citizen, even of the Constitution. If it be objected that these documents are themselves dogmas of a faith, the reply is that they are
facts of experience verifiable by reason and as such are subject to
the *libre examen* which vindicates their validity if they are valid.
For under free examination they survive the tests which would
destroy them if they were natural delusions or willful deception:
"Truth can stand by itself." And so the Rights of Man stand. The
civic loyalty which men are to learn is first and last a loyalty to
these rights. It is the true patriotism, having no part in the dogmatic nationalism of the "patriotic charlatans." For it is the
patriotism of ideas, the ideas of liberty, equality and fraternity, that
are both the means and the ends of truth and progress.

The educational establishment which should be the carrier of
this loyalty upon the ways of the *libre examen,* would be arranged
in five stages. There would be elementary and secondary schools,
institutes and lycées. They would be tax-supported, and free to all
the children of the land. There would be one elementary school
for every four hundred families. It would provide a uniform four
years' course in the three R's, geometry, geography, agriculture and
citizenship. Schools of the secondary stage would be set up in the
chief cities of each district, one for every four thousand families.
Essentially, they would continue and extend the studies begun in
the elementary schools for another four years; but the content
would now have the form of the pure and practical sciences, and
would add commerce, foreign languages, social science and political
history. Every secondary establishment would be equipped with a
library, a laboratory and a botanical garden. The institutes, of
which there were to be 110, appropriately distributed through the
nation, would be similarly equipped and would further advance
training in the same fields. But they would add "political arithmetic," and provide Greek and Latin as electives. Finally there
would be ten lycées, one in Paris, and the others so located as to
offer the greatest attraction to students from abroad. Their curricu-

lum would cover *toute connaissance* and their equipment would correspond. It would need to be adequate for research in mathematics and the natural sciences, the theory and practice of political science, the application of science to art, and lastly belles-lettres and the fine arts.

Concurrent with each stage of the education of youth would be a continuing process of adult education. This would consist of weekly or monthly Sunday lectures by the schoolteachers on civic rights and duties, scientific discoveries, mechanical inventions, and military developments which might save them from becoming "docile instruments in adroit hands."

The program would be planned and executed by the savants of the National Society of Arts and Sciences. This society is to be the final step in the progression of inquiry and education. It is to be the final step and the supreme power. Its seat would be Paris. It would have 318 members, the most distinguished citizens of the nation in their respective fields. The fields would be the four studied at the lycées—mathematics and physical sciences; the technological sciences; the moral and political sciences; literature and the fine arts. As against that prime source of error, the antiquarianism of existing educational authority, the four divisions would emphasize the matter and the methods of the sciences.

To the members of this society Condorcet would entrust the control of education. He would give them power to prepare and appoint teachers, to safeguard tenure, to insure academic freedom, to supervise the awarding of scholarships to the worthy, to prepare texts and oversee instruction, and so on indefinitely. Their task is to "save the future generations from experiencing new prejudices that would ravish them of both their independence and dignity rather than protect the present generation from exploitation." They are thus at once the custodians and the chief instrument of progress. Although associated in four distinct groups, they are to seek the maximum of intercommunication and cross-fertilization for their separate disciplines; they are to effect the confluence of research, *libre examen,* with education; they are to bring about a diffusion of knowledge such as will reduce social distance to a minimum and establish in the daily life the same sort of equality that the law decrees for political status.

Whatever tendencies to autocracy this system might conceal

would be checked, Condorcet argues, by the requirement of full publicity for both elective lists and scientific labors, so that free public opinion would be always in play. Moreover, the proposed establishment would not be a monopoly, exclusive and totalitarian. There would arise many voluntary societies united by a common interest in this or that field of study and instruction. There would be numbers of private schools, privately supported. The societies would naturally watch the ways and works of the savants. The private schools would naturally rival or emulate the national establishment, and might indeed come to be themselves yardsticks of the public service. And always and ever there would be the power of the state. Unless, however, the proposed autonomy were provided for the educational establishment, the teaching of the teachers and the learning of the pupils would, as in the past, undergo distortion at the hands of the despot, the mob or the priest especially the priest. For the sake of truth and freedom, the priest must be kept from laying hands upon the school.

Such was Condorcet's proposal. The anticipated objection was made nevertheless: the philosopher was proposing to set up a state within a state. The defense that he was but safeguarding the liberties, of which the state should be the vehicle and insurance, from encroachment by state as well as church, was disregarded. The report was rejected and a new committee was appointed. Time, now, has vindicated Condorcet's intention, and in free countries, especially in the United States, there are indications that the event may be catching up with the intention.

Chapter Nine

THE SCHOOL IN THE STRUGGLE FOR DEMOCRACY

Condorcet worked out in a comprehensive and pointed plan the philosophy of education which Jefferson formulated briefly in general terms, and which he found he could implement only piecemeal, intermittently and inadequately. To the French *philosophe* education could not perform its prime function unless the entire educational enterprise were made autonomous, the teacher recognized as a responsible democratic leader and the *libre examen* employed as the method paramount in teaching and learning. Only when these requirements were fulfilled could the schools provide each human being with the knowledge, the skills and the understanding that would "make real the political equality decreed by law."

Neither Condorcet nor Jefferson conceived such equality as internal and qualitative. Both were too deeply aware of the individuality of individuals, of the many ineffable differences which distinguish them. Both wanted, however, free play for those differences, free co-operation and free competition between them, and to both the inward meaning of equality lay in such organization of the different individuals that each could become more freely and fully himself by means of the organization than he could without it. Education, they held with Danton, "next to bread . . . is the first need of the people." Both regarded the school as among the foremost of such organizational instruments. Through the school, they felt, individuality might be liberated, equipped, and sent on an open road of personal development and social achievement, where it might run the race of life and labor on its merits and not on privilege of birth or station or on the favor of wealth. The world to which they were proposing equal educational opportunity for different individualities was a hierarchical world, a world of status organized on lines of caste and class. The multitudes of men lived and moved and had their being in separate social strata whose differentiae were provided by social condition and not by personal quality. The all-important boundaries between men were horizontal ones, separating gentleman from workingman, nobleman from commoner, orthodox believer from dissenter. Very rarely could a man move from a lower level of the hierarchy upward, and no matter how low downward he fell, he retained the privileges of the gentleman. These were at least as profitable as the privilege of clergy. Never could nobleman and commoner stand beside each other on equal ground, on the same level of status and respect, each counting for one and neither for more than one, as is the case when different sorts and conditions of men who make up the citizens of a democratic republic cast their ballots in a free election.

Both Jefferson and Condorcet believed that education could obliterate, or at least reduce to a passing instrumentality, these imposed horizontal divisions between human beings that shut them off from one another in caste and class. They believed that education could cause the artificial horizontal divisions to dissolve before the natural vertical differences between person and person. They believed that education could liberate those differences, that it could enable men to live together on the one level of equal right to life, liberty and the pursuit of happiness, and to move on their own powers freely up and down and back and forth through every story of the fabricated social pyramid. This pyramid, they were sure, was a secondary and not a primary structure. They held its hierarchies to be derived and associative merely, not basal, not constitutive. They believed the hierarchies to be artifacts made by the contractual relationships of mobile individuality and altered, eliminated or recreated by this mobility. They regarded the changing structures as organizations of liberty. Franklin Roosevelt, renewing their insight amid the global civil war of the twentieth century, envisaged these organizations as ways of life achieving what he called the Four Freedoms. In the debates leading to the Charter of the United Nations they were given the form of a bill of human rights.

The spring and matrix of all of them is the right of the human person at his own risk to seek the truth wherever the search may lead; to think, to speak and to write what he thinks without fear and without favor; under the protection of the laws to keep to himself or to join with others; to earn his bread in freedom and to eat it in peace; to be the master of his own body and in secure possession of the fruits of his own labor. Right, in this context, designates the acknowledgment by all men that certain powers and qualities are essentials of the existence and growth of any man, and that his freedom consists in the expressive functioning of these properties. The properties are conceived as constitutive of his nature, and his right, hence, is thought of as a natural right.

The passage from the idea of property as quality or power to the idea of property as possession may not be logical, but it is psychologically inevitable. Every human being experiences the event that production terminates in product, and product—which is personal power projected by labor, personal power gone over into something else, power thus become external, detached—is property as possession. The traditional conception of the relation of parents and children retains much of this proprietary sentiment. The labor theory of value has diffused this sentiment into the political economy of goods and services. And in political thinking it persists in the still prevailing idea that "property," whatever its mutations, is a natural right. Before Jefferson, the triad of rights had been life, liberty and property, and a most troublesome issue in the struggle to realize freedom through organization has lain in the relation between liberty and property.

Thus, the making of American institutions began formally as a loose association of thirteen self-declared "free and independent," separate and distinct, sovereign states. Under the Articles of Confederation, a military alliance against a common foe, the alliance began to dissociate into its component and competitive sovereign units just as soon as the foe was overcome. What afterwards held them in their precarious togetherness was a number of common liabilities and the prospect of common gain—external and internal debts, paper money, an indefinite reserve of unappropriated land. The interests most ardent "to form a more perfect union" are said to have been more concerned about the disposal of property than about securing the general welfare and the blessings of liberty to themselves and their posterity. Many wanted such a union of states as would be sure to pay 100 cents on the dollar for continental scrip that they had taken up from discharged soldiers of the Revolution for practically nothing. They wanted an invidious distribution of state and federal lands. They also wanted a central rule of law and order which would take for its supreme duty keeping property safe rather than men free. The debates between the spokesmen for those interests and the men who sought to translate the doctrines of the Declaration into the law of the land are recorded by James Madison. They make the background of the articles in the *Federalist* of which he, and Alexander Hamilton and John Jay, were the authors. The Constitution whose adoption they urged, was, as we have already seen, a compromise. It established a republic. But of its six articles only one was formulated in the spirit of the Declaration. This is the last one, which provides for its own, the Constitution's, alteration and amendment. The people, however, wanted liberty as the precondition and aim of government. To get the Constitution adopted the framers had to pledge the addition of a Bill of Rights, and from then on the steps of the American republic toward democracy and "the blessings of liberty" are signalized by the successive amendments to the Constitution.

Each amendment—except the repealed eighteenth—has been said to mark a victory for human rights over property rights. Each has been possible because every citizen could freely vote for his preferred alternatives of policy and law. Lacking this freedom, there can be only tyranny. To maintain it and assure it, hence, called for more than one political party, each with a program and candidates between whom the people could choose. As an organization every such political party is a minority. Campaigns and elections are the ways in which it seeks the support that would enlarge it from a minority into a majority. Its ways and works flow from the general recognition that change of rule is necessary and desirable, that its direction can be freely defined and freely chosen. Competing political parties are among democracy's foremost instruments of peaceable change. With them as the vehicles, alternatives of persons and policy freely confront one another, their virtues and vices undergo analysis and exposure at each other's hands, and finally the people choose between them at the ballot box or voting machine. The party that the majority has rejected loyally accepts its rejection. But it does not therefore either abandon or suppress its program or its leadership. On the contrary, it serves by their means a necessary organic function in democratic government; as the opposition (in England, "his majesty's loyal opposition") it employs them as standards of appraisal and judgment upon the causes of the victorious majority. And the majority faithfully acknowledges and loyally protects this equal right of the minority to its difference, to its free endeavor to become in its turn the majority.

Rather than hazard the diminution or loss of this equal liberty, democratic government endures the inconveniences, even the dangers, of filibusters; the pressures, the hypocrisies, the delays and incompetencies of competing interests; all the law's delays, all the insolence of office, all the hubris and vanities that in an authoritarian society are instantly intolerable. Democratic society lives in the hazards of equal liberty and by the duty of the eternal vigilance which is liberty's well-known price. The social and economic history of liberty in the United States sufficiently exemplifies what this indicates. The American way not only permits the formation and development of societies whose structure and purpose are the opposite of democratic, it secures to them the protection of the laws and the nourishment of the economy. They grow into mighty concentrations of wealth, power and influence. Many are business enterprises; others are religious establishments; some purport to be patriotic or friendly societies; many are political organizations such as feed off New York or Jersey City and other great urban centers. They find ways of so applying the law intended to safeguard equal liberty—such a law, for example, as the Fourteenth Amendment, or such an expression as the "general welfare clause" in the Preamble of the Constitution—as to subvert their purposes and turn them into facilitators of authoritarianism, dogmatism and monopolistic privilege. In terms of Jefferson's conception of the necessities of freedom in the organization of liberty, in terms of Condorcet's affirmation of the *libre examen,* it is right and just that the undemocratic should receive the equal protection of the laws, and that a free society must assure it to them. It is this quality of the American way which provides the experience for George Santayana's observation that democracy moves "by a series of checks, mutual concessions and limited satisfactions. It counts," he further noted, "on chivalry, sportsmanship, brotherly love, and the rarest and least lucrative of virtues—fairmindedness; it is a broadbased, stupid, blind adventure, groping toward an unknown goal."

No one aware of the processes of democracy doubts that democratic society is often stupid, or that one aspect of its stupidity is the logic which impels many of the most devoted champions of democracy to follow their democratic principles to the point where the democratically protected foes of those principles come thereby into the position and power to proscribe them. This stupidity is a function of the fair-mindedness and the sportsmanship which are, above all, the unique differentiae of the democratic spirit. In them lives and moves the morale of free enterprise wherever in a community free enterprise truly exists; and they are most needful where the principle of the parity of the different is exposed to the passions and powers of property. It is by segregating property to itself, by putting it to the service of hierarchical authoritarianism, that the latter is able to undermine and ultimately to abrogate the liberties which nourish it. A propertyless church must prevail by the merits of its doctrine and by these alone; a business unprivileged by handicaps of money and monopoly must prevail by the merits of its goods and services and by those alone. But let the privacy of property pass from the diversity of individuals to the singularity of the corporation, then servility is in the offing.

The well-known story need not be repeated of the support that the idea of equal liberty for different men received from men's untrammeled access to public lands, and then from their opportunity with hands and head to work them over into private property. When the national economy was nearly as agricultural as Jefferson once wanted it to be, the majority of the American people, were, or could become, independent farmers. Property could be deeply private. A farmer's relation to his land was as personal as a modern machine-worker's relation to his toothbrush. But with the industrialization of the national economy this appropriation of nature through the laborious expenditure and projection of personal energies was displaced by absentee ownership of farms and factories. Farmers became tenants on the land they worked even as craftsmen became tenants in the factories which employed them. Both now lived without any continuing personal stake in the materials and tools that channeled and precipitated their personal energies. As the structure of the national economy became more and more that of the corporate monopoly and the banking chain, property became less and less private. Critics of the economy who cry out against abuses by private property do not know what they are talking about. The abuses they denounce are not due to the privacies of property but to the destruction of those privacies. The need is not to eliminate what private property still exists, but to make the achievement of private property once more equally open to all the citizens of the land. Too few Americans are freeholders of land and houses and tools, not too many. Too many Americans are now without roots in the soil, and have lost, or never had, their personal identification with the things and tools they use or possess. The cause of this rootlessness, of this depersonalization, writers from Jefferson to Henry George and after, attribute, not to a superiority of skill and knowledge among the small number of successful competitors, but to their non-competitive aggression with force and fraud. Carl Sandburg is a contemporary voice of this representative yet traditional judgment:

> Get off the estate.
> What for?
> Because it's mine.
> Where did you get it?
> From my father.
> Where did he get it?
> From his father.
> And where did he get it?
> He fought for it.
>
> Well, I'll fight you for it.

Impersonal absentee ownership, defined by legal instruments, such as deeds and stocks and bonds, is set by the community over against personal appropriation achieved by the projection of personal energies upon impersonal things. The former is the artifact of a rule of law, and can exist only so long as the community acquiesces in the fiction created and sustained by the law. The right to it is a civil, not a natural right. The latter, on the other hand, is a natural event which comes to be wherever a human being works consciously upon any non-human stuff. The working is a personification of that stuff and renders it psychologically a property of the worker, regardless of whom the law may designate as owner. Whatever alienates it from his personal being does so, to his feeling, either fraudulently or by *force majeure*. The trades-unions and their apologetics, the various socialist philosophies, all are enchannelments and rationalizations of this feeling. Behind them all lies the sanction of the man's power and readiness to fight for what is thus his own.

Now this power, this readiness, are, in the democratic idea, proper equally to all sorts and conditions of men, and for all necessities which only education can supply. Nor, in view of the permanent exigencies of the democratic situation, can the ways and works of such education ever fail to be those of Condorcet's *libre examen.* Its initiation must needs be controversy; its termination consensus. The pedagogy of democracy, if it is to be a teaching *for* democracy, must rest in the sportsman-like confrontation of alternatives, their dialectic analysis and the scientific elicitation of their possible consequences. Even the validity of the multiplication table is more surely realized controversially through challenge by alternatives, through doubt and verification, than through its dogmatic repetition as a self-evident truth by an infallible teacher. "A student of philosophy," declared John Mill [1] "would be the better for being able to stand an examination both in Locke and in Kant, whichever of the two he takes up with, or even if with neither: and there is no reasonable objection to examining an atheist in the evidences of Christianity, provided he is not required to profess a belief in them."

But traditionally, education has gone with requirement; it has been inculcation and indoctrination, excluding the sportsman-like consideration of alternatives, and the techniques of free inquiry. It has degraded freedom into a dogma to profess instead of establishing it as a habit of deliberation and action. And it has done so because the democratic ideal of education for democracy never quite broke away from the authoritarianism which has pertained to education from its beginnings. The old and new authoritarian interests—ecclesiastical, economic and political—which find shelter and soil in democratic society still further inhibited the conversion of the schools to the ways of democracy. Structurally, the great secular public systems became echoes of factory organizations with their authoritarian hierarchies. Politically it was safer and less trouble to abolish controversy than to join issues of knowledge and belief in the spirit of sportsman-like fair play. There are very few public schools—or for that matter, private ones—in whose classrooms the pupils may freely and openly discuss controversial social issues. There are very few where the dynamics of govern-

[1] *On Liberty.*

ment may be considered as they actually are. Release-time for sectarian indoctrination is *de rigeur,* the scientific study of religion is taboo. And a candid analysis of economic behavior is usually denounced by economic establishments who have precise ideas of what image of their attitudes and doings they demand that young America should carry away from school. Honest and fair consideration of alternatives is decried as sedition. Teaching is made the art of wearing intellectual blinkers. In the circumstances, what else can the schools provide as education save that barrenness and irrelevancy of matter, that contradiction of instruction by experience and of principle by practice, which confirm the ground of the class-war between teachers and pupils. The contradictions have often been declared to be consequences of the democratic idea.[2] Obviously they lead to the idea's nullification and complete defeat.

For the education of free men, hence, the question is momentous whether certain traditional and powerful ways of thinking and learning and teaching even of freedom's self [3] are not such imminent threats to man's liberties that they are fraught with death to freedom? The question presents itself whether the democratic principle by its very nature makes for its own nullification. The question presents itself whether democrats are required by their democratic faith to shelter and to nourish in equal liberty the foes of democracy until those foes feel safe and strong enough to destroy their host and his ways and works. And the question presents itself most immediately as issues of the conduct and management of the nation's schools. The industrial state of New York, for example, is one of the most progressive in the Federal Union. Her people and her laws stand well forward on the frontiers of the democratization of the industrial economy. Yet a recent survey [4] of the state's school system shows that classroom lessons and school activities are independent variables; that pupils either know nothing or know falsehoods regarding the political economy of their home towns; that school administrations are dictatorships; that student self-government is a sham and a pretense; that teachers, being afraid, not only are aloof but are unaware of the problems of the communities whose children they are supposed to educate

---

2 See Marie Syrkin: *Your School, Your Children.*

3 See B. F. Pittenger: *Education for Democracy* (New York: 1942).

4 The Regents' Inquiry into Social Studies Teaching in New York State.

into freedom; that *what* they teach has no relation to the interests
and passions of their pupils and presents them with no vital,
momentous or forced options; that they neither inquire into, nor
analyze, nor appraise the moral judgments and social preferences
of the pre-eminent and élite, merely receiving them from the tradition and repeating them as received.[5] In sum, education in
progressive New York State is indoctrination in a dated grammar
of assent. Lacking the liberty and denied the skills to explore
the dynamics of the state's total economy, neither the teachers nor
the pupils can attain that insight into its process on which an
organization of liberty can be advanced and the arts of its intelligent cultivation be developed into habits of the free man's life.

The schools of New York may be taken for a true enough
sample of the schools of the nation. The question which they pose
to all who see education as an organic integer of the democratic
idea is the question which Condorcet answered by his proposal
that the educational establishment should be made autonomous
and self-governing. It also envisages the situation which caused
John Mill and Herbert Spencer to fear lest education become a
monopoly of the state. The condition interposes a barrier, to
this day broken through only at rare intervals, between the school
as ideal and the school as fact in the struggle for democracy. The
resolution of the doubts which the situation engenders is still not
an issue of experience, still but a projection of the will to believe.

---

[5] See H. E. Wilson: *Education for Citizenship* (New York: 1938), pp.
221-27.

Book III

OF SOCIAL ORGANIZATION AND PERSONAL
LIBERTY

Chapter Ten

THAT YOU CAN CHANGE HUMAN NATURE

In the history of teaching, such words as "indoctrination," "instruction," "inculcation" give away the persistent relation of teacher to pupil, of adult to child. It is a relation of superior to inferior power, of hardness to plasticity, of authority to dependence. The primary activities, upon which the later meanings of the words are variations, are activities of building in, stamping in, talking in. Among the armed forces "indoctrination" has been the word for all teachings of ideas, while the teaching of only actions is called training. Teachers tend automatically to resort to it when pupils appear unable or unwilling to learn that which teachers purport to teach. The component of force in the meaning of the terms points to a certain recalcitrance and aversion in the learner.

Yet commonly the doctrines of the indoctrinators are presented as self-evident ineluctable truths. But it must be obvious that if they were such, indoctrination would be unnecessary. If indoctrination is necessary, the doctrines can be neither self-evident nor ineluctable. If indoctrination is necessary, it is necessary because the doctrines cannot come to acceptance on their competitive merits and need support from strengths other than their own. They need support against alternatives which dispute their claims upon the learner. The alternatives may be unconscious beliefs or conscious judgments. Their resistance may be active and deliberate or passive and automatic. But it is operative and it lays upon indoctrinators the burden of meeting and overcoming it. Whereever alternatives fight for place, wherever an issue is controversial and options are live, weighted and momentous, indoctrination becomes an applauded educational method, a pedagogic troubleshooter which strips away the hesitancies and trials and errors of natural learning. Few people dispute about how to teach the multiplication table. So long as it is learned and used, *how* it is learned stays of little concern, although it is true that during more than a quarter of a century the teaching of all arithmetic has moved steadily away from indoctrination. Pass, however, from the multiplication table to statistics, to non-Euclidean geometries, to relativity, the quantum theory and biophysics, and you enter worlds of active controversy. Schools among the Communists, the Catholics, the Nazis, the Fascists will treat those as issues of doctrine. The dogmas and regulations of the churches, the mores directing the ways of a man with a maid, the professions and practices of war, the sanctions of property, are among the most notable of human interests and relations which societies tend to keep taboo against free inquiry and reserve for inculcation. Each society and each group within a society may have its own way of rationalizing these ultimately arbitrary preferences and decisions. Each employs a certain conception of the nature of man and of the world, and of man's place and destiny in the world. Each labors to hold its conception invariant against its own inner changes and against the outer impacts of the *libre examen*. Hence, although the schools have been considerably secularized and pedagogy makes large pretensions to science, education retains many of the traits of the religious establishment it was freed from. It also has its singular definitions of human nature, its diverse fixed techniques of faith and works, its salvational goals, some of them still for immortal souls at rendezvous with eternity. The argots and the procedures are different. The attitude remains. It ages but it does not change.

And perhaps this is why only something like a religious conversion can bring a professionally trained teacher to realize that pupils are people, that colleagues are people, that the living child is by no means the same as the classroom pupil and the human being as the classroom teacher. The latter are occupational fictions, artificial characters shaped to occupational ends by abstracting a few possibilities of behavior from the lasting *totum simul* of personality and by suppressing and ignoring the enormous organic residue whence the abstraction draws whatever life it may have. Even in the classroom, it is this residue which gives force to the interpersonal relations that the words *pupil, teacher, colleague,* enchannel or the bookkeeping of the school system can or does take account of. In the schoolroom also, pedagogy seems happy to forget that teachers and pupils are people, each different from the others and each under greater or less duress to live together with the others. By the acts of indoctrination the pedagogue weights and intensifies this initial duress; while the arts of the *libre examen* remove it from the spirit of the learner, converting compulsion into co-operation and authority into consent.

Which comes to prevail, indoctrination or *libre examen,* is largely a consequence of *how* people envisage each other, realize each other, understand each other. No living person can enter the perception of his fellow save as a body. This holds in the most spiritistic of systems. Even the bodyless dead must have a living body for a medium of their manifestation; nor can any event of heaven or hell make sense except by way of bodily reference. In a word, presence, existence, being *there,* always means some experience of seeing, hearing, smelling, tasting, touching, acting on, feeling, a something not the same as the sensori-motor adience which answers the thing's call. In the case of people, living or dead, this something is the body or some symbol or image of the body. But it is true that the bodies are not the people. By themselves alone, bodies, humanly speaking, are not human. By themselves alone bodies are only animal organisms reacting to stimuli. The humanity which attaches to them envelopes them like an atmosphere, radiates from them like an aura and illuminates them like an aureole. This effulgence is an added something, for which the name in any individual is personality, and which is the self that the individual struggles to preserve as he "struggles for self-preservation." Though we see people as bodies, we experience them as persons. Every person is a unique body which somehow is uniquely embodying a unique personality-image.

A clear, distinct, scientific definition of how personality and the personality-image relate themselves to the body is still out of my reach. There are many theories of what mind is and of how it is related to the body. I have received small aid and less comfort from any. There is only one thing on which all are agreed: this is that body is not mind and mind is not body. The recognition that the two are different may be as old as humanity itself. Certainly every known species of human culture builds a considerable part of its commonalty of organization upon or around this difference. And even sophisticated cultures with totally monistic philosophies, that make all different things modes or mutations of one thing and only one—one spirit or one matter—are compelled to employ the distinction in order to liquidate it.

In the prescientific world the most widespread as well as the most conventional equivalent for personality is "soul." Tradition is apt to designate education as the culture or discipline of the

soul, and the soul as an immaterial simple entity, create or un-
create, having functions but no parts, but in any event immortal,
receiving the body for a dwelling place at birth and moving from
its ruinous shelter to another habitation at death. The soul's
functions are to think, to will and to feel. Its career during life
is an exercise of those functions which may require a warfare
with the flesh in which it dwells, or with its own self as a being
whose will is free. Its choices and decisions while it is in life
will establish its fortunes when it is dead. The duty of education
is to instruct in right doctrine and to inculcate right discipline.
This will render any choice but the right choice and any decision
but the right decision impossible. Education, that is, should be
indoctrination in orthodoxy of thought, of judgment, and of conduct.[1] Different cultures cultivate different orthodoxies, but each
develops as a variant upon this ground plan of belief relating
body, soul and destiny. The multitudinous societies of mankind
hold, each in its manner, to these beliefs. Their religious and
political economies are addressed to enchanneling these beliefs
in the conduct of life. Education, as we have seen, has been held
internal to these economies, their instrument for transmitting their
principles and practices to the generations. The personality into
which any member of such an economy develops will absorb into
his singularity at least the dominant features of this transmitted
cultural inheritance. Willy-nilly he will pattern his works and
ways to the lines of force which this projects.

---

[1] The Democratic Revolution, with its faith in reason and progress,
superseded this conception with another which has been winning an ever
wider allegiance since the age of Jefferson and Condorcet. This other is
intrinsic to the Jeffersonian philosophy of education. "We should be far,
too," he wrote in 1811 (The Rockfish Gap Report) "from the discourag-
ing persuasion that man is fixed, by the law of his nature, at a given
point; that his improvement is a chimaera, and the hope delusive of rendering ourselves wiser, happier or better than our forefathers were . . .
Education engrafts a new man on the native stock, and improves what
in his nature was vicious and perverse into qualities of virtue and social
worth. And it cannot be but that each generation succeeding to the
knowledge acquired by those who preceded it, adding to it their own
acquisitions and discoveries, and handing the mass down for successive
and constant accumulation, must advance the knowledge and well-being
of mankind, not infinitely, as some have said, but indefinitely, and to a
term no one can fix and foresee."

That neither the conception of personality as "soul" nor the conception's implications—however widely and strongly they continue to be held—is acceptable to the modern spirit, need not be argued. The sciences of life and of man deny that personality is a lodger, or even a freeholder, in the body, that it is from the body detached or detachable, that it is independent and subject to the law of its own nature alone. In the light of these sciences, personality and body belong to one another. Their relationship is not external but internal, the first being a growth of the second, a sort of effulgence from its structure and activities. But concerning the *how* of this dynamic inwardness, the sciences provide no unambiguous deliverance. Analogies abound—analogies from ideas of force and field, of heat and light, channel and stream, sun and ray, and so on to no end. Nevertheless what is said of the relation between mind and body belongs rather to speculative than to experimental psychology. The latter assumes the relation, exploits it, but does not explain it. The former purports to explain it, but cannot exploit it; and when it can, turns out to have used in the explanation that which it undertook to explain. Faculty psychologists, psychoanalysts, behaviorists, connectionists, gestaltists, hormicists, topologists and all the rest; philosophers as diverse as Bergson and Russell and Dewey and Whitehead—each starts from assumptions only to return with that alone which they took with them. A consensus seems as remote as ever in these modern times.

This should cause a certain inconvenience to education, and certainly does when the educational establishment calls for a philosophy. And when, indeed, does the establishment not call for a philosophy? Being always, however, a pressing, present enterprise, education cannot wait for a consensus. It must act on working hypotheses, whatever at last may be the religious or scientific and philosophic ultimates regarding the mind-body relation, and whatever may be their bearing on the many devices of postulation, determination and measurement which make up so much of the educational psychology of our time. The schools avail themselves of whatever assumption and whatever devices and techniques authority sanctions or fashion suggests. And in using them they tend to exalt them from postulates into principles, from working hypotheses into infallible dogmas, from tools into idols. Because of their uses, these servants of education become its masters.

With this in mind, let us assume that personality is to the body as, say, music is to the violin. Obviously its music is not the same as the violin, nor as the moving bow that causes the fiddlestrings to vibrate. True, music is not until the bow strikes the strings; if the former should be called stimulus, the latter's vibration must be called response. Those vibrations are the immediate antecedants of music, and music ensues upon the sequence of the relationships to one another of the fiddle's parts and of the whole fiddle and the bow. That fiddle is a special, if you like, a singular, organization of stuffs which because thus patterned are able to respond, among others, to certain selected stimuli external and internal. The bow is but the stimulus acknowledged by convention. But the fiddle may also vibrate because of difference between its woods, of a step on the floor, a wind outside, and many other impacts which do not customarily figure in the formation of music. So it is also with body and personality. Personality is the vector relationship between a body and its environments. It is not actual until the diverse environment stimulates and the body responds. Its being is not however response merely, it is response impatterned, projected, changing, yet developing continuously. Aristotle was among the first to observe this fact of relationship. He noted that soul is to body as cutting is to an axe. Soul thus is an activity or "actualization" of the body. Aristotle also thought that the most human, the most rational part of the soul had no organ of which it was an activity, that it was actual of itself, in itself and for itself, an independent and autonomous power. We know that this is not the case, that personality and body belong together as field and magnet or music and instrument. We know that they affect each other as function affects structure and structure function.

Taking the analogy with music for a working hypothesis, how does any person realize his personality? [2] How does he envisage and

───────────

[2] We must always keep in mind that even the most perfect analogy is inadequate, and that every one of them can cause error. The music which comes from a violin is a terminal event for the violin. It figures as the final effect of a sequence of actions whose energies are used up in the music, as the force of a spring is consumed in the pattern which the water makes as it fountains into the air. The music might be compared to the incandescence of a tungsten filament in an electric light. Music is the goal and consummation to which all other operations of a musical performance lead. Although the fiddle does undergo structural and other modifications in the

understand the selfhood of his self? Is it in the manner of the image that a snapshot catches or the pose a photographer arranges or the form and features that a mirror reflects? Every man knows that it cannot be any of these by itself nor all of them together, alone. They are events of a moment that passes and though they are substance of his substance and form of his form, the self he is not- only passes but continues as it passes. The self endures. Images, postures, gestures, actions, expressions, like the notes of a tune, are passing events; what permanence they attain, they attain, again like the notes of a tune, when and as they have ceased to pass and become the past. The self's continuity and existence is the activity of passing; it is process; it is transition wherein some-how, as in a melody or other musical progression, the shifts of

---

course of being played upon, it is generally believed that those modifica-tions are mechanical only. The speculations that interpret them as a sort of learning are not many. To be genuinely learning, the violin's changes would have to resemble those of a singer learning to sing. Her vocalizations are also an incandescence, also the final term to which all her other activities are preliminaries, and in which they are at once spent and consummated. But if her singing were only that, she could no more learn her art than the violin. She would be to the music she produces what the violin is, or a record is—a mechanical occasion of a mechanical effect. Since the violin is not a living organism and she is, the violin does not remember, and she does. All her body remembers, her vocal chords remember. In minding the experiences to which her response is singing, she takes in some items, shuts out others; she so assimilates and compounds those she takes in, that her organs of musical perception and expression modify in form and diversify and expand in function. During each lesson, exercise or performance, her printed notes, her instrumental accompaniment, and other matters rele-vant and irrelevant, are contributing accessories to the functioning of those organs. The process is continuous, and it is such that each event of it com-pounds with its predecessors and all together exercise a shaping influence on the future ones still unformed. Currently, this process is declared to be "feedback," and to resemble the stimulus-response circle that the physiolo-gist calls "homeostasis." This requires that the end-term of a given activity as an effect shall serve at the same time as an initiator of repetitions as well as new consequences until the action completes itself. Thus, the analogy between music and mind has its application limited by the fact that mind is not only terminal incandescence, but also consequential "feed-back." Minding changes the organism which minds. So far as we know, music does not similarly change the violin. Mindful changes are funda-mentally processes of remembering and constitute what is usually called learning.

transit stay on as they disappear. Those that do so become the living past, the past out of which presently flows that next movement we call the future. They are biography that makes itself as the hours of the day and the days of the years and the years of the life, until the making stops and the personality does not even linger on. The composition has finished or is stopped. As Bergson wrote somewhere, the individual makes his own road as he travels, for none has traveled that road before. Though his body grows up, grows old and dies, the spirit of that body, his personality, lasts. The fiddle may wear out as the tunes played on it diversify and multiply and compound. And similarly every body sustains more than one personality, whose multiplicity nevertheless orchestrates into simplicity. The years do not diminish it, the years increase it. For its growing is learning and its living is remembering. There is more of it at the body's death than at the body's birth, and its nucleus is an organization of activities whose singularity is an orchestration of the body with the diversities of the world it has taken for field.

Which diversities are largely matters of the *Zeitgeist,* of the "climate of opinion," of the "culture" patterns prevailing. One is born into a family, in a place, at a time, when people dress in a certain mode, do their hair in a certain style, carry themselves in a certain posture, make use of a certain vocabulary at a certain pitch with a certain rhythm and with certain gestures, prefer this music and not that, read these books and not those, eat these things in that way and not otherwise, and admire and emulate these contemporaries and those historic types but no others. And so on. Words like "Victorian," "Georgian," "Elizabethan," "pre-war," "post-war," signify such constellations of preferences and practices, of manners, morals, attitudes and judgments. They name a social and cultural atmosphere. They designate the traits which are common to its types. Their import is the characteristic of the age.

An age's philosophers, poets, novelists, painters and sculptors for the most part embody, and so conserve it, in types. The core of Aristotle's ethics is a delineation of Greek types. The brave man, the prudent man, the foolhardy man, the free man, the slavish man, the man of magnanimous mind, are each a type. Plato, Aristotle's teacher, began it by delineating types in his Republic, and Theophrastus, Aristotle's pupil, made of types or characters the explicit theme of his writing. And what else, for that matter, does Victorian Carlyle make of his heroes of history, with all their singularities on their heads, but types, or as Emerson would have them, "representative men"? These are first living men of blood and bone and brain, with all the juices of individuality in their veins. The image-maker abstracts from these singularities the de-limiting shape, the gradient of form. The thinker breaks up the form into a collocation of traits and rules, recomposes them in a set of relationships exemplifying his "laws of thought" rather than the original's way of life, and thereby transmutes the whole into a system of abstractions which is called a philosophy of life and character. After the tongue has uttered what the eyes have seen, the ears have heard and the heart has felt, the head can transpose the utterance from empirical description into dialectical definition. But always the image of the Self begins in the direct impact of another person, in the form and feel of him as a living force, as a gradient of one's own growth toward freedom and fulfillment. The image begins as a recollection of something netted from that impact, as a dynamic line along which the imagist's energies readily flow, as a role to enact, a character to achieve, and as achieving to alter, even to outgrow.

Every soul, every personality, starts its life course upon a track thus chosen and thus followed. *Curriculum vitae* is more than a metaphor. Every personality is a manifold music which the finger-ings and blowings and percussions of the world awaken from its body, and the diapason swells, with all the discords and dissonances that enter such harmonies, until the body dies and can no more respond. Psychologists will endeavor to reduce the aggregate event to a single dynamic. According to the dogmas or the postulates of their sects and schools, they will talk of extravert and introvert, eroticisms oral or anal, feelings of inferiority and masculine pro-tests, behaviors, connections, frustrations, aggressions, vectors and *Gestalts,* and so on in ever-diversifying volume. But whatever its drives, how limited, how varied, how scattered or how con-centrated, a life story is a succession of personality-images thus enacted, compenetrative or mutually exclusive, toned alike by ir-reduceable conflicts or by ever-heightened orchestrations.

How an individual's personality-images relate to one another sustains the kind of person he is. And one's kind of person is always an event going on and never a static condition. It is the sustaining of a constellation of adiencies and withdrawals, a role maintained, a limit sought, surpassed or kept up to. Its dynamic is well exemplified in the expression "keeping up with the Joneses." This phrase, which significantly has become a part of our American idiom, is a title of a comic strip. The inward theme of the strip is how people choose and embody their ideals. "The Joneses" are a generic name for the ideal. They are neighbors. Where they live does not matter: they may be American Middletowners, Chinese in China, Ghandi's Hindus, Stalin's Communists, Main Street's "best people"—the local banker or businessman or minister or politician or woman's club leader. But wherever and whoever they are, they will impress the mind as figures of force, freedom and fulfillment, at once life's going and life's goal. They will be taken for objects of emulation and imitation, for characters to enact until habit makes the self-characterization the "second" nature which, as Pascal somewhere observes, is more primitively and expressively a person's self than the original nature of his birth and heritage. In the comic strip, the Joneses embody the personal ideal. They set the standards and make the pace. What they are is good, how they act is right. They are both the measures and the measurement of all things. And so it is in the daily life. The persistent vogue of the comic strip rests upon the fact that it does bring out and up into the open, and does, under the guise of laughing at it, confess to the workings of this central drive in every man, at once his secret substance and his secret shame.

The range of emulation knows no limit, nothing is too strange, no item is too little, no principle too sweeping. Sometimes it will focus exclusively on Mrs. Jones's hat or tableware, or Mr. Jones's necktie or golf score or motor car. Often it will embrace the entire Jones career, again limit itself to his love-life, or his hobbies or his special abilities in sport or profession, or his ways of walking and talking, of eating and drinking and smoking, of sitting down and standing up. It will draw from comic strips like *Dick Tracy* or *Superman,* from motion pictures, from stage-plays, from novels, from newspaper reports and other more authentic forms of poetry, making of these emulative shapes that impattern for the individual the upkeep and enlargement of his life, liberty and happiness.

That children live and grow through such emulative embodiments is a commonplace observation. Their play is a make-believe. Whether they make-believe they are Orphan Annies, cops and robbers, Dick Tracys or Supermans, all the personalities that they enact live through adventure, channel love and hate, achieve the struggle and overcoming of misfortune, the war and the victory over poverty, wickedness and stupidity alike in the commonplaces of the daily round and in the deep fantasies of "escape" and "compensation" such as are Aladdin of the Arabian nights of old or Walter Mitty in the Thurberian nights of our new day.

The knowing explain this play in many ways and every single one of them may be right. But its dynamic reality is the embodiment of the succession of personality-images, each somehow impatterning energies, liberating and expressing powers, making over the players into something they are not. Such impersonation may also be called learning, and the learning even of the most abstract of abstractions calls for a modicum of some such impersonation. Not until powers have failed and stimulus no longer receives response does it come to a stop. In adults it goes by other names than make-believe and seeks other consequences than the consequences of play (which is supposed to be its own reward). As each new enactment becomes an old memory, it condenses into a vestige, a sign, a symbol of that richly diverse image whose present incarnation was freedom and fulfillment. It may condense into the potent ideo-motor tension we call habit. It may persist only as attitude, tonus, psychic timbre. In whatever form it continues, it is of the persistent stuff of personality.

The initiating model appears always to be some psychologically near exemplification of force, freedom and fulfillment. With children it is as a rule a parent, an elder brother, a playmate, whose form is directly perceived and whose power is directly felt. To this perceptual base are then assimilated the images supplied by the comic strips and other contemporary transpositions of ancient faerie; then there accrues the faerie land of tradition itself, and all the outlying kingdoms of make-believe. As children grow they change old images for new, and make all sorts of starts at new personalities with new careers. Those which they achieve are always, at the core, some hero of the place and time whose adventures among men and things and ideas sets before their attention and effort "the standard of living" of their aspiration, the image of

the personality they would live into. They also become the proto-
types of myth and tale as well. Miss Pyrtle's reference to Lindbergh
signalized the beginning of one such mutation—"the lone eagle"—
now forgotten, but the starting point for so many comic strips. The
canonization of Henry Ford among the Soviets is another instance
of the same process. The stories of the heroes' lives are first
confronted, then confused, then compenetrated, with the life
stories of other heroes from other times and other places, from
history and legend, and from the artist's creation. The images do
not serve as models to emulate only. Automatically they are taken
as well for measures to appraise with. So in the eighteenth century
the actual Indian of the North American continent was worked
over into the child of nature whom Pope and Rousseau and Voltaire imagined; he became the personality whom Marie Antoinette
and her ladies-in-waiting simulated in the Gardens of Versailles;
and the Man Friday who served shipwrecked Robinson Crusoe on
his desert island. Crusoe himself was a compounding and refinement of English "cits" whose powers of self-help and self-respect as
colonials won them mastery and liberty. The Persians and Chinese
in whose mouths Montesquieu or another put his judgments of the
French were but costume versions of admired actual English ways
and ideas. So "the man nobody knows" who is one of the twentieth
century images named Christ, is some contemporary man of affairs
and master of publicity assimilated to the reverence-evoking figure
of the gospel legend.

Personalities who signalize to their neighbors concretions of the
force, freedom and fulfillment they desire for themselves are, of
course, not only admired, loved and emulated; they are also despised, hated and attacked. These very traits and attainments which
exalt them into the Joneses men want to keep up with may affect
other men not as configurations of liberty but as powers of oppression. The model, instead of being freely chosen from among alternatives present, may impose itself. To Hitler, for example, Kaiser
Willhelm II was so releasing an image, that like many other
German-speaking males, he long wore his mustachios pointed up
like horns, in emulation of his Jovian Kaiser. After the German
defeat of World War I, the figure of the Kaiser could no longer
symbolize a German dream of self-consummation. Hitler cut off
the horns of his mustachios, and gave his upper lip the adorn-

ment of which the most widely recognizable wearer was Charles Chaplin's mirth-making, servile weakling, whose misadventures somehow make him stronger and freer than he was before. German mustaches ceased to be kingly horns and became the abrupt sub-nasal smears of the *führer*. But they signalized the same gradients of force, freedom and fulfillment that Wilhelm's horns had ex-pressed, only loosed from the refinements, the politenesses and the punctilios that clothed the elder tradition, and with its tyranny, its sadism, its egomania and its stupidity stripped naked and exalted. The new version of the German Jones was made into a systematized image of the conqueror of the world. The schools, the press, the churches, the arts and sciences were ordered to pro-ject and inculcate and indoctrinate the image of this Jones by every means of communication in their power among Germans and everywhere in the world. Those Germans who despised, hated and would oust this image and its embodiment in works and ways for another were, however, estopped by the police power from model-ing this other image upon the originals in other lands, as Voltaire and Montesquieu modeled upon the English, and Voltaire and Rousseau and Defoe upon the American Indians. They could turn only to figures of history and art, in so far as the latter might be envisaged and projected free from the moldings to the dominant image imposed by a teaching whose purpose is propaganda and whose method is indoctrination. Since only education could supply such a knowledge of the past, a primary duty of the educator would be to prevent or to pervert such knowledge. Whatever the images of record might be, the image to which the arch-educator permitted his pupil access would be his party's prescribed equivalent of Plato's "noble lies." Authority and its spiritual police—the teachers, the censors, the preachers—undertook to see that no aspiration of the heart should be unconformed to the dominant image. Hitlerism of course, has its antecedents as well as its successors. Stalinism is the most important, both as antecedent and successor. In matters of the personality-image it has a parallel history. Nor did Hitler Germany improve upon its initiating example.

Nevertheless, as the record sufficiently shows, for any individual to accept an image that he may grow into, imposition and coercion are rarely enough. Plastic as spirit may be, it has, we know, an ineffable limit, beyond which its individuality will not conform.

The adiencies of curiosity are as diverse as they are numerous, and all are procedures of psychosomatic energies seeking free way and fulfillment. Commonly that channel is accepted which opposes the least obstruction and calls for the least effort, which is most congruous with the form and flow of the personal consciousness from its springs. Although our adiencies go in all directions and our curiosity reaches out to all things, we follow only those roads that enlarge and satisfy our being and get to grips with those things that nourish and advance our powers. These are countless, and which of them we take and follow is always, within the bounds set by our powers, more a personal option than a social or natural necessity. To experience, there is never one and only one road to Rome, or one Rome; one and only one nourishing stuff, one and only one personality-image. Alternatives continually present themselves simply or in multitude. There are not only planes and ships or trains to go to our Rome in. There are different companies traveling different roads. There are not only white breads and dark breads. There are breads of different bakings, different compositions, different forms. There are not only the career of engineer or poet, or what have you. There are different modes of each career, exemplified in different personalities between whose images we choose for our going and goal.

And as a rule, that which we freely choose must promise or possess congruity with our spontaneous powers. Our choices must offer fulfillment of our natures, not violations; liberations, not inhibitions. The once fashionable notion of the behaviorist school that the human organism is a plastic which that expert in human engineering, the psychologist, can mold as he chooses, has turned out a wishful postulate which the behaviorists' own experiments have falsified. Whatever may be done to us or by us in the making of our personalities, if the making is not to be a mere breaking, its events must be assimilable to the singularity of our organic becoming whose wholeness is our self. If this do not confirm the making, it remains alien, excremental.

There is, Edward Thorndike tells us, a "confirming reaction." It acts, he says, "biologically, not logically. It does not pick out infallibly the connections which the person wishes to strengthen, and confirm, that is, strengthen them. It strengthens primarily the connection that has just been acting, but may strengthen a neighboring connection in addition, or instead. It acts more like a hormone than a syllogism . . . is more like a knee jerk than like either a syllogism or a cash register." It goes on all the time and compounds. It sustains the skills and knowledge we have attained and are attaining. It applies, not to details, but "to 'large' trends and total thoughts." It "has its source in the over-all control of a person at the time. This over-all control may be any one of the numerous selves of a man . . . [It] has its origin outside the situa- tion → response unit upon which it acts . . . there is no simple opposite [of it] . . . The confirming reaction may be the act of a free agent, a free will, in the most useful sense of those words. Science has hitherto denied this or seemed to deny it. Science com- monly thinks of the modification in human beings as caused by the environment, including the social environment constituted by other living men and the intellectual and moral environment constituted by all surviving institutions of such men living or dead. The en- vironment, in this very broad sense of the world with all its persons, customs, arts, religions, and sciences, undoubtedly determines most of what occurs in man and most of what is rewarded. Most, but not all.

"To some extent man modifies himself. The confirming reaction is issued by a man when a man is satisfied. That man originates in a certain collection or battery or output of genes which is by definition apart from and contrasted with its environment. Day by day that man has changed his nature partly by the influence of his own confirmations of connections whose consequences satisfy him. Each person is to that extent an *imperium in imperio naturae*. Each person is a center of creative force modifying himself more or less to suit himself."

So Thorndike affirms by his lights what Bergson has declared by his. In the workings of "heredity and environment" which the conventions of science single out to be causes of personality, the "battery of genes" is assigned a certain autonomy with respect to which the geneticists and environmentalists invoke contradictory postulates. One is that we are that which we were born to be; in the last analysis, the world where we grow up and grow old and die can serve only to suppress, to release or to destroy our inborn powers, but cannot alter them; it can stop up the springs of an- cestry or set them free, and that is all; heredity is destiny. The other postulate is that "the battery of genes" is but a collocation of plastic energies with no inevitable inner gradient, and that the world of their struggle, not the powers we inherit, makes us what we are today and is never satisfied; destiny is environment. In neither case is personality cause; in both, it is effect and only effect, a passive "this and no other" with no role and no influence on its own making.

A fundamental consequence of this position for the theory and practice of education is that "science" provides its own aid and comfort to the traditional conception of human nature as invariant, and its own justification of the Platonic notion that education is at best a kind of sorting machine—in military parlance, a "screening" device for separating and training according to their inalterable powers the generations of mankind. The good society, whose rule is justice, is a society with a place for everybody and everybody in his place, minding the business for which he was made and not sticking his nose into other people's business. Justice requires that those should rule who are born to rule, those watch and fight who are born to do so and those serve whose nature can no more exercise another function than a donkey can be an elephant. Slaves are such by nature, not by nurture; free men are born to freedom, and cannot owe their capacities and status to any institution or other environment. The evils of the common life ensue when society instead of perfecting confuses the natural order of things and slavish natures receive the power and prerogatives of freedom, while free men go in bonds. Servility is the true freedom of the slave—by nature but a tool with life in it, as a tool is a lifeless slave. Power and rule are the true service of the free man whose worth is in himself and whose self is the discipline wherewith his spontaneous powers are shaped toward perfection. Each form of government—the tyranny, the oligarchy, the polity, the aristocracy, the plutocracy, the ochlocracy, the timocracy and the democracy— imparts its own singularity to this general confusion. But the worst sinner is democracy, which enshrines the disorder of the social faculties at their height, with nobody in the place where by nature he belongs, and everybody in the place where by nature he does not belong.

This idea of human existence, of the relation of the individual to society and of the task of education in society, has never lost its hold on the power-holders among the peoples of mankind. The idea that nurture can transform nature, that education must provide nurture before it can discern and discipline nature, is its revolutionary counter. The idea's vogue began with the critique of the inequities of the social order that is one of the labors of the illuminati of the eighteenth century. It received a great increment of meaning from the ideas of the American Revolution and the French Bill of Rights, and the early essays of biological and social science were held to bring it confirmation. It is a dogma of the Marxist faith and a directive for biological research in the Russia of Stalin. But as both free biology and free psychology became more experimental and specific, evidence accumulated that seemed to give support to the older view. From the initiation of the Binet-Simon efforts to define and measure intelligence until this day and beyond into the indefinite dark future, schemes of accountancy of human traits follow one another, device upon device, formula upon formula, rule of interpretation upon rule. The distance from the first Binet-Simon test to the last Rorschach test is spanned by a succession of measuring gadgets and bookkeeping devices, each carefully called by the name of its inventor, to assure his immortality, and each purporting to be in its own way a demonstration of the fixity of human nature, enabling assurance in counseling and certainty in prediction. World War I gave the entrepreneurs of these devices an immense opportunity and established the devices as a permanent part of the schools' equipment. It opened up new careers in the domain of education—school psychologists, testers, counselors. In World War II all that had been brought to market since World War I was mobilized to the end of finding the right place for the right conscript in the hierarchical division of labor imposed by the requirements of a mechanized organization of the armed force on the land, on the sea and in the air.

In the schools, especially in the overgrown urban schools, with their overlarge classes, their formal and passionally and practically irrelevant curricula, the measuring devices provided reliefs from the responsibilities of teaching. As the children are passed on from grade to grade, their I.Q.'s go with them. Those have ostensibly revealed in thirty minutes what it would have taken a teacher weeks to discover concerning her pupils as learners. They constitute a grid upon which the pupils may be ranked in a hierarchy from

superior to dull and moronic, with a precise number for each—
69 for the "feeble-minded," 90-109 for the "normal," 130 and over
for the superior. The grid will compose a "normal distribution
curve" with defectives at one end, 2 per cent of the whole, the
borderline cases 6.7 per cent, the dull normal, 16.1 per cent, the
average, 50 per cent, the bright normal, 16 per cent, the superior,
6 per cent, the very superior, 2.2 per cent. In the order set down,
children of Jewish, English and Scotch extraction will outnumber
all others among the superior and very superior; Germans, Norse,
Bohemians, Chinese and Japanese will bulk large among the average, while the dull normal and the rest will be drawn from Italians,
Poles, Portuguese, French, Canadians, Mexicans, Indians and
Negroes. Pupils of private schools reveal higher I.Q.'s than public
school pupils, city dwellers than country people; the city-slicker
and the country hick, then, are born, not made.

And if these findings are taken for constants, in which the actualities of variation are so small as to be negligible, I.Q. foretells the
destiny of each child. How can you make an intellectual silk
purse out of an intellectual sow's ear? Knowing the limits of the
pupil's capacity, the school's task then is to suit the curriculum to
the capacity, to bring to the future citizen that personality-image
and to train him for that station in life which his nature fits him
for. Education becomes in modern practice the sorting or screening device that Plato held it must be. It accepts the existing hierarchical correlation of vocations and powers and inducts the growing American into that vocation best fitted to his inalterable
powers. The school becomes a caste-ing device, an instrument of
classification and distribution of the generations of Americans
in the national economy, and thus the keystone of the arch of
economy's continuing structure and operation. As a time-and-labor-
saving tool in the management of instruction, the I.Q. and the
other numbers produced by the other tests are a godsend alike
to administrators and classroom teachers. They now truly know
what their pupils can and can't do, and it saves them a lot of
heartache and trouble. The measures determine for them what
their educational ideals may not fail to be. Variation, and the
practice called "enrichment" can have no place in those ideals.
Wisdom points to a method more indoctrination than free inquiry,
to a simple homogeneous content and discipline—a refinement and

perfection of what exists, not a variation *from* what exists. The educational goal must needs be excellence, not growth.

Excellence accrues to a thought or an action or a personality when it reaches the optimum of economy, efficiency and order appropriate to its essence. Excellence is performance with the least material in the simplest and quickest way and the most suitable form. Machines, particularly scientific machines, are the usual models of such excellence. Human beings attain it through drill or practice. By dint of unrelaxing repetition they become virtuosos in some occupation, art or science, masters of a "mystery." The attainment of virtuosity would thus be the goal of education, general as well as special, and virtuosities would vary only with the invariant endowments of the men and women whose virtuosities they are. Business enterprise leaped at the idea. It would enable employers to choose employees that would produce the most with the least trouble. All over the land testing was taken for a trouble-and-money-saving device. The idea was taken to be true, as Mr. Hutchins asserts, that the poor truck driver does not need to learn physics, nor for that matter, the nuclear physicist how to drive a truck. The virtue of the former would be his virtuosity with trucks in motion; of the latter with protons and electrons in motion. The two would be organic parts of the same society as the wheels of a clock are organic parts of the same machine. Each would mind his own business utterly unaware of the business of the other, and the union of the two would be the care of some very superior I.Q. with a liberal education acquired through drill in the liberal arts; or else some divine overseer of a pre-established harmony by God's grace granted and God's grace maintained.

To the postulates upon which this image of human nature and of its education is grounded there have been counters from the very beginning, nor was their environmentalist form the most effective, though its force is undeniable. The other counters appeared early in the controversy over the level of American intelligence raised by the alarums of propagandists using inferences from the army Alpha and Beta tests of World War I as provocations to xenophobia. A number of studies were launched, a variety of experiments were initiated, to establish that, far from being constant, the I.Q. and other ratios stating the amounts and degrees of human quality vary with the environment. There were the studies of Burtt in England, during the early '20's. In America there were Freeman's studies of the late '20's. In the '30's there came from the Iowa Child Welfare Experiment Station the reports of Skeels and Fillmore, and of Stoddard and Wellman.[3] The studies dealt not only with young children. They investigated twins both fraternal and identical. They analyzed the effects of alterations of the same home and of changes from one home to another. They studied the workings of changes from homes to schools, and the like. The investigators found that changing conditions brought large changes in the I.Q., both up and down, average to genius and average to dull. An especially striking record of change was made by Miss Bernadine Schmidt, now of the State Teachers College at Terre Haute, Indiana. She had launched, when she graduated from the Chicago Teachers College at the onset of the Great Depression, a school of her own for feeble-minded children. In a loft above an undertaking establishment, she assembled 70 boys and girls, aged 7 to 16, with I.Q.'s from 40 to 70, and school grades corresponding. She taught these children for three years. Her idea was that all too often feeble mind is weak will, deficient initiative, not deficient intellect. And she set about developing initiative, by methods of self-help and self-orientation. Her projects were progressions from immediate to remoter needs and interests. Her results were such at the end of three years that she was put in charge of Chicago's Opportunity Center for Subnormal Children. There, the city sent her 254 boys and girls 12 to 14 years old, none with an I.Q. higher than 69, most lower, so that the average for the 254 children was 51.7. With eleven other teachers to help her, Miss Schmidt worked with these children for eight years in all. Standard tests given at the end of the third year showed them to have an average gain of four grades. During the next five years tests were given eighteen months apart. At the end of the eighth

---

[3] Cf. Brigham, *American Intelligence* (Princeton: 1921); F. M. Freeman, "The Influence of Environment," *27th Yearbook, National Society for the Study of Education* (1928); H. M. Skeels, "Mental Development of Children in Foster Homes," *Journal of General Psychology* (1936); Beth L. Wellman, "The Role of Cultural Status in the Intelligence of Pre-school Children," "The Effect of Pre-school Attendance on the I.Q.," "Growth in Intelligence under Differing Pre-School Environments," *Journal of Experimental Education and of Genetic Psychology* (December, 1937).

year the standard tests demonstrated that upward of 80 per cent
of the children had gained 30 points, that only 7.2 per cent remained "feeble-minded." Even more recently, Irving Lorge, of
Columbia University, reported upon comparative changes in the
I.Q.'s of the schooled and the unschooled. His study covers a period
of twenty years. It establishes that I.Q. varies as much as 15 to 20
points directly with the amount of schooling. "An adult's measured
mental ability is related to his intelligence as a boy and to the
extent of his subsequent schooling."

None of the studies in the variation of the I.Q., all of them
controversial, convincingly separates hereditary endowment from
environmental influence. All of them establish that change does
take place and that the absence of any noticeable measure of
change cannot be accounted for on the ground of biological necessity. Together, the studies establish that the constancy observed or
inferred has been rather a consequence of the fact that the wish
for constancy shaped inquiry and determined its assumptions and
procedures, and that the latter could hardly fail to satisfy the wish
that set them going. As soon as investigators began to look for
variability, they saw it. Genius and feeble-mindedness can be made
as well as found.

Now for democracy the observation that human traits can be
made is of prime importance. For democracy rejects the idea that
there is one place and only one place for each and every person,
and that the good society must be one in which there is a place
for everybody and everybody is in his place. Democracy assumes
that people are free, that they have no sole inevitable place and
function, but move from one to another as their hearts prompt and
their powers carry. Democracy rejects social hierarchy for social
mobility and invariant personality for changing personality. And
the careful studies of such mobility and change bring democracy
aid and comfort. But they are not enough. For the making here
reported does not take into account the role of the individual in
his own making. It pays no heed to that aspect of a life which
Thorndike names "the confirming reaction" and Bergson *élan,*
and which the tradition, perhaps less aptly, has called free will.
The idea, that one's heredity or one's environment are causes external to the personality of which the personality is the effect,
leaves no room for the most intimate and the most lasting of

Everyman's experiences—the experience that he is, even at his most passive, diversely up and doing, selecting, rejecting, excreting, assimilating, from among the multitudinous alternatives which present themselves for his response, those that then and there engage and enchannel his powers most livingly and variedly. These he incorporates into his changing self with the "confirming reaction."

No such confirmation can be a repetition merely. Even the drill and repetitions that compound into excellence are not simply repetitive. The new event, identical as it may be with old, in so far as it *is not* the old, changes the latter. Every genuine repetition is alteration. The two together are a quality different from either alone. As in struggling to preserve ourselves we change ourselves, so in repeating a same, we alter it. As the study of human development becomes fuller, more detailed and more prolonged, there is a disposition among students such as Arnold Gesell to see development as a series of mutations, analogous to the form changes of insects from egg to adult, rather than as a continuous enlargement of childhood into maturity. The experts discriminate well-marked stages, each with its characteristic traits and preferences, with the antecedent surviving in the consequent, and altered by being suffused by the consequent. They do not take growth as a waxing of sames, but as diversification of the same into the different and a transformation of the same by the different.

This happens even with the born idiot, and an idiot is by definition a human animal incapable of acquiring a personality. He can repeat the past but he cannot differentiate and thus transform and enrich the past. He cannot learn as better-endowed creatures learn. But he, too, struggles to live and makes himself different if his struggle succeeds. He too has his confirming reactions, his life story singular to himself, whose plot he weaves as he lives, tomorrow, and tomorrow, and tomorrow, to the last syllable of his recorded time. No more for the idiot than for his *soi-disant* betters, can the life line be fixed by a cross-section of tests and a graph of measurements. These are to his personality what a frame from a motion-picture is to the whole event which is the picture's action, or a single tone to the whole event which is a melody. Neither the tone by itself nor the single frame by itself can make any revelation of the total past nor any prophecy of the future. The turn of events before either was reached was multitudinous, and multitudinous are the turns to follow. Of which were taken, of which will be taken, the present instance can give no unambiguous warning. Its best is like the Delphic oracles: the inquirer pays his money and takes his choice. Looking back he can always see true prophecy if he wishes. But as the present image or sound is different from all that went before, so those will vary that follow it.

The further a life grows from its starting point the more numerous and diverse are the differentiations its rocket-like energies shoot forth. In order to take a hold on it and harness it up we think the days of a life as repetitions of identicals. We separate out their compenetrations and measure their passage by that which they passed through. We restate the events of them in the categories of the psychologies and the other social sciences; we undertake to arrest them mid-passage in concepts they pass through and that are themselves a passage. As we struggle for self-preservation, and change the more because we struggle, so we struggle to hold in identity the diversifying multiplicities around us that alter as our concepts rein and check them. Their existence is not a rubber band that stretches, returns to its original form, and goes on as if it had never been stretched. In fact its every stretch is a transformation, into a different structure with an altering function. In fact heredity is not a force outside us, compelling us; in fact heredity is our past alive and present within us—in the ways and works of our organs, in the posture and patterns of our minds transformed by experience and transforming it, as new skills and new knowledge are learned, and being learned, suffuse the old and give them new characters and new meanings. It is a static illusion to hold we cannot change the past. What else is there *to* change? If the present is not the enduring consummation of all past, if the future is not the enduring diversification of the present, what can they be? Change is change of the past, from the past in the present; it is making the future. Heredity and the genes are to personality and memory what the atom is to the energy locked in it and released by it. As the atom is both particle and wave, so the personality is both soma and psyche, and the psyche is a continuous learning, a remembering thrusting forward into form. Let a man lose his memory and he loses himself. All of him that is not animal body is an orchestration of memories which are the continuing music of that body as its environments play upon it. The impacts from without are assimilated and digested into growths from within.

This is why the eugenists rest their case on a fallacy. They fancy that the qualities of men are ancestral constants like property in entail. They can little foretell what personality any body will enact from an examination of its parentage or a knowedge of its genes. Nor are the speculations of such investigators as Kretschmer and Sheldon, with their classification of human beings into constitutional types, any less ambiguous and retrospective. It is an ancient adage that you cannot argue a soul from a body, that you cannot deduce Socrates the personality from Socrates the pyknik or Socrates the athletic or Socrates the asthenic; nor Churchill, nor Roosevelt, nor Frank Sinatra, nor Jesus Christ. We are not born with souls, with personalities; we acquire them, and acquiring them alters the endowment we *are* born with. Personality is self or soul ever-in-the-making, a continuing embodiment of an image chosen from a multitude, nourished by contributions from every member and every institution of society that affects the image. The I.Q.'s and the other fractions number a point in its passage, not the force and figure of its going.

Take that number for inalterable and you take with it hierarchy, authority, indoctrination and all the other postulates of anti-democratic society as the latter cultivates the static illusion. Take that number for what in philosophic fact it is, for a starting point for new change, to be used in the process of accomplishing its own alteration, its own diversification, and you take with it the diversity and mobility intrinsic to the democratic way. I.Q.'s and other measurements need not be enclosures; they can be doors and gates. They need not be limits which teachers may only confirm and repeat; they can be taken for prisons whose doors teachers must open for pupils to pass through. They can be employed as indicators of the teacher's task of enabling her pupils to outgrow them. That which the pupils require from the teacher is not instruction in things, nor even perfection in skills; it is the facilitation of power, of growth in self-rule and self-help. Excellence is good, but not good enough. For excellence is a limitation of the static illusion. If excellence and growth were mutually exclusive alternatives, the democrat would be committed to growth. But they are not such alternatives. The records show that living men attain to both, with excellence as a phase in the initiations of growth. The possibilities are known to be far greater than the achievements. Long ago William James called attention to the fact that the energies of men appear to exceed every last demand ever made on them. And recently Dr. Howard Rusk deplored the fact that most human beings live far, far below their psychic income. They make the least effort they dare in order to exist, and even crises will not call forth all their available powers. Dr. Rusk had been looking at the rehabilitation of both disabled war veterans and civilian workers. He had come to the conclusion that few were disposed to exert more than one-tenth of the power they were capable of exerting and that the rest were a fair sample of mankind as a whole. Schoolmen educating free men for a free society could well study the arts of releasing the immense energies of the spirit and powers of reason locked up in each personality, so that each might enact many roles and live many lives so orchestrated to one another that they nevertheless compose one happy and abundant growth from birth to death.

Chapter Eleven

OF PERSONALITY AND HYPHENATION

Those who see the ground of personal being as the reacting body, and its singularity as an action-pattern chosen from the diversities composing a culture, sometimes refer to the personality's sustaining energies as empathy. Empathy is the late Edward Titchener's equivalent in English for the German word, *einfühlung*. It is not to be confused with sympathy. The latter designates a diffusion of one's own drives and passions in another's. It goes with a sort of abrogation and losing of the self and is sometimes regarded as an attribute of insight; "sympathetic understanding" is a common expression. The center of reference in such understanding is "the object." Empathy, per contra, takes "the subject" for center of reference; it takes the works and ways of others as channels for itself. Where sympathy is receptive, a liquidation of the self in the Joneses, empathy is projective, an appropriation of the Joneses by the self; it is an expansive and emulative diversification of self through otherness. Together, the two action-patterns enfold all the modes of motion that personality shapes for itself. They are intrinsic to every choice a man makes from the day he is born to the day he dies.

If he grows up as well as grows old, these choices diversify, and multiply as they diversify. The world in which he counts as one, and a dynamic one, at birth, is likely to be a very small, a very intimate and a very narrow world. It is the world of the family, the world composed of his mother and his father, most of all his mother, perhaps a brother and a sister. These give him his options for his initial model of himself. From the very beginning the pitch, rhythms and timbre of voices, the postures of people as they stand and sit and move, their gestures and expressions, will come to present ideo-motor alternatives, and somehow, friends and visitors beholding him will say, "he's the spittin' image of his father," "he's so like his mother," "he could be Sammy's twin."

In due course the boy goes off to school, with its classrooms and playgrounds, its gangs and cliques and clubs, its public assemblies and private enterprises. Each will issue to his being a new challenge to a new choice. Again he takes up an option. By emulatively appropriating someone as a leader he is himself appropriated to an allegiance. School life becomes a diversification of fellowships and a multiplication and identification of personality-images. It may be supplemented by the Boy Scouts and by Sunday School, each with its own singularities of associative interest demanding attention. The Sunday School may be followed by a full and formal aware- ness of the specific quality of belonging to one church and not another. It may bring into the foreground of attention, in a posi- tive way—if the boy lives in a community drawn from a "national minority"—the cultural qualities of his nationality; its "foreign" speech, and the modifications which the habit of it introduces into the English that the citizens of this community employ; its singu- larities of dress and diet; its songs and dances, its folk tales and legends, its dominant visual images, even its occupations. The total composes a community's way of life, the complex of its customs, traditions, aspirations and expressions, preferences and rejections, from which he will have drawn ideo-motor forms that then mark him as Scotch or Irish or French or Negro or Jew or Jap or Mexican or Chinese or Yankee or Hillbilly. Religion may be an item, even an important item, in that total; or it may not. If he is of Irish or Spanish or Jewish or Polish parentage, it is quite likely to be such, since the communities which these words point to have brought, from their struggles abroad for freedom and fulfillment, the will to use their religion as a mode of self- identification and an engine of survival. For the boy growing up, nationality and religion may fence him off from many varieties of association and cause him to be shut out from many others. Nevertheless, whether within or beyond the confines of a cultural community, the number and variety of his associations multiply as he grows. He may add to the groups in which he already counts as one, several others with competitive interests such as baseball or football or debating or chess; he may be initiated into a high- school fraternity or be taken on the staff of a school paper, or enrolled in a dine-and-dance club, or in a necking confraternity. Out of school at last, he may join the National Guard; or, if he is a veteran, go into the Reserve, and join the American Legion, or the American Veterans Committee or another such group. When he is twenty-one he becomes a full citizen with the right to vote, and associates himself to one or another of the political parties.

Now he is not only the inhabitant of a locality and the member of a community, he is simultaneously a citizen of his state and of his country: he is an American.

And if he thinks of his country's relations with other countries, of its commitments in the United Nations Organization, he may regard himself as a member of that world-wide society. Perhaps he enrolls in this or that one of the voluntary associations which endeavor to support and to nourish the international society so that the global union may receive precedence over all others. Perhaps, during this time, he has been a self-supporting worker, earning his own living, from his fourteenth or fifteenth year, at some skilled trade, or as a semi-skilled factory worker, or even as an unskilled laborer. Perhaps he is among those who have had access to "higher education" such as it is, so that he comes to the status of self-support at the age of twenty-eight or twenty-nine. But whether he earns his living as a carpenter or machinist or plumber or garbage collector or bond salesman or department-store clerk or teacher or doctor or lawyer or clergyman or undertaker or college professor or soldier or sailor or farmer, there will be vocational and professional associations which he will seek to join or be coerced into joining—bar associations, medical societies, education associations and teachers unions, ministerial conferences, learned societies, trades-unions within and without the American Federation of Labor and the Congress of Industrial Organizations.

Then, too, he may have married young, and been the head of a family of his own while adding all these other associations to those with which he started. Or, as is more likely, he marries late, after he feels sure he can "support a family" and in his turn becomes a father and a husband, and his spouse a mother and a wife.

And so at last we have our youth come to man's estate. Let us specify one set of the many sets of associations in which he may figure. He is at one and the same time his mother's son, his wife's husband, his children's father, his brethren's brother; he is a graduate of his high school, an alumnus of his college, a fraternity brother, a debater, and what other collegiate survival you have. He is also a Congregationalist, an Elk, a Mason, a Legionnaire, a Rotarian, a Republican, a lawyer, a director in a corporation, a trustee of a charitable society, a member of the Bar Association, of a social and athletic club, a dining club, and so on indefinitely.

If he is the kind of person who gets listed in *Who's Who,* the number and variety of the companies he keeps may run into the hundreds. Each one of these companies is the organization of an interest that he shares with a limited number of companions. These companions, each in the beginning different from the others, each coming together with the others because he feels or believes that he can better serve this interest of his with a company than he could alone, have in the course of serving this interest taken on certain common characteristics which are marks of their togetherness: a special language, bred of the united interest, with meanings solely for members of the fellowship; articles of dress, modes of behavior, ceremonial and functional, and so on. To an outsider these marks of togetherness may seem foolish and inconsequential; to the insider they may, with many other items, be bonds of a union that could range from a formal, externally compelled aggregation to an inwardly impelled intimacy of association. Every association of men, if it lasts, develops such attributes of community, each according to its purport and mystery. That the doctors, the lawyers, the clergy and the other learned professions, so manifest their communion is common knowledge; it is common knowledge that each has its private language, its modes of dress and address, its singular measures of propriety and good, and that each has a leadership who identify the security and well-being of these with their personal well-being and security; a leadership, that is, who make the society their careers. But it is not so well known that all such fellowships of arts and crafts, such trades-unions and sport societies, such every other species of human togetherness, signalize the communion similarly, each with words and works and ways singular to itself. Those make up the differentiae of the society; their syndrome enacts its group-personality, impatterning its culture and suffusing each individual member of the group with its quality. By that quality you know them as school-marms or glamour girls, pedagogues or politicians, Adams or Zaccheuses.

In the nature of things the relations of organizations of this sort to one another can be neither simple nor lasting. Each will struggle like the individuals who compose them, to attain force, freedom and fulfillment. Each will compete with the others for the exclusive allegiance and devotion of their common memberships. Each may endeavor to isolate the individual member from its competitors, cutting him off and shutting him in. Each evinces the propensity to fight and labor like any religious denomination for exclusive rule over the attitudes, the deeds and the thoughts of its members. And in their struggle for their group sovereignty and group autonomy all may come into collision, crossing, overlapping, conflicting, separating, combining. In the last resort, a "world brotherhood" dedicated to the creation of a parliament of man and a federation of the world can behave not otherwise than a Ku Klux Klan dedicated to shutting out and cutting off all who are of another color, faith or nationality than the sought membership. Each association, in its endeavors to hold the old members and to seek new ones who shall undertake its purposes, presents itself to both the old and the new as an option, as one alternative among many competing. It does so even when it claims that membership is organic and unalienable and that none can put asunder what has been somehow mystically joined together. Nor can any help doing so. For generally, leadership comes to know that a coerced allegiance is not a dependable allegiance, that unless the individual member accepts the duties of his membership willingly, with his whole heart and his whole soul, the organization can not rely on him; his membership is not inwardly impelled, and his participation but an outward seeming, like a hold-up victim's who gives his money so as not to give his life.

That membership may be inwardly sustained the individual must enter his association freely and stay with it willingly. The powers of its government must be the creation of his consent, and its force must somehow serve his personal freedom and fulfillment. In no instance is the relation he feels to any society of which he is a part internal and organic. To him the society is no organism of which he is an organ, but an organization which is an organ of him, set up in his service. He is the vital center alike of the collaboration and the conflict of his organizations. If they collide, overlap, attract, repel, it is in him, the member of them all. If they federate, work together, orchestrate, grow each more abundantly through its union with the others than any could by itself alone, it is in the singularity of his personal being, his and his brethren's, whence alone things draw their collective force for freedom and fulfillment. In his existence they may make up a co-operative whole of united interests each of which is strengthened and enlarged by being orchestrated to the others: contrariwise, they may present themselves as vital options, alternatives for acts of choice that by merely settling on one, cut off the other and shut it out.

This is the democratic understanding of society, of its structure and of how the person is related to it. In the democratic view the individual personalities and not their forms of association are the active and deciding partner of this relationship. Associative form is but the process of interpersonal relationships taken as a state of things instead of a sequence of events. This is why, in a democratic nation, citizens are not born, but are made. Birth may be accepted as a claim to citizenship, but the claim must be put forth and proved; not only is it not conceded in advance but certain conditions must be met in order that it may be conceded; the native claimant must have reached a certain age, must have refrained from some actions and performed others. For the foreign-born the conditions are different but the relationship is the same as for the native. In this sense both native and foreign-born must alike be "naturalized." For both native and foreign-born citizenship is a voluntary association which may be severed as well as joined. Among multitudes of others, Messrs. William Waldorf Astor and Henry James were one-time Americans who made themselves Englishmen. Millions of Americans were once subjects or citizens of one or another among all the countries of the world and are now Americans. Nor, in the democratic view, is church affiliation any less voluntary than political. Yesterday's Judaist may be today's Episcopalian, yesterday's Methodist today's Baptist or Quaker or Unitarian or Atheist; yesterday's Atheist may be today's Romanist, and yesterday's Romanist today's Communist and back again. Nor are men's vocations taken as hereditary and inevitable: an Irish immigrant of peasant origins may be in turn laborer, policeman, lawyer, city attorney, army officer and mayor of the greatest metropolis the world has yet known; the son of an immigrant Jewish tailor may be in turn a boxer, a fight manager, a stenographer, an impresario and a feuilletonist. The son of a Negro slave may be a carpenter, a schoolteacher, a chemist, a farmer and one of the nation's foremost scientists. Any man, any woman, born anyhow, anywhere in the land, and educated any which way may be a news-boy today, a law student tomorrow, a "realtor" the next day, a carpenter and builder the next, a physician the next, a banker the next, governor of a state, cabinet member, vice-president, president. So long as he has the will and the heart he may move from occupation to occupation and interest to interest, abandoning one for another as emulation prompts, insights guide and opportunity permits. The choices are his, even though their consequences are eventuations of change and chance.

Being a living center in an indefinitely diverse and indefinitely extended network of associations, each with its own singularity of being and meaning, the individual may find himself able to orchestrate their diversities into an ongoing configuration of things and ideals, passing from one to another as a music moves from theme to theme and key to key. Or he may find himself confronted by ineluctable decisions between alternatives mutually exclusive—*either or: either* miner *or* farmer, *either* Democrat *or* Republican, *either* unionist *or* scab, *either* priest *or* natural scientist, *either* scholar *or* businessman, *either* jingo *or* patriot, *either* isolationist *or* internationalist, *either* libertarian *or* totalitarian, and so on, without end. Often a decision is a choice between orchestrations. Sometimes the decision which incorporates one such orchestration in the personality-image and cuts another off is an act of faith, guided by the ideal or image of personality and involving a role in life whose prosperous consummation cannot be guaranteed in advance. The difference between an idiot and a man of sense, between a man merely of sense and a man of culture, is measurable by the number, the diversity and the vitality of the associations among which each lives and moves and has his being, by their dissonances and harmonies, their unions and conflicts.

In times of social crisis, of wars, conspicuously, such compenetrations of groupings become issues of patriotism or of religion. What had been a rich harmony, an integrative combination, becomes a mutuality of violent repulsion and irreconcilable conflict. Associations that have lived together in peace and fellowship no longer so live together. They say to the individual *either or: either* wife *or* mother; *either* love *or* duty; *either* the Federal Union *or* States Rights; *either* liberty *or* slavery; *either* property *or* people. For example, at the turn of the century, the relations between Germany and the United States were of the most intimate. Americans went to Germany for higher study, for music, for the arts and sciences,

Germans emigrated to the United States for a living, for a life, for security, and for liberty. They lived in their own communities together, according to their German traditions, in their German ways, with their German journals, their fraternal and gymnastic societies, their *männerchor,* their cookery, their churches. In due course they became Americans without ceasing to be Germans. Each society, each individual in the society was a link between the old country and the new. Of course, this was the case with every new come people, everywhere in the land. Not alone the Germans, also the Englishmen and Frenchmen and Swedes, the Italians and Russians and Irishmen, the Jews and Scotchmen and Danes and the Negroes and Chinese and Hindus and Malayans—also communities from the miscellany of the inhabited globe—had come into the land with their folkways and mores, their folk arts and crafts, their words and their music, their faiths, their loyalties, with all their rememberings conscious and unconscious. They had brought, as they could not help doing, their entire cultural economy, and each was knowingly or unknowingly weaving it into a pattern of communication with the others, and shaping on the warp of the American Idea the woof of the American life and culture. But where these others were ignored or despised or deprecated, the Germans were approved. *Deutschtum* received a significance beyond that of mere contiguity. The relationships between it and Americanism were cultivated almost as assiduously by Americans as by Germans. But in due course came the tensions of World War I. There were large numbers of Americans, not of German affiliation alone, who put *Deutschtum* above Americanism, and saw Americanism as a sort of handmaiden to *Deutschtum.* Events largely in German control forced the nation from a neutrality of equal good will to a neutrality friendly toward the Allies, from that to a neutrality of positive unfriendliness toward the Germans, from that into a declaration of war against the Germans. Woodrow Wilson coined the expression "hyphenated American" to describe all those who would subordinate the American to the German in "German-American," who chose to make Americanism the support of Germanism, instead of dedicating themselves to the defense and nurture of the American people and American ideals. The war "to make the world safe for democracy" brought an option, vital, forced, momentous—*either* Americanism *or Deutschtum.* Both could no longer live together on equal terms in the same private conscience. The hyphen had been transvalued into an occasion of suspicion and reproach.

Yet the excellent expression "hyphenated American" disappeared from usage with the war's end. Positive, productive relationships with Germany were resumed, to hold sway until Hitler, this time with a sadist violence unknown in history, made Nazi *Deutschtum* the irreconcilable alternative to Americanism and again degraded the hyphen from a bond uniting the different into a boundary cruelly dividing and ruthlessly opposing the different. Nazi Germany has been succeeded by Communist Russia, and today's hyphen of conflict is Communist-American. The case of each is but a critical instance of the nature of the relationships between all groups— political, familial, ethnic, religious, economic, esthetic, scientific, and so on, to the latest coming together of men and women in new ways to work for new purposes by new means, and to devise new words and a new language to express the meanings of their new event.

Personality, it follows, is at once unique and multitudinous. Each person is, as we have seen, ineffably different from the others. These associations it moves in are also multitudinous and unique. Each has its own culture, its own singularity of purpose, operation and expression. A society's existence is strengthened, its life is enriched, in the degree that its members may pass unhindered from it to any other, making free exchange of the thoughts and things of each; in the degree that the members are hyphenated, and the hyphen is a bond of union, a bridge from each to each and all to all. Education, when it is successful, is such a bridging. It equips the learner with the knowledge and skills by whose means he can come into empathic realization, sympathetic understanding and co-operative association with individuals, occupations and cultures different from his own. Education provides him with both the power and the freedom of that intercommunication on which cultural excellence and cultural abundance depend. Education turns him from a barbarian and xenophobiac into a civilized man. Education is civilization and civilization is hyphenation. In the relations between peoples, states and economies, civilization is all the processes of free trade in things spiritual and things material. In the relations between churches and denominations, civilization is the passage from a state of war of each against all, through the phases of tolerations which begin as the mere endurance of what is regarded as evil or an unpardonable heresy, to the co-operative union of the different of which the Federal Council of the Churches of Christ in America and the interfaith movement are rudimentary initial forms. To whatever uses a culture may be put by superior power, its fruits whether in a city-state like Athens or Florence, a kingdom like Great Britain or Denmark, a republic like Switzerland or the United States or France, grow from this equal freedom of the different in communication and exchange, from this mobility of men, of their thoughts and their works.[1] In ultimate terms, the roots of culture are the democratic idea as the Declaration of Independence voices the democratic idea. It is where the movement is stopped, it is when the point of stoppage is declared to be the infallible apex of human existence, to which all else is but servant and forerunner, it is where man and his works are subdued into supporters of this stoppage, that culture is degraded into *Kultur,* civilization into barbarism and education into mere training, into indoctrination, inculcation and instruction. Then hyphenation becomes a reproach again; then co-operative difference is converted to irreconcilable conflict; then men must choose between alternatives that cannot survive on the same terms in the same world together.

There are many names for such stoppages, as there are many interests that tried, and try, them on. Current usage applies the term *Totalitarianism* to them all. Education may be for totalitarianism or for freedom. Occasionally philosophers of education have made the two interchangeable, or taught that the methods and content of the first are indispensable to the development of the second. That the disposition to such stoppages springs eternal, need not be urged. The totalitarian propensity is as primal as it is inveterate. At its spring lies the blind expansive impulsion of any living thing, that must eat and drink and be warmed and sheltered in order to live and grow and would in its blindness refrain from nothing that it has the power to do in order to satisfy its wants.

---

[1] "Athens has brought it about that the name Hellenes no longer suggests a race but an intelligence, and that the title Hellene is applied rather to those who share our culture than to those who share a common blood." Isocrates, *Panegyricus,* 60.

The only animal limit to this blind expansive propulsion of the totalitarian is equal power in the others, its neighbors. The human limit is the removal of blindness by understanding achieved through education. Totalitarianism, however, rejects education. It confirms its original blindness by means of indoctrination. Consequently, when checked by that resistance or counter-expansion of the neighbor, it will, as the record tells us, turn its weakness into imperialist pretension, its deficiency into authoritarian demand. If opposed, but not successfully checked, it will inflict an autocratic rule of force, fraud, censorship, espionage, inquisition and exaction. To justify its works and ways before its victims, it will attribute them to some theological or metaphysical principle which it will pronounce to be universal, infallible, beneficent and omnipotent.

Chapter Twelve

ANTI-HYPHEN

All the world's peoples have at one time or another been triumphant bearers or miserable victims of powers claiming heaven-sent right to total rule and absolute authority. Such powers are the implacable foes of all that hyphenation can be and do for the freedom and safety of the people of the earth. In the twentieth-century West, four such have preached their gospels and urged their purposes, each with its own doctrine and discipline for the schools. Knowingly or otherwise, each took for its educational premise the situation—Aristotle, remember, was among the earliest to make explicit note of it—that that which contributes most to the permanence of constitutions is the adaptation of education to the form of government. The adapters, of course, are the persons who hold in their hands the instruments of government. Owning the power renders them the lords and nobles; thereby they and no others are that part of society which Aristotle called the polity; and in a position to employ the schools as the instruments of their own magisterial perpetuation and aggrandizement.

The theory and practice of education among the four illustrates these observations. Two of them—the Italian Corporative State and the German Racial State—have for the time being been disposed of as power-holders by the victors of World War II. Their views upon doctrine and discipline are however by no means rendered impotent. The other two are the Russian Communist State and the Papal Sacerdotal State. These two continue to confront each other in a battle whose logic does not permit both to live and grow in the same world together. This is not because of their teachings. These are by no means incompatible. It is because both assert the exclusive right to the total devotion, submission and obedience of mankind, and employ, so far as each is able, identical means to gain their similar but irreconcilable ends.

That the Papacy is materially by far the weaker, as well as the far, far older and more experienced of the two, does not affect the fact, and may have less influence on the outcome than just appears. For the Papacy makes up in political adaptability and diplomatic subtlety what it lacks in material force; it has known how to achieve through "secular" agency that which it was unable or found inexpedient to undertake by direct action. It knows when to bend and when to stand, when to press its purposes and when to withhold its force. It knows how to infiltrate and use societies whose doctrines and disciplines are to its own "fraught with death," conforming those societies to its purposes until as the late Monsignor John Ryan declared in *The State and the Church*, "the political proscription of them may become feasible and expedient."

The Soviet Republic and the Papacy make their identical and irreconcilable claims upon identical grounds. Each asserts that it is the custodian of the one and only Truth, the sole guide upon the one and only way to the safety and happiness of the human race. Each says to the other, and to all mankind: "I am right; you are wrong. Where you are in power, you are bound to support and protect me, because I am right. Where I am in power, it is my duty to abolish you because you are wrong." Toward a free society of free men they take an identical stand. Of this the words that Veuillot addressed to the democrats of France are still the completest expression, "When you liberals are in the majority," he told them, "we Catholics claim liberty in accordance with your principles, when we Catholics [or, alternatively, we Communists] are in the majority, we refuse liberty to you in accordance with our principles."

What, then, are these principles to which mankind must conform and assent without question, which all must believe, obey and fight for? Of course they are philosophies of life. Of course they are principles of religion. Of course they are revelations of the nature and origin of the world, of the nature and destiny of man, and of the methods and matters by whose means man may himself achieve this destiny. They tell what the world is, how it got that way and what will become of it. They tell what the world is good for, as a whole and in its parts. And they tell how they know, with a certainty certain beyond all doubt and challenge, that which the world is and that which it is good for.

In the Catholic revelation, this information is a "deposit of faith" which God has entrusted to the Roman priesthood, and only to the Roman priesthood. They and they alone are the bankers of this supernatural treasure, its dispensers and interpreters to the profane multitudes to whose credit of salvation it has been de-

posited. They constitute "a perfect society" established by God,[1]
a society hence endowed with complete and absolute sovereignty
inherent in "a moral person" owning such an origin, and therefore
the singular and universal creator, sustainer and ruler of all other
lesser "moral persons" which may compose the membership of the
total "perfect society." [2] As against the supreme authority thus
derived directly from God, no other on earth can have any standing or validity. All must bow before it. In the figure of the pope it
is made flesh and walks on earth, occupying on this globe "the place
of Almighty God," [3] being the visible presence of Jesus Christ as the
Blessed Sacrament is his invisible presence. All men are required
hence and should render "complete submission to the will of the
Church and to the Roman Pontiff as to God himself." [4] His sacred
sovereignty "must not be, nor must it appear to be, subject to any
human authority or laws whatsoever." [5] His judgment is infallible,
and an avower of the Catholic creed declares: "I likewise receive
and profess without doubt all things delivered, defined and declared

---

[1] Pius XI *Quas Primas* in the *Encyclicals of Pius XI*, ed. James H.
Ryan.

[2] Cf. Canon 100 of the *Codex Juris Canonici*.

Cf. Brendan F. Brown: *The Canonical Juridical Personality with Special Reference to its Status in the U.S.A.*: "The Catholic Church occupies
a position analogous to that of a sovereign State, being perfect, supreme,
and possessing the right to have inferior corporate bodies for the accomplishment of her ends" (p. 76). ". . . In the United States the Catholic
Church, as such, is not recognized as a juridical personality endowed with
civil rights." Mussolini's *Concordat* with the Vatican—Pius XI saw Mussolini as "that man sent by Providence"—did so recognize it (Art. 29):
Hitler's *Concordat* had the same effect as Mussolini's (Article 13). Those
popes of "secular" religions—supplementary rather than competitive—
gave, like the masters of Spain and Portugal and other Catholic countries,
practical effect to the Papacy's pretensions to exclusive sacerdotal dominion, phrased to Americans as "the favor of the laws and the patronage of
public authority" and to the cartelization of the ecclesiastical economy of
the Christian world. The sympathy between Catholicism and Fascism rests
on a more carnal basis than their common authoritarian and hierarchical
intentions. So does the antipathy between Catholicism and Communism:
if issues of property and privilege could be harmonized, issues of irreconcilable doctrine could be forgotten.

[3] Cf. Leo XIII, *Encyclical Praeclara Gratulationis Publicae.*

[4] Leo XIII, *Encyclical Sapientia Christianae.*

[5] Pius XI, *Encyclical, Ubi Arcano.*

by the Ecumenical Vatical Council, especially concerning the primacy and infallible magisterium of the Roman Pontiff." [6] What is contrary to Catholic teaching hence may, indeed must, be rejected and opposed even by force. "If the laws of a State," writes Leo XIII,[7] "are manifestly at variance with the divine law, containing enactments harmful to the Church or conveying injunctions adverse to the duty imposed by religion, or if they violate in the person of the Supreme Pontiff the authority of Jesus Christ, then truly, to resist becomes a positive duty, to obey, a crime." So Pius X declared null and void the French law separating Church and State.[8] This the Vichy Government piously revoked when it took power; as Salazar's dictatorship revoked the Portuguese law to the same effect [9] and the entire Constitution of the Republic of Mexico was similarly nullified by Papal fiat. Concomitantly, the Church may and did bless the war waged by Mussolini against helpless Ethiopians and by Franco and his Nazi and Fascist coadjutors against the free men and free government of Spain; nor did churchmen refrain from doing their bit to involve the United States in action against the liberation of the thought and conscience of the Mexican people.

The Roman Church does such things so that mankind may have no other recourse for help and healing than the doctrine and discipline of the Church: so that its dogmas, its sacraments, its rules for living and prescriptions for dying shall not encounter the competitions of alternatives of knowledge, faith and morals; so that the religious economy of mankind shall be an exclusive monopoly of the Roman Catholic establishment. Whatever is different is *ipso facto* menace; therefore to be suppressed and extirpated, by all available means, direct and indirect. If the different be similar but opposed, it is similarly condemned; if it be both different and opposed it is beyond all reconciliation. The proscription embraces everything that the Declaration of Independence envisages and that the Americanism it defines has from the first sought to attain. A catalog of the proscribed principles and practices was published by Pius IX in 1864 as the *Syllabus of Modern Errors,* to accom-

---

[6] Cf. Woywood, *A Practical Commentary on the Code of Canon Law.*
[7] *Encyclical Sapientia Christianae.*
[8] *Encyclical Vehementer nos* (1906).
[9] *Encyclical Jandudum Lusitania.*

pany the *Encyclical Quanta Cura*. They had taken four of the
Curia's theologians some ten years to assemble and formulate. They
were in effect a declaration of war upon the free society of free men.
The encyclical condemned the humanist or naturalistic idea of
human relations, liberty of conscience, public worship, freedom of
the press, and communism. It excommunicated all who would in
any way restrict the powers and privileges of the Church in matters
of status, immunities and property. The Syllabus, by explicitly
anathemizing the contrary, affirmed the indisputable right of the
sacerdotal establishment to the accumulation and employment of
temporal power, the unchallengeable scope of the authority of the
pope, the supremacy of canon law over all other, the eternal subordination of State to Church, the exclusive jurisdiction of the
hierarchy over marriage and divorce, so that marriages uncon-
secrated by a Catholic cleric would not be marriages.

The idea that the Roman Pontiff should or could "agree with
progress, liberalism and modern civilization" was declared anath-
ema.

Later popes have in various ways reaffirmed both the condemna-
tions and the pretensions of these documents. As the National
Catholic Welfare Conference declares in its formal announcement,
The Church and the Social Order,[10] God's mandate to his one and
only Church "permits no curtailment of the law, no matter how
diverse the circumstances and conditions under which a man
lives . . . The obligation comprehends the action of a man in his
private and public life as an individual and as a member of society."

But in practical fact, while the pretensions to a divine commission would make the Papal State nothing less than global, its performance takes what it can and relinquishes what it must. Among
its interests are many more consequential than those appraised by
Erasmus in his *Praise of Folly*. The relations of the sexes are one
such, and its prescriptions regarding marriage and divorce, its stand
on venereal disease and birth control have been the makers of
tragedy untold for multitudes of Catholic women since the Counter
Reformation. According to the canon law, diversity of belief is
even more intolerable. The unbeliever and the misbeliever merit
the death sentence and are therefore open to all lesser sentences;

---

[10] Washington, D.C., February 7, 1940.

of Christian charity they should be "compelled to come in." As for any Catholic converted to another faith—and in the United States the numbers are greater than is admitted—the wages of this unpardonable sin is surely death.[11] Others among such heresies are all higher criticism of the Bible or "deposit of faith," and all scientific research into the Catholic doctrine and discipline. Great Catholic scholars to whom Catholicism remained the sacramental and symbolic religion it always was, but who could not accept it as a sacerdotal government engaged in defending and extending its rule—men such as Döllinger, Loisy and others guilty of the modern heresies which the *Encyclical Pascendi Gregis* condemned—are excommunicate, and had the Inquisition in fact the power it has never relinquished in claim, their fate would have been traditional. Philosophical works like those of Henri Bergson, whence Catholics draw metaphysical support for their modernistic reinterpretation of the faith, are on the Index of Forbidden Books; and a secret Council of Vigilance sits for ever at alert against all modern heresies.

That the findings of Darwin and his successors should be such goes without saying. The economy of the Papacy is postulated on the doctrine that every man is an infinitely precious and immortal soul inhabiting a doubtfully valuable mortal body; that his doings and sayings in the flesh, in so far as they submit to or disobey the prescriptions of the Church, will determine how long his soul shall lodge after death in a place called Purgatory, and what, after due penance more or less modified by indulgence and the like, shall be its position in a place called Heaven; or, if it die reprobate, unshriven, unannealed, in an opposite place called Hell. Darwinism confronts this conception of human nature with an insufferable competing alternative, even as modern astronomy confronted the geo- and androcentric topography of the cosmos with a competing alternative which had to be condemned. A consistent Catholicism would be an anti-Copernican Catholicism. It would have to condemn modern astronomy and its evolutionary and mechanistic postulates. In point of fact, the condemnation obtains. It is official. It is explicit. It is binding upon the faithful. As Andrew D. White

---

[11] Cf. M. de Luca, S.J., *Institutiones Juris Ecclesiastica Publica*, I, 141-50; 270.

points out,[12] in the year 1664 the Pope, Alexander VII, prefixed to
the Index of Forbidden Books a bull, "signed by himself, binding
the contents of the Index upon the faithful." This bull confirmed
and approved in express terms, finally, decisively, infallibly the
condemnation of "all books teaching the movement of the earth
and the stability of the sun." The condemnation now has the status
of a Connecticut blue law, but it is law, unrevised, unrepealed, and
it stands there to be invoked whenever ecclesiastical power might
find it, in the late Monsignor John Ryan's words, "feasible and
expedient." And it *has* to stand; for to revise, to repeal, to withdraw, is to concede fallibility, and to concede fallibility is to abandon all the justifications which the Sacerdotal State invokes for its
strategies and tactics. It is aware that even definitely to deny is an
admission, so its rule of procedure is: *numquam admittere, rarum
negare, semper distinguere.*

Of this sort, then, is Catholic truth; absolute, infallible, intolerant of alternatives, the one and only medium of salvation. To the
generations of men salvation can come only as they learn this truth;
and if they cleave unto it, it shall make them free from sin and
eligible for salvation. To ensure that they learn it, they must be
protected from what is not this truth. Competition to it must be
shut out and cut off: "Error," writes Monsignor Ryan,[13] "has not
the same right as truth." Education, hence, is inevitably a God-
given monopoly of the Sacerdotal State. "As a mandate to teach,"
asserted Pius XI,[14] "Christ conferred infallibility in educative work
on his church." "All Catholics," Leo XIII proclaimed,[15] "must believe what the Pope says, especially as regards modern liberties.

"As regards opinion, whatever the Roman pontiffs have hitherto
taught, or shall hereafter teach, must be held with a firm grasp
of the mind, and so often as the occasion requires, must be openly
proposed.

"Especially with reference to the so-called 'liberties' which are
greatly coveted these days, all must stand by the judgment of the
Apostolic See, and have the same mind."

And how could any human being have any other mind, but for

---

[12] The Warfare of Science with Theology in Christendom, I, 58.
[13] Catholic Principles of Politics, p. 318.
[14] Letter on the *Christian Education of Youth.*
[15] *Immortale dei.*

the Father of Lies and Maker of Infidels and Heretics, since the teaching of the Church is infallible? Does not the salvation of men require that the control of education, both public and private, should be the inalienable right of the Sacerdotal State, and that its jurisdiction should extend over every branch of learning which is implicated in religion and morality? and what branch is not? The Papacy's mission to educate extends, indeed, to every sort and condition of man and to all peoples, non-Catholic, no less than Catholic. "And there is no power on earth that may lawfully oppose her or stand in her way." [16] And so the Law of the Church prescribes: that Roman Catholic children may be taught nothing contrary to Roman Catholicism,[17] that no Catholic may attend a non-Catholic school—except by special permission of the pope or the bishop;[18] that a complete system of Catholic education should be established.[19]

In free countries, where Catholicism is not in power, this requirement calls for the establishment and support of a Catholic school system in competition with the free tax-supported public school system, and an ever-pressed and never-relinquished claim, in contempt of the First Amendment, for especial government support of this denominational enterprise.[20] For with all the sacerdotal influence less than half of all Catholic children are enrolled in parochial schools. The burden on the obedient Catholic purse is too heavy, the competition from the public schools, too competent—they do the job of educating so much better and their relevancy to the realities of life and labor is so much greater. According to the rescript from Pius XI,[21] ". . . all the teaching and the whole organization of the school and its teachers, syllabus and textbooks in every branch must be regulated by the Christian spirit, under the direction and maternal supervision of the Church."

---

[16] Pius XI: *Divini Ilius Magistri.* The paragraph which this sentence concludes sums up the argument of this papal letter.

[17] Canon 1372.

[18] Canon 1373.

[19] Canons 1375, 1379. See also Woywood's *The New Canon Law,* rubric "Catholic Schools."

[20] See Supreme Court of the U.S. No. 52—October Term, 1946. Arch R. Everson Appelant v. Board of Education of the Township of Ewing *et al,* for the views of the Court on this issue.

[21] *On the Christian Education of Youth.*

What this Christian spirit comes to when the Church is relieved
from the competition of alternatives on equal terms in a free
society, is of record in the authorized texts employed in Catholic
Franco Spain for the Christian education of youth. Here is a work
by R. P. Angel Maria de Arcos, S.J., entitled *A Brief and Simple
Explanation of the Catholic Catechism,* said to be selling in the
hundreds of thousands. It treats, of course, not only of the affirmations of the Papal deposit of faith, but of its negations, viz:

Q. What are liberal principles?
A. Those of 1789: so-called national sovereignty, freedom of re-
   ligious cults, freedom of the press, freedom of instruction,
   universal morality and other such.
Q. What consequences result from these?
A. Secular schools, impious and immodest periodicals, civil mar-
   riage, heretical churches in Catholic countries, abolition of
   ecclesiastical immunities, etc.
Q. What does the Church teach about these?
A. That they are most disastrous and anti-Christian.
Q. What more?
A. That they can never be accepted as good, and may be tolerated
   only for so long and in so far as they cannot be opposed with-
   out creating a worse evil.[22]

_____

[22] Translated by John Langdon Davies in *The Spanish Church and
Politics.* American versions of the same intent may be more moderately
expressed, but their social and political meaning is identical. Cf., for
example, the *Manual of Christian Doctrine,* pp. 132-33. J. J. McVey,
Philadelphia, 1926 (Imprimatur of Archbishop Dougherty).
Q. "In what order or respect is the state subordinate to the (Roman
   Catholic) church?" A. "In the spiritual order and in all things refer-
   ring to that order."
Q. "What right has the Pope in virtue of this supremacy?" A. "The right
   to annul those laws or acts of government that would injure the salvation of souls or attack the natural rights of citizens."
Q. "What more should the state do than respect the rights and the liberty
   of the (Roman Catholic) church?" A. "The state should also aid, protect, and defend the (Roman Catholic) church."
Q. "What then is the principal obligation of heads of states?" A. "Their
   principal obligation is to practice the (Roman) Catholic religion themselves, and, as they are in power, to protect and defend it."
Q. "Has the state the right and duty to proscribe schism or heresy?" A.
   "Yes, it has the right and the duty to do so both for the good of the
   nation, and for that of the faithful themselves; for religious unity is
   the principal foundation of social unity."
Q. "When may the state tolerate dissenting worships?" A. "When these

The substantial sympathy between the Sacerdotal, the Fascist, the Nazi and the Communist doctrines and disciplines here comes fully to light. Disputes between them have been and will be only over power and spoils, not over the essentials of authoritarianism and totalitarianism. Count Kalergi-Coudenove says of the Sacerdotal State that it "is the Fascist form of Christianity. The Catholic hierarchy rests fully and securely on the leadership principle, with an infallible Pope in supreme command for a life-time." [23] Franz von Papen wrote of Hitler-Germany as "the first power which not only recognizes but which puts into practice the high principles of the papacy." [24] It was not merely coincidental that the Catholic prelates of the National Catholic Welfare Conference urged the reform of the American economy by means of "a guild or corporative system which will establish sound prosperity and which will respect the proper hierarchical structure of society." [25] This is the

---

worships have acquired a sort of legal existence consecrated by time and accorded by treaties or covenants."

Q. "May the state separate itself from the (Roman Catholic) Church?" A. "No, because it may not withdraw from the supreme rule of Christ."

Q. "What name is given to the doctrine that the state has neither the right nor the duty to be united to the (Roman Catholic) Church to protect it?" A. "This doctrine is called Liberalism. It is founded principally on the fact that modern society rests on liberty of conscience and of worship, on liberty of speech and of the press."

Q. "Why is Liberalism to be condemned?" A. (1) "Because it denies all subordination of the state to the (Roman Catholic) Church. (2) Because it confounds liberty with right. (3) Because it despises the social dominion of Christ, and rejects the benefits derived therefrom."

[23] *Crusade for Pan-Europe,* p. 173.

[24] Voelkischer Beobachter, Jan. 14, 1934.

[25] "The Church and the Social Order." The pope, writing to Professor Charles Flory, president of the *Semaines Sociales de France,* expressed himself, according to *The New York Times* of July 21, 1946, as favoring a "corporative form of social life," and holding that form to be "more advantageous from the social point of view and also more conducive to efficiency." Presumably the "corporative form" is consistent with "Christian [i.e. Roman Catholic] doctrine concerning the individual, community, labor and private property." The known examples of "corporative form" are the mediaeval guilds, the fascists' corporative state, and the communist coordinations of trades-unions and state trusts. All these are inimical to the liberties of labor organization and the structure and functions of trades-unions in democratic and capitalist countries. Basically, the Sacerdotal State must treat the latter as it treats religious freedom and free public education in those countries.

system that Hitler set up in Germany, following Mussolini's example in Italy. "We represent," the latter had announced to a great audience at Milan,[26] "a new principle in the world, we represent the clear-cut, categorical, definitive antithesis of the whole democratic world . . . to say it in one word, of the immortal principles of 1789." His novelty was but secular imitation of religious tradition, a repristination, not an innovation. At another time he vaticinated: "In this dark world, so tormented and vacillating, salvation can come only from the truth of Rome, and from Rome will come."[27] The ambiguity of the phrase "the truth of Rome" was not unintentional.

The Russian Union of Soviet Socialist Republics offers an alternative system of totalitarian authority for the salvation of mankind which willy-nilly all will come to believe in, obey and fight for. That, the articles of Communist faith notwithstanding, this creed was but the elder brother of Fascism and National Socialism and the younger brother of Sacerdotalism, the observations of both Italian Fascists and German Nazis testify. "In Russia and in Italy," wrote Mussolini way back in 1922 in an article discussing *Compulsion and Consent*,[28] "it has been shown that men can rule without, over and against the whole liberal ideology. Communism and Fascism stand apart from liberalism." And this, he urged, is what men crave. They are tired of freedom. They would rather have discipline, order and hierarchy. They want to be safe, not free. This is why the Fascist Revolution didn't come merely to bring power and privilege to Italy, but to serve as "the idea of the world-wide order which is the hope of the world."[29] "Where Marxism ends," wrote Moeller van den Bruck, explaining Nazidom to the world, "there begins German National Socialism . . . whose mission is to supplant in the intellectual history of mankind all liberalism." And the heroic, disciplined, perfectly-ordered pyramid of society, with a place for everybody and everybody in his place, from *fuehrer* to foetus, is the Third Reich.

On the testimony of their foremost theologians, then, Fascism and Nazism are at one with Communism in their enmity to the liberal

---

[26] October 25, 1932.
[27] Works, VIII, p. 140.
[28] Gerarchia, April, 1922.
[29] *Collected Works*, VIII, p. 254.

spirit. If World War II has broken the bodies of the first two, it
has done nothing to their souls, which go marching on in Communism's Holy Russia. Diverse as their doctrines may seem, they flow
from a common philosophical spring, whose stream Fascism suffused
with its etatist conceptions, and Nazism with its racist fantasy; and
all three are confluent with sacerdotal authoritarianism. The spring
is the political metaphysic of the Prussian philosopher, Friederich
Hegel. His doctrine and deliverances continue to be momentous
issues of Soviet fundamentalism.[30] Giovanni Gentile, the Italian
schoolmaster, who became Mussolini's apostolic minister of education, and whose reordering of the schools of Italy Mussolini called
"the most fascist of fascist reforms," flatly built his educational
doctrine and discipline on a Hegelian ground. Nothing, he had
instructed the teachers of Italy, in 1922,[31] really exists or can really
exist but the State. For the State is the concretion of both the
collective and the personal will, growing to ever greater power.
The self-expression of the State in the living remembrance of its
past history and the deep awareness of its future mission constitutes
it as nation. Of necessity, every individual entering it, whether by
birth or otherwise, can live and grow in the organization of interests, images and ideas that is the nation, only as their vessel and
vehicle. They give him what reality he has, and without them he is
nothing. And it is in the school that he receives this reality most
truly. Through its doctrine and discipline the State incarnates
itself in each and every one of its subjects. It, and it alone is the
teacher; and in teaching, "in the school, the State comes to consciousness of its real being." Gentile's reform of Italian education
purported to be an application of this idea of education to the
Italian schools. He gave primacy to conforming instruction to the
requirements of the Vatican. In 1931, at a meeting of the International Hegel Congress in Berlin, Gentile avowed his debt to Hegel
and his deviation from Hegel. Hegel, he was glad to say, was
the first totalitarian. Hegel was the first to see clearly that the
libertarian conception of the natural man with his natural rights
made of the State a servant, instead of the master it objectively
is and should be; that its structure and functions, hence, would

<hr>

[30] See John Somerville: *Basic Trends in Soviet Philosophy*, Philosophical Research, May, 1946.
[31] Circular of November, 1922.

only constitute the limiting conditions of free men's living together. Hegel saw that the State was thus reduced to being but a necessary evil, whereas in metaphysical reality it was the absolute good that it has to be. Hegel demonstrated that the State was God on earth, that it was the highest form of objective mind, the ultimate consummation of self-consciousness. Unhappily, although Hegel's dialectic co-ordinated everything else into the State, it left out art, religion and philosophy. It allowed them separate and distinct sovereignties conflicting with that of the State. He, Gentile, had remedied this defect. He had co-ordinated all the dimensions of spirit in the single concrete universal, the State.

With some difference of emphasis and perspective, Soviet fundamentalism has done the same thing. Looking at thoughts and things, Hegel had been obsessed by two of their common attributes. One was their togetherness. This seemed to him so intimate, so tight, that no single thing could exist, no single reflection could be made unless everything else also existed, unless all other reflections were simultaneously implied. Everything was like Tennyson's flower in the crannied wall. And the principles of the coexistence of things and coimplication of thoughts was the same principle. By virtue of it each thing was inwardly related to all things, and was constituted and maintained by these relations. In itself, by itself, and for itself alone, a thing was nothing, it had no reality. All it was, all it could ever hope to be, it owed to its place in the whole, according to the workings of this principle. Indeed, the whole was the principle, and the principle was the workings.

This was the second of the common attributes of thoughts and things. It could be observed anywhere, at any time, under any conditions. The name for it was *Negativity*. The exemplification of it was the event that everything which happens starts as a combination of opposites, and ends by itself turning into its opposite. Hegel called the process *Dialectic*. He distinguished in it three events: a *Thesis,* an *Antithesis,* a *Synthesis.* And he found that all experience could be described in these automatic sequences of polarity and self-polarization. It was impossible, he was convinced, to think of anything without thinking its opposite: no man can think "right" without thinking "left," "up" without "down," "straight" without "crooked," "light" without "dark," "hot" without "cold." Yet antithetical to one another though these pairs are, none of any pair can exist without its other; they can neither live together in peace with each other, or at all without each other. To retain their identity they must be opposed; to come to peace, to synthesis, they must lose their identities. Only the Dialectic according to which this must happen is not "sublated" in the happening. The principle of Negativity remains its unaltering self, universal and eternal, through all the processes of "the negation of the negation," which are nature, history, religion, art, science and government. Negativity is the very inwardness of Reason, and the substance of the idea—of the universal and eternal *totum simul* which alone has no relations but is the absolute ground and force of all relatedness.

Every event in nature, every institution of society, every moment of history exemplifies, Hegel taught, this eternal Dialectic. And his works, his logic, his philosophies of history and religion and art and law and the State were demonstrations of the Dialectic-at-Work. The Dialectic was the absolute. It never occurred to him that this absolute ultimately could be anything but "spiritual," that is, of the substance of mind, not of matter. Matter, was to him, but the self-negating projection of spirit. Spirit had always to be *Thesis,* matter *Antithesis,* and the *Synthesis* spirit again, on the higher, more complex level of this everlasting, self-negating, self-compounding Dialectic. Human thinking was the completest act of self-negating composition man could experience. It meant the continuous relating of all things to one another until Pure Spirit, the-Absolute-without-relation-to-anything-but-itself, was reached. It meant the attainment of the ultimate range and acme of self-consciousness, in which the part aware of the totality of its relations becomes coextensive with the whole, its concretion and symbol. In this awareness, Hegel held, is man's freedom. Thus, in the Dialectic of politics, history moves, *Thesis, Antithesis, Synthesis, Thesis, Antithesis, Synthesis,* until it reaches Hegel's own time and the Prussian monarchy of his allegiance. Here the King is the State and the State is the King. Conscious submission to the will of the King is the freedom of the subject; embodiment of the law of the State is the freedom of the King. He is the concrete universal, the political absolute. Only through their relationship to him do his subjects possess any reality or enjoy any liberty.

The Hegelian Dialectic impressed the younger minds that first came in contact with it as a sure and facile method of organizing the data of experience and of bringing to order the chaos of events without battling or deploring the reality of the warfare which was their burden. That history is judgment, that whatever is, is right, followed from the very nature of the Dialectic. But it also followed that every particular judgment must be a self-negating judgment, and every particular rightness a self-negating rightness. Thus, to a generation which considered that their time was out of joint and that it was far from a curséd spite that they were born to set it right, the Eternal Dialectic was a beacon of hope and a guarantee of salvation.

Of this generation, Karl Marx became a leader and apostle. The Dialectic, he argued, was not a dialectic of spirit or idea at all. It was a dialectic of matter, and the ideology of any age was but a derivative and effect of the dominant material urges of that age. The core of those was always "the mode of production." Its intrinsic polarity and its self-negation underlie all social, political and intellectual life processes. "It is not the consciousness of men that determines their being, but on the contrary, it is their social being which determines their consciousness." Change the mode of production and the entire system of society changes with it. An agricultural economy breeds one kind of culture, a craft and commercial economy another. The industrial and financial or capitalist economy breeds the culture in which individuals live and move and have their being today. Each such economy and its culture has its characteristic poles; each lives only as there grows at its heart the force that is destined to kill it, the force of its own negation. History is Dialectical Materialism working universally, infallibly and totally. Individual men can acquiesce in the Dialectic's ineluctable determinations or resist them. But whether they acquiesce or resist, the inner logic of the dialectical event will have its way with them. It will polarize them into classes. Men acting on natural objects invest those objects with their skill, knowledge and energies. They expend labor on them, and this expenditure is a projection of themselves. It converts something that was without worth into a thing of value. It negates a human power into non-human property. This property is capital, and capital is the self-negation of labor; capital is "congealed labor." About that polarized labor men then gather, like iron filings about a magnetic pole. The labor therein congealed may have the form of a thing or a tool. If there is more of it than any one man can use up, he makes it available to other men—at a price. The price is the difference between what the other men need in order to subsist and what their new product brings in the market. In money terms this difference is "surplus value." It is the capitalist's profit, his rent, his interest, while the cost of subsistence which the laborer draws from it is the laborer's wages. By dialectical necessity, the surplus value becomes the pole of a struggle between "labor" and "capital." As it goes on, with never a respite, the rich get ever richer, the poor get ever poorer. Capital is drawn to capital. Monopoly capitalism replaces free competition. The dialectical process continuously decreases the number of capitalists, continuously increases the number of workers. It turns them all into proletarians although they produce ever more goods. They do not receive enough of the value of their own labor to buy the goods they produce. A business cycle, of booms and depressions recurrent as the seasons, characterizes the capitalist economy.

Those with insight into this working of the Dialectic know that the best thing for the workers is not to seek reform, but to acquiesce in the inevitable process and help along the negation of the negation. They become the Communist Party, apostles of the gospel of Communist salvation to the workers of the world. Patriotism, racism, nationalism, religion, philosophy, these are but the ruling ideas of the ruling class. The workingmen of the world have no stake in them. They have no country. Religion is but their opiate. They have nothing to lose but their chains, and they have a world to gain. Let them then unite in the waging of the class war. The eternal Dialectic of Matter assures them the victory. In the fullness of time the capitalist system must crash of its own contradictions. There will be a Proletarian Revolution followed by the dictatorship of the proletariat whose vocation it is to establish unto everlasting a classless society of equals where each will contribute according to his powers and receive according to his needs. In this Communist commonwealth the free development of each will be the condition for the free development of all, and all will live happily ever after.

For God or Divine Providence, read Dialectical Materialism; for the Sacerdotal State read the Soviet government; for the infidel and the heretic (the Jew, the Mohammedan and the Protestant) read the Liberal, the Capitalist, the Fascist, the Catholic, the Social Democrat, the Syndicalist, the Menshevik and the Trotzkyite. For the warfare of the true believers with the misbelievers and unbelievers, read the class war of the proletariat and the capitalists. For the final establishment on earth of the rule of the Church as the perfect society, read the final ordination of Communism as the global economy. For Catholic, read International. For Apostolic, read Party-forming. For Rome, read Moscow. For the Vatican, read the Kremlin; for St. Peter's, read the Red Square and Lenin's Tomb. For the images of the Virgin, Christ, the Apostles, put the ikons of Marx, Lenin, Stalin and the lesser divinities of the Stalinized pantheon. For the pope, read Stalin; for the Curia, read the Politburo; for Communist Party, read Society of Jesus. For the "deposit of faith," read the writings of Marx, Lenin, Stalin, and the other documents of the Communist canon. For the Church fathers, its theologians and metaphysicians, take the fundamentalist pundits of Marxo-Leninist and Marxo-Stalinist Dialectics, making reason the handmaiden of their theology of matter.

Such transpositions will bring home the similar but antagonistic purpose and practice of the Catholic and Apostolic Sacerdotal State extending from Rome its ecclesiastical organization and rule to the entire world, and of the Communist International or Cominform, determining from Moscow the strategy and tactics of the Communist parties of every land of the globe. Until the nineties of the last century this new salvational religion received as little attention as did the Christian during the first century. Then, because German trades-unionism had to be political trades-unionism, because Christian Socialism and Owenism seemed not to suffice the English intellect, Marx's "scientific socialism" received an access of significance. His doctrines became, in circles wider than those of his sect, debaters' issues and organizational interests. Marxists assembled in sects and groups as diverse as the English Fabians and the Russian bolsheviks, the French Syndicalists and the German Social-democrats. It was, however, for the Russian revolutionists, in exile and hunted by the Czarist government, to invest Marxian precepts with the dynamic of conspiratorial force and fraud. Living furtively, precariously, in exilic squalor, waging a war that, but for the infallible providence of Dialectical Materialism, would be a hopeless struggle against gargantuan odds, men like Lenin, Trotsky and the other old Bolsheviks rationalized their anti-Czarist strategy with new doctrine. Was not their entire vocation the proletarian revolution? Then, for the true believer whose Communism is a fighting faith, this revolution should be his profession. He should be an engineer of revolution, the practitioner of a science and an art that he and his peers would create, and study as they create, giving it at least all the concentration, working it out in all the detail that engineers of less momentous undertakings give and work out. With the dialectical laws of matter for their method and guide, how could the engineers of revolution fail to bring the classless society to consummation? Thus Lenin initiated, among his fellow-Communists, a purpose and a program for which the aptest parallel in the Sacerdotal State are the purpose and program of Ignatius—now Saint Ignatius—Loyola.

The changes and chances of World War I brought the Germans to an exigency which gave Lenin and his fellow-Bolsheviks their opportunity. Their initial success in Russia was far more a consequence of the democratic majority's sportsmanship, weakness and generosity than even of Bolshevik ruthlessness. Having seized power, the latter in time burned, bled, cajoled and shackled the peoples of Russia into the configuration of their Soviet Socialist Republic. Since it required what the gospel according to Marx had declared to be an impossible leap from a feudal agricultural to a Communist Industrial State, it was necessary to reinterpret Marx, and to replace Marxism with Marxo-Leninism and Marxo-Stalinism. In the name of these revised revelations of the universal and eternal Dialectic of Matter, they established a totalitarian state with an authoritarian hierarchical political economy—every item and organ of it is readily transposable into the parallel structures of the Fascist and Nazi police state—an economy which permits free movement for neither the bodies nor the minds of the hungry Russian peoples, who receive from it less than a subsistence wage and are compelled to surrender to it all of the surplus value of the products of their labor.[32]

---

[32] In July 1947 the average workman was paid 200 rubles a week. Commodity prices at that time were, in dollars, as follows: Bread, per loaf, $5.67; Butter, per pound, $44.25; Eggs, per dozen, $13.00; Milk, per quart, $2.65; Honey, per pound, $15.00: Sugar, per pound, $41.25; Cheese,

For all practical purposes these peoples are the terrorized prisoners of their government, which wages both an open and a secret war against them—of course, for their own salvation. It prevents them from exchanging ideas or anything else with any other people. It refuses to let them travel abroad or to let travelers from abroad move about in Russia, especially journalists. "It is inconceivable," wrote Lenin, "that the Soviet Republic should continue to exist for long side by side with imperialist states—in the end, one or the other must conquer. Meanwhile a number of terrible clashes between the Soviet Republic and the bourgeois states are inevitable." Stalin's *Problems of Leninism,* quotes this deliverance and reaffirms it; and the Soviet hierarchy employs that bible of politics for Russians as one book of the gospel which teaches its subjects that what is not of the Soviets is of the devil of Capitalism and Fascism, and that the entire non-Soviet world is by dialectical necessity and psychological jealousy and malice, the deadly enemy of their Marxo-Stalinist fatherland. It teaches also that their *Vazhd,* Comrade Joseph, is their infallible little father, their savior and protector, whose knowledge and understanding is their shield. He knows far better than they what is good for them to think and to read and to write and to do, on all things in all forms—poetic, dramatic, fictional, musical, terpsichorean, philosophical and political. Their salvation depends on their obeying his commandments. From those follow the form and methods of their work and of their play, their learning and their teaching. They have but to believe, to obey, to work and to fight.

To ensure that this is truly what the Russian peoples do, their government maintains an Inquisition into their obedience and conformity. Like mud and dung to the farmer, they are a means to be used, not ends to be served. To the Soviet government the human beings with inalienable rights to life, liberty and the pursuit of happiness are not yet but ever to be born. They are the inhabitants of the future classless society which the submerged and bound in-

---

per pound, $20.00; Ham, per pound, $24.57; Chicken, per pound, $13.20; Herring, per pound, $13.20; Bologna, per pound, $13.20; Mutton, per pound, $11.34; Soap, 1-2 oz., $5.00; Shoes, men's or women's minimum price, $156.00; Stockings, rayon, $25.00; Suit, men's minimum price, $133.00; Sweater, $20.00. The purchasing power of 200 rubles was then the same as $16.50 in the United States.

dustrial castes of the Soviet Socialist Republic are being used up to create under the lash. To the masters of Russia, the murder and willful famine of millions of peasants in the interests of "collectivization" is a deplorable but necessary incident in the building of their socialism; the enslavement and starvation of upward of fifteen million men, women and children suspected of some sort of deviation of faith or works, is quite a proper instrumentality in the preordained march to that glorious climax. Nor could the assassination of political opponents or disillusioned believers who have escaped to foreign lands, of men like Trotsky and Krivitsky and many others, be anything else. What means, indeed, does such an end as Lenino-Stalinism not justify?

So, for the greater glory of the Scientific Socialism of utopian tomorrow, the Communist State of realistic today takes from non-Socialists as of right and withholds as of duty. It has sent its missioners among the latter and set up its converts to preach the Holy Crusade of the Class War against the entirety of mankind. Its spokesmen in the councils of the nations and its emissaries among the peoples of the globe have acted as procurers of dissention, isolationism and sabotage. It has boycotted the World Bank, the International Monetary Fund, the International Labor Office, the United Nations Educational, Scientific and Cultural Organization, the Civil Aeronautics Organization, the International Trade Organization. It has been the sole obstacle to the conclusion of a reasonable peace, to co-operative action by the Security Council in order to enforce peace, to effective international co-operation in the control of atomic energy in order to maintain peace. The Soviet government's acts of commission and omission follow from its infallible certainty that the Communist providence in Dialectical Materialism is shaping the relations of men and societies to the Politburo's ends, which are its ends.

And here a divergence from the governments of Hitler and Mussolini becomes manifest. In the latter, precept and practice were confluent. Their decrees were implementations of their dogmas. But the Communism of the primitive Communist gospels bears to the practices of the Communist State, of its international, of its emissaries, leaders and functionaries at home and abroad, the same relation that the Christianism of the gospels of the New Testament bears to the organization and activities of the Sacerdotal State, or

that the gospel of free enterprise bears to the form and conduct
of monopolies and cartels.

The Communist educational establishment, like that of the
Sacerdotal, the Nazi, and the Fascist States, is an organization of
doctrine and discipline which conforms all learning to the Stalinist
orthodoxy and teaches that what varies from this right doctrine
must be heresy and error, which to think or speak is mortal sin,
worthy of death, and expiable only by public confession and re-
cantation. Whatever the experimental facts of genetics may show,
Soviet geneticists must be environmentalists. However convincingly
physics, chemistry and astronomy may establish relativity and the
quantum theory, they cannot hold in Russia unless they are proved
not to be in conflict with Dialectical Materialism. Soviet philosophers, to all of whom Dialectical Materialism is revealed truth as
infallible and undebatable as Catholic dogmas are to the theologians and politicians of the Sacerdotal State, must know how to
make the positive sciences of matter and man handmaidens of the
Stalinist faith. Periodically there are meetings of the organizations
of scientists and thinkers as there are party meetings and meetings
of functionaries. At these meetings the correct view is voted the
eternal truth until the Soviet hierarchy decides that it is feasible
and expedient to declare a different view as the correct one. Those
whose judgments and opinions had differed, however innocently
and unintentionally, from the now true doctrine, publicly confess
their error, do appropriate penance, are absolved and go and sin
no more or are purged. That instruction in the arts and sciences
can under such conditions present teachers with the most exciting
of problems need not be argued.

On the other hand, instruction in the art of war can be and is
a simple and straightforward business. The Communist State has
been from the beginning an armed State, geared for war. Its constitution makes military service a necessary duty. The purpose and
policies of the guardians of that Constitution place any individual's
meeting of this necessity early in life. They formally start military
training in the fourth grade—though informally the militarism
extends to the kindergarten and the militarist spirit pervades the
entire school system—and active service in the tenth. Lenin set the
goal of the training in 1920. The alterations of content and the
modifications of method made since then are simply a hopeful

bettering of the means wherewith the more swiftly, surely and cheaply to reach this goal. Everything that is devised in schooling is such a means. The goal is "the Communist regeneration of society." The schools can accomplish it if they, as Lenin required, "imbue youth with Communist ethics" and make them "all-around, determined, possessors of knowledge and of the proletarian world-outlook, devoted to Communism and to Communist morality, builders and defenders of a socialist society." [33] What sort of personality thus emerges, the total record of the Soviet élite at home and abroad sufficiently attests; Victor Kravchenko provides a specific picture in his book *I Chose Freedom*.[34] The educational emphasis falls entirely on the élite, and the élite, drawn from youthful Octobrists, Pioneers and Komsomols, are developed into reflexological vehicles of the doctrines and disciplines declared orthodox by the highest authority. To them, even to imagine that an alternative may have validity or a variant possess an equal right to live and grow, must be as nearly impossible as anything in this world can be; a co-operative union with the different must be ever out of question; a free trade in thoughts and things must be as alien as living without breathing. The people must be conditioned to ineluctable conformation to a state they hold to be omnipotent, omniscient and infallible, and the leaders and functionaries of the State must be the power plants of the establishment.

[33] Albert Pinkevitch, in an address before the Bubnov Pedagogical Institute, 1937. The stress on war and military duty has been consistent and progressively more emphatic. History textbooks began to be rewritten with a military nationalist slant in 1934. The directions for rewriting the textbook were drafted by Stalin, Kirov and Zhdanov. In 1943 coeducation was abolished in the Elementary and Secondary schools of those communities large enough to maintain separate ones for boys and girls. The declared purpose was to differentiate "the military physical preparation of the youth of the two sexes." More and more emphasis was laid on indoctrination in "Soviet patriotism," loyalty to the "Motherland" in the duty to believe, to obey and to fight for the Soviet leaders pre-eminently of course, *Vazhd* Stalin, and to passionately hate and combat the different in works and ways.

[34] See in addition Alice W. Field's bibliography, *Education in the Soviet Union;* Harold D. Laswell, *World Politics and Economics;* David J. Dallin and Boris Nicolaevsky, *Forced Labor in the Soviet Union;* Human Events: *Blue Print for World Conquest;* Harold J. Noble, *Conflict in Korea* (New Leader, May 31, 1947); House Document 754; *Communism in Action in the Soviet.*

Call them commissars or call them cardinals, call them Curia or call them Politburo, call them *Vazhd* or *Batachka,* or call them pope, their pretensions are similar and their practices are similar. They are equally anti-hyphen, therefore anti-democracy. Though their conceptions of the world and of human destiny are different, their works and ways to embody them are of the same totalitarian character. Alike they move to destroy diversity and to impose conformity; to destroy equality and to impose hierarchy; to destroy mobility and to impose status; to destroy discovery and impose dogma; to destroy liberty and to impose authority. If hyphenation is civilization, their totalitarianism and authoritarianism are the antithesis of civilization. They are the Anti-Hyphen.

Chapter Thirteen

PERSONALITY AND THE RELIGIOUS INTEREST

Until recent years, the trends of democratic sentiment in democratic society have been steadily less and less favorable to the privileged status which custom and tradition allow to "religious" organizations, "religious" interests and "religious" personnel. This status is a survival from the so-called "age of faith," an age in which one particular ecclesiastical establishment was powerful enough to maintain an exclusive monopoly of doctrine and discipline, to crush competitive religious societies, and to suppress or destroy religious alternatives as heresies. When this monopoly was first ordained it was a new thing in the world. Except in Judea, the republics and kingdoms of antiquity did not know the practice. In them the gods and their service were either an affair for each family, each occupational group or each political government; the state religion was one among others, with its special functions, and the idea of a struggle between religious and secular interests for supremacy was not easily thinkable. The Christian churches took the form and grew up in the emotional climate of this pluralism of cultus. Indeed, they were themselves pluralistic, and their fertile early history was characterized by marked differentiations of doctrine and discipline about which gathered many sects. These sectarian differentiations were reduced to uniformity not by the desire and intention of their communicants but by the command of the secular imperial power, which rewarded the unity it enforced with a privileged status ordered by fiat. From Constantine to Justinian, emperors multiplied the privilege of clergy until, when there were no more Roman emperors in Rome, clerical prerogative had become identical with the exclusive control of what was left of the intellectual enterprise of the Western world, and of not a little of its property and power. Imperial favor had been granted always in the certainty, on the part of the Christian successor to divine Augustus, that the church would remain an instrument and agency of the state and the head of the state be always the Pontifex Maximus of the church. Justinian had described himself without challenge or denial, "vicar of God," "supreme master of beliefs."

Events falsified the certainty and for a time reversed the relations between Church and State. Some eight hundred years after Justinian, Pope Benedict VIII's Bull, *Unam Sanctam,* claimed for the Papacy, as against all other powers, the imperial especially, complete obedience in all things. But this Bull's totalitarian claims were put forth when the wherewithal to make them good was lacking, if it ever existed. It initiated an era of steady recession of ecclesiastical power, without, however, any abatement of ecclesiastical claims. In various parts of Europe, in France, and conspicuously in German-speaking countries and in England, the ancient subordination of church to state was restored; the chief of the state was acknowledged as the head of the church, and the religious establishment was made once more an instrument of policy, foreign and domestic.

Nor did this condition remain stable. In Protestant countries, in spite of initial suppression and persecution, religious societies multiplied, as we have already noted. Each set up its own doxy with its own ritual and its own way of life. Each made the same claim as its alternatives and rivals to possessing the one true infallible revelation of the will of God to man, and the sole vehicle of his grace and salvation. At first the state demanded conformity of doctrine and discipline to those of the state church. It censored, it persecuted, it killed. But ultimately it abandoned both its claim and its effort. Religious societies grew and multiplied. Their number and variety, and the number and variety of their doctrines and disciplines, became too great to be coerced, or to coerce one another. James Madison pointed out in *The Federalist*—there is safety in numbers. "In a free government," he wrote, "the security of civil rights must be the same as that for religious rights; it consists in the one case in multiplicity of interests and in the other in a multiplicity of sects." [1] This Monsignor John Ryan accepted as his point of departure when he wrote in his book, *The Church and the State,* "Constitutions can be changed, and non-Catholic sects may decline to such a point that the political proscription of them may become feasible and expedient." Non-conformist sects had increased to such a point that political proscription of them had become unfeasible and inexpedient. The Christian communions had found

---

[1] *The Federalist,* X.

their way back to the pre-Nicene freedom of differentiation in
doctrine, in discipline and in association.

The event that there had come into existence many religious
societies, neither sanctioned by the state nor bound to it, and that
the state had to deal with each of them on equal terms, was consummated in the principle of the separation of church and state.
On this principle, the state is seen as a political association which
adheres to no religion but extends the equal protection of its laws
to all, ultimately including those, like Judaism, Mohammedanism
or Buddhism, or any other of the multitude of cults of the supernatural which tradition had excluded because infidel and mis-
believing.[2]

As the idea of the separation of the church from the state spread
and was made effectual, its principle was transferred to other than
religious societies. Business undertakings, professional associations,
colleges of scholars or craftsmen, trades and artisans' unions, racial
groups, women—each organization of interest begged, labored and
fought for a similar liberation from coercion and a similar equality
of status before the law. The world over, but most thoroughly and
successfully here in the United States, the direction of social change
was as we have seen, *from* an order fundamentally of fixity, status,
caste and authority, *to* an order fundamentally of social mobility,
contract, free association and civil, religious and intellectual liberty.
Mankind had begun that movement toward democracy as a rule
of association and a way of life, which constitutes a free society
of free men.

Now, it has long been a commonplace that the growth and diversification of a way of life depend upon how it is passed on
through the generations. The tools and techniques of transmission,
the personality of the transmitter, are often all that there is to
education, whether direct or indirect. The free tax-supported public
school that in the course of the last hundred years democratic
society has succeeded in establishing—not easily, not freely, but by
dint of harsh and bitter struggle against the powerful resistance of
all sorts of vested interests, ghostly and material—is the foremost

[2] This is the situation which the Sacerdotal State continues to outlaw.
As Leo XIII declares in the encyclical *Immortale Dei,* "It is not lawful
for the state, any more than for the individual, either to disregard all
religious duties or to hold in equal favor different kinds of religion."

embodiment of all this in the United States. But its struggle is by no means over. The free, public democratic education exemplified in the American educational establishment continues, as in the days of its first victory, to perform its tasks under something like a condition of siege. It is beleaguered by all sorts of pressure groups, the advance guards of all sorts of special interests, each with a special plea for special privilege for its own especial doctrine and discipline. And in the forefront of these, the most clamant, the most insistent, stand the interests of sectarian religion. Where others are more or less aware that they argue on sufferance, the religionists demand, as of right. They assert, in the words of Mr. Dyer Blair, the director of the Weekday and Vacation Church School and Community Relations for the International Council of Religious Education, that religion must be "a part of the basic curriculum of the public school." And short of this consummation, they require that one or another of the facilities of the public school shall be put at their disposal, so that they may "reach the unreached" and "church the unchurched" until the whole enterprise of democratic education is once more subsumed under the doctrines and disciplines of the churches. In one way or another these claims are sounded on all levels of the educational establishment: in the great private colleges like Harvard or Yale or Brown, that once had been seminaries for the indoctrination of clergymen and now purport to be organizations for the pursuit of truth; and in the great land-grant universities like Michigan or Wisconsin or California that make less pretense of "the higher learning" and search and seek in field and laboratory after useful knowledge.

The reasons given for these claims are various and not always candid. We have already inspected their upper limit, the pretension of the Roman Catholic hierarchy that it has inherited a mandate from God to teach the deposit of faith, supernatural and infallible, which God has entrusted to his vicar on earth and to his ecclesiastical subordinates, and to them alone. Taking advantage of the equal protection of the laws and the principle of the democratic separation of church and state, the Roman Catholic establishment in the United States early began, as was its privilege, to set up and maintain "parochial" schools, separate, self-contained and self-containing, and to demand that lay Catholics should send their children only to Catholic schools. Pio Nono, writing in 1864, described the United States as "that most flourishing American nation which affords such grounds of hope to the Church," and directed that American citizens of the Catholic faith who do not send their children to parochial schools should not receive absolution in the sacrament of penance. His famous Syllabus condemned all non-Catholic schools and all Catholics that made use of them. To send children to the public schools, the Bishops were advised in 1875, was to violate both the laws of nature and the laws of God. And the third plenary council of 1884 ordered the building and upkeep of schools in every parish. Priests who failed to carry out this order were liable to removal; others, who failed to help the priests, to censure. The building program thus commanded and launched has been carried out with ever-increasing momentum. Benedict XV's new code of canon law served to whip it up, and this he re-enforced in 1919 with admonitions to the American hierarchy to build; for "the Christians of the future will be those and those only whom you will have taught and trained."

In 1920 Benedict's successor, Pius XI, addressed an Encyclical letter to the American hierarchy on the Christian education of Youth. The point of the letter is important enough to deserve restatement: it was that ". . . all teaching and the whole organization of the school, and its teachers, syllabus and textbooks in every branch, be regulated in the Christian spirit, under the direction and the maternal supervision of the Church;" that it was the duty of the state to help bring this condition about; "the basic plan for spiritual training must be that of the Catholic Church."

Significantly, such orders were not at first received by all Catholics with unquestioning submission. Devout but truly American Catholics like Professor Thomas Bouquillon and Father Edward McGlynn challenged both the ground and the value of the Papacy's claim to control education. But between the two world wars such overt public challenge was rarely heard. Building goes on. According to figures released by Monsignor Hochwalt of the National Catholic Educational Association, Catholic secondary schools have increased from 1552 in 1920, to 2111; enrollment has risen from 130,000 of that year to the present 475,000. Monsignor Hochwalt says that in 1920, there were fewer than 2,000,000 children in Catholic schools and colleges; today there are upward of 3,000,000 distributed in 10,800 schools and indoctrinated by 101,000 teachers.

Monsignor Hochwalt says that this number is 35 per cent of all Catholic children of high-school age; but that 65 per cent of all such children of elementary school age are enrolled in elementary parochial schools.

Not only the pretensions of the Papacy, also the costs of the parochial school to the Catholic layman, its separatist pull away from his non-Catholic neighbor with the suspicions it arouses regarding his loyalty to democracy, have led Catholic authority to press ever harder and by ever diversified methods, direct and indirect, for public subvention to Catholic schools—from local bus service to federal aid.

In that, over a period of years, the Catholic interest had had the tacit, if not the active support of many of the Protestant denominations. This is no longer the case. But between World War I and World War II numbers of the functionaries of these denominations, each a private corporation enjoying the privilege of freedom from taxation upon its properties and enterprises, had come to feel that their establishments were not holding their own among the institutional, cultural and intellectual interests competing for the attention and service of the generations of Americans. The religious interest which had once stood dominant at the center, was receding to the peripheries of the personal life. The churches, even the most fundamentalist, were developing a condition of technological unemployment. Their functionaries are naturally and quite properly eager to remedy this situation, and are disposed to diversify their traditional occupation of mediators of otherworldly salvation with more worldly tasks better performed by secular agents specially trained for the purpose. This diversification is noticeable also in the Roman Catholic establishment and has been condemned by Pius X in the *Encyclical Pascendi Gregis* as the heresy of Americanism. In the Protestant enclaves it runs the range from sports to psychoanalysis.

But these contributed little toward bringing the people back to the churches. Whence, quite naturally, churchmen seek a cause for this trend toward an economy of scarcity from which their craft currently suffers. To original sin and the inborn perversity of human nature, they add the secularization of the public school. It is, they contend, the school's fault, not the church's, that churchmen so largely fail to hold the interest and loyalty of youth. Without religion in their schooling, the churchmen argue, original sin holds sway in their careers, determines their personalities and forms their characters.[3]

Public education, declares a pamphlet published by the American Council on Education, must give due recognition to the place of religion in the culture and convictions of our people. Since religion supplies the "unifying principle which modern society lacks"; must not, then, the school supply intelligent contact with religion? Must it not affirm religion's essential role in social and personal living, in order that this role may be "uncovered" outside the school? It is for the school to "impel the young toward a vigorous decisive personal reaction to the challenge of religion." Indeed, it is for the school "to impel students toward the achievement of a faith." But not a "common faith," for a common faith would omit this or that article which one denomination or another holds essential. This is proposed, perhaps in ignorance of the fact— certainly without regard to it—that Catholic authority rules out that commingling of the faithful on the secular level which the American Council on Education implies. Not only does Pope Pius XI declare in his Encyclical on the Catholic Education of Youth that the school, if not a temple, is a den. He constrains Catholics from admitting "that type of mixed school (least of all the so-called *école unique* obligatory on all), in which students are provided with separate religious instruction, but receive other lessons in common with non-Catholic pupils from non-Catholic teachers. For the mere fact that a school gives some religious instruction (often extremely stinted) does not bring it into accord with the

---

[3] The argument is a perennial in the recurring debates over establishment, whether of one denomination or more than one. A signal American instance is the bill offered in the Virginia legislature of 1779 as an alternative to Jefferson's famous Statute of Religious Liberty. The situations that evoke the debates are also perennial. See Irving Brant's *James Madison, the Nationalist,* p. 347; see Madison's own *Memorial and Remonstrance against Religious Assessments;* see Thomas E. Finegan's *Free Schools: A Documentary History of the Free School Movement in New York State;* Carl Zollman's *Church and State in American Law;* A. W. Johnson's *The Legal Status of Church-State Relationships in the United States;* Conrad Moehlman's *School and Church: The American Way* and *The Church as Educator;* NEA Research Bulletin: *The State and Sectarian Education;* Wilfred Parsons, *The First Freedom.*

rights of the Church or make it a fit place for Catholic students." [4]
What price "unifying principle," then?

And with the Catholic authority rejecting participation, how is
modern society to be brought to the unity, which the Council on
Education says it lacks, through sectarian instruction in particular
non-Catholic religions? Not, God beware, by means of teaching or
indoctrination, but by means of "study" such as is directed to all
"controversial issues about which rational people differ."

This paradoxical proposal comes after a long period of experi-
menting with "release time." "Release time" is a Protestant initiative which at last received Catholic support. "Release time" had
been devised to compensate for the felt inadequacy of the Protestant
religious school and the recession of the Protestant parochial school.
There had been a time when the Protestant Bible was used as
almost the sole source book of elementary education: spellers,
readers, even arithmetics had drawn upon it. In the early days of
the Republic, the liberal Dr. Benjamin Rush had even written a
"Defense of the Use of the Bible as a School Book." But against
every resistance, the public school spread and grew, the Protestant
parochial school diminished. According to the religious census of
1936, of the hundreds of Protestant sects only some 31 were maintaining parochial schools, for some 275,643 pupils, the majority of
them Lutherans; the rest of the 31,000,000 Protestant school
children were attending the public schools. Their religious education was the task of the Sunday religious school and it somehow
failed to hold their allegiance to the parental church. It is this
situation which the device of "release time" was expected to
remedy. Local school boards, state legislatures, and pressure groups
of all sorts were mobilized. Between 1937 and 1947 it was variously
reported that released time was required or permitted in 45, 44, 46,
38, 33 and 27 of the states, according to the interest of the re-
porters. The number of children reported to be involved by it
varies from 265,000 to 2,500,000. Whether there were ever many
more than 1,000,000 of the 24,600,000 school children may be
doubted. The most numerous have been the Catholics—about 81
out of every 100; Protestants have numbered 14, Judaists, 5. Moreover, in one place or another, the release of time was followed by a

---

[4] *On the Christian Education of Youth (Divini Illius Magistri) Encyclical of His Holiness Pope Pius XI* (New York: the America Press) p. 27.

requirement of service, the requirement of service by demands for space and personnel, thus explicitly challenging the separation of church and state established by the First Amendment.

That the challenge would get into the courts was inevitable, as it was inevitable that the courts, low and high, would decide according to the prejudice and politics of the judges.[5] One such challenge reached the Supreme Court of the United States. This is the now famous New Jersey "Bus Case," in which a taxpayer of the state of New Jersey sued to prevent the transportation of Catholic children to parochial schools by public school bus. The court divided five to four on the issue, the majority holding that the provision of such transportation was proper under the general welfare clause, but no more than so; the minority holding that such provision was a direct violation of the First Amendment. Paradoxically, the five also pronounced themselves forcefully in behalf of the strict observance of the Amendment. It means, wrote their spokesman, Mr. Justice Black, "at least this: Neither a state nor the Federal Government can set up a church. Neither can pass laws which aid one religion, all religions, or prefer one religion over another. Neither can force nor influence a person to go or to remain away from church against his will or force him to profess a belief or disbelief in any religion . . . No tax in any amount, large or small, can be levied to support any religious activities or institutions, whatever they may be called, or whatever form they may adopt to teach or practice religion. Neither a state nor the Federal Government can, openly or secretly, participate in the affairs of any religious organization or groups or vice versa. In the words of Jefferson, the clause against the establishment of religion by law was intended to erect a Wall of Separation between Church and State." [6]

---

[5] See *The Bertrand Russell Case* (John Dewey and Horace M. Kallen, editors) New York, 1941.

[6] Everson v. Board of Education, 15 Law Week 4224 at 4228. Since this has been written, the Court has made another decision which amplifies this position. A study released by the Institute of Church and State and published in part in the *New York Times* (April 15, 1948) develops the implications of the court's judgment on this instance of the relation of church to state. The writers say: There is a good deal of confusion over the scope of the decision recently handed down by the Supreme Court of the United States in the *McCollum* case. The ruling itself, by an 8-1 vote,

But as the four see it, the majority's decision breaches the wall which they purport to strengthen and defend. The powerful dissents of Mr. Justice Jackson and Mr. Justice Rutledge show how and why this must be, the first by a review and analysis of the

---

determined that the system of religious instruction conducted inside the physical structure of the Champaign, Illinois public schools, on public school time, was illegal under the First and Fourteenth Amendments.

The confusion has been occasioned in some part by the separate concurring opinions of Justices Jackson and Frankfurter, and by the dissent of Justice Reed. Further perplexity over the implications of the *McCollum* holding has arisen because of the many unofficial pronouncements publicly made regarding its applicability to practices not before the Court in that case. . . .

A careful reading of the Jackson, Frankfurter and Reed opinions, together with the majority opinion written by Justice Black, raises these collateral questions: (1). Is released-time religious instruction conducted *outside* of the public school buildings legal? (2). Would federal aid to education, if extended to sectarian institutions, be legal? (3). Is the *McCollum* decision anti-religious in its nature and does it endorse—as has been charged—atheism?

Reflection will disclose that this confusion and uncertainty really spring from loose, vague and even erroneous thinking on the American doctrine of separation of church and state. This was true before the *McCollum* ruling and has not been ended by it, despite the revealing discussion of the history and context of the doctrine by Mr. Justice Frankfurter, in his separate opinion. . . .

The adjustment worked out in America between state and church is one of the unique contributions of this country to statecraft. Indeed, there is no precedent for the American doctrine of separation, although the problem of the delimitation of authority between church and state has long confronted society.

This American principle of separation is grounded on two concepts which are embraced within the First Amendment to the Constitution, and derive from developments within the states as embodied in their constitutions, and from the reading of the Fourteenth Amendment into the First by the United States Supreme Court, by which the prohibition of the First Amendment was made applicable to the States. The first concept contained in the First Amendment is that of disestablishment, the express interdiction of a national or state church. This is the guarantor of religious freedom and freedom of conscience. All persons understand and agree that disestablishment is guaranteed by the First Amendment.

The second concept demands the restriction of religion to the realm of a private as distinguished from public concern. This takes religion out of the sphere of public control and maintenance and makes of it a voluntary activity. Religious organizations thereby become private corporations, de-

Vatican's idea of the purposes, and its pretensions to the control, of education; the second by an exposition of the cause and occasions that led to the adoption of the First Amendment.

The generally repeated justification of the breach may be taken

---

pendent for their support solely upon voluntary contributions. Separation of church and state thus goes further than mere disestablishment. Were it not so, there would be nothing distinctive to this uniquely American doctrine. The old world knew it in the abbreviated form of disestablishment but did not know complete separation of church and state. But here, in this country, the principle has come to mean the prohibition, in Justice Black's words, of public aid "to any or all religious faiths or sects." This second concept of separation means that in the field of education, public funds and public pressure cannot be used or exerted on behalf of sectarian interests.

In operation, this doctrine of separation has for a century and a half been a unifying force holding together people of diverse religious and racial backgrounds. In fact, the degree of civic unity attained in America is credited by historians in good measure to the classic principle of separation.

There has, however, been occasional rejection of the second concept, and in recent years the American doctrine of separation has been increasingly subject to attack along two lines. One is the attempt to introduce sectarian instruction into the public schools. The second is the effort to secure public funds with which to aid sectarian institutions or interests. For example, released time practices are common throughout the United States; they exist in well over 40 states, spread over 2000 communities, and affect between 1½ to 2 million children in public schools. Cracks in the wall of separation have also been made by two decisions of the United States Supreme Court, authorizing in the one case the use of public funds for the purchase of free text books for parochial school pupils and, in the other case, the transportation of pupils to private parochial schools at public expense.

The spread of the released-time movement throughout the country and other developments tending to weaken the doctrine of separation of church and state therefore make the decision in the *McCollum* case one of utmost importance to the American people. It not only re-affirms the American doctrine of separation but, moreover, if carefully analyzed, it also lays down valuable criteria with which to test practices not specifically before the Court in this case, despite Justice Jackson's fear that the decision does not lay down any standards to define the limits of the effect of the holding.

What are the conclusions to be drawn from this decision?

(1) It closes the door finally upon all attempts to secure federal and state funds in support of "non-public" or parochial schools. The clear-cut statement in the majority opinion to the effect that government as-

as the lower limit to the churchmen's claim to prerogatives in education. It is the assumption, made even among the most liberal Protestants, which underlies the argument in the American Council on Education's Janus-fronted pamphlet on the relation of religion

---

sistance of a financial character to "any or all religions" . . . "falls squarely under the ban of the First Amendment (made applicable to the states by the Fourteenth)" appears to spell the defeat of efforts on behalf of federal and state aid for sectarian schools. Besides, the decision brings into question both the provisions of the Mead bill of the last Congress (S2085) which authorized the Federal Works Agency to provide educational facilities, other than housing, to non-public educational institutions and the practice of furnishing buildings, equipment and facilities to these same institutions out of federal surplus stock.

(2) From criteria developed in the majority opinion and particularly in the separate concurring opinion of Justice Frankfurter, which was joined in by Justices Jackson, Burton and Rutledge, it is likewise clear that any and all programs of religious instruction on released-time which utilize public school machinery to secure enrollments and maintain attendance, fall under the constitutional ban. They point out that, even more important than any possible financial assistance which may be rendered through the use of personnel in insuring enrollments and regular attendance upon classes, such programs of released time unconstitutionally bring pressure to bear upon children. Justice Frankfurter and his colleagues specifically forbid situations in which the school brings "obvious pressure upon children to attend" sectarian classes, or in which "a feeling of separatism" is created in children "belonging to non-participating sects." They reject any situation that "furthers inculcation in the religious tenets of some faith, and in the process sharpens the consciousness of religious differences at least among some of the children committed to its care" or that create conditions such that "children will have religious instruction in a faith which is not that of their parents."

Hesitating, perhaps, to ban all programs of released-time in the abstract, Justice Frankfurter seems to suggest that a possible legitimate method of cooperation between public schools and church groups is "dismissed time"; under such a system, all children are dismissed at a given hour (the school-day perhaps being shortened for this purpose) in order that parents, rather than school authorities, can cooperate with religious groups in the maintenance and conduct of classes in religious education. This method may avoid all of the evils which seem inevitably associated with "released time" classes whether conducted inside or outside school buildings. Certainly dismissed time avoids using the "momentum" of the "school atmosphere and school planning" . . . "precisely in order to secure for the religious instruction such momentum and planning." It may also avoid affording "sectarian groups," the illegal invaluable aid, the majority found present in the Champaign system, which was accom-

public education. It is the assumption that in some peculiar and organic way, "religious" education is character education, that it is uniquely education of the personality, whereas non-religious education is not and cannot be. What kind of character is not said, but assumed; but one may safely add that it must at least be

---

plished by helping "to provide pupils for their religious classes through use of the State's compulsory public school machinery."

The above interpretation of the decision of the United States Supreme Court would seem to be confirmed by the lone dissenting voice of Justice Reed who states "I conclude that their teachings are" (that is, the teachings of the Justices) "that any use of a pupil's school time whether that use is on or off the school grounds, with the necessary school regulations to facilitate attendance, falls under the ban."

Finally, it should be emphasized that the *McCollum* decision is in the interests of religion, and not opposed to it. Solely because Mrs. McCollum is a professed atheist some earnest people assume, erroneously, that the Supreme Court is giving aid and comfort to anti-religion. This is the reverse of the truth.

The men who wrote the First Amendment were the friends and not the enemies of religious conviction, as are the members of the Supreme Court today. Madison and Jefferson and their colleagues were resolved to write into the Constitution the indispensable conditions of religious freedom. They knew, from tragic experience, that many church groups claim for themselves a monopoly on religious truth and that in a conflict between absolutists there can be neither peace nor freedom. Consequently they resolved to remove sectarian doctrines completely from the sphere of governmental control, regulation, and maintenance and to conceive of religious conviction as a private concern and of church groups as private organizations. This is the basic meaning of separation of church and state in the United States.

The *McCollum* decision thus merely reaffirms our traditional policy that religious institutions cannot use the resources which belong to all of the people for the purpose of inculcating sectarian doctrines. In addition it guarantees children the right to attend the public school free from religious coercion. Once a child crosses the threshold of the public school he is protected from the injurious consequences of separatism and he enters upon what Justice Frankfurter terms "a training ground for habits of community." "The claims of religion," states the Justice, "were not minimized by refusing to make the public schools agencies for their assistance. The non-sectarian or secular public school was the means of reconciling freedom in general with religious freedom."

It is a fair appraisal of the *McCollum* decision to hold that, because of it, the wall of separation erected between church and state by the First Amendment is once again as high and impregnable as the fathers intended it to be.

a character conformed to the pattern and interest of the sect molding the character, and disciplining it to special church loyalties, sentiments and practices by means of sectarian instruction in the Bible, and in the dogmas and the rituals of the sect. Instruction in non-religious subjects such as arithmetic, history, chemistry, music or housekeeping somehow cannot be character education and falls outside the field of morals. Morality is peculiarly bound to religion and religion peculiarly identified with a special and specific doctrine and discipline. Thence it follows that character must be weak and morality lacking where children have not been molded, body and mind, to this doctrine and this discipline.

The pretensions of the clergy to a superior ability to shape character and maintain morality constitutes the least common denominator of their claim of special privilege for the doctrines, the doings, the property and the professional personnel of the sects. It is an ancient claim which has its root in the fact that the Emperor Justinian, having rid his churchmen of the competition of the secular schools by closing them, gave education to be the exclusive monopoly of the clergy. During a thousand years, so long as there was any schooling, it was schooling first in religion, with the clergy as teachers and church dogma as the ultimate limit of what might be safely said and taught concerning the life, the labors, and the destiny of man.

Thus the claim of the more or less exclusive intimacy of religion with morals possesses the authority of age, and is generally accepted without scrutiny. Yet wherever scrutiny is made, the claim seems to rest on very debatable evidence. For example: recently Columbia University's foremost psychologist, Professor Edward G. Thorndike, made a study of the American way of life in American cities. He reported that in cities where the general goodness of life is high, church membership is low; that in cities where church membership is high, the average in good reading, home ownership, continuance in school is low, while illiteracy and child labor are high. "Unless the better communities under-report their church membership," said Dr. Thorndike, "or the worse communities over-report theirs, we must suspect that the churches are clubs of estimable people and maintainers of traditional rites and ceremonies rather than powerful forces for human betterment." [7] These findings of Thorndike's confirm earlier and current findings of educators, psychologists and penologists, psychiatrists and criminologists regarding the claimed influence of religious instruction on delinquency and crime. Thus, that leader of the Essentialists in educational theory and practice, the late Professor William C. Bagley, writes:

> The states and sections of our country where religious 'fundamentalism' shows the fewest signs of 'collapse' are the states and sections which have the heaviest ratios of the most serious crime (homicide) and which in proportion to their population, have produced the greatest number of criminals. And among the states that have the lowest ratios of serious crime and apparently produce the fewest criminals in proportion to their population are certain states in which a more liberal spirit unquestionably prevails.[8]

"Most criminals," writes Professor Carl Murchison, "belong to some church and frankly admit the fact. The big majority attend church services every Sunday Morning in the Maryland Pen . . . 14.3 percent are frankly agnostic. The Criminal is religious, the vast majority belonging to some established religious denomination." [9]

In *The Individual Delinquent,* Dr. Healy declares:

> It is quite evident that formal religious training has not prevented delinquency in many of our cases, when other strong personal or environmental conditions were not, as such, squarely met. Participation in religious education and religious communion has been quite general among our offenders, but of course the answer given by pastors of all congregations is that these have had the word, but not caught the spirit. Occasionally in certain unstable types there is a tendency to religious emotionalism and anti-social conduct at the same time. It is curious that in not over a dozen cases have we heard expressions of formed irreligious opinions . . . certain it is that, through not taking into account these other backgrounds of delinquency, such religious experience as most of our offenders have had has not proved thus sustaining. Many a parish would be bettered if the

---

[7] E. L. Thorndike, *Your City* (New York: Harcourt, Brace). See also *Human Nature and the Social Order* (New York: Macmillan).

[8] W. C. Bagley, *Education, Crime and Social Progress* (New York: 1931), p. 43.

[9] *Criminal Intelligence* (Worcester: 1926), p. 144.

fundamental sources of misconduct were studied, enumerated and treated in a scientific spirit.[10]

William Healy and Augusta Bronner studied 1636 delinquents before the Chicago Juvenile Court in 1910, and found that 90 per cent of them were of religious background (56 per cent of the total being Roman Catholic) and less than one-tenth of one per cent definitely of no religion. Father Leo Kalmer O.F.M., chaplain at the Illinois State Penitentiary, Joliet, Illinois, from 1917 to 1936, published in the latter year a book entitled *Crime and Religion*.[11] On the basis of data supplied to him by thirty-six Roman Catholic prison chaplains throughout the country, he found that although in some twenty-eight states the average Catholic population was from 16 to 17.24 per cent of the whole, the average Catholic prison population of those states was 33.62 per cent of the whole.[12] "During the first four months of 1943," the Roman Catholic chaplain at Columbia University was quoted by the newspaper *P.M.*,[13] "64 per cent of the juvenile delinquents in the Children's Court were Catholic. This means that the Catholic Church has something to be greatly concerned about." And the militant Catholic Bishop Noll, of Fort Wayne, Indiana, editor of a Catholic weekly with a million circulation, author of a broadside against the "godless" public school, under the rubric "Our National Enemy Number One," declared to a session of the National Catholic Conference on Family Life, sitting in Chicago in March, 1947, that "nearly all the evils of society prevail most where we [the Catholics] live and not where Protestants live . . . It is where they live that the big motion picture houses are located, the filthy magazine racks, the taverns and gambling halls." It is in the large urban centers, he pointed out, where "Catholics constitute from one-third to two-thirds of the entire population," that crime abounds [14]—and, he might have added, but did not, parochial schools are most numerous and well-attended.

---

[10] (Boston: 1924), pp. 151-52.
[11] *Crime and Religion*, by Leo Kalmer, O.F.M. Preface by the Very Rev. Francis J. Haas, Ph. D., Franciscan Herald Press, Chicago, Illinois, 1936.
[12] Cf. *Ibid.* Table III, p. 76.
[13] February 25, 1944.
[14] As reported in the *New York Times* of March 13, 1947.

On the record, does it not seem as if the claim of the sects to a special prerogative in the education of youth is based upon two special pleas: one, that "religious" education exercises a peculiar salutary influence upon the personality and its morals; the other, that churchmen once upon a time did have a practical monopoly of schools and schooling and the Catholics among them continue to claim this monopoly, while the Protestants ask merely for a privileged relation of their various doctrines and disciplines to the general educational establishments.

Neither plea is a reason, both are rationalizations of a special interest. If, everywhere in democratic society, the clergy have been deprived of their monopoly over education and public education has been largely separated from religious education, it is not because of any antagonism of the people to religion, but because of the opposition of the clergy to the equalization of educational opportunity for all the people. By and large, the American public school system was, we know, established and enabled to grow and to serve, through the efforts of plain people, of workingmen's organizations and of intellectuals or philanthropists like Horace Mann, whose fundamental faith was in the democratic ideal and the democratic way of life. By and large, what has been achieved has been achieved against the obstructionist tactics and unremitting resistance of the sectarian interest.

That this interest should be in conflict with that of free, public education was natural enough. It sought and in some respects still seeks a fundamentally different method. The goal of the free public school of democratic society has to be the support and strengthening of the common faith in the democratic way of life and thought by the development of habits of thinking and doing which, to repeat Aristotle's phrase, should contribute most to the permanence of the democratic constitution. The trend in free society is to accept the instincts and impulses with which children are born for what they are; to provide them with enchanneling action on the environment that disciplines them into habits by the methods of free inquiry rather than authoritarian rehearsal; and to open up new ways for the continual growth and reconstruction of personal traits and social relations. John Dewey says that the primary business of the school, in democratic society, is to train all the children in co-operative and mutually helpful living.

But regardless of how unanimous may be the verbal agreement of churchmen with this notion of education, it is contrary to their actual interest. The primary business of sectarian instruction is naturally enough the growth and prosperity of the sectarian organization. Each needs devout communicants who will believe beyond any question that their special sectarian discipline and doctrine and theirs alone can save the human soul. Their method requires the minimizing of observation, experiment, analysis, reflection, and of choosing between alternatives; it requires the maximizing of indoctrination, repetition *memoriter,* and exhortation. Their goal requires that minds should be molded into automatic acquiescence in dogmas regarding all sorts of matters, from the Immaculate Conception to birth control. It is true, of course, as Mr. Dyer Blair pointed out, that in many of the weekday church schools programs have been enriched, methods have been changed, in the direction of the democratic way. That is, efforts have been and are being made to meet the competition of the free public school and to do the same job, if not better, at least as well. But as truly religious observers note, when such efforts are successful they tend to bankrupt their primary business. The content of instruction becomes secularized; the denominational interest is deprived of its privileged position among the other interests that compose the diversified theme. The method of instruction introduces that fair consideration of alternatives which opens the way from conformity to dissent and differentiation. Interest shifts from *A* religion to religion, and religion becomes a personal attitude, instead of an infallible creed. Character, then, is detached from any special doctrine and discipline, and becomes a habit of doing and thinking which may be developed as response to any material with which the environment challenges personality. There ceases to be a privileged material: arithmetic, English, history, art work, social studies, botany or chemistry become no less shapers of character than denominational doctrines and disciplines. Those become secularized and are assimilated to their proper place in the social studies. This, if I am not mistaken, is why lifelong students of religious education, devout Christian experts in its techniques and goals, like George Coe and Harrison Elliott, are skeptical of both its pretensions and results. In his book, *Can Religious Education Be Christian?*, Harrison

Elliott declares that "a fundamentalist procedure and true education are not compatible."

Nevertheless, "the fundamentalist procedure" must be insisted
on, if the claim of any denomination to a privileged position is to
be enforced. Such lay pundits of Catholicism as Mr. Mortimer A.
Adler [15] thunder in the index, with epithets and gestures, the
commonplace old charge of the clerical against the modern world
—that it has fallen into materialism, irreligion, sin and war because fundamentalist doctrine and discipline have been displaced
by the conceptions of science, the methods of democratic education
and non-invidious subject matter. The free public schools, the
charge is, are ultimately responsible for the state of the world.
Because of them, churches are empty, the religious schools are
poorly attended, the churchmen are poorly supported, and the

---

[15] Concerning this manifestation at the Conference of Science, Philosophy and Religion in New York City, September 1, 1940, *The Christian
Century* said: "It is doubtful if a more indecent spectacle has ever been
staged in the long tradition of American culture and scholarship than
that which the members of this conference had to sit through. The spirit
of tolerance has rarely been subjected to a test quite so exacting. Mr.
Adler was answered by Professor Sidney Hook, of New York University,
and others, who unfortunately, and perhaps forgivably, replied in kind.

". . . Mr. Adler's proposal that we return to the thirteenth century
philosophy and theology of Thomas Aquinas, which is the official doctrine
of the Roman Catholic Church, inevitably conjures up the bugaboo of
authoritarianism and priestly control of knowledge and education. Ecclesiastical fascism is no more palatable to modern scholarship which has
tasted the sweets of intellectual freedom than is political fascism. Mr.
Hutchins himself is distinctly tinctured with this same scholasticism, but
he writes and speaks with a degree of reserve . . . which suggests that
he is better satisfied with his diagnosis than with his prescription.

". . . But the introduction of the category of revelation backed by a
scholastic theology which makes revelation a form of knowledge and the
official church its custodian, simply scares a modern scholar into a state of
intellectual vertigo.

"And he has good reason to be scared. The hard-won freedom of intelligence to inquire into every field of reality, including that area where
certain 'truths' are held to be sacrosanct because they were once delivered from above—this freedom the modern man will not easily surrender.
It is unfortunate that, in one university at least, where the teachers and
students have made a fair start toward emancipation from the parochial-
ism of science, the primary issue should have been momentarily obscured
by the introduction of irrelevant issues such as Mr. Adler has raised."

earth is given over into the hands of the wicked. When the historical and sociological record is called up, when the data studied by Drs. Shaw and Myers and Bagley and Healy and Bronner and Kalmer and so many others are cited, the excuse is given that the types studied by these experts did not really and truly learn religion. But if this excuse has anything to it, then exactly those persons least exposed to the doctrines and disciplines of the denominations, being the least criminal or delinquent, are the most religious. What is called "religious" education, it may be noted, had been in control of the training of Western mankind during a thousand years, what is called secular education less than a hundred. If there were any such connection as is claimed between character and some special doctrine and discipline, all clerics would by this time have been shaped into paragons of their morality. As John Stuart Mill [16] noted in 1859, when the churches still had control of such education of the people as England provided: "Not one Christian in a thousand guides or tests his individual conduct by reference to the laws of that morality . . . Its doctrines in their integrity are serviceable to pelt adversaries with . . . they have no hold on ordinary believers . . ." In point of fact, men have long learned from experience that it is as vain to require that a physician must enjoy good health as that "religious" education should result in good character. The causes do not reside in that domain of social life.

Where, then, do the causes reside? Not in the singularity of any one doctrine and discipline, demanding dominion and empire for itself, refusing freedom and safety to those that are different, and because they are different penalizing them, cutting them off, shutting them out, beating them down. The personality and character of free men are growths of free communication between the different, of free union among the different. They are prospered by hyphenation, and the hyphenation is accomplished as alternatives to one's own faith are envisaged, understood, appreciated and accepted as good neighbors on equal terms with one's own. Such envisagement and respect need no more diminish one's first allegiance than his appreciating the personality and beauty of another man's wife need make him unfaithful to his own. But churchmen

---

[16] *On Liberty*, p. 75.

seem to require that in his religion every man shall be a Don Quixote, and every denomination a Dulcinea del Toboso; they will not be content unless the lover of any other woman is compelled with sword and spear to confess the greater excellence of his conqueror's lady fair. Since the Counter Reformation Roman Catholicism has exemplified the ultimate of this rule of chivalry. The doctrine and discipline of the sacerdotal establishment gives to tradition the same authority as revelation. In the sixteenth century the Council of Trent had decreed the tradition of the Church to be equal in authority with the word of God in the Bible. In the nineteenth century the Council of the Vatican in effect superseded both by having infallibility decreed a Papal attribute. To the observation that a thousand years of churchly tradition carried no hint of Papal infallibility, the newly infallible Pius IX replied, "I am tradition." And English Cardinal Manning, a leader in the effort to invest the pope with this inability to make mistakes, disposed of a parallel observation with the remark, "All difficulties from human history are excluded by prescription." It was the Roman Catholic historian, Lord Acton, who called attention to the implications of this innovation in the eternal and universal doctrine for free inquiry and education. It makes of Catholics, he said, "at once . . . irreconcilable enemies of civil and religious liberty. They will have to profess a false system of morality, and to repudiate literary and scientific sincerity. They will be as dangerous to civilized society in the school as in the state." The record verifies Lord Acton's prediction, which holds for other sects hardly less. However any of them regard other people's religion, none do willingly accept that their own shall be held one among the "controversial issues about which reasonable people differ" and which they study by the methods of inquiry and judgment that the record of the social, no less than the natural, sciences has proved to be the most efficacious, peaceable, unifying, and certain that the mind of man has yet devised.

That the schools might, and profitably could, install such studies, cannot, I think, be gainsaid. The springs of religion are inveterate, and the religions of the world are among the latest as well as the most ancient and the most pervasive components of the world's cultures. But their mutual exclusions and intolerances are also among the most passionate and inveterate, and their pretensions are among the most absolutist and totalitarian. Yet, given their numbers and variety, none, in its character and consequences, can be an ineffable; nor, in a democratic society which takes democracy in a truly religious spirit, may the study of any or all be ordained as a grammar of assent, or the argument of a foregone conclusion. The truth of their relations to one another, to the qualities of men, and to the peace and freedom of humankind can be studied only as each and every human enterprise is studied, not by the rehearsal of a doctrine and the indrill of a discipline, but by way of inquiry into causes and consequences, on their merits, without privilege and without favor. Unless the study of religions is such a humble and devout inquiry, the hyphen in American-Catholic or American-Communist or American-Methodist or American-Muslim or American-Judaist or any other denomination-American, ceases to be a sign of free communication and orchestration. It becomes a sign of overruling aggression conspiring to subdue the non-denominational member of the hyphenation to the domination and service of the denominational one. On the record, where such aggression is resisted, its final term, if the aggressor has the power, is armed assault whose other name is war. The personality which such an aggression nurtures is not that of a free man in a free society.

Chapter Fourteen

THE PLACE OF WAR

By and large, as Washington observed,[1] the hatreds of religion have been the bitterest and most vindictive which the peoples of the world have borne, so ineffable, so final and urgent have seemed the options with which ardent believers confront their neighbors, near and far. Let us observe again that only of recent years have the rules of *live and let live, live and help live* which characterize free society, come to modify the practices of the cults, to bring them toward union and co-operation. Perhaps, had they retained the power as they retain the pretensions, they would continue to insist on the exclusive infallibility of their respective schemes of salvation, and the irresponsible absoluteness and sovereignty of their several churchly economies. But generally, direct power has passed from the ecclesiastical interest to that of the political economy; generally, sovereignty is now held to be the ineffable possession of the national state, which hence may in its turn employ without reproach any and every form of force and fraud its power-holders regard needful to its security. Certainly, the wars waged since the Democratic Revolution have been wars to vindicate, to impose or to defend the "sovereignty" of peoples or states. Defenders have called that which they defended "liberty," "political independence and territorial integrity"; aggressors have sanctified their aggression on the score of "national honor," "vital interests," "keeping the peace" and other rationalizations. Democratic states justified World War I as a War to Make the World Safe for Democracy. They have exalted World War II, which is now in a "cold" phase, as a War for Survival, a War for the Four Freedoms, a War for One World, a War for Democracy. To the American people this World War II is the eighth of the major wars which the nation has fought, beginning with the War for American Independence—one war about every twenty years. The fear of the next rides the American people like an incubus.

Yet it is only since the cessation of the shooting phase of World

---

[1] "Of all animosities which have existed among mankind, those which are caused by difference of sentiments in religion appear to be the most inveterate and distressing and ought to be most deprecated."

War II that the American people have changed their attitude toward training for such war. Hitherto the great majority had consistently opposed all forms of universal military training and had resisted all proposals to that end. But in the summer of 1947 a Gallup Poll indicated [2] that three-fourths of the nation's voting population had decided in favor of peacetime military training.

---

[2] If the country were to vote today in an official referendum on peacetime military training, the results would be as follows on the basis of the estimated 61,000,000 eligible voters at time of last Presidential election: 45,700,000 voters in favor, 11,000,000 voters opposed, 4,300,000 not voting.

That reflects the results of the latest Gallup Poll on military training— an unofficial sampling referendum among the voters in all 48 States. A cross-section, scientifically selected to represent all walks of life, was interviewed on the following:

In the future, do you think every physically fit young man (who has not already been in the armed forces) should be required to take military or naval training for one year?

The vote: Yes, 75 per cent; No, 18 per cent; No opinion, 7 per cent.

One thing the survey brings out is that indorsement of peacetime training is uniformly high in all major population groups. There are no striking differences by age, amount of education, geographical section, sex or party.

The vote by groups follows:

By age:	Yes Per Cent	No Per Cent	No Opinion Per Cent
21-29	75	19	6
30-49	75	18	7
50 and over	74	18	8
By sex:			
Men	74	20	6
Women	76	16	8
By education:			
College	72	23	5
High School	78	17	5
Grade or no school	71	17	12
By party:			
Democrats	76	16	8
Republicans	75	20	5
By section:			
N. Eng. and M. Atl.	74	18	8
E. Cent.	73	20	7
W. Cent.	72	20	8
South	80	14	6
Far West	73	20	7

The change is the more remarkable when one remembers that it is concurrent with the nation's replacing its traditional isolationist position with a forthright internationalism expressed by the American initiative in setting up the United Nations, the United Nations Educational, Scientific and Cultural Organization, and other agencies of collective security and international co-operation. The one would seem to be a contradiction of the other, to be the kind of confused and self-defeating running hither and thither which fear without knowledge often induces in societies as well as in the individuals who are their force and life.

Is this, however, the case? May not the contradiction be merely an illusion of form rather than a substantial fact? May not the turn to both military training and collective security be evidence that Americans, at long last, have learned the lesson which the record of the League of Nations has taught—that right without might is empty, just as might without right is perverse? Unless the law of the nations has the will of the nations and the power of the nations to enforce it, such law, as all experience has shown, is not law but the hypocrisy of the strong toward the weak. Now the law of nations, which we call the Charter of the United Nations, is by intention an instrument to guarantee and to protect the equal liberty of unequals in inter-personal as well as international relations. It proposes to vindicate and to secure the rights of the individual as against aggression from a state or nation, no less than the rights of all nations, states and other societies as against aggression from any. Together with the remaining instruments of the team play of the nations, it constitutes a hyphenation of the peoples of the world. By their means, upon their ways, it is hoped, the societies of men may so arrange their lives and relationships in equal liberty, that each will grow more powerfully and abundantly into its own characteristic culture and economy than it could if it struggled by itself alone. The most comprehensive implementation of the principle *e pluribus unum* men have ever yet undertaken, the international organization of liberty which the Charter of the United Nations attempts, is the beginning of the purposeful self-orchestration of mankind.

On the record, the achievement of this orchestration, the support of this hyphenation, is an enterprise as hazardous as it is difficult. It seeks everywhere in the world an intellectual life characterized by free inquiry, free thought and untrammeled communication; a religious life characterized by the free conscience and open worship; an economic life constituted by free trade of truly free enterprise. It aims at an economy of cultural as well as economic abundance everywhere in the world. Where, in the past, societies have lived under the dominations of authority and have been closed to variation and difference: where their power-holders have penalized difference and imposed conformity of faith, of thought, of act, the United Nations looks to an open world of open societies. It undertakes to protect plurality and diversity, to encourage initiative and innovation, and to operate through democratic consensus instead of imperialist conformity. It looks to a world of free men confined to no fixed status, no inevitable association. It looks to a world of men whose existence is mobile, who have, in each and every field of the human enterprise, alternatives freely to choose from: alternatives of belief, alternatives of sect and party, vocation and culture. This freedom, for a personality or a people to consider and to choose at its own risk, without fear or favor, is the ultimate good which an international organization of liberty aims to establish and to make secure. All the organization's instruments are endeavors to insure that the ultimate act of consent shall be the uncoerced chooser's and the chooser's alone.

A fundamental agent of such insurance is inevitably education. As a personality is educated, his skills improve and multiply and his knowledge diversifies; his choices increase in variety and number, and his power mounts to orchestrate them into a personal history ever richer, more flexible, more varied, harmonious, smooth-moving and self-reliant. His existence is growth in freedom. This is the democratic faith concerning the personal biography, concerning the national being and concerning international society. Those whose faith it is, however, have not been sufficiently alert to the fact that such growth in freedom is far from inevitable, that its continuance is a hazard, and its very being a choice effectuated by choosing. Growth in freedom is not an automatic process cumulatively consummated. It develops as a succession of undertakings achieved by the conscious will. In each man and society its spring is effort, its dynamic is laborious struggle which diminishes and inhibits the pulls and pushes of some alternatives while it enhances and facilitates the pushes and pulls of others. It requires a genuine nullification of a person's vital energy there and a genuine increment here. Its initiation and support, in a word, is that personal fiat, that act of faith which we all, at one time or another, perform but do not recognize when it is named "free will." We know it better, perhaps, as the dynamic and quality of self-directed self-differentiation. It is the liberty of the "life, liberty and pursuit of happiness" which the Declaration of Independence affirms to be each man's equal and unalienable right, and is the aboriginal spring of all the other rights and liberties and obligations whereby a free man lives a free man.

> Out of the night that covers me
>   Black as the pit from pole to pole,
> I thank whatever gods may be
>   For my unconquerable soul.
>
> In the fell clutch of circumstance
>   I have not winced nor cried aloud
> Under the bludgeonings of chance
>   My head is bloody but unbowed.
>
> It matters not how strait the gate
>   How charged with punishments the scroll,
> I am the master of my fate:
>   I am the captain of my soul.
>   William Ernest Henley, *Invictus*

Such is the free man, inwardly at least, the master of his fate, the captain of his soul, the man who has chosen his destiny, who has held fast to his difference, his individuality, and not yielded. His faith in his choice is the efficacious energy of his power not to yield. His choosing is a condition of active tension, of holding his own without any assurance that the rest of the world will cooperate, with the future open and unguaranteed. William James, in a letter to his wife [3] describes this initiating act of freedom as "a sort of deep enthusiastic bliss, of bitter willingness to do and suffer anything . . . which authenticates itself to me as the deepest principle of all active and theoretic determination which I possess."

And so, first and last, the orchestration of mankind by means of the United Nations is a personal choice, an alternative elected from among its competitors as the means most propitious to the growth

---

[3] December, 1878. See *The Letters of William James*, Vol. I, p. 199.

of freedom. The competing choices which are opposed to this global union of the diverse in fact are the ancient, traditional ones. They are exclusive national sovereignty, total national authority, national honor, national interest, imperialist pretension and the like. Sometimes used to rationalize aggression, at other times to nullify international consensus on programs for international good, these alternatives surge irreconcilably against a genuine and efficacious union of the peoples of the world. Their protagonists in the councils of the United Nations employ the veto—as anciently it had been employed by the members of the Polish Seym—to disrupt undertakings toward collective security into events of distributive anarchy. Of hyphenation they make fission, not union; of orchestration, cacophony, not harmony. The divisions they bring about are far less those of the democratic process than those of totalitarian domination and exclusion. For in the democratic process an issue is explored for its nature, origins and diverse consequences; discussion consists of such exploration, not of unsupported charge and countercharge, insult and recrimination. In the democratic process, the labor of a parliament is discussion in which the diverse wills and interests that make up the parliament search out, assemble and bring to one another's consideration all information that may serve to build up a clear and distinct idea of the problematic situation: of what it is, what it may develop into, and what alternative plans of action may change it into. In the democratic process the formation of such a clear and distinct idea is completed in a consensus of pros and cons. Upon such consensus division follows. Each person votes in the light of information which he has endeavored to make as fully every other voter's as his own. By his vote he counts himself into the majority or the minority of the division. In the democratic process the minority on any issue loyally accepts the decision of the majority. The majority is then charged with implementing the decision by action; the minority with exercising the vigilance which is the price of liberty over the methods and consequences of the executive action; with criticizing, warning, checking. The minority acts as the "loyal opposition," and the majority is bound by the democratic terms of its mandate to see to it that the opposition may perform its proper tasks of vigilance and criticism fully, freely and unafraid, until another division may establish the minority as the majority and the majority as the minority, and the roles be reversed.

That which distinguishes democratic decision from authoritarian fiat is obviously the continuous free exchange of knowledge and judgments between competitive interests. Initially, both are choices. But authoritarian choices are blind acts of faith—autos da fé—in the decisions of a *vozhd,* a *führer,* a pope or a *duce,* whose infallibility is the ineffable substance of things hoped for and the opaque evidence of things unseen. Democratic choices are similar acts of faith supported by the free exchange of knowledge and enlightened by free exercise of reflection upon alternatives. Democratic choices are thus educated choices, and indeed, one way of understanding education is to realize it as the support and enlightenment of choice by knowledge and reflection. Knowing and thinking thus pursued are the practice of hyphenation, the process of orchestration. By and large they bring the unique and the diverse in being and spirit to mutual appreciation and respect, to pleasure in one another, to co-operation with one another, or at worst to agreeing to disagree.

There are occasions, however, alike in a personal life or the life of a community or a people, when the height of knowledge and the depth of reflection may only make certain beyond all doubt how irreconcilable an irreconcilable conflict is, how infallibly some existences that are different from each other or similar to each other simply cannot live in the same world together; how, inevitably, if one is to be free the other must be bond, if one is to survive, the other must perish. This, in the personal life, is the substance of tragedy, in the lives of nations and churches, it is the potentiality of war.[4]

---

[4] This is a fact of the human record which UNESCO perhaps unintentionally ignores. The Preamble to the Constitution of this very hopeful agency of the orchestration of mankind reads as follows:

THE GOVERNMENTS OF THE STATES PARTIES TO THIS CONSTITUTION ON BEHALF OF THEIR PEOPLES DECLARE that since wars begin in the minds of men, it is in the minds of men that the defences of peace must be constructed;

that ignorance of each other's ways and lives has been a common cause, throughout the history of mankind, of that suspicion and mistrust between the peoples of the world through which their differences have all too often broken into war;

Like authoritarian societies, predemocratic ones, whether free
or unfree, have always been geared for war, and prior to the
Democratic Revolution, free men everywhere were fighting men.
Such was the case in the city states of antiquity, in the mediaevel
free cities, in the Renaissance republics, and among the landhold-
ing noblemen of all times. The last defined what Lincoln called
"the genius of their own independence" in an ideal of personal
worth and personal honor that kept them ever involved in ven-
dettas, in duels, in warfare or the threat of it. As free men they
were conspicuously fighting men. But not less so were the citizens
of the ancient cities of Greece—of Athens and Sparta and Thebes.
They likewise were fighting men, and that for which they fought
was to establish and confirm their honor, which to them was the
outer acknowledgment of their inward worth by other men.[5] In
free society this acknowledgment is reciprocal and all men are
equal in honor. In authoritarian society the honorable are only

---

that the great and terrible war which has now ended was a war made
possible by the denial of the democratic principles of the dignity, equality and mutual respect of men, and by the propagation, in their place,
through ignorance and prejudice, of the doctrine of the inequality of
men and races;
that the wide diffusion of culture, and the education of humanity for
justice and liberty and peace are indispensable to the dignity of man
and constitute a sacred duty which all the nations must fulfill in a
spirit of mutual assistance and concern;
that a peace based exclusively upon the political and economic arrangements of governments would not be a peace which could secure the
unanimous, lasting and sincere support of the peoples of the world,
and that the peace must therefore be founded, if it is not to fail, upon
the intellectual and moral solidarity of mankind.

There is no recognition in this Preamble or elsewhere in the Constitution of this agency that when authoritarian and totalitarian principles are
held as a fighting faith that justifies missionary aggression and penalizes
every variation as a heresy worthy of death, full understanding of this
faith cannot fail in the last resort to imply war against it. For mere peace
can be had, and could have been had, by appeasement, submission and
service to the authoritarian militancies. But the global peace of free societies of free men, such as this preamble envisions, could not thus be
had. Appeasement was followed by resistance, resistance by war. The survival and growth of freedom may require that every form of unfreedom
shall either die a natural death or be destroyed.

[5] Cf. Aristotle, *Nicomachean Ethics*, I, 5.

the well-born, the powerful and the rich. The education of the free Hellenes was learning a social doctrine of honor and a discipline in the ways of honor as practiced and transmitted by the heroes of their breed. Plato, although he deplored the wars of Greek with Greek, conceived of his ideal Republic as a state geared for perennial warfare against non-Greeks, whom he called "barbarians," and who, not being "of one blood" with Greeks were hence their "natural" foes. In his Republic the fighting men are the master men, and the working men are the serfs and slaves doomed to obey the laws but not to make them; while the lawmakers, after a youth as soldiers and law enforcers, are free from the laws they make. To Platonic guardians religion is an instrument of policy, the arts and music nourishers of the warlike spirit. The educational system which they establish and control is a system of education for war and government. Among its implements were not only "noble lies," there was also battlefield experience for children. The citizen-to-be must learn by seeing how blood is shed and lives are taken.[6] But as between Greeks, Plato wanted that war should not be an effort at mutual destruction. He wanted that war should be what John Ruskin called a game expressing the full personal power of the human creature, a game which "when well-played determined who is the best man." Plutarch tells of those victims of imperial Athens, the Megarians, who never interfered with non-combatants at work, never ravaged or sought to annihilate the foe. Battle, for the Megarians, was a trial of strength and skill, aiming to disarm, not to kill; and the vanquished submitted himself as the victor's prisoner, and undertook to ransom his freedom with a stipulated sum of money. When this was paid, the victor became the "spear-friend" of his former foe. Payment was a point of honor. To default was to be considered "a person unjust and unworthy" by the defaulter's own people as well as his victor's. Chivalry implied a similar ordering of combat. And both have been points on the gradient along which warfare as a mode of settling disputes was tamed and civilized. In so far as warfare belongs to civilization it does tend toward the character of a game which "when well-played determines who is the best man."

But the civilization of warfare, even as expressed by the laws of

---

[6] Cf. *Republic* 467 E, 537 A.

war which the trials of the Nazis at Nuremburg vindicated, has been its least stable, its most precarious characteristic. It has regularly tended to corrupt into total war, especially for persons and peoples to whom combat was the supreme expression of spirit, "a part of God's world-order"; to whom, as Helmuth von Moltke urged, it was the savior of that order from materialism. Yet it is among the latter that civilized war regularly degraded into total war, and its aim perverted from victory over the foe to destruction of the foe. At the same time it is for the latter that the survival of the foe with his power and knowledge is indispensable. Because by destroying the foe the idealizers of war take their own lives as warriors. For if the peak of the spiritual of life is reached in combat and through combat alone, only the continued confrontation of a foeman taxing the warrior's strength and skill can bring the one or the other to that peak. In the degree that either holds the warlike life to be the best life, he commits himself to the survival and equal prosperity of his antagonist. Neither may seek the other's destruction; each must seek victory in a struggle whose outcome must never be such as to prevent the other from fighting again. Both need their enemies as they need their breath. For both, war would be, as von Clausewitz points out, a mode of human intercourse, like business and politics, but the mode most excellent. In both, wars would call upon two kinds of courage—that which Plato designated as wisdom concerning dangers and that which is constituted by the resolution to endure and not yield but conquer; however often down, never to be out, but to rise again and renew the battle.

In the end, this resolution is the warrior's mainstay. Change and chance beset every moment of his struggle; the weather of events may nullify his weapons, defeat his skills, and abort his knowledge and his plans. But if he retains his fighting faith, he rises up again, staunch and unyielding in repeated disaster, and wins to victory at last.

But, if war is a mode of human intercourse, like business and politics and the arts and the sciences, so also the ultimate fighting faith on which war is postulated must be the ground of the labors and hazards constituting those more peaceable forms of the competitive human enterprise. The farmer in his fields, the worker in his factory, the scientist in his laboratory, the artist in his studio, the scholar in his study, draw upon this fighting faith no less than the soldier in his battle. Such war is a war different in kind, however, from the total wars of religion, state and race whose ultimacies of sadism and horror World War II exemplifies. If the latter is war, the former is truly but sport, but a game. If the former is war, the latter cannot be. It can be only a struggle for survival of the same sort that men make against any irrational cataclysm of nature, such as earthquakes, tidal waves or floods, against plagues like syphilis or cancer or leprosy. Those who launch it magnify refined and sadistic aberrations into institutional techniques. In fact they do not wage war but only practice murder and destruction. Both by their faith and their works they wilfully make themselves as different from humanity as are the spirochetes of syphilis, the cells of cancer, or the germs of leprosy. Mankind must check them lest they destroy mankind, and until education transform them, nothing short of preponderant force can check them.

This has always been a principle of the free societies of the world. They have known through tragic experience that it does not take two to make a quarrel, but one only; that peace is a contract which it takes two to keep but which any one can break by himself. Hence, they have been painfully aware that war degenerates into blind destruction when it shuts out peace and the co-operations of peace, for then men cease to be human and for their faith's sake torture each other to death instead of sustaining one another in battle and enabling victory. Free societies have been aware that peace endures only as it incorporates into its own structure readiness for war; that those wars are shortest which, like police action, are waged as events in the organization of peace and in order to keep the peace. They have come to know, better than ever before, that peace can last only as men are ready to give battle to every breach of it. To be educated for peace, hence, free men do need at one and the same time to be educated also for war. To establish lasting peace, the men of peace must learn the sciences and arts which, in the great John Milton's definition of education shall enable them "to perform justly, skilfully, thoughtfully and magnanimously all the offices, both private and public, of peace *and* war."

In a free society these "offices" are members of one another. Thus, during the wars between Athens and Sparta, the ways of

Athens—which Plato depreciated and denounced, were those of a free society; the ways of Sparta—from which Plato drew the paradigm of his Republic, were those of an authoritarian state. Owing to treason and disunion in Athens, Sparta was the victor in those wars. Yet here is what the historian of the critical Peloponnesian War, Thucydides, writing after the victors had razed the fortifications of Athens and stationed a garrison in the Acropolis, puts in the mouth of Pericles speaking in remembrance of fellow-citizens fallen in battle. Athens, this chieftain was made to remind his fellow-Athenians, is a free society, all her institutions—her government, her commerce, her athletic contests, her religion, her building, are rooted and grown in freedom. So are her military training and her education:

> Our military training, too, is different from our opponents'. The gates of our city are flung open to the world. We practice no periodical deportations, nor do we prevent our visitors from observing or discovering what an enemy might usefully apply to his own purposes. For our trust is not in the devices of material equipment, but in our own good spirits for battle.
>
> So, too, with education. They toil from early boyhood in a laborious pursuit after courage, while we, free to live and wander as we please, march out nevertheless to face the self-same dangers. . . When the Spartans advance into our country, they do not come alone but with all their allies; but when we invade our neighbors, we have little difficulty as a rule, even on foreign soil, in defeating men who are fighting for their homes. . . . Indeed, if we choose to face a danger with an easy mind rather than after rigorous training, and to trust rather in natural manliness than in state-made courage, the advantage lies with us, for we are spared all the weariness of practicing for future handicaps, and when we find ourselves among them, we are as brave as our plodding rivals. . . For we are noted for being at once most adventurous in actions and most reflective beforehand. Other men are bold in ignorance whilst reflection will stop their onset. But the bravest are surely those who have the clearest vision of what is before them, glory and danger alike, and yet notwithstanding go out to meet it.
>
> . . . We are alone among mankind in doing benefits, not in calculation of self-interest but in the fearless confidence of freedom.

Pericles was the spokesman of perhaps the freest of the predemocratic societies to whose members the idea of lasting peace was largely fantasy. To modern democratic societies lasting peace is however a positive practical goal planned for, worked for, also fought for, from their very beginnings. In many ways the first citizens of the first of modern democracies were not free men but freed men. They had been the multitudes of the laborious under-privileged, the peasant-serfs and artisan-subjects of landlord and prelate and king. They had been restrained from carrying arms and forbidden the use of them. The Democratic Revolution started them on the careers of the self-governing farmer-citizen and citizen-worker of modern democratic society. They carried with them into those careers a certain resentment, sustained by generations of liberties taken and wrongs suffered wherever they encountered the privileged and free men at arms. The new free man, though he had won his freedom by warfare, was, like the bondsman his ancestor, a man of peace who preferred pruning hooks to spears, and ploughshares to swords. Nevertheless, he aspired to do everything possible to abolish slavery and put an end to war. John Quincy Adams, sixth president of the United States, and son of our second president, was in-vincibly sure that this was the divine mission of modern democracy. "The ultimate extinguishment of slavery throughout the earth," he wrote to the president of the Andover Theological Seminary, "was the great transcendent earthly object of the mission of the Redeemer . . . the Declaration of Independence was a leading event in gospel dispensation . . . its principles lead directly to the abolition of slavery and of war, and . . . it is the duty of every free American to contribute to the utmost extent of his power to the practical establishment of these principles." [7]

And from the founding of the nation, Americans did their prac-tical utmost to establish these principles, and found that the most pacific measures needed soon or late to be supplemented by war-like ones. From the formation in 1815 of the American Peace Society, right up to World War II, pacts followed treaties, and aggressions broke pacts. Treaties were appraised as "scraps of paper." The League of Nations was demoted into a hypocritical debating society; in 1929, forty-five nations, all the great powers of the world, joined in the pact of Paris to condemn "recourse to war for the solution of international controversies and renounce

[7] Brooks Adams, *The Degradation of the Democratic Dogma*, Introduc-tion, p. 29.

it as an instrument of national policy in their relations to one another." But they continued to wage war.

On the record, a freedom which lacks the force to maintain its integrity collapses into bondage, a peace unenforced breaks up into war, within states as between states. The men who framed the Constitution of the United States knew this. They thought of the Constitution as a ground plan of co-operation between diversities and those who voted it ordained and established it "in order to form a more perfect Union, establish Justice, insure domestic Tranquillity, provide for the common defence, promote the general Welfare and secure the Blessings of Liberty to ourselves and our Posterity." Domestic tranquility and the common defense turn upon the immediate and historic actuality of faction or rebellion among fellow citizens and of war with other countries. Most of the participants in the Constitutional Convention of 1789 were men with a classical education. They knew of Athens and of Rome as the poets, historians and philosophers of those societies had written of them, and there was nothing in the record to encourage hope of a domestic tranquility or international peace that did not rest upon power and will to enforce both. Nor had they missed the mediaeval record, alike of the feudal fiefs and the free cities, with their horrors of continuous oppression and revolt. In the immediate past was not only the War for Independence, and the part that Indians had been induced to play in that; there were also the War of the Spanish Succession and the Seven Years' War, with their extensions from Europe to America. The authors of the Constitution were acutely aware that principals in these wars, Britain, Spain and France, still had great colonial holdings on the North American continent, and that the rulers were past masters of the intrigue that entangles the innocent bystander in one's own quarrel. And in the Confederation, Shay's Rebellion was just behind. They knew hence that they had to provide police power for domestic tranquility, military force for the common defense of the union—of its justice, its general welfare, and its blessings of liberty.

But what they knew of the effect of war on the fortunes of freedom made them wary of a standing army, and led them to reject professional control and professional leadership of the needful military power: in the forty-first paper of the *Federalist*, Madison argues that Roman liberties had been lost to Roman militarism. The agencies of the common defense could be only such as were consistent with preserving the people's liberties. The army of a free society would have to be a citizen army, and its control would have to be civilian control. Accordingly, although the convention gave the Congress unlimited power to provide and maintain agencies of the common defense on the land and at sea, they limited appropriation of money for such purposes to two years. Among the agencies to be created and maintained a militia stood out. And the commander-in-chief of the whole was to be the nation's elected civilian head, its president. Thus military power, though by the very nature of its function unlimited—for it must be ample as well as skilled and wise enough to overcome and disarm the enemy—was absorbed into and set under civilian interest and civilian rule. War was envisaged as a part of peace and one of its agencies.

Nevertheless, the sense that war is a menace to liberty was not quieted. And the time was not far off when the Napoleonic overturn of the French Revolution would vindicate the fears of the Founding Fathers and the American people. The memory of multitudes without arms, held down as serfs and servants of minorities whose arms were the badges of their privilege and liberties, ran too deep. If, historically and actually, the free man was the armed man, and the profession of arms an occupation of the privileged aristocracy to whom commoners are mere cannon fodder, then all men shall be equally aristocrats with arms and none shall be deprived of his inalienable right to his sword and spear. Thus in the Bill of Rights on whose acceptance the adoption of the Constitution was made conditional, it is the very second article which guarantees this right: "A well regulated militia, being necessary to the security of a free state, the right of the people to keep and bear arms shall not be infringed." The amendment puts behind the collective power of government to provide for domestic tranquility and the common defense, the individual power of each citizen. It implies a self-insurance of the citizen from aggression against his liberties by government itself. For the ultimate sanction of law, whether in nature or in human relations, is the force whose law it is. Also a government of powers delegated to it by the people, who ordain and establish the government in order to secure their equal rights to life, liberty and the pursuit of happiness, must be strong enough to compel conformity to its works and ways. But neither may it be so strong as to leave the men and women from whose consent its just powers derive unarmed and helpless against possible usurpation and oppression by its delegated officers. The Second Amendment guards also against the last contingency, which could turn a free republic into an authoritarian despotism. It not only looks to a militia, a citizen-army to defend the free state against foreign enemies; it looks to an armed citizenry equipped to defend their liberties against domestic usurpation and aggression, from whatever source.

Thus the interdependence of force and freedom is a first principle of free society. Among the Founding Fathers the foremost spokesman of liberty was Thomas Jefferson. He was as sensitive to the dangers of domestic usurpation as of foreign aggression. "What country can preserve its liberties," he wrote to Madison from France in 1787, "if its rulers are not warned from time to time, that this people preserve the spirit of resistance. Let them take arms. The remedy is to set them right as to facts, pardon and pacify them. What signify a few lives lost in a century or two? The tree of liberty must be refreshed from time to time with the blood of patriots and tyrants. It is the natural manure." That he preferred peace and the ways of peace is of record. This is the message of his First Inaugural, which in effect reaffirms the principles of the Bill of Rights and which besides invokes the ballot as against the bullet, and points to majority rule as "the vital principle of republics, from which there is no appeal but to force, the vital principle and immediate parent of despotism." He is ever for the rule of reason; and hence for "the preservation of the general government in its whole constitutional vigor, as the sheet anchor of our peace at home and safety abroad." He is for "peace, commerce and friendship with all nations—entangling alliances with none." But he knew that sooner or later resort to force might become unavoidable, and he preferred the free man's readiness to the bondsman's unreadiness. So he advocates, under civil authority, "a well-disciplined militia—our best reliance in peace and for the first moments of war."

Peace-lover as Jefferson was, he never doubted that war—either as domestic strife or foreign conflict or both—was a part of peace, or that the ultimate sanction of freedom was its own force to maintain itself at home and defend itself abroad. This is the force which resides in the citizens keeping and bearing arms as by unalienable right; and disciplined to the right use of arms. "None but an armed nation can dispense with a standing army. For a people who are free and who mean to remain so," Jefferson advised the Ninth Congress in 1808, "a well-organized and armed militia is their best security."

But such militia as was developed had proved itself of little good in the War of 1812, and Jefferson believed that its failures were due to the attitude of regarding the study and use of arms as an interruption merely and not an organic part of the education of the free man. "We must train and classify the whole of our male citizens," he wrote to Monroe in 1813, "and make military instruction a regular part of collegiate education. We cannot be safe till this is done." Jefferson had early come to see that military education had best be a part of the general education of the free man. He founded the United States Military Academy at West Point in the first years of his presidency. And when he finally launched his University of Virginia, dedicated to the "illimitable freedom of the human mind to explore and expose every subject susceptible of its contemplation," he made military training an integral part of the course of study. "It is at this age (the college years) of aptness, docility and emulation of the practices of manhood" he wrote in 1818, "that such things are soonest learned and longest remembered."

If Jefferson may be called the statesman-educator, Woodrow Wilson may be called the educator-statesman. Jefferson passed purposefully from his leadership of the nation to the leadership of his university; Wilson passed accidentally from the leadership of his university to the leadership of his nation. Between 1818 and 1914 pacifism had become a world-wide movement. Governmental and voluntary undertakings to displace war as an instrument of policy had become numerous and potent. International tribunals had been established. International co-operation in such matters as posts and patents, piracy and prostitution, health and hunger had become continuous and diversified. The laws of war were being progressively civilized; here an item and there an item, they were being shaped toward that sportsmanship and fair play of which the

practices of the Megarians have been the high place. Economists
and publicists exposed as illusion that in modern society war might
in any way profit the victor. Peace foundations, peace societies,
peace congresses, peace missions, peace mobilizations became numerous and vocal, and in the United States, even potent. Then
during the presidency of Woodrow Wilson the Germans made of
their international contracts "scraps of paper" and launched
World War I. In the United States, as everywhere on the globe, the
hyphen, which had been a sign of national union was immediately
employed as an instrument of division, although that use of it but
strengthened the people's loyalties and brought into operation the
nation's police power. In 1914, the war in Europe seemed none of
America's business, without threat and without promise for the
national interest. We would be neutral and do what was needful to
keep our neutrality secure. For the rest, we would be about fulfilling our happy destiny of peace and freedom. "We will not," the
educator-become-president told the Congress on December 8, 1914,
"we will not ask our young men to spend the best years of their
lives making soldiers of themselves. There is another sort of energy
in us."

But before many more years had passed Woodrow Wilson was
asking the Congress to draft the youth of the nation to do just
what he would not. For the first time in the nation's history its
young men were compelled by law "to spend the best years of their
lives making soldiers of themselves," or as Mr. Wilson now put it,
"a citizenry trained and accustomed to arms." The action of the
belligerents had made of the nation's neutrality but an empty
dream which alone a force great enough to subdue both the
Germans and British and all their allies could turn into reality.
And force of such dimensions would have to be force sufficient to
overawe the world. America could hold onto her isolation and
neutrality only if America built up armament strong enough to
overcome the compulsions of all belligerents. To preserve our soli-
tude we would have to fight every power that challenged it. Defeat
would mean bondage to those powers; victory could mean only rule
over those powers. And such rule, to be effective, must be imperial,
as all history shows. The logic of isolationism and neutrality thus
leads straight into militarism and imperialism, not into the pacifism
American isolationists pretended to. The one alternative to a peace

assured by the preponderant force of one imperial power is a peace assured by the collective force of all. This Woodrow Wilson soon realized, and the final goal of the war that he presided over, in order to end all wars and make the world safe for democracy, was the collective security of a League of Nations.

However, the sovereign and independent states which set up the League were not concerned with establishing collective security but with employing the league as an instrument of their competitive sovereignties. Powers that could not so employ it deserted it, and in deserting it they scrapped all those decencies of war and peace that the nineteenth century had so hesitantly and painfully either extended or initiated. With Stalin, Mussolini, Hitler, Tojo, and Franco, politics became the rawest of raw power politics. International relations deteriorated once more into techniques of force and fraud, a Hobbesian war of all against all. When, in 1939, the diplomatic war became also a shooting war, no decencies were left. The totalitarian states waged total war with no crime that they could commit against the human spirit left uncommitted. Nevertheless, those whom they had so treacherously attacked won the war. Having in mind the betrayals, acutely aware of the futility of the League of Nations, the victors set up the United Nations as a new instrument of the collective security they had hitherto so vainly sought. Undertaking the hyphenation of mankind in an order of equal liberty for unequals under the law of nations, which the global charter was to renovate and assure, they provided in it for international force as the sanction of the international peace and international freedom which the charter purported to ordain and is being invoked to nullify.

Perhaps it is because the frightfulness of totalitarian warfare with weapons has been transposed to the councils of the United Nations in the totalitarian warfare with words, that the American people are at one and the same time for the United Nations and for universal military training. Perhaps the observation that also the free English people under a labor government, are for the first time coming to something like peacetime conscription, is an added influence. Perhaps vigilance aroused by the doctrine and discipline which the educational establishment of the Soviet power imposes on the generations of Russians is an influence. For the Soviet Union continues as a totalitarian state which has shut its subjects away from all free communication with peoples elsewhere. Unlike the American, its isolationism is a true isolationism enforced by all the powers of a politico-economic despotism alike in the world of thoughts and the world of things. Its dogmas may not be exposed to the free challenge of alternatives, nor to the tests of experience. And they include the false doctrines of an irreconcilable conflict with the different everywhere in the world, a conflict in which one or the other must perish. Soviet Russia has been from its beginnings an armed state with a conscripted armament which includes workers as well as soldiers, women as well as men, machines as well as weapons. Article 136 of the Soviet Constitution of 1936 declares, "Universal military service is law. Military service in the workers and peasants army is an honorable duty of the Union of Soviet Socialist Republics." Before World War II all males from eighteen to forty-one served, up to twenty-five, in the regular army units; after twenty-five in the reserves. In 1939, following the Soviet pact with Hitler, military training was made part of the regular school curriculum. From the fifth grade to the eighth grade it is required two hours every week. In the eighth grade it becomes definitely what Americans called basic training. At the tenth grade, youth is sent into active service. The entire curriculum embodies among much else, physical training, military science, and "military-political orientation." To direct the multitudes so disciplined, Soviet authority provides for a segregated military caste, whose training begins at the age of ten. These selected children are taken to the specially created Suvorov Military Schools. There they are isolated to the military enterprise, and acquire a mentality analogous to that of the Prussian military aristocracy, geared however to the ruthless fanaticism of the Communist faith.

The influence of such training on the free spirit is not happy. That war itself should impose serious limitations on liberty is acknowledged in free societies as a necessary evil. Wartime powers held over into peacetimes easily become instruments of usurpation and oppression, and citizens are vigilant and government is required to be careful that the constriction on civil liberties shall be the least and the briefest that is compatible with security. Since Frederick II of Prussia, a soldier, however, is less free than a civilian in peacetimes as well as during the war. His military occupation reduces him from a citizen into a subject, from a free personality into a biological tool. "As to the soldier . . ." Frederick wrote in his secret testament of 1768, "it is necessary that he should fear his officers more than the dangers to which the latter expose him. Otherwise nobody would be able to make them charge across a storm of fire from three hundred cannons shooting at the same time. Goodwill never can take the common people into such perils; it has to be fear." Of course, Frederick was a despot and autocrat, and his observation may be offset by that of Herodotus who wrote that the Athenians, under despots, were no better than their enemies, but when free were "far and away the first of all. This then shows that while they were oppressed they willed to be cravens, as men working for a master, but when they were freed, each one was jealous to achieve for himself." Herodotus' Athenians were not called, however, to charge three hundred cannon shooting at the same time. Grant's and Lee's Americans were, on the other hand, and by and large do not seem to have falsified the Greek historian's judgment of the relation of courage to freedom. But it remains true that military training in the modern sense does not seek the habits of inquiry, deliberation, judgment, decision and action which are the first qualifications of a free man in a free society and the ultimate reserves of the individual after battle is joined. The blind faith, physical skills and automatic obedience which are militarism's primary objectives underlie both the force and form of totalitarian societies geared for war.

Thus military training presents no problem to the masters of Russia, but is a very knotty one to the citizens of the United States. How may American free men be formed into effective soldiers and retain the spirit and disposition of free men? This problem is not changed by the character of the new armament—the airplanes, the atom bombs, the rockets, the tanks. It is not affected by the new tempo at which weapons become obsolete and the skills necessary to their care and use irrelevant. For it is a problem in ethics and psychology, a problem of personality. And it is peculiarly a modern problem. Although "the battle is the payoff" and every soldier, whatever his special function, must first learn the personal skills of personal attack and defense in company and alone, the number ever likely to be engaged in combat is an eighth part of the number required to supply, to sustain and to repair the fighters' needs and the fighters. The *know-how* of these eightfold men behind the front is first and last industrial *know-how*. Modern war draws no sure line between war skills and peace skills. The military establishment solicits men to "join the army and learn a trade." Although infantry may be the consolidators and custodians of victory, engineers, meteorologists, chemists, pilots and other highly skilled technicians are modernly the prime essentials of victorious combat.

In the light of these observations, what price military training as usually conceived and practiced? What could universal military training do for the liberties of men in a free society? Could it do more at best than create an illusion of security, a sort of psychological Maginot Line that the first attack with modern weapons would shatter? Might it not be wiser for the nation to devote the vast sums that such training must cost to making efficacious the collective security of which the United Nations is today but a pretense? For several generations now, oil has been a chief subject of contention in power politics. It still is important, but is entirely overshadowed by rivalry to monopolize uranium and thorium and other fissionable materials. Unless all nations can soon make themselves the insurance of each nation against the menace of atomic warfare, each will succumb to the rule of fear. The moral, intellectual and material isolationism with its imperialist implications, as now practiced by the masters of Russia, may become the practice of all the peoples of the world. A new sort of war of all against all may take form, and end either in a peace made by a bona fide union of the nations at last, or a sort of Pax Romana enforced by the victorious arms of a single victor, imposing its imperial rule upon the entire earth.

This next war would be absolutely a total war. It would be a long war. Whether it ended in imperial rule by one of the combatants or in a self-governing union of all, it could not have failed largely to destroy the works of man, and the records and tools by whose means the sciences and arts, needful for producing those works, are transmitted to the generations. Concentrated on mere survival, the arts and the sciences—Hitler Germany provides an apt instance—would not only regress: disuse would atrophy them, and they would perish. All civilization might lapse as Spengler predicted it would in the West. The condition of peace would then be ignorance, and the bondage of ignorance.

Clearly, the education of free men must needs envisage this

contingency, as one of the options presently before mankind. The alternative would be to endow the United Nations and its agencies of communication and co-operation with genuine powers, strong enough to defend the global union against all nullification and secession, and to establish and enforce globally a way of life which Woodrow Wilson designated as "the reign of law, based on the consent of the governed and sustained by the organized opinion of mankind." The generations would need to learn the hyphenation of their own country with all the other countries of the world. This hyphenation would need to become the supreme object of their devotion, their faith paramount, their ideal to fight for, to live for and to die for. Learning it would require transposing the customary patriotism of place and people into the wider patriotism of all places and all peoples—the patriotism of the democratic ideal which the Declaration of Independence voices—into the loyalty to the equal liberty of different human beings everywhere in the world, which Condorcet urged.

The change would be slow, it would be arduous, and in all likelihood, bloody. But it is a process of union that every one of today's sovereign states derives from and continues in. Every instance of it—whether in Great Britain, or Switzerland, or France, or Germany, or Russia, or China—has had for its efficacy a shift of individual allegiance from a place and people self-isolated, shut in and cut off, to the same place and people, united to their neighbors on equal terms in a free trade of thoughts and things. The United States of America began as a confederation of sovereign and independent states whose bond of union was resistence to the oppression of a common master. The war for independence freed the confederation from the master. But once the menace of his power was removed the alliance tended to disintegrate in a variety of conflicts, and the Constitution with its Bill of Rights held the North and the South but doubtfully together till after the Civil War to save the Union. Then somehow, local loyalties, without having diminished, were superseded in most men's minds by national allegiance. Personal devotion shifted from the particular state to the United States. The man from Maine, or from Ohio, or from Virginia, or Mississippi became hyphenated in faith and feelings with the men from all the other states in the Union. He became inwardly an American.

The defeat of Germany in World War I was also followed by centrifugal actions of the powers which degraded the League of Nations into a hypocritical pretense, and no crisis occurred intense enough to shift the personal allegiance of the multitudes from their countries in sovereign isolation from one another to their countries self-hyphenated into a family of nations. Can World War II be reinterpreted as such a crisis? Now once more the defeat of *Deutschtum* has been followed by division among the foes whom its aggression had united, division that in effect nullifies the union and stalls the co-operation which their Charter of the United Nations provides for. Against this division fear and hope are building certain illusions, already touched upon. A doctrine is current that if only the combatants could thoroughly understand each other, such understanding would be followed as surely as day follows night by reconciliation and peace. Policies are projected and programs enacted on the assumption that the United Nations can survive and grow as a union of states merely and not as a hyphenation of peoples. There are voluntary pressure groups and state governments that cling to the ideas of peace maintained without power and freedom sustained without force. The doctrine, the policies, the ideas are either sentimental fantasies or false faces of a ruthless game of power politics. It need not be repeated that understanding may show how utterly irreconcilable irreconcilable interests are, and its upshot may be not conciliation but war. If the past is any guide, the United Nations can survive and grow only as it freely becomes the fighting faith of each one of the multitudes that people the earth, only as they study what it is, what are its goals, what are its instruments, how they work and how they may be bettered; and only as they learn that they must defend its integrity with all their powers. In sum, a realistic, as against an illusory program of international peace must rest on the education that John Milton postulated for the free man—the education whereby he will be equipped to perform justly, skillfully, thoughtfully and magnanimously all the offices, public and private, of peace and war.

This means that the education of the free man as soldier shall not be segregated from the education of the free man as citizen and worker but shall be fitted into the latter as a natural part of the education of the whole man. It means that military education and

liberal education must be members of one another, and both be
directed to the works and ways of freedom, by freedom, for freedom, as the greatest good of the diverse and diversifying peoples of
the world. Since the United States has taken the initiative in the
organization of the United Nations, and in the establishment of the
United Nations Educational Scientific and Cultural Organization,
it follows also that the initiative falls to the United States in the
reorientation of the national curricula. The President's Advisory
Commission on Universal Military Training has in some degree envisaged the nature and need of this initiative.[8] In addition to
other agencies for the common defense it recommends for all boys
of seventeen or eighteen, first, six months "basic training" in camp
or aboard ship; then, six months of one or another form of training
that each may choose for himself, or his admission, if he be found
capable, to a military or naval career. Then, it urges civilian participation, almost control, both of the policy and practice of training, and that the training should have a relevancy also to the
trainee's life as a man and a citizen. The Commission recommended an improved program for conscientious objectors harmonious to the democratic idea. And it calls attention to the global
record which makes force the foundation of freedom:

> It is apparent from the lessons of history and from the experi-
> ence of the post-war period that the only way in which we can
> lend authority to our voice in international affairs and inspire
> confidence in the ability of the United Nations to enforce peace
> is to maintain our armed forces at a level of efficiency and com-
> prehensiveness that will defy challenge by any would-be ag-
> gressor. If the people of this country will declare in convincing
> fashion their determination to support such a program in all its
> elements for as long as may be necessary to guarantee the attain-
> ment of a stable world order through the United Nations, they
> will make the greatest contribution to perpetual peace within
> their power. . . . We recognize that weakness is an invitation to
> extermination. Without the strength to back up our moral
> positions or discharge our international commitments, we are

─────────────

[8] A Program for National Security: Report of the President's Advisory
Commission on Universal Military Training. The Commissioners were:
Karl T. Compton, Joseph E. Davies, Harold W. Dodds, Daniel A. Poling,
Anna C. Rosenberg, Samuel I. Rosenman, Edmund A. Walsh, Charles E.
Wilson.

impotent in a world where force is still, unfortunately, a determinant of right. While we try to rebuild, we must not at the
same time invite further destruction. A weak nation can only
beg, not command respect and reciprocity.

The specific program which the Commission proposes, however,
in no way adequately links military enterprise to international co-
operation or the soldiers' skills to the patriotism of an international mind which sees one's own nation as an equal member of a
union of nations linked to them by every form of free communication. The program is based on the idea that soldiering is a vocation
which interrupts rather than extends and enriches the citizen's life,
and it speaks of military training as if it had to be a vocational
discipline independent of the culture it occurs in. But that, in
effect, is exactly what in a democracy military training must not be.
Given the same armament, training in its care and use is much
the same whether in a totalitarian or a free society. Given the
human body, training in bodily skills tends to be much the same,
whatever the other values, works and ways of the community. The
important difference between Fascist, Communist or Falangist
soldiers and soldiers of democracy is not in their military training
but in the ideals and the ways of life composing the culture which
the training is supposed to serve, and which is supposed to suffuse
and channel the training. On the record, military training isolated
from its culture by its very nature inhibits freedom and sustains
authoritarianism.

The problem for modern democracy is to achieve under modern
conditions and for the ages to come that fusion of vision and will,
insight and readiness, which the Athenians whom Pericles led and
served seem spontaneously to have established as the Athenian
way. There is an organic connection between this way and the
fact that the Spartan victory did not long endure, that Athens
rose again and came to be considered the light and leading of the
Hellenistic world; that to so great an extent and for so long a time,
the civilization of mankind was largely synonymous with the
Hellenization of mankind; that within a generation after the
humiliation of his country a successor of Pericles was able without
bragging to say: "Athens has brought it about that the name
Hellenes no longer suggests a race but an intelligence; that the
title Hellene is applied rather to those who share our culture than

to those who share a common blood." [9] Can the democratic faith,
as it has developed in America, come to an analogous consummation in the works of democracy? This is today's critical problem
in the education of free men. It is more or less acknowledged when
a crisis in the common defense occurs. So, the Morrill Act of 1862,
establishing the land-grant colleges and prescribing "military tactics" as a part of the general curriculum, was such an acknowledgment. But when the crisis is over the soldierly function of the
citizen is again cut off and shut out from the wholeness of life,
to be intruded with the next crisis.

The danger to freedom which most military training carries at its
heart can be lifted alone by an education which assimilates military
education to the liberties of men and holds steadily before the
minds and hearts of the generations how only those peoples retained
their liberties who were ready to fight for them, how only those
nations had peace who were able to enforce it. Alone education can
transfigure the vocation of arms with the culture of liberty and
shape military training to the service and not the subversion of
equal liberty for different people everywhere in the world. From
the close and faithful examination of the career of freedom and of
the faith and "natural manliness" that supports their liberties in
the lives of men, the generations may learn to pass on as tradition
that emulation of the noble dead by the hopeful living which
Pericles commended. They may then in their turn live on as unyielding defenders of free society "knowing the secret of happiness
to be freedom, and the secret of freedom a brave heart."

---

[9] Isocrates, *Panegyricus*, 50.

Chapter Fifteen

THE DISCIPLINE OF FREEDOM

Although a certain sect of philosophers are just now very vocal
about a discipline of freedom they do not mean by freedom what
is usually meant. They mean in fact an unwilling conformation to
rules imposed, not chosen, whereas freedom regularly goes with
willingness and choosing. Neither tradition nor usage couples
discipline with freedom. Both couple it with authority. Such coupl-
ings as "military discipline," "religious discipline," are characteristic of both. Education, when a military enterprise, is regularly
called "indoctrination," while the catechisms and other ecclesiastical instruments of instruction have always been engines of indoctrination. By first intention the phrase "doctrine and discipline"
is an authoritarian expression bespeaking the hierarchies of faith
and works which sustain "the army" and "the church." "Discipline"
in either establishment designates far less its operational procedures, its ways of working—ways of working are the substance of
discipline in the sciences and the arts—than the powers that compel
following the ways and punish not-following. By tradition "freedom" breaks up "discipline" and "discipline" shuts out "freedom."
Plato thought of them as mutually exclusive, and so the philosophic
educators of his cult regard them to this day.

However, this antagonism in concept nowise diminishes the interdependence of discipline and freedom in experience. The two
compenetrate wherever choice displaces coercion and group action
is the result of a group consensus which grows out of free inquiry
when such inquiry is aimed at attaining a general understanding
of an issue and its solutions. What in fact do we mean by a free
society if not one where the associations and establishments which
compose it are such because of these ways of working together?
When different individualities join together freely on equal terms,
when the consequent group accepts, appreciates and takes the fullest
possible account of the personality of each of its members so that
everyone's place and function in the team play of the whole expresses his character and powers, changing as those alter, the society is free. It survives and grows both as a whole—and in its
diverse lesser groupings—as a community of purposes and prac-

257

tices. Each of its members so participates in their definition, diversification, and enlargement that the community's laws and statutes are then but symbols of its spontaneous dynamic. Its spirit or morale is then but the orchestration of the pride and satisfaction of each of the members in his being an associate of the others in the communion of going and goal wherein the society's wholeness consists.

Where these relations obtain, the group spirit and the members' allegiance evince the discipline of freedom. You see it in families where parents take their children into a free partnership in the shaping and upkeep of the total family economy. You see it occasionally in religious groups, such as the Society of Friends. It is indispensable in athletic teams where it constitutes the sportsmanship and sustains the co-operative skills of competitive games such as baseball, football and the like. Even military organizations may achieve it, if the structure and operations of Evans Carlson's "Raiders" are an indication.[1] In fact there is no problem of theory or practice that human beings need to solve jointly and not severally, which cannot be met by team play developing as this discipline of freedom. In all cases, the tasks to be performed, the tools, the materials and the relevant technics may be the same as those which are customarily available to the discipline of authority. What is different is the human relation—the relation of each person to cach, and of the person having authority, that is, of the leader, to all. What is different is the principle, the direction, and the pattern of interpersonal communication. These release or inhibit the employment of means and determine the attainment of ends.

So it is with the educational establishment. By tradition and actually, school organization is hierarchical, school administration is authoritarian, school discipline is coercive, teaching is indoctrination, learning is repetition of doctrine. The peak of this condition may be observed in the profession of attitude which Ignatius Loyola laid down for the members of his Society of Jesus as one of the "Spiritual Exercises" he prescribed for them: *"I will believe what seems to me to be black to be white, if the hierarchical Church*

---

[1] See *The Big Yankee* by Michael Blankfort, especially Part V, Chapter I.

so teaches." [2] The rule and disposition which this remarkable profession evinces are by no means confined to the Jesuit order. They appear in diverse forms and with different degrees of awareness in every walk of life and in every kind of group. Even those school people whose professional education has exposed them to the most scientifically verified insights into human nature and human development are molded by the school system into acquiescence in this surrender of the free spirit of inquiry. They can repeat as by rote that any individual child's heredity is not an inalterable force coercing it from without, but a pattern within the singularity of its personal energies changing from within, as it grows and develops. Such schoolmen are aware that if this were not the case, biography could have no content and history no meaning. They have words for the idea that heredity is not a set of premises enfolding foregone conclusions but an initiation of processes, of changes and learnings, whose psychosomatic equivalents are attitudes, memories, habits none of which a personality has been born with. They have the words but either do not grasp or ignore the meaning, and its bearing on the science and art of teaching. Among those who do grasp the meaning and its implications, some of these changes are appreciated as arbitrary, irrational, perverse, non-adjustive, suggesting spontaneous variations from within; most are seen as consequences of education, the outcome of the interaction of the human animal's biological heredity with its social inheritance. A generic name for this social inheritance is culture, and the process by which anyone comes into possession of it is often called acculturation. By acculturation, bodies receive souls, born animals acquire human traits, inarticulate psychosomatic organisms grow into articulate human personalities, "original nature" transmutes into the "second nature" of the civilized man.

The perception of this process and what it implies is far older than its demonstration by the sciences of man. Pascal observed three hundred years ago:

---

[2] A Jesuit college head much in the public eye gave this prescription one contemporary expression in 1942. "Students," he said, "should be taught obedience to the constituted authority, because it is the constituted authority." He denounced academic freedom as a "mumbo jumbo" allowing any teacher "the privilege of uprooting all the true foundations of life."

What are our natural principles but principles of custom? In children they are those which they have received from the habits of their fathers, as hunting in animals. A different custom will cause different natural principles. This is seen in experience; and if there are some natural principles ineradicable by custom, there are also some customs opposed to nature, ineradicable by nature, or by a second custom. . . Parents fear lest the natural love of their children fade away. What kind of nature is that which is subject to decay? Custom is a second nature which destroys the former. But what is nature? For is custom not natural? I am much afraid that nature is itself only a first custom, as custom is a second nature. The nature of man is wholly natural, *omne animal*. There is nothing which he may not make natural; there is nothing natural which he may not lose.[3]

Curious paradoxes are to be noted in the ideas devised to explain the interaction of the two heredities, original nature and custom. An assumption that biological heredity is inalterable goes with an educational technique which presupposes that it can be molded and shaped, but only by applying a force great enough to overcome both its passive and active resistance. Tradition attributes this resistance to original sin and original sin to man's free will. It holds that free will is bad will, whose sign is disobedience; that it can be overcome only by the supernatural force of grace. Grace must invest the rod, if the child is not to be spoiled. In the schools, this traditional appraisal pushes aside the untraditional insight and calls upon the doctrine of freedom to justify the lazy continuation of the discipline of authority. Since that discipline largely fails to produce the character and personality which are its goals, the failure is attributed to the inalterable recalcitrance of original nature. The doctrine that original nature is original sin is thus verified and confirmed. The logical circle is closed, complete, perfect. Teachers, in school and out, may thus remain sure beyond challenge that the fault is ever the learner's, never the teacher's nor the teaching's. Every so often the excuse of the learner's total depravity is re-enforced by endowing him also with an unconquerable stupidity, as do those lamentations over the nation's destiny which build upon calculations that the average American intelligence cannot rise above the thirteen-year-old level. Such transferences of responsibility or guilt from the holders of authority

---

[3] *Pensées*, 92, 93, 94.

to the subjects of authority, make authoritarian explanation of authority's failures simple, sure, and consoling. They save its face while the ground falls away from under its feet. The class-war between teacher and pupil, the contrasting and antagonistic mores of classroom and campus, with their diverse devices for evading obedience and submission are all modes of this falling away. They are frustrations and defeats of the discipline of authority. They may start as spiritual withdrawal and the refusal of consent; and this may remain inward so that the body is present and the mind absent. They develop as outward non-participation; sometimes they pass over into active sabotage and full-dress strikes. In politics the same process may take the form of what Gandhi called non-co-operation, civil disobedience; this mounts to secret, then public rebellion. In industry withdrawal of consent begins as a slow-down, heightens to sabotage, sit-down strike or walk-out, breaks loose as violent resistance.

When original sin and total depravity ceased to be acceptable explanations of this rejection of the discipline of authority, when free will was no longer made the same as bad will, philosophy was relieved of its pessimism. Philosophers appeared who interpreted the defeats of authoritarian rule as demonstrations that the good society and the good life cannot be reliably postulated on the miracle of grace and the authority of the elect whom the miracle thus favors. The good life and the good society, it followed, must be growths of the unalienable liberty and the deliberate consent of the people whose life and society they are. Jefferson, Rousseau, Condorcet, Emerson, John Mill, Charles Renouvier, William James, John Dewey, among others, are diversely interpreters of this idea; they set forth, each in his fashion, the doctrine of a discipline of freedom which might exemplify this doctrine in persons and events. In the history of freedom they count among the great philosophic spokesmen of the democratic faith as experience engenders and sustains this faith, as observation sanctions it, and study and reflection bring to light its grounds in the processes of original nature, subsequent formation and ultimate hopes of men.

Although, however, experience, observation and reflection anticipate experimental test and scientific verification, they are not equivalents for these, their consummation. They do not bring the assurance and certainties that go with "proof." Those come only as the methods and measurements of the scientist confirm theoretical expectation in practical consequence and transpose working hypothesis into operative law. Between the two world wars scientific proof of the democratic faith came from both industry and education.

The requirements of World War I had set problems regarding the human conditions of industrial efficiency, which the postwar reaction and the notorious "American Plan" for industry made the more acute. Concurrently, various forms of totalitarian dictatorships were taking power in Europe and each proposed a doctrine and discipline which held democratic society up to scorn, denying its principle and challenging its power as well as its right to exist. Wartime studies of the human conditions of industrial efficiency led to several somewhat surprising perceptions. It was observed that although workers are hired and fired as single individuals, on the job they do form groups. It was observed that interpersonal and intergroup relations affect industrial efficiency. It was observed that the effectiveness of foremen and other leaders depended far less than was supposed on their place and powers in the hierarchy of plants. It was observed that all these relationships have a dynamic role in determining the quality and quantity of productive work. The studies leading to these observations were begun during World War I by Elton Mayo while he was still at the University of Pennsylvania. With a group of collaborators, he extended, and deepened, the field after he joined the Harvard Business School as professor in the Department of Industrial Research. This group inquired into the psychosomatic conditions of the personality, its relations to others on the job, in the school, and in the community, the effect of the physical environment, and the like, and how these influence competition and co-operation and conflict. They studied the consequences of leader attitude and leader action to the group, the person and the plant; the workings of employment and unemployment on the personality. The inquiries were directed to different businesses, different parts of the country, different communities at home and abroad. They were carried into and through World War II. There are many reports of them. But Mayo's trilogy, *The Human Problems of an Industrial Civilization, The Social Problems of an Industrial Civilization* and his projected *Political Problems of an Industrial Civilization* provide a conspectus of this work of a generation. They demonstrate that the administration of things is anything but independent of the government of men. They establish that the government of men can either speed, smoothen and heighten the administration of things or delay, obstruct and diminish it. They make evident that production is not truly facilitated where organization is based on traditional concepts of "efficiency" and "human engineering"; that treating men as biological parts of automatic machinery only obstructs the most fruitful use of such machinery. They make evident that such use ensues when work is orchestrated to a team spirit resulting from free and flexible team work in which each participant feels himself a person with a personal part to play. They indicate that foremen, superintendents and industrial brass are effective leaders in the degree that their social distance from the worker diminishes and that all intercommunicate and share in knowledge and direction of the organization and economy of the plant. They establish that the efficiency of an industrial organization follows from the assent of its personnel to the directives they receive; and that the authority of the directives is in the will of the hearer, not the purpose of the speaker. Without a feeling of belonging, without a high level of common understanding and personal responsiveness, authority is external and gets whatever results it does get through fear or greed or both. When the demonstrably desirable conditions are established, on the other hand, authority becomes inward, its directives are in a functional sense self-directive, the feeling of personal dignity and worth is heightened, the esteem of one's team mates outweighs as incentive the desire for gain or the judgment of special interest; production jumps. The survival, to say nothing of the growth, of democracy, Dr. Mayo implies, requires that such relationships between men and managements shall become constitutive of the folkways and mores of industrial civilization. To render them so we need not only "patient pedestrian work at the wholly neglected problems of spontaneous participation;" we must also heighten the national level of knowledge, skill and social understanding. "The forms of democracy are not enough;" democracy must become the dynamic of all interpersonal relations in industry. This requires a much higher than the presently prevailing "general standard of technical skill and literacy;" a much higher general standard of living, and "the effective participation and cooperation of every one." It requires, in a word, an educational policy and program which shall take the findings of a generation of study of human relations in industry as at least one of its foundations. These findings embody a discipline of freedom.

Similar conclusions, similarly grounded, come out of experiment and research in our educational establishments. In one direction, these were concurrent with the studies in industry, in another, they were consequent to the nazification of Germany.

The first were functions of the progressive education movement which was organized close to the conclusion of World War I. Although during a hundred years Pestalozzi's initiative had been emulated by this educator here and that reformer there, in Europe no less than in the United States, an influential progressive education movement developed only with the organization of the Progressive Education Association in 1918. That year, teachers employed in a handful of private schools came together with parents of their pupils to plan and advance a program of teaching and learning requiring a discipline of freedom for the education of free men.

Their immediate philosophical "frame of reference" was John Dewey's *Democracy and Education,* published in 1916, and still the light and leading of all that is being written on education alike by those who vary while agreeing with him and those who keep keening that his philosophy of education is a hateful error fraught with death. Children, Dewey reminded his readers, are people. They grow into tomorrow only as they live today. For them, as for everybody, but for them especially, living is learning and learning is living, and living and learning both are processes fulfilling their actual interests and satisfying their actual needs. They will make every effort to serve their interests and to still their needs. They will make every effort to avoid frustrating their interests and starving their needs. A school's curriculum should always be devised so as to call up activities which will work out in the knowledge and skill required both to produce and consume things and to work freely and merrily together with others.

In this philosophy there was nothing utopian or humanly irrelevant. It was a summary and projection of experimentation, analysis and observation that Dewey had been carrying on for a generation.

Indeed, it was the beginning of a genuine science as well as a new art of education. And all undertakings in progressive education endeavor to base themselves, fully aware, on all that scientific method can discover about the growing pupils, their relations to their tasks, to one another, to their teachers, to their parents and to their environments. The progressives have given a veritable *poussée formidable* to the study of children, not piecemeal, but as whole living persons. They base their activity programs on the findings of the medical and social sciences—from the various psychologies, physiologies, and anthropologies, to the histories of culture and the principles of sociology. They understand that children are not merely performers with words and things. They know them to be persons and characters who in their performances feel, perceive, choose, reject, decide and judge, both people and things. They regard learning as the formation of diverse patterns of personal conduct which are at the same time adjustments of the personality to its world and its world to the personality. So progressive schools tend to be "child-centered" schools, yet schools as little unlike home and the rest of the world as is educationally feasible. They are designed to be schools in which the task agreed upon generates the discipline which its performance requires, where learning is a process that implements spontaneous curiosity with the methods and media of scientific research, where knowledge and skill are the consummation of this discipline of freedom.

But to believe in the principles of progressive education is one thing; to embody them in practice is quite another. Often, the protagonists of these principles knew far better how to undo what they did not want, than how to accomplish what they did want. In many cases sentimental vagueness was taken for pedagogic competency, and aversion to the discipline of authority for skill in the discipline of freedom. A good many schools became scenes of anarchy which was interpreted as progressivist order. Parents came, in many instances, to doubt the educational effectiveness of the enterprise they had espoused. Pedagogic champions of the discipline of authority, antagonistic from the beginning, became ever bolder in their denunciations. Sympathetic ones saw pupils leaving the progressive schools without having learned to read, to write, to reckon, and without being disciplined to concentrated attention and correct systematic thinking. They wanted a reform of progressive education which would center on "essentials" and make "informal learning" the fringe instead of the focus of the educational enterprise.

The leaders of the progressive movement accepted the challenges. They recognized that some schools called progressive were guided by extremists in theory and were only crackpot. But they knew also that the most representative of them were solid suburban establishments, many private, some public, with pupils whose parents were comfortable American liberals and conservatives, who would not accept the alleged miseducation of their children without investigation. And over a period of years, one investigation after another was carried through. Among them was a detailed study [4] of some five hundred youngsters from about the same social level, of relatively equal intelligence and under reasonably similar teachers. Half were pupils in progressive schools, half in traditional schools. This inquiry demonstrated that the essentialist charge of failure to teach the three R's satisfactorily was groundless. It demonstrated that while the pupils in traditional schools knew more about rules of health, those in progressive schools were healthier. It showed them also to have a wider and more reflective knowledge of current events, to be more apt at writing, drawing and arguing, and in their personal relations to be more honest, more co-operative, better able to lead. It showed them to have a wider and deeper range of interests.

Another test was the Eight Year Study.[5] This study was launched by the Progressive Education Association in 1932. That year it set up a Commission on The Relation of School and College. An agreement was entered into with some three hundred liberal arts colleges throughout the nation, under which they would admit graduates of thirty progressive schools unconditionally. The college records of the graduates of these schools would then be compared in detail with those of matched graduates from non-progressive schools. Some of the progressive schools were public high-schools like those of Winnetka, Illinois and Denver, Colorado; others were private schools, like the Lincoln School in New York

---

[4] J. Wayne Wrightstone: *Appraisal of Newer Elementary School Practices,* Bureau of Publications, Teachers College (New York: 1938).

[5] Wilford M. Aiken, *The Story of the Eight Year Study* (New York: 1942).

City and Milton Academy in Milton, Massachusetts. Under the agreement students began to enter the colleges in 1936. Between that year and 1939 some four classes were enrolled, with 1,476 progressive students. Each of these was matched with his like in family background, sex, age, interest, and intelligence from a non-progressive school. The matchers were college judges, who, if they had any bias at all, would have it for the customary and traditional. Their comparisons showed that the progressive school graduates received slightly better marks in their courses; that they were awarded more academic honors, that they could think more logically and precisely, that they were apter in handling practical problems, that they read more books, listened to more music, were more concerned with public affairs, had a more diversified social life and won elections to more student offices. The highest record on all counts was made by the graduates of the six schools regarded as most progressive.

Where high schools are "terminal," the human implications of the discipline of freedom are even more crucial. For it is the discipline of freedom alone that can correct the evils of the social prolongation of infancy required by industrial civilization. A representative instance may be observed in the workings of the Nadeau Township School,[6] located in the Upper Peninsula of Michigan. The people of this township are by derivation of the miscellany of Europe—French from Canada, Poles, Germans, Italians, Russians, Scandinavians. Many of the 1,680 are first generation Americans. Theirs is basically an agricultural economy. Their children tend, for Americans, to marry early, and to settle down not too far from their parents. In 1943 they got a new superintendent of schools, a young man still in his early thirties. Education, as this schoolman envisages it, must be "functional" and what he means by "functional" is what the progressivists mean by "progressive." That is, the three R's, history, literature and the like, are to be treated not as isolated and self-sufficient departments of knowledge, but as both means and ends in the total business of living. This business all turns on the earth, the water, the grasses, the trees, the cattle, the people, and where and how they live. A schoolhouse is an instrument of the common life. If geometry and algebra are

---

[6] Cf. Karl Detzer, "The Whole Town Goes to School," *Farm Journal*, (January, 1948).

learned there, they are better learned when they are integrated with surveying, with map-making, with bookkeeping for a business that brings the school income and the students wages. Botany is more alive as a function of the gardening, forestry, and the like, which may provide cash crops. If home economics is a topic of study, it is best studied as the economy of an actual home, where things are done to serve living ends and not as abstract school exercises. Chemistry and dietetics become important as frames of reference for canning food one is going to eat. Literature acquires a more than escapist significance when it is bound up with writing letters on matters of vital import to the letter writers, to prospective customers or merchants, or with reports to public officials. The care and repair of tools and machinery actually in use is more vital than training in an expensive school machine shop in actions so detached from anything significant as to be meaningless. For all these activities the school buildings are the center. The elders and the youth use them together and the social distance between them is correspondingly reduced. Recently Nadeau Township voted sixteen hundred dollars for a war memorial. A "functional" one, the superintendent of schools suggested, could be a lighted baseball diamond on the school grounds. The people having agreed, a geometry class laid the diamond out, and the class in manual training helped with the wiring. Children and parents by general consent made a team, each generation doing its part for the achievement of an end equally important to both. In this and many other undertakings the school, instead of prolonging infancy, re-enforced growth toward maturity. Its discipline is the discipline of freedom.

Between the world wars, the nation's educational establishment became spotted with progressive units; most, definitely committed to the theory and practice of progressive education; some, like New York City's school system, forced by public opinion to reluctant experimentation. In the technical sense, none of these undertakings was scientific. None was a controlled experiment, identifying, isolating and manipulating the processes under study, subjecting them to measurement and verification. Now the time was come for such an experiment.

The place was the Iowa Child Welfare Experiment Station at the University of Iowa. The experimenter was the late Kurt Lewin. This Jewish man of genius was a refugee from the Hitler terror.

Prussian-born, Lewin grew up under the handicap of the Jew unafraid to count himself a Jew in imperial Germany. His parents
were able to give him the usual academic education available to German nationals of a certain economic status. He completed his work
for the doctorate in 1914 at the University of Berlin, and then was
called to the army. He began his war service as a private and ended
it as an officer with an Iron Cross—an unusual record indeed for a
Jew in the German Army. After his discharge, he returned to the
University. He concentrated on psychology. His familial background and personal connections set his attention upon the ruling
Weimar Republic's problems of industrial efficiency. Among other
things, he studied the psychological consequences of the Taylor
system; he was continually concerned with the impact of war on
the minds of men; the nature of relations bothered him and he
studied the differing conceptions of them held by physicists and
biologists. They were central to the problems inherent in perception, and for the matter, in the behavior of children. Lewin became
more or less a convert to Gestalt psychology. But he was too aware
of the importance of quantitative techniques in scientific method
to rest content with the orthodox attitude of gestaltists toward
them. Keenly conscious of the inadequacies of statistical and sum-
mative procedures, he turned to the geometric disciplines. He
thought out a geometry of living quite other than the physicalist
geometries of Euclid and the mechanists. He devised new psychological terms such as "life space," "field theory," "vectors" and
built up with these a "topological psychology" which brought to
fruitful union topological conceptions and psychosomatic traits. He
was far less intolerant than his companions of the gestaltist faith
and was able to transpose Freudian inferences and insights into
topological interpretations of personality and its dynamics. His
curiosity reached out to human relations in all sorts of groupings—
educational, industrial, military, dietary, religious, cultural, political, and he kept constantly modifying or altering his postulates,
revising and improving his methods, his agencies and his recording
instruments. At his death Lewin was head of the Research Center
for Group Dynamics at the Massachusetts Institute of Technology,
Consultant to the United States Public Health Service, and one of
the Advisers on Human Relations of the Navy Department's Office
of Naval Research.

Significantly, most of this development took place after Lewin had settled in the United States. He happened to be in this country as visiting professor of psychology at Stanford University when the Nazi sadistocracy took power in 1932. Soon after, Lewin resigned his professorship of psychology and philosophy at the University of Berlin and sent back his Iron Cross to the Hitlerite cabal. He labored long at a project to set up a department of psychology at the Hebrew University in Jerusalem, which came to nothing, although Lewin's concern with the problems of Palestine and the problems of his people, generally, was intimate and active. His political devotion, like his scientific destiny, turned out to be American of the Americans. His central problem developed into the scientific verification of postulates underlying American society and its structure, as those came into the focus of public and professional discussion condemned by the totalitarian systems of Europe, and challenged by sacerdotal and other admirers of those systems in the United States.

Early in his ten-year service at Iowa City, Lewin, with a group of enthusiastic associates, laid out and carried through the firmly controlled experiments in social atmosphere with which they wrote a new page in the history of social psychology as an experimental discipline. The problem he set for his group was, by means of experiment, to bring out, to describe, to compare, and so far as possible to measure what happens when individuals in a group live and work in free association and again when their relations to one another are determined on order by authoritarian rule. They were to judge what happens to ideas and ideals; to group cooperation and group conflict, to the group's stability, to the alternatives of loyalty between which group members come to choose, to the status of individuals as affected by the group's attitudes, and the like.

To find answers to these inquiries, Lewin asked for volunteers from the fifth and sixth grades of the Iowa City Public Schools to join a new kind of club. The clubs were to do something the children had never done before; they were to make masks. From the numbers of volunteering those were accepted whom expert observers found to have similar attitudes and qualities of leadership, to be equally popular, but not otherwise alike. Rules were adopted: It was agreed that each mask made would be the possession of the whole group; that all the group's members would participate in making the masks; that one and the same group leader would have charge of all the groups; that the groups would meet once a week for twelve weeks in sessions two and one-half hours long. A club which, when compared with a "normal" Iowa City classroom, developed a freer atmosphere, would be appraised democratic; one developing a stricter than normal classroom atmosphere would be autocratic. The methods of organization would decide. In one club, policies would be the result of a consensus reached through all the members and the leader consulting together. The leader would explain the nature of the club's task, analyze different ways of performing it, leave the way to be used to the decision of the members, and the formation of subgroups, in order to get the work done, to individual initiative. The leader would be in, but not of the group, serving as a catalyzer, always appraising the group's performance but not any individual's. In the other club, policy would be prescribed in directives by the leader. Instead of analyzing the task as a sequence of interdependent steps in a total action and pointing out alternatives of procedure, the leader would prescribe each step by itself and give orders as to the techniques to be used in each. Instead of allowing the members to arrange the work for themselves, he would assign his task to each. Instead of judging the results in terms of the performance of the entire club, he would appraise the work of each individual without relation to the rest.

The experiments were carried through in a room enveloped by a one-way screen. Stationed at strategic points on the translucent side of the screen were four observers with instructions to pay special attention to relations of superior and inferior, if and as any developed during the life of the clubs; to manifestations of positive and continuous concern with the objective task, and conversely to withdrawal from the sabotage of the task; to the formation and role of subgroups in relation to the whole group and its aim; to variations in the intensity and direction of attention and interest. A stenographic record was taken of everything said, and motion pictures were made of activity going on. Each session of the twelve was written up by the leader as soon as it was over. The write up was then analyzed. When the experiment was finished, the whole record was gone over and the findings were checked and rechecked.

This is what emerged:

In the democratically organized club, tension was low, subgroups were stable, the members were concerned about what they were doing and not about themselves and each other. They did not create scapegoats. Such hostility as arises in the nature of things was at a minimum; the conspicuous social fact was the amount of co-operation volunteered, asked for and achieved. Production was more competent; the masks were better made. In the making, initiative and invention were more in evidence. The club had a high morale, a very notable *we-feeling* in virtue of which it was a united and stable organization, each member manifesting a marked concern for the club's possessions and goal. By contrast, the autocratically organized club showed definitely high tensions. Its subgroups were unstable, forming and reforming. Members developed strong self-regarding sentiments, with tendencies to shut out and cut off others. They projected these tendencies especially on two of the group, who became its innocent scapegoats. Indeed there was thirty times as much hostility in this autocratic group than in its democratic peer. Praise, friendliness, co-operation were very noticeably deficient; the work was sloppy and carelessly done; a good deal of it was left unfinished nor did it call out much initiative or invention. The prevalent feeling was *I*, not *We*. The club didn't hang together very well and there was little concern either for its possessions or its purposes. When clubs exchanged members, an individual from the autocratic group, entering the democratic one, changed under the influence of the democratic atmosphere into the likeness of a democrat. The effect was reversed when a democratic individual became a member of the autocratic group.

The experiments were varied and repeated. Later, others were devised to generate an atmosphere of what Lewin called *laisser faire* —grouping without purpose, without plan, without leadership, with consequent slackness, confusion and anarchy, and with achievement even lower than under autocracy. (It was the mistaken identification of progressive education with mere *laisser faire* that led to the justifiable reproaches to progressive education.) The series of experiments confirmed and vindicated the claims made for the discipline of freedom and its record in the institutions of civilization.[7] Later, anthropologists called attention to similar groups with analogous cultures.

The conclusion of the matter seems to be that a discipline of freedom, unlike the disciplines of authority, by providing direction and shape for all a person's powers and passions, absorbs the whole of him in its goings and goals. Authoritarian disciplines reach only parts of him. The residues they drive underground. By inhibiting, suppressing, coercing, condemning, dispositions and interests not gainful of the exclusive authoritarian ends, they split the personality whose submission and obedience they exact. It is in this wise that the corporate economy of industry, with its hierarchies of management and men, have generated the fission between man as producer and man as consumer which makes industrial a schizophrenic civilization. It is in this wise that hierarchical military structure, with its boundaries between officers and men, splits the whole man into soldier and citizen, worker and warrior. It is in this wise that the sacerdotal order disintegrates total personality into god-fearing and sinful parts. It is in this wise that the educational establishments maintain the hierarchical ancient gaps between culture and vocation, that they feed and support the invidious distinction between the liberal education which culture is assumed to consummate, and the vocational training which an occupation crowns. The discipline of freedom reunites what these divide, heals and makes whole what these wound and break into parts. Doctrine to the contrary notwithstanding, such is the record.

---

[7] See K. Lewin, "Experiments on Autocratic and Democratic Atmospheres," *The Social Frontier*, 1938. "An Experimental Approach to the Study of Autocracy and Democracy" (with R. Lippitt) *Sociometry*, I, 1938: "Democracy and the School," *Understanding the Child*, April, 1941; "Dynamics of Group Action," *Educational Leadership*, 1944. All of Lewin's publications converge on the patterns of human relations that might enchannel a discipline of freedom. For a complete bibliography see *Sociometry*, 10, 1, February, 1947.

Book IV

THE LIFE AND LABOR OF THE FREE MAN

Chapter Sixteen

CONSUMPTION AND PRODUCTION IN THE DISCIPLINE OF FREEDOM

The role of the teacher under the discipline of freedom is unprecedented and difficult. As the record shows, it requires of the traditional taskmaster to become a fellow-worker, of the classical pedagogue to become a democratic leader. A teacher can be either. By dissolving hierarchy in fellowship, the discipline of freedom releases the whole of the teacher's personality to her task; her management of her group of learners then calls for a sensitive responsiveness to their characters and capacities that a mere commander—whether the commanded get a "crush" on her or not—can do without. In fact, whatever be its field of action, the power of democratic leadership may be measured by the degree that the interest and feeling of the followers are absorbed by the action; by how far its ends and means, its going and goal, are appreciated as continuously compenetrated and one. Let the action be what you please—making masks, a baseball game, the study of an ancient tongue, the cooking of a meal, the solution of a problem in mathematics, the perfection of a dance, a laboratory experiment, the preparation of a play—we have in the evidence recorded by the Iowa and other studies a sample, a measure and a test of the teacher as leader. Democratic team play ensues whenever she so deals with her pupils that their energies of mind and heart are taken up by the *what* and *how* of their project, while the *who*—even though the team consists of the teacher and but a single pupil—disposes itself according to the requirements intrinsic to the materials and ends of the enterprise. In function the teacher is then actually a team leader; her initiatives set free and heighten the passions and skills of learning; they release the learner into ways of self-direction, self-help and spontaneous co-operation.

These consequences are far from easy, for the pupil as well as the teacher comes to the work with a multiform shell of resistances. In the teacher they are the inertias which lead us humans to find in command or instruction a minimum of trouble joined to a maximum of self-exaltation taking form as a sense of power. That sentiment is often the greater part of her psychic income from the teacher-pupil relation. In the pupils the resistances are usually persistent feelings of infantile dependence and insecurity against which command brings reassurance and obedience safety. These feelings pervade the personality and often hold back the natural self-liberating processes of growth: following a party line, any party line, is so much easier than taking responsibility for a road of one's own. The discipline of freedom brings to learning recognized as natural growth the synergy of the group: it enables freedom and responsibility to develop as actual functions of one another; it makes learning again the consummatory activity it is by nature; it takes study back from the servilities of labor to the liberties of leisure wherein, as Aristotle knew, it first flourished, and thus renders the scholar studying a vocation a freer person than a conventional scholar of the liberal arts.

This is a critical consequence in view of the fact that the great majority of people who pass through our schools are perforce working people; that is, men and women who must earn their livings by means of one or another of the manual arts—machinery renders most clerical occupations manual—and who in all likelihood might not survive unless they did. All that each according to his singularity knows and can do is liquidated in a conceptual composite for which the generic term is *labor*. Modern culture has a great deal to say about "the dignity of labor." Modernity has enveloped the words "worker," "workingman" with a prestige-giving emotional aura in whose glow they stand each a rival of the word "gentleman." Since World War I there is hardly a country on the globe where a new right, "the right to work" is not affirmed and proclaimed, while revolutionary constitutions one after the other are careful to name the right to work among the prescriptive rights of citizens. In the United States, the antithesis to "workingman" is "loafer." Yet the gentleman of leisure is not the same as a loafer. His means of support are somehow "visible"; they are free income on which he can live without working. A loafer, per contra, is a person who would need to be "gainfully employed" yet is not, and has "no visible means of support."

The change of sentiment resulting in the climate of opinion which exalts labor and condemns leisure became noticeable in the eighteenth century. It is exemplified in William Hogarth's comic sequence (*strips* to the modern) entitled *Industry and Idleness*.

These show two youths whose destiny is labor. One pursues the ways of leisure, like a gentleman, drinking, gaming, whoring, spending other people's money and ending on the gallows. The other works hard and long, courts and marries his master's daughter and shares in his master's fortune. This "success story" is protean in its mutations. It had a sort of philosopher in Samuel Smiles, a fabulist in Oliver Optic, and his imitators and adapters have become legion. One variety of the story is exemplified by George Horace Lorimer's *Letters of a Self-Made Merchant to His Son,* and the weekly journal which this writer once edited keeps success stories as perennial contributions to its own success. The blue-shirt figures occasionally but the white-collar sets the standard and provides the pattern. That which is portrayed and exalted is busi-ness as "gainful occupation" absorbing brain and brawn. The dominant personality-image is a composition which fuses the excellence attributed to Henry Ford with the putative virtues of a certain aviator when his public name was "The Lone Eagle." The inwardness of the whole is far less financial than is believed. Its moral is not, *Be smart and you will be rich.* It is an ideal of the rightness of work as work, the faith that being industrious, having a business, is morally worthier than being at leisure and having none. Rousseau gave it the representative eighteenth-century expressions: "To work," he wrote in *Émile,* "is then a duty indispensable to social man. Rich or poor, powerful or weak, every idle citizen is a knave . . . Of all the occupations . . . that which comes closest to the state of nature is manual labor; of all the conditions the most independent of fortune and of men is that of the artisan. The artisan depends only on his labor. He is free—as free as the husbandman is slave, since the latter is dependent on his field. The enemy, the prince, the powerful neighbor may take his field away from him; may harass him on account of it in a thousand ways." The artisan is immune to all that. Not tied to the land, he can pack up and walk away. Let Émile, then, learn a trade. A trade "will give him a rank he cannot lose, a rank which will honor him so long as he lives. . . . It is important to learn a trade, less for the sake of knowing one than for overcoming the prejudices which despise trade." If you don't have to earn a living, "do not work from necessity but work for glory." Twentieth-century Thorstein Veblen brought the whole development to its high place in his *Theory of the*

Leisure Class, with his exaltation of the producer and production and his bitter scorn of the leisured consumer and consumption.

Now what this sequence of events signalizes is in no small degree an infusion of the economy of our civilization with the same sort of transvaluation of values that turned over the political order during the Democratic Revolution. With this event goes another so counter to the central drives of human nature as to bring on and keep up a sort of schizophrenia of both the personal lives and the social arrangements of our industrial civilization.

The combined ideas, the first dignifying labor, raising the workingman to the status of gentleman and labor to a parity with leisure, the second separating the life of man as producer from his life as consumer, give history a new turn. Throughout the millennia of recorded time, the plain people were not free men. They worked but could retain only enough of the product of their work to restore their spent energies and keep them at work. They had no power over their own support. The decision as to when or whether they should labor or not labor or what should be done with the fruits of their labor was not in their own wills but in the will of a landlord, a master or an owner. In the classical civilization from which both the literary and the theological "humanists" of our own time draw their tradition, labor was not held to be worthy of free men. "The dignity of labor" would have been a contradictory phrase to Plato and Aristotle, the thinkers who are taken as the spokesmen for what is best and noblest in that tradition, and whose views and judgments are so powerfully a part of our own living past. In the society for which they spoke, as in every society until our own, the entirely free men were the gentlemen, the men of birth and station, and they were free because they could live their lives without earning their livings. They were free because they were at leisure, and were very busy in their leisure. But their business was not the business of the farmer, the artisan, and the mechanic, earning his living. It was the business of the man who does not need to earn his living—and who is therefore free to perform all functions public and private whereby he could diversify and ennoble his life; free to live more abundantly. Their business was the business of the soldier and the ruler, of the sportsman, the connoisseur, the athlete, the orator and the philosopher. It consisted—Aristotle said it—in the enjoyment of leisure which is better than occupation and is the end, being the practice of the "liberal arts," the achievement of "pleasure, happiness and the delight of living." By contrast, labor, useful or not, is painful, ignoble, inimical to the virtue proper to free men. By contrast, labor is the activity appropriate to slaves; it is a means only, never an end, and its nature is ever to serve leisure. The laborer is a slave by nature, by nature incapable of freedom. The laborer is a tool with life in it, even as a tool is a lifeless slave. The laborer is to be trained in his useful function as an animal is trained or a tool is modeled, and no more. Contrariwise, the education of the free man should not equip him with the servile skills of the artisan, the farmer or the mechanic; it should equip him with the liberal and noble arts. These are arts of consumption, not of production, and the free man is consumer, not producer.

Religion confirmed philosophy in this judgment of the relative values of labor and leisure, of production and consumption. The pagan gods, being free, were at leisure, and their existence was an immortality of free activity with its "pleasure, happiness and delight in living." Aristotle gave this general appreciation of divine existence as consumer existence a philosophical formulation. "God's life in eternity," he wrote, "is that which we enjoy in our best moments, but are unable to possess permanently: its very being is delight." The men who imparted its characteristic shape to the Christian view of human nature and human destiny combined the judgments of classical thought with the implications of certain narratives of the Hebrew Scriptures regarding labor and leisure, consumption and production. It was not, they noted, the six workdays of the creation that the Creator blessed; it was the seventh, the Sabbath, that God blessed and sanctified, "because in it he rested from all his work which God created and made." And heaven, consequently, is one eternal Sabbath. In the life of man, again, it was not in the Garden of Eden that Adam ate his bread in sorrow and earned it in the sweat of his face. God had created Eden to be the happy habitation of the first man and the first woman. The economy of Eden was an economy of abundance, and life in Eden was life without labor, a consumer life, all free activity bringing pleasure, happiness and delight in living. But God had forbidden Adam and Eve to eat of the fruit of the tree of knowledge. Eve, persuaded by the serpent, had eaten, and Adam had followed suit. This disobedience was the original sin. It altered the inward nature of Adam and Eve. And this now corrupted nature of theirs is transmitted to their descendants. And all the generations of man are tainted with it. Because of it God expelled Adam from the abundance and leisure of Eden "to till the ground from whence he was taken." Because of it God laid a curse upon Eve to bring forth her children in sorrow. Because of it God laid a curse upon Adam, to eat his bread in the sweat of his face, to win his bread from a now condemned earth that would bring forth for him "thorns also and thistles."

In sum, labor is a curse, leisure a blessing. Labor is a sentence for sin which we work out on an earth whose abundance had by that sin been corrupted to scarcity. Labor is a consequence of evil, itself an evil, made necessary by sin; labor is the price which most of us pay for survival in a world where we must work or perish. By contrast, leisure is a state of innocence, of the free and joyous functioning of all our powers whereof consists the life more abundant. The good life is not the laborious life but the contemplative life, wherein we may see God and enjoy him forever. The state of labor, thus again, is a state of bondage, the state of leisure is a state of freedom. Production is servility, consumption liberty. Society condemns its criminals to hard labor. "The life of labor," Emerson wrote, "does not make men but drudges. The Farmer is an enchanted Laborer who after toiling his brain out, sacrificing thought, religion, taste, love, hope, courage at the shrine of toil, turns out a bankrupt as well as the merchant. It is time to have the thing looked into and with a transpiercing criticism settled whether life is worth having on such terms."

It is against this judgment of the ages upon the men who labor that the democratic faith revolts, clothing labor with dignity, making employment a right, occupation a supreme good and work a beatitude. The principles that also the workingman must be a free man, that the dignity of labor is nobler than the dignity of leisure derive from the democratic faith whose basic articles are those of the Declaration of Independence.

These principles however, do not contradict the traditional religious and humanist conception of the relation of leisure to labor, of consumer to producer. They confirm the conception, but they reject its traditional application. They refuse to confine it to the small numbers of men and women who from the beginning of civilization were, because of birth or station or other forms of privilege, free to live their lives without needing to earn their livings. They purposefullly extend it to the great multitudes of human beings who are cut off from living any life because nothing of their lifetime is spared from earning a living. They affirm that the workingman, no less than the gentleman, is a consumer by nature; that his natural goal is leisure, not labor; freedom, not bondage; that he becomes a producer by necessity and that he strives all his life to unshackle himself from this necessity. Else, why the struggle to devise "labor-saving" devices? Why the honor and gratitude to inventors of such devices? Why not leisure-saving devices? Why the efforts of labor unions ever to raise wages and reduce hours, that is, to increase leisure and the possibility of consumption?

Indeed, whatever may be a modern man's professions regarding "the dignity of labor," his practices confirm the judgment passed upon it by both the humanities and the religions of our civilization. As he contrasts labor to leisure, he likewise contrasts play and sport to work, art to industry, creation to production, profession to occupation, culture to vocation. Leisure, play, sport, art, creation, profession, are free activities, whose ends are in themselves. Their orchestration is culture. Labor, work, industry, production, occupation, are means; they are exertions toward an end other than themselves, qualified by fatigue and pain, and endured not for what they are but alone for what they bring. Their apex is vocation. Now the expression, "gentleman of culture and refinement" is a commonplace of usage, but say "workingman of culture and refinement" and you cause surprise if not shock. Cultural activities are consummatory activities. They are the traditional means and matter of a liberal education, that is an education "befitting a free man." The liberal arts were originally only the trivium and quadrivium. They were three arts of speech and four arts of contemplation: grammar and logic and rhetoric; arithmetic and geometry and music and astronomy. These were the arts which classical Rome held appropriate to the education of its free men. To them Renaissance humanism joined the famous humanities of the now great tradition. They compose the classical equipment that is often deprecated as "useless knowledge." They are sharply contrasted with the useful knowledge which equips a worker to practice a trade. We speak of *educating* in the liberal arts, of *training* in the practical. The student of the college of liberal arts having his bachelor's degree, may afterward immerse himself in business or industry, but by and large, he enters the society of heads, managers, bosses, and his work does not carry the stigma of servility which attaches to working with the hands. Social convention approves his occupation as free activity: appraises it as consummatory. The youth with vocational training, starting on his first job, enters into the society of hands, of labor force, of employees, of producers of a product to which they stand as means. The multitudes of them go to work not because they want to, but because they must. Like the heads, they were not born to work. They were born to live, and first and last, living is consuming.

This observation regards the innermost nature of the human creature. It embodies the truth about all the freedoms he gropes after and labors for to the end of his days. We are born consumers and consumers we remain all our lives. But in most of us, the society we live in overlays the consumer we are born as by the producer it compels us to become. By original nature, consumers, and producers only by nurture, nevertheless we must, most of us, produce or perish. Not many may all their lives consume without producing, while too many must all their lives produce without consuming, produce, consuming only enough to keep them producing. And every soul of those unfree multitudes dreams of the day when he may be purely a consumer again; every soul struggles to be freed of the chain gang of production in which survival shackles him.

Imagine the years of any such man who must earn his living, as he spends it from the cradle to the grave. When a babe in arms he produces nothing. He is absolutely a consumer. He is fed, clothed, sheltered, amused and defended. His needs are served, his wishes gratified, his activities encouraged and praised. He is protected from the consequences of his mistakes. His life is the life of Riley. He grows into childhood living his life without needing to earn his living. As his powers develop his environment is enlarged, his opportunities are multiplied. He goes to school, to the ball game, the church, the dance and so on. Then perhaps at the age of fourteen or fifteen this carefree consummatory daily life of his stops. The fourteen year old must now earn his living. He gets a job on a farm, in a factory, in a shop. He spends his day repeating a few single, simple actions in which his work consists. If he wishes to continue doing the things he had been doing before he was required to earn his living, he must do them at night. His existence, which had been one and whole is now split in two. He has a day life in which he earns his living; he has a night life in which he lives his life.

This boy is, almost, Everyboy. There are, we know, a more fortunately placed few who do not need to become workingmen at fourteen. They are not called upon to earn their livings. In high school, in college, they continue to live their lives. Tradition allows them certain privileges, certain liberties, which constitute "college life." They are liberties and privileges analogous to those enjoyed by gentlemen of leisure everywhere in the world. They are the liberties and privileges of infancy: not to be held accountable for violations of the adult social code; to consume without producing, food, clothing, shelter; to engage in sports and play and every sort of free activity, without any splitting into day life and night life. But if, when they are graduated, they also must devote their days to earning a living, then they, too, can have only a few hours of night for the free activities to which, in school and college, they could give their days. For them, too, night becomes the time for living, day for only earning a living. During the day they are but producers, working for money. At night they are consumers, converting the price of their labor into goods and services which nourish and please the body, which exercise, enlarge and delight the mind.

Day life is the means, night life is the end.

The farmer, for example, is often envied on the ground that he lives a more natural life than does the factory hand. A man's life is natural when what he does to earn his living and what he does to live his life are not separate, but flow together in such a way that the freedom and the pleasure of night life are felt in the labors of day life, and the satisfactions of consumption are enjoyed in the activities of production. A life is natural when its means and its ends flow together in such a way that even though they are distinct, they are not different. A life is natural when work yields the same feeling as play, and play is as productive as work. A life is natural when production and consumption flow together and are not to be separated.

Thus it is not natural, either to eat to live or to live to eat. It is natural to enjoy living as eating, and to take delight in eating as living. Rightly or wrongly, the farmer's existence is supposed to possess this naturalness. Yet his life too divides into day life and night life. By his work on the farm he is engaged in earning his living. Most of what he produces—let it be grain, or cotton, or milk, or fruit, or vegetables—he produces, not to consume for himself, but to sell to others for money. With this money he buys, of course, the tools and materials which he has used up as producer and which he must replace if he is to continue producing. But if those were all his money could buy, he would indeed be no more than a tool with life in it. To be a free man, he must be able to exchange his money, not for producer goods only, but for consumer goods, material and spiritual: not only for work clothes, but leisure clothes—clothes for church, for parties, for political meetings; not only for a farm truck but a passenger car; not only for manuals on farming, but for newspapers, magazines, books, radio, an occasional motion picture, a play or concert; for something to risk on the races, at checkers or at bridge; or a baseball game; for hunting and fishing in the season; not only for good barns, but for a good school and good teachers for his children; for a well-built, well-appointed house with adequate plumbing and heating and good furniture to be his home.

Obviously, a farmer's interests as a consumer are many and varied in kind and quality, his interests as a producer are of one kind and few. Yet as a rule, his mind and heart are concentrated on the narrow arts of production. From sunrise to sunset, and beyond, he performs his backbreaking labors for money to spend; and he joins with other farmers in order to buy his producers' goods as cheaply and to sell his product as dearly as possible. Then when he has his money, he, for the most part, continues to leave the art of spending and using, which is the art of consumption, to shift for itself. Through his working day, from morning till noon, from noon to night, our farmer burns up his energies in his hard labor. When he stops for lunch, the food he eats is merely so many calories of fuel which his working oxidized into fatigue products and which his meal replaces. He bolts his bread and meat and pie; he gulps his coffee; he snatches his smoke. He is scarcely aware how his food has tasted. He has no effective interest in how his food has tasted. He has no effective interest in how it was served. The food only stokes the labor-expending animal engine, restoring its "horse-power." It does not nourish the human being.

For the human being cares about exactly those qualities which the animal engine, the labor-expending organism, the wage-earning or profit-seeking producer must needs disregard. But the laborer, the producer, is not freed to be a man again until the day is done and the day's work is over. In this respect, the factory worker is far worse off than the farmer. His life is far more unnatural. Let us recall that on the job he is not a man with a proper name but a "hand" with a number; that his work is not varied like the farmer's nor does he have the mobility of the farmer; that his tools are not moveable like the awl of the shoemaker or the needle of the tailor, which those craftsmen take up or put down at will. We have seen that it is the "hand" which is moveable, and attached to a stationary machine like any other attachable and detachable gadget. If that man is a tailor who makes a whole suit of clothes, and that man is a shoemaker who makes a whole pair of shoes, the factory worker is neither a tailor nor a shoemaker. For the act of making suits or shoes is divided into a great number of separate operations, with one worker to repeat each operation endlessly throughout the working day. In terms of a whole suit or a whole pair of shoes, it is the factory that is the tailor, the shop that is the shoemaker. In terms of the whole product the operative is only one-fiftieth or one-hundreth of a shoemaker or a tailor. The operative's lunch, even more than the farmer's is a replacement of burnt up calories, not the gratification of a human being's hunger. It stokes the animal engine, it does not feed a man with a heart and a mind.

But finally, like the farmer's, the factory hand's workday ends. Here they are now, the farmer and the factory worker, released from being producers earning their livings, free to be the consumers they were born as, living their lives. They clean up. They wash away, so far as they can, the marks of their producer day. They put off their labor clothes and put on their leisure clothes. By contrast, they now move without haste and speak without strain. The supper they sit down to may consist of exactly the same dishes they ate at noon. But their food is not now just so many hundreds of calories to be swallowed but not savored. It is now an exciting and delightful combination of sights and flavors and scents and textures. The cloth it is laid on, garnished perhaps, with flowers, the dishes it is served on, the knives and forks and spoons it is taken with, feed the eye and the hands with sight and touch as much as the fragrance, the taste, the chewing and digesting please the palate and comfort the body. Communion with others, table talk, music or news on the radio, may accompany the meal. Compared with the noonday event, this meal is eaten without haste, lingeringly, and the qualities of each dish may be discussed like the contents of a good book, or the events of an exciting game or movie or play.

This is how we take our meals as human beings, that is, as consumers. And significantly, both the physiologist and the psychologist advise us that in taking our meals thus, we not only do not diminish, we heighten the caloric or producer value of our nourishment. But we are free to eat thus only at night and perhaps on Sundays, when we are at leisure. The waking hours that remain are taken up similarly by actions which farmer and worker perform for the fun of it, freely because they want to, not necessarily because they have to. They may read, or sing or play cards or play billiards, or go bowling or attend a movie or a concert or a lodge meeting or a church social or a political rally or they may go shopping for clothes or baseballs or shotguns or boxing gloves. Whatever they do, they will be spending the money they earned as producers, and in spending they will be doing those many different things for the sake of which they labor monotonously to produce one thing; they will be living their lives.

Here, then, in the splitting of existence into the day life of earning and the night life of living is the schizophrenia of our age. That it is evil nobody will deny. The question is rather, is it, like labor, necessary evil? Can the values of leisure be infused into labor, the goods of consumption into production? Or must art and industry, play and work, culture and vocation, be forever considered so put asunder by God that no man can join them together?

Our original nature is consummatory. Our spontaneous energies are energies of consumption. Every hour of the day these impulsions, coerced and hemmed in by the necessities of earning a living, break through or overflow those necessities and at one time or another become momentarily identical with them. After all, the same psychosomatic personality and its organs, that it employs in the skills of earning, function also in the arts of living. The different modes of association and action that producer and consumer stand for have an identical individual for their human term. Whether as producer or as consumer, the individual functions, the individual expends his vital energies. The fact that we use two words for this expenditure and not one, that consumer has somehow come to denote intake and producer output, misleads the mind. To eat may mean in fact to burn up more food calories than are swallowed down. Games and sports can be far more dangerous, exhausting and painful than many hazardous occupations. Playing requires the identical nerves and muscles we employ in working, and similar skills. The difference resides not in the nature of an activity. The difference resides in its gradient and goal. Production is appraised as required and planned procedure ending in a product; consumption is appraised as spontaneous activity, intent on itself as a process. The producer's worth is not a function of the process but of the product; and since industrial men and women are attachments to the processing machinery, they cease to be individual personalities and become generalized labor. Production, as we have already noted, involves depersonalization while consumption stays ineluctably personal. Expending, and in expending, expressing or restoring a human being's spontaneous energies, consumption, unlike production, not only uses them, it uses them up. It is an end-term and the last word about anything is said by its "ultimate consumer." We neither think nor speak of an ultimate producer. The folkways and mores assimilate pleasure and delight to consumption, but pay little attention to the pains and pangs which are also intrinsic to it. For the hurt of them is also consummatory, and without masochism. Hurt is consummatory whenever it occurs in the course of a free activity whose values are first and last process and not product, whose product is the process, producing more of itself.

Any work a human being performs may be thus free, whether he works alone or with others. Whatever a person is busy about, it can channel his manipulative propensities or instinct of workmanship. "I am convinced both by faith and experience," wrote Henry Thoreau, "that to maintain oneself on this earth is not a hardship but a pastime, if we would live simply and wisely; as the pursuits of the simple nations are still the sports of the artificial. It is not necessary that a man should earn his living by the sweat of his brow, unless he sweats easier than I do." "The truly efficient laborer," he says in another place, "will not crowd the day's work but will saunter to his task, surrounded by a wide halo of ease and leisure, and then do but what he loves best. Let a man take time enough for the most trivial deed, though it be but the paring of his nails." Thoreau is speaking of the consummatory personal conversion of work into play and labor into leisure, which we call craftsmanship or artistry. Where the work is team play, the discipline of freedom accomplishes the same result and the mechanical division of labor is converted into the free union of men by the sharing of plans, purposes, skills and knowledges. When work has been transposed into play or industry into art the event is signalized by the confirming reaction. Observers get the impression of a heightened general intelligence, for as we have seen, intelligence also responds to emotional climate and can on occasion be as contagious as courage and infectious as hope.

Now that assimilation of labor to leisure and production to consumption, wherein must consist the healing of our communal schizophrenia, is a task of which the first phase falls peculiarly in the field of education. It is not a task, however, that educators recognize, not to say give thought to. Since we are all by nature consumers, the Joneses, whom the multitudes who must work without living choose to emulate, are the élite of "culture and refinement" who can live without working. This is why the new rich become patrons of the arts and protectors of artists, build palaces and collect objects of "virtue." Here is why the schools pay continual tribute to this keeping up with those Joneses, why they hold up "the liberal education" of tradition as the measure of excellence. However piously the dignity of labor may be preached, the dignity of leisure is the dignity prized and adored. However idleness may be deprecated and busi-ness approved, everybody who works hopes a time will come when he can live without working, when he can savor his culture and not sweat his vocation.

Here again the trend of the schools of democracy has been willy-nilly counter to the intent of democracy.

Chapter Seventeen

OF CULTURE AND VOCATION

If it is true that necessity is the mother of invention, it is even truer that invention is the mother of necessity. To a Chinese coolie, a Hindu untouchable, or a Soviet peasant, an American unskilled laborer's necessities would be luxuries. The luxuries of that same blue-shirt are often easily the necessities of his white-collar neighbor, and so onward and outward to the necessities of a tycoon with a city house and a country house, mediaeval tapestries or Renaissance paintings, half-a-dozen motor cars, and far more shirts and shoes and suits of costly fabrics and costlier fabrication than he could in fact use up in a long life. Luxury and necessity are variables that change with the state of the industrial arts. These arts alter with every application of the multiplying natural sciences to harnessing the forces of nature up to the service of man. These sciences are our knowledge of nature. Their application is our industrial establishment. Its judgments, tools and skills compose our industrial arts, and their state consists in the degree of refinement and the range and level of effectiveness to which they have been brought. For the most part the state is transitional, not static, always being varied by discovery, by invention, and by the new knowledge and new skills those generate. Discovery, invention, knowledge, skills, together with the tools they energize, join up into the machinery which embodies man's creative intelligence. Lacking them, millennia of generations succeeded each other as but dependent creatures of a world not made for them, passively adapting to its harsh unalterable substances and its heedless intractable seasons. Then came the time when man began to see, and became able to measure the chemic potencies of substance and the astral mechanics of the seasons. He transposed the ancient "mysteries" of his handicrafts into the patent sciences of machine industry. He found himself able to alter the inalterable and bend or neutralize the intractable. He could not only provide himself with seasonal goods out of season; he could find water without prayer, and scatter natural darkness without recourse to supernatural aid. He could build himself a winter in the midst of summer and a summer in the midst of winter. He could transvalue the land and the water and the air from hard natural environments into plastic natural resources. On a breath-taking scale he could transmute the wastes of nature into the wealth of man.

It is the state of the industrial arts which sustains all the difference there is between this waste and this wealth. These arts are the energies of the changing relations between labor and leisure, production and consumption, vocation and culture. They are the reason for the fact that three-quarters of the Americans "gainfully employed" occupy themselves with interpersonal service, and that while only the remaining quarter labor at material production, they yet produce enough to provide for all our material needs at home and to leave a surplus for export abroad.

That this abundance has come with a dehumanizing division of labor, that its ample provisions are not well distributed, that "one-third of the nation" still live at far less than the minimum of "the American standard of living" is another story. The relevant consequence here is the re-enforcement which the sciences and arts, whereby modern man transvalues luxuries into necessities, bring to the champions of the traditional liberal education in their fight against these very arts and sciences. For insofar as the industrial arts enable more and more people to live above the level of subsistence, they render striving to be as good as one's betters a practicable thing. And since the betters are customarily distinguished as beneficiaries of "liberal education," it is this liberal education that people emulatively acknowledge as the most desirable. Graduates of colleges of liberal arts enjoy, among other "collegiate" Americans, not only a certain prestige which is more or less unaffected by other sources of prestige. They are also presumed to have acquired and absorbed "culture"; that is, the curriculum of accomplishments which the folkways continue to attribute to the wellborn and wealthy. They are supposed to have come to know and understand "the great books," and to have mastered the arts of reading, writing and speaking well. They are supposed to have received through the "great books" a knowledge of *the* truth; that is, philosophical, if not theological information, which, being truth, is "everywhere the same." This knowledge, at the same time, is expected to have nothing in common, even when it consists of the arts of communication, with the principles and practices of the industrial arts. Although everywhere the same, it is peculiarly a personal possession consisting of "true and deeply held convictions about the nature of man, the ends of life, the purpose of the state and the order of goods." To receive these doctrines requires undergoing a discipline wherein the freedom of the free man is made perfect, and his person whole. The missioners of this ideal of acculturation look back to Aristotle, sometimes via St. Thomas. Recall that the *paideia* or culture for which Aristotle spoke held the industrial arts in low esteem. Aristotle called them servile and unfitted to the dignity of a free man. He could not admit their practitioners to be citizens, since civic virtue requires leisure, that "first principle of all action, better than occupation, and the end." Farmers, moneylenders and traders, artisans and all others who work with their hands for pay, do that which would be vulgar and degrading in a free man. If the latter were to occupy himself with such activities, even in study, he must do so *en amateur,* for the fun of it. Let him do so for money, or as a service to others, and the action becomes "menial and servile." Fundamentally, the implication is, of course, that whatever a person may be busy about, the business befits a free man if it is consummatory, an end in itself and not merely a means to other ends. But Aristotle was not concerned to teach the laborious multitudes that liberty begins and ends in the primacy of the consumer; he was concerned simply to keep it beyond their ken. And although disputed, his class prejudices remained the principles of education until the Democratic Revolution.

Their basic illogic and inhumanity has, however, been exposed every so often throughout the ages, and by perceptive men and women who had themselves received their invidious advantages. We have already seen how the generous Condorcet dealt with them, at the very beginning of the Democratic Revolution. Let us now look at the judgment of a man of the Renaissance, of the generation to whom the *nachlass* of classical antiquity was still a vital liberating power and who felt themselves actually freer men by virtue of the humanities. The man is Francis Bacon. However logicians, moralists and men of letters may judge him, he had a long experience of the impact of the new learning and the old on his own spirit, and on the hearts and minds of the Elizabethans among whom he was a signal figure. He was in a position to consider and to appraise them, which their protagonists of the twentieth century may envy but can assume only by getting themselves born in his time. He set down his judgments in Latin as well as in English, and his *Essays,* his *Advancement of Learning,* his *Novum Organum,* his *New Atlantis* repeat them variously for the generations to come.

If the world in which men find themselves is to yield them a good life, Bacon held, they must know what it is, but even more, how it works. It is in knowledge that mankind comes to its humanity, and its career from the beginning of history has been a career of knowledge. In the making of this career, it is the ancients who are its childhood and youth, it is the present generation who are its manhood. To take the ancients for old and their successors for young is like taking a man's infancy for his old age and his old age for his infancy. Beside the men of earlier times, we are the ancients. But as regards the arts of knowing, mankind have merely prolonged their infancy, indoctrinating the present with what had been held for true and right by the past. They have valued knowledge as a bed to rest on, a terrace to view the scene from, a tower to raise one above one's fellows, a fort to fight from, or shop to profit from. So, they have molded the body of knowledge into a temple of idols differing as the sources of its material differ. Many are idols of the tribe—reshapings and distortions of the deliverances of experience by our senses and appetites and passions that tend ever to shut out what is not agreeable, to accept what agrees, and seek to impose their own quality on everything. Many are idols of the cave. Their stuff is drawn from the singularity of our personal beings as that is altered by accident, training or habit, distorting the given to conformation or unlikeness as interest blindly requires. Many are idols of the market place. They are the figures which words have shaped; the colorings wherewith words so tint reason that the sciences and philosophies of which they are the vehicles are made sophistical and inactive. Finally, there are the numerous idols of the theatre—the sophistical, empiric, superstitious philosophical systems past and present that disregard experience, hardly consider experiment, but build upon perverted rules of demonstration that "fashions a world out of categories." "For the wit and mind of man, if it work upon matter . . . worketh according to the stuff, and is limited thereby; but if it work upon itself, as the spider worketh his web, then it is endless, and brings forth indeed cobwebs of learning, admirable indeed for the fineness of thread and work, but of no substance or profit."

Thus, knowing is either an autonomous activity like a spider's spinning his web, or such a passional distortion of things and their ways, as to enfold them all in the misleading disguises of our fantasy. The knowledge we so pride ourselves on is merely delicate, or fantastic, or contentious. Delicate knowledge is the body of accomplishments that mark the gentleman and courtier; it is the outcome of concern with *litterae humaniores* and the liberal arts. It is to the mind what court dress is to the body—decorative, ceremonial, ostentatious, a mode of what Veblen called conspicuous consumption. Fantastic knowledge is not so much personal accomplishment as personal pretension to power over nature. Bacon says that it apes true knowledge: magic, alchemy and astrology are its outstanding representatives. Contentious knowledge is even more personal in its pretensions than the fantastic. Its purpose is power over men. Its method of getting that power is the scholastic procedure, as that implements or modifies the logic of Aristotle. Assuming that the mind already possesses but is not aware of the universal truth of reason and nature, the contentious man undertakes to elicit it dialectically and to compel others to accept it by demonstrative proof or by his powers of persuasion. He is concerned only with the already-known and the ready-made. His aprioris rule out discovery and invention. Yet the apriori is the father of lies. With all its prestige, it cannot reach to the causes of things, although "it is a correct position that true knowledge is a knowledge of causes." With the apriori the contentious man may win an argument, but cannot control an event. It is rather a weapon of what Veblen called exploit, like a duelist's sword, and the causes that it emphasizes, those "barren virgins," the final causes, corrupt rather than advance the sciences.

In sum, the humanities and the liberal arts, the crafts of magic and disputation, are gentlemanly activities, cultivated modes of behavior using up the energies of a virtuoso, whose vocation is his culture, and whose product is his prestige, not his power. This prestige is his power in so far as it affects other men; and the skills that sustain it impose their authority by their appearance, not by their performance. They are completely consummatory. If man depended on this kind of knowledge alone, he would long have

perished from the earth. But this kind of knowledge has ever been
mixed into another kind of knowledge, to which it in fact owes
much of its prestige, and whose credit it appropriates. This is the
despised and menial knowledge which the workman gathers like
a bee by laboring with things. It is the knowledge which is truly
power. Men win it when the mind so tries things that its experiments will bring to light the operative causes of which their stuff
and form are the effects. Natural philosophy is this other knowledge. This, says Bacon, "is not yet to be found unadulterated, but
is impure and corrupted by logic in the school of Aristotle; by
natural theology in that of Plato; by mathematics in the second
school of Plato (that of Proclus and others) which ought rather to
terminate natural philosophy than to generate and create it."

Bacon wants to say goodbye to all that. No democrat, he nevertheless is disillusioned with the aristocratic personality and its
relation to mankind. He is sure that the function of knowledge is
not the exhibition of either accomplishments or prowess but the
service of man. He is sure that only the knowledge which is power
over nature can render this service and cause the earth to yield to
mankind the good life that they all seek. Against the subjective
self-assurance and certainty which men draw from the delicate, the
fantastic and the contentious, Bacon matches the objective certainty
and assurance they could draw, world without end, from the power
of truth discovered by successful inquiry into the causes of things.
The Salomon's House, of his *New Atlantis,* is in no way a model
of what scientific enterprise has grown into today, yet the House's
purpose and perspectives are the purpose and perspectives of that
enterprise: "The ends of our foundation is the knowledge of the
causes and secret motions of things, and the enlarging of the
bounds of human empire to the effecting of all things possible."

Since Bacon's times, the Western world has gone far on the road
to the knowledge which is power, and those who have it receive
some of the envy and admiration which we give to power-holders
of any kind. But they are still far from being accepted as the ultimate Joneses of the emulative globe. Fundamentally, to the countless multitudes who must work without living the denumerable
élite who can live without working remain the Joneses, since their
state endows them with the leisure, liberty and well-being which
all men, being consumers by nature and producers by necessity,

crave from birth to death. The arts and sciences of the delicate, the fantastic and the contentious embody the traditional satisfaction of those emulative cravings. Although the fantastic, displaced by the sciences of nature, has passed from the purviews of the secular educational establishments, the delicate and the contentious hold the field. And they represent also the preferred disciplines of the new educational enterprises of the trades-union movement, and of private undertakings in adult education. In those establishments, too, the "fine" arts are segregated from and exalted over the "industrial" and "commercial," and "culture" is preferred over "vocation." Studies which are undertaken in order to remedy a defect, or to learn a trade, or to improve a skill have not the prestige of those which communicate knowledge and judgment of the arts, of letters, of philosophic systems and dialectic skills. The latter are culture, the former are vocation. The wall that keeps them apart is as old as human education. Its architect, indeed, is man's own innermost nature. It is the primacy and ultimacy of the consumer in him. This it is which leads every man to appreciate productive labor as the curse of God, fitting for menials and slaves, while consummatory leisure is the providential endowment of men noble and free. This keeps education always *either* "cultural" *or* "vocational"; it attributes the creative impulse only to the liberal arts, and transfers the instinct of workmanship from the industries and trades where it is in fact operative to the otiose disciplines where it can only make believe. Even where the power-holders have imposed the dogma that the word "worker" shall carry all the connotations usually attached to the word "gentleman," the same thing holds. So the Soviets, having concentrated all their powers of military and moral policing to imposing the dogma that labor is more worthy than leisure and production than consumption, have reduced the people of Russia to a servility beyond that of Czarist times. "The worker," wrote André Gide, in his *Retour de U.S.S.R.*, "is at the bottom of a highly stratified hierarchy . . . (He) adjusts to changes he does not initiate . . . I doubt whether we can find any other country, including Hitler Germany, where the spiritual life is less free, more subservient, terrorized, servile."

Can one deny, then, the springs in human nature of the principles and program of those who would give primacy to cultural education? I do not think so. It is not their ends any would-be educator of free men need quarrel with. It is the means they propose to gain those ends. Because the means require maintaining and fortifying the wall between culture and vocation, perpetuating the hierarchical stratification of the occupations and professions, the means would merely defeat the ends they are declared to serve. It is only as culture and vocation can be compenetrated, so that there shall be no vocation without culture and no culture without vocation that the schools can educate free men for a free society. It is only if they accept the different occupations of men with the same democratic faith they are presumed to accept their persons, that they can bring to event the task of democratic education as Condorcet defined this task: to vindicate the equality of the different, in dignity, excellence and worth, thus making real the political equality ordained by the laws.

Can the schools do this?

Seeking an answer, let us look a bit at the mutations of the idea of culture since Bacon's day. He himself used the word both literally and analogically. In *Sylva Sylvarum* he uses "culture" literally, in the sense of tillage and growing of crops; he notes that certain stands of wheat were slower than "the ordinary wheat of itself, and this culture did rather retard than advance them." In *The Advancement of Learning* his use of "culture" is analogical. Concerned with the consequences of education, he writes: "The culture and manurance of minds in youth hath such a forcible (though unseen) operation as hardly any length of time or contention of labour can countervail it afterwards." Here culture already denotes the planned and purposeful formation of the mind. It carries the meaning which became dominant during the nineteenth century.

Cicero had used the word in that denotation, and the usage recurred intermittently among the Western peoples from his day on. During the Renaissance, wherever monarch and populace came to a certain positive community of interest, and increasing autocracy deprived feudal noblemen of even their hypothetical functions in society, culture became, as we have already observed, a matter of prime courtly importance. The change tended to demote the vocation of arms from an obligation of subjects into an occupation of mercenaries; it disemployed the landed noble without impoverishing him. It left him with time on his hands and rents in his purse; and on his lands, no place to spend them. So he went to town, and he went to court. He became a courtier, learned in displaying the courtly accomplishments. Instruction in these accomplishments is the cultivation of the courtier, and the aspiration of the *bourgeois gentilhomme*. Presumably, whatever it makes of the latter, it makes of the former the "gentleman of culture and refinement." Baldasare Castiglione's *Book of the Courtier* describes what that is and how a gentleman born is thus acculturated. It repristinates the ancient inwardness of the aristocrat's liberal education: training to perfection in certain skills of consumption, the skills of the swordsman, the wordsman, the lover and connoisseur of aesthetic and philosophical good things called "the humanities" uncontaminated by any of the productive arts and crafts.

Among the English, Bacon's criticism had little influence. Courts and colleges continued on their delicate and contentious ways. In 1630 Peacham produced a version of the ideal as *The Compleat Gentleman*. In 1631 Braithwait followed with *The Compleat Gentlewoman*. Every generation produced its own renewal to this day. Each also had its renewal of Bacon's judgment, which has been variously repeated. Jean Jacques Rousseau's discussion of the relation of human nature to social privilege is such a repetition. His discourse on the arts and the sciences argues that their cultivation, instead of bettering, corrupted the natural virtue of human beings. Three years later, his discourse of inequality points out how much is artificial and unnatural in the prevailing culture. His *Nouvelle Heloise* pleaded for that different way of life which he called "natural" in contrast to the cultured, with its invidious distinctions, its insincerities and artificialities. The natural man to Rousseau was the honest, the sincere, the self-supporting and self-ruling citizen, the man whose practices expressed his principles and whose principles were those of a liberty-loving member of a free society, as, of course Rousseau conceived of free society. Opinion to the contrary notwithstanding, Rousseau did not mean by his "return to nature" abandoning culture. He meant man's perfection of his natural being by means of culture. "Man," he wrote, in *Nouvelle Heloise*, "is too noble a being to be obliged to serve simply as an instrument for others, and should not be employed at what he is fit for, without also taking into account what is fit for him; for men are not made for their stations, but their stations for men." He makes this idea explicit in *Émile,* which is a plea for an education aiming at naturalness within civilization. Significantly, the argument focuses this naturalness in the growing child's *vocation,* in its life-work and career, its art and their correlative sciences. Learning this *what* and those *hows* called for methods of instruction no less natural; methods contrasting sharply with those prevalent at the time. Pestalozzi and Froebel, who endeavored by applying, to transvalue the constructions of Rousseau from a set of sentiments into an educational program, were no democrats. They nevertheless built their plans of teaching upon vital economy instead of architectonic doctrine; they gave food, clothing, shelter, defense against enemies and disease an educational importance which the dominant "liberal" education never did. These were the plain man's whole habitation, and they provided only the ground and cellars of the courtier's dwelling.

And not, as we know, of the courtier's alone. Of everybody's who could make himself rich enough to live at leisure, without labor. Merchants, artisans and craftsmen everywhere sought the culture in virtue of which they could feel themselves to be as good as their betters: Moliere's gentleman-cit is still representative. Where their wealth exceeded their vital and vocational needs to grow, it was expended on the fine arts and liberal disciplines: the culture of the free cities emulated the culture of the courts. Although they added values singular to themselves, the "merchant princes," the "great bourgeois," and the little as well, of Holland or England or Germany paid the noble courts of Madrid or Paris or Rome the compliments of sincerest flattery. In Germany, moreover, where a sort of renaissance grew and spread during the late eighteenth and early nineteenth centuries, a new philosophy appeared, rationalizing and justifying the cultural event. At a time when in France, in England and in the American colonies of Britain the social trend was toward participation by more and more of the governed in the liberties and responsibilities of governing, rule in German states became, if anything, more autocratic. Richer than many of the wellborn, but with worth-while military and political careers not available for their leisure, thus, on the loose in their communities, German cits turned, each according to his desire, for self-realization and personal fulfillment to the arts and the sciences. Freedom became their word to conjure with and *Kultur* came to designate for them the body and soul of freedom. The courtly military and churchly establishments which shut these commoners out from equal participation, they transvalued dialectically into mere tools and vehicles of self-expression and self-aggrandizement. The individual, the person in his singularity, blown up into a world-soul or Ego, was presented as the sole real existence, sometimes as Will, sometimes as Feeling, sometimes as Reason, "positing the non-Ego" and playing a game with itself according to rules of its own devising. Its freedom was identified with the playing and the rules, which consequently had to be absolute, spiritual, eternal and universal.

The ultimate logic of this philosophy of freedom ended in a paradox which Hegel consummated. But it was intrinsic to the way of thinking. For, of course in the world of appearance, of time and space and the economies of hunger, love, and war, of play and sport and thought, each Ego had a different incarnation, a different vocation and a different history carrying all the felt and recorded distinctions between person and person, and each person had to accept that totality, and submit to its authority. His individual liberty was transcendental, not ciscendental; only absolute, not relational. Hence as a living man of flesh and bone, he was merely secondary and derivative. Whatever personal reality he had was not cause but effect; as actual existence, nothing.

However, this romantic transvaluation of the initial romantic rebellion into romantic submission was a long time coming. It was subsequent to the tremendous upheavals following the Democratic Revolution. It voiced the victory of Europe's ancient regime over Napoleon. In its first mood it had the solipsism of the socially detached and spiritually uprooted. It is manifest in the earliest phases of Fichte's expression. As a young philosopher passionate about freedom, he affirmed that culture consists in "the exercise of all a man's powers toward complete freedom as a goal"; that what occurs in our experience is valuable only as it figures in culture, and that the task of the state is to enable the individual to achieve complete freedom. The poet Schiller found the goal of culture in *die schöne Seele,* the spirit which fuses *anmuth* or grace with *würde* or duty. A man of culture so orchestrates beauty with duty, obligation with delight, that the conflict between means and ends is resolved in the harmony of his personality. But the most eloquent prophet of culture as the vocation of man, was the poet Goethe, whose *Faust* is the classical revelation of romantic libertarianism. The individual, Goethe wrote a Swiss friend, is ineffable. His destiny is *sich bilden,* that is, to cultivate his selfhood by reaching out to "the highest" and best. This is to be found in the achievement of the Greek spirit; to recover it, to possess it, to utter it is to achieve culture. So, the career of Faust is largely shaped by his quest of Helena; in Arcadia where at long last he lives wed to her only to lose her, he comes as near as may be to the perfection of the gentleman of culture and refinement.

The German word is, of course, *Kultur,* and for what the young Fichte and Schiller and Goethe had in mind, the English word *culture* did well enough. But *Kultur* had a career of its own in Germany which renders English culture its contrary in spirit and purpose. In the course of a century the meaning of *Kultur* became one with the ideas of racism, totalitarianism, frightfulness, and youthfulness as such. These not only make it untranslatable by culture, they also set it at the opposite pole of the urbanities, the reasonableness and tolerance of civilization. As Spengler used the term, civilization was the old age and *Kultur* was the youth of a racial life cycle.

In the English-speaking world meanwhile, Matthew Arnold's employment of culture gained such prestige as to make this meaning very hard to change. The occasion of his use was John Bright's praise of the United States as a land where liberty, democracy and education flourished. To this Arnold retorted in effect that Americans were not the Joneses the British should keep up with. They were merely provincials; they were merely Philistines. They put all their stress on machinery and were heedless of culture. They were unable to see life steadily and see it whole. They lacked understanding of perfection. They could realize the piecemeal material externalities of life but had no sense of spiritual inwardness, and no idea of the all-sided development of the whole man which is culture. Their fractionated concerns made but for spiritual anarchy. Culture is a progression in "harmonious self-development;" we men of culture have attained "sweetness and light," by "the acquainting ourselves with the best that has been known and said in the world, and thus with the history of the human spirit." And strangely enough, the best knowers-and-sayers seem agreed that this best is "the glory that was Greece," Faust's

Helena and the Hellenism of whose beauty and excellence she is the eternal symbol. It is this, signalizing the Greek "spontaneity of consciousness," the "disinterested play" of it that Socrates exemplifies, which Arnold opposes alike to the Americanism of "faith in machinery," to the Hebraism of "strictness of conscience," and to the people of his country whose noblemen are but barbarians, tradesmen but Philistines, and workingmen but mere populace. How mean is this England of Victoria, poring over the Bible as the revealed word of God, yearning with Huxley after "useful knowledge," beside the England of Elizabeth splendid with the culture of the classics, alert to the best that has been known and said in the world! Culture makes the greatness of this England; lack of culture makes the meanness of Victoria's! [1]

That Arnold speaks here no longer for a caste but for an academic and literary cult, his appraisals of the British aristocracy as barbarians attests. But this indicates only that Arnold had arrogated to persons of his own ilk the spiritual snobism of the courtly man of culture, who strutted his stuff in the England of Elizabeth. It is significant that not a peasant or workman in Shakespeare's plays but is burlesqued and lampooned; nor a bourgeois in Ben Jonson's but some gentleman cuckolds, derides and cozens him. It is equally significant that the heart goes out to these despised types when they are encountered in the novels of Dickens and Hardy and Kingsley and George Eliot, or in the poems of Wordsworth and Cowper and Hood, and the compositions of how many other writers, most of whom had been made acquainted with the glory that was Greece by the masters of that glory in the public schools and universities of Victorian England. In that England there had come, after the Democratic Revolution, sympathetic insight into the equal humanity of the miserable working multitudes and their equal hunger for the good life of free men.

This new humanism was the true humanism, the humanism of democracy. Among the gentlemen of culture to whom it became a fighting faith it transvalued the courtly humanities and the liberal arts with a revolutionary meaning. It was not from these humanities that the Victorians drew this meaning. It was from the demo-

---

[1] Cf. *Culture and Anarchy*, 1869: "Literature and Dogma" (the preface), 1873.

cratic faith, from the potentials of science, from the productions of machinery.

Because of it, the idea of culture itself—set in the unprecedented perspectives of universal process initiated by Darwin's *Origin of Species*—took a new turn, the turn given it by the new science of anthropology. Culture as gentlemanly accomplishment or harmonious self-development was confronted by culture as the total complex of attitudes and judgments, beliefs and knowledge, morals and manners, folkways and mores resulting wherever human beings, living and working together, shape their experience of thoughts and things into arts and sciences. Culture so understood has vocation for its center. It becomes the word for a total way of life, an economy which does not segregate consumption from production and labor from leisure. This culture does dignify labor at long last. In its light the England of Victoria shines with a brightness, and the figure of it is luminous with a humanism which the England of Elizabeth never dreamt of.

Victorians themselves could burn with the fire but could hardly see the light they gave. Like their forebears and descendants, they too felt that their own times were not the times they would choose to live in. They yearned for the Greek's "spontaneity of conscience" with the imaginative Arnold, for the mediaeval's work at leisure with dreamy Ruskin and nightmarish Carlyle, for the utopian delights of Nowhere with William Morris and all the socialist sects. They were all looking to repristinate a Golden Age long past or to bring to immediate birth a New Jerusalem forever to come. The Victorians like their twentieth-century descendants conceived "the best" as that which has been or is to be, but never as that which is, save as the images of ancient past and unborn future *are* present aspiration and ideal. For education, in this conjuncture, the past is the thing. What can learning be if not "the acquainting ourselves with 'the best' of what has been known and said," with acculturation—if so plebeian a word fits so aristocratic a connection—in the "history of the human spirit" thus transfigured.

But "best," alas, is an arbitrary term. It represents the preference of a person, not the perfection of a thing. Matthew Arnold's "best" deprecates the Bible and exalts the classics; it takes Elizabeth and refuses Victoria; other men's "bests" exalt the Bible and take Victoria. If disciples of the Arnoldian cult make lists of "best books" they give some an un-Arnoldian preference, like exalting works of mediaeval disputation over expressions of Greek reason. The fact is that "best" designates no finality, no first thing or last thing, but is a judgment of value bearing on a time, a place and occasion, and all these change.

Among the Christian sects a consensus prevails that the universal ideal of human perfection is not Helena but the figure of Jesus Christ. In its functional incarnations, however, the figure is protean. Not only do artists' images vary; theologians' definitions, moralists' and historians' interpretations vary even more. We know that each generation, each age, each sect, and each interest of each age and generation and sect remolds the figure to conform to its own dominant personality-image. Which is Jesus? Bruce Barton's "man nobody knows," Upton Sinclair's "Carpenter," "Christ the King" of recent Papal proclamation, "the historical Jesus" of the scientific students of the New Testament, the sun-myth of others, Mary Baker Eddy's "healer"? Or are these all different "bests" attuned to different times, serving different people and different needs, but called by the same name? Agamemnon or Ulysses, Socrates or Thomas Aquinas, are similarly protean. Their being and intent are functions of the knower's needs far more than their authentic characters. Indeed the entire body of culture is not less protean than these figures of it. Change is its life, and tradition is no less a process of change than mutation. The difference is not between alteration and constancy; it is between slow movement and speedy. The traditionalists, however, who segregate culture from vocation are disposed to hold it a universal essence of unaltering and inalterable ideas and accomplishments, everywhere the same, thence "best." "Freedom like Industry" wrote Matthew Arnold, many years later,[2] "is a very good horse to ride:—but to ride somewhere. You seem to think that you have only to get on the back of your horse Freedom or horse Industry, and to ride away as hard as you can, to be sure of coming to the right destination." The destination's the thing and the destination is culture. But if a culture thus final exists, a goal separate and distinct from the going, it is beyond human experience; if it falls within human experience it cannot be final, the going and goal must be fused. Our records

---

[2] *Friendship's Garland,* 1896.

of the known and said are stratum upon stratum of scribe's mis-writings, printer's errors, scholars' misreadings. Be it the Bible, the literature of the Greeks and Romans or what one chooses, the scholarly enterprise changes what now is into something that it now is not yet but that may or may not have been; scholars call the deed restoring the authentic, unaltering and inalterable original. Uni-versal and eternal meanings, everywhere the same, may be stood on their heads by the scholarly shifting of a comma.

The decision that a meaning is this and not that is an act of faith, not truth revealing itself. The new event suffuses, and in suffusing transfigures whatever had come before—as each new note suffuses and transfigures its predecessors in a melody or a new word transfigures its predecessors in a sentence. Each bring different wholenesses and new meanings. If self-development is the personal differentia of the process, this comes as an extension and refinement of inquiry, not as a taking possession of the final answer. Death or weakness or fatigue may finish off the act as readily as satisfaction or realization. But in no case is the finish the same as a final goal. It is not the end of the unending road. Decision is literally a cut-ting off of something that might have gone on. Every stoppage occurs by fortune or choice; no knowable providence shapes its end. As an act of choice it culminates a felt need to stop questing, and the need can arise anywhere and the inquiry resume everywhere. At its primal core, culture is curiosity at work. It lives and grows as the arts of inquiry which, by learning and knowing, digest ac-complishment in power and contention in insight. In contrast to the cult of culture cherished in the snobbish humanism of the traditionalists who ordain prejudices of taste to officiate as prin-ciples of being, this culture labors to reconcile exclusive alternatives into orchestral unities; and where it must reject, it endeavors to understand before rejecting and to reject without condemning. A personality thus "acculturated" would be a cultural pluralist. Civili-zation would be to it neither the senescence of a culture nor its optimal mode. It would envisage civilization as the union of the cultures. It would live and move and have its being in one civili-zation of many cultures, in an orchestration of mankind through their works and ways, whether of the communities of the homeland or the peoples of the earth.

Where culture falls short of such a dynamic, educated choice seems more like animal response verbalized than human preference illumined and clarified. It looks like automatic discharge of blind instinct or coerced conformation to an outer authority, alike for what it affirms and what it denies. Its pattern is self-repeating, especially in its exclusions, and these are self-defeating. In cutting itself off from vocation it dooms itself to be a cut-flower culture, fragrant, costly, and self-destined for quick death. The economy of culture is of a piece with the economy of all things human. Cut it off from the sources of its being, keep it the decoration and accomplishment of leisure instead of developing it as the power and consummation of labor, and you keep it a precarious parasite with no force or destiny of its own. The springs of culture are agriculture, animal culture, the culture of the machines. The root of culture is vocation; the fruit of vocation is culture, alike in the institutions of society and the personal life. The glory that was Greece had to be the works and ways of men and women before it could shine out in glory. The delights of leisure which Aristotle appraised as the end of life had to be the productions of servile labor before they could become the consumption of enfranchised leisure.

And save that producers were despised as menial and slavish, and consumers honored as noble and free, because the consumers kept themselves the masters and held the producers servants, there was no reason why the delights of consumption should not suffuse production, or the powers of production find their ultimacies in consumption. They do just this in the fine arts and the sciences; they need do no less in the commercial and industrial arts or the applied sciences, where function is the determinant of form, and beauty the crown of use. Ancient Homer and Theocritus, Phidias and Praxiteles, Euripides and Aeschylus and Sophocles, Aristotle and Plato and Socrates, all the architects and masons and builders, all the sculptors and painters and writers and thinkers whose surviving productions we acclaim as the glory that was Greece, were men of bone and blood and sinew that needed food and drink and health as well as skill and knowledge and taste to practice the vocations whose products are declared the fundaments of our culture. The *what* and *how* of their production were not culture to them, the producers. They were culture only to the consumers of that production. Primarily ways of earning a living, they may also have been ways of living a life. There was nothing intrinsic to their natures to prevent them from enjoying a life while earning a living. On the contrary, any action men enter upon can give form and tempo to their powers, nourish their "instinct of workmanship" and fulfill their being and free their personalities by relating them creatively to existences not themselves.

It is the relationship that creates or destroys the difference in the economy of culture, the economy that its traditionalist champions disregard. But the men and women whose vocation is music, literature, drama, painting, sculpture, dancing or architecture, have always been as aware of it as their fellows, the butcher, the baker, the candlestick maker. In the advancing division of labor, any man's vocation is every other man's culture. For the dynamic of culture is free trade between vocations. Hence, the closer a man of culture gets to the vocational roots of his culture, the deeper, the more discriminating his judgment and accurate his understanding; the nearer his insight of the personality of the producer, and his fellowship with the latter's life and labors. The achievement and expression of such a fusion of sympathy and empathy, and its communication to others, is the especial vocation of the teacher. Where the fusion obtains, the invidious distinction between "useful" and "useless" knowledge lapses; what is invidious in the distinctions between fine art and commercial, sacred and profane, precious and vulgar, classic and popular, dies away. The head understands and the heart acknowledges the singularity of the worker and his workings, their symbolic transposition into other media for other purposes, orchestrating them all to the other singularities that environ them. Such orchestration makes the culture of democracy.

Every progressive kindergarten can exemplify the process. Each assumes that the young children entrusted to its care are to learn to serve their own needs and help themselves. Provision is made for their feeding and resting and for guidance in such necessary actions they cannot yet perform for themselves. At a given time they have milk, perhaps biscuits or bread. The milk drinking is a vital complex of experiences. The children arrange and set the tables, place the chairs, maybe pour the milk which they see and taste and smell before they savor and swallow. Drinking milk is experiencing satisfaction of a vital need. It could be treated as an interruption of the school period, could be isolated and disposed of with as little attention as possible. It is so treated in conventional kindergartens. A progressive kindergarten is progressive, however, precisely because it undertakes from the first to relate learning to the needs of survival and growth which are the fundamental drives in learning. Before long the children are taken to visit a dairy and to explore the producer-economy of the milk they consume. The experience places the milk in a hitherto unknown order of relationships, with cows and bulls, fields and feeds, barns and milking sheds, dairymen, milking machines, sterilizers, separators, butter churns, and other instruments for processing milk. All these become for the children added context of the milk they drink. Returned to the school, the experience does not lapse into the forgotten. It is recalled and discussed. It is relived as story, as poem, as song, as play, as picture, as dance, as model in clay. The reliving brings in new words and new arrangements of words, new images, new symbols, new ways of the children's being together. The reliving is culture crowning vocation. It makes of milk the perceptual core of a process of meanings, embodied in symbols and images which link with other percepts far away and long ago. The culture to which milk-drinking is the vocation is the system of linkings, thus symbolically present and envisaged. It is the way of making the absent present, of vicariously experiencing it. And how else have ancient drama, ancient dance and song and tale, ancient myth and ancient rite come to be? How indeed can any come to be at any time, save in some such modes of reliving, direct or indirect?

Those who grasp truly the dynamic interdependence of culture and vocation realize also why and how the poor truck driver of a certain college president's parable may well find in physics nourishment of his driver's art, or the college president himself find in physiology sustenance for his invidious pedagogics. Of course human beings grow up, grow old and die ignorant of numbers of arts and sciences which might enlarge their powers and improve their chances of survival and growth. How many drive motor cars totally unaware of the mechanism which puts them at the mercy of the cars they drive? How many eat meals innocent of all knowledge of nutrition and health, easy victims of their diets? The goods and services we consume, the stuffs of our culture, are the creations of a production we take on faith, the end-products of the vocations of multitudes we never know, yet whom we trust implicitly. The wonder is not that the trust is ever betrayed, but that it is not betrayed more frequently. When men work freely they work honestly and well; and ever under compulsion, the instinct of workmanship often overrides the enforced servility and the qualities of freedom suffuse their necessities. Nevertheless it is better for them that the consumers of their products should know the ways of production, and better for the consumers if the producers who serve them participate in their standards of consumption.

The world being what it is, most men must work to live, and men being what men are, work is evil, but necessary evil. Most who are gainfully employed, let me say again, do what they must, not what they wish, and endure as they can. Fortunate are those whose occupation dissolves necessity in consent, and who wish to do what they must do anyhow. But consented to or not, for industrial man his job is the dominant fact of his day-to-day life. Its dominance cuts off his days from his nights, rendering his day life vocation and his night life culture, and making the function of culture not fulfillment, not consummation of the day, but flight from the day and compensation for it. Is not night life organized to console and restore "the tired businessman"?

Here, then, we come once more to the crux of the split between vocation and culture for the education of free men. For school days to heal it requires centering in the study of a vocation all the linkages with other vocations that make up its culture. The original point of departure is the satisfaction of some organic need, such as the need of food. A young child cannot do without eating but can do without playing Indian; it may play house instead. Food is passion, enacting an Indian is diversion. Enacting an Indian busy producing and consuming food makes the diversion into the channel for the passion. Passing from the acts of direct gratification of organic needs to training in a vocation, is passing from the level of the equality of the different to the levels of inequality and hierarchy. Vocations, as we have already seen, vary immensely in social status. The more nearly they are taken as mere means, the more menial they are held to be. How immense is the social distance between an archaeologist and a garbage collector!

Yet in a free society, social distance is a foe of freedom. True, the teachers may teach "a man is a man for a' that," but democrats must take a man to be a man not despite but *because* of a' that, *in* and *through* a' that. Since the democratic idea envisages men as equal in right to life, liberty and the pursuit of happiness whatever their vocations, it requires that schools of democracy impart an abiding loyalty also to this vocational aspect of the parity of the different. The national enterprise of keeping up with the Joneses labors to reduce social distance by means of emulation and imitation. But people assume the inferiority of the condition they would abandon and the superiority of the condition they would attain. How win acknowledgment of the equal worth of the rejected and the pursued? How bring democratic emulation nevertheless to honor equally the garbage collector and the archaeologist?

Perhaps, for reasons beyond their province, the task is beyond the capacity of the schools. In what do archaeologist and garbage collector differ? Hardly in the stuffs they deal with. Both gather the excrementa of human existence—the garbage collector the excrementa of the living, the archaeologist the excrementa of the dead. By this token garbage collecting is a social necessity, archaeology is a social luxury. A community could live well and grow without archaeology, it would soon sicken and perish without garbage collecting. Yet the mere thought of garbage collecting brings an automatic reflex of disgust; however rightly the mind may approve the garbage collector and his labors, the sensibilities are averted from his person; encountering him, we do not even look; we shudder and walk aside. Psychosomatic reflex overrules social insight. On the other hand, not only do we not avoid the archaeologist, we may seek him out and linger with him, handle his collections even though they stink, discourse about their form and meaning and history, all for the fun of it. Reduced to its simplest terms, the difference between the garbage collector and the archaeologist resides in this discourse, and the discourse is the substance of culture gathered by education. A bone or a shard from a kitchen-midden ceases to be merely this bone or this shard when it is set in the imaginative perspectives of the anthropologist, the historian, the aesthetician, the psychologist. It becomes the concretion of a human era, the symbol of an entire social economy with its knowledges and skills, a museum piece and a theme of liberal education. No such transvaluation accrues to the garbage of the garbage collector, nor to his person and labors. Yet only psychosomatic reactions re-enforcing survivals of caste judgments stand in the way. In a chemical laboratory the same stuffs and the same smells evoking the same aversions can be quickly digested into their social and intellectual contexts, and may even be found to give pleasure, like limburger or gorgonzola cheese in a luxurious hostel. The same individual, avoided as a garbage collector, may be sought out as a sanitary engineer, who is only a garbage collector with a college education. The point should stick out, then: Condorcet, remember, made it long ago—education it is which brings the difference; for education, when successful, makes real the equality of the different decreed by law. No education serves democracy which segregates the values of production from the values of consumption, vocation from culture, labor from leisure. The boundaries between these ways of action are artificial and external; without the alien greeds that maintain them they would flow together in one continuous consummatory stream of living. Kept apart from culture, vocation is servile, brutish and blind; vocational education is animal training. Kept apart from vocation, culture is parasitical, cruel and sterile; liberal education is the cultivation of futility. The education of free men requires reuniting the two so long divorced, the orchestration of the producer's knowledge which is power with the consumer's discernment which is delight.

Chapter Eighteen

THE LIBERAL EDUCATION OF THE MODERN MAN

In the United States, school and society interpenetrate as nowhere else in the Western world. This is true is spite of the traditional isolation of the school and school life from the community and its enterprises. Whatever success the school has had in turning the minds of American youth toward freedom, has grown from the influence of the aspirations of the community on the practices of the classroom. These aspirations keep American society a mobile, and to that extent a free, society. Expressed by our manifold endeavors to keep up with our diverse and diversifying Joneses, they channel and shape our interpersonal, interoccupational, interdenominational, in fine, our intercultural, relations. They figure in the ways that the nation's schools are managed and controlled. Inadequately democratic as the latter may be, they are not, as among the Europeans, removed from the people, an institution of the state ruled by a remote ministry of education, which fixes the educational purpose, makes the educational policy and commands the nation's teachers as one more hierarchical bureaucracy of civil servants. For the educational establishment of the United States, the community is primary. Government of the American school is entrusted, from kindergarten to university, by each community to a body of elected or appointed officials representing the dominant majority of region or locality. These officials appoint the teachers, decide the curricula, select the texts. Not infrequently political policy or the mores provide that representatives of minorities shall also serve on school committees and boards of education.

Community by community, hence, the schools are a barometer of its prevailing climate of opinion and of the winds of doctrine that blow through. Consequently, the extraordinary thing about the theory and practice of education in the United States is not the stodginess, the inertia, the superficiality, the vocationalism and "scientism" of which its critics accuse it. In those respects education is really no worse in the United States than elsewhere, and in many ways, is better. The extraordinary thing about American education is its abundance, its flexibility, its diversity and its power. The pressures upon it of widely diverse and manifold interests, economic, ecclesiastical, political, cultural, have evoked both autogenous and associative defenses which help maintain the autonomy and integrity of the nation's schools as a national ideal. They have led to the birth and growth of a science and art of education without parallel elsewhere for vigor, originality and richness. And to these, soon or late, there comes a grass-roots response which in its turn affects the churches, the chambers of commerce, the labor unions, the rotaries and the ethnic groups no less than those affect the educational establishment. The American people have, as a people, a care for education unique in the world. They believe in it and support it as the foremost bulwark of their liberties. If they exalt the liberal education of tradition, they do so because they know about it as the education provided for the élite, and because they see in the élite the models of the truly free, the Joneses of their world.

Not that the American people are unaware of the more than sufficient reason to hold that the claims made for that kind of education are a cruel deception, like those made for a patent medicine cure-all. The epic of education in America establishes that they are not. But the tradition has the vitality of a tapeworm. Take one more sample of the reasons, as given in the high schools of New York City. Some time ago, a teacher of many years' experience in those schools, published a book under the title *Your School, Your Children*. It was a summary and appraisal of the state of high-school education in America's greatest and most cosmopolitan city. This sensitive and intelligent lady with a genuine vocation for teaching, and a deep devotion to the American Idea, observed, among her colleagues, the characteristic gap between profession and practice. She found pervasive what she called a "tart scepticism" regarding the teacher's art. To me her story suggested that the teachers only earned their livings through their vocation, that they lacked genuine professional interest; that since little else seemed to offer them a life, they used their occupation as a funnel for their personal retreats and aggressions from and toward the frustrations of their personal worlds. These worlds are made up, of course, of the churchly, fraternal, familial, and other groupings whose purposes and prejudices make the more or less conscious frame of reference of the classroom lesson. The pupils are, similarly, carriers of all the prejudices of family, faith and race. They too were in school because they had to be rather than because they wanted to, and with their hearts, even more than the hearts of their teachers, on quite other matters than those which the lesson period set before them. An official syllabus prescribed what the lessons should be, but rarely did any of the prescriptions present a content with vital significance to either teacher or pupil. The routine of the syllabus seemed to produce a sort of stalemate in the class-war between teachers whose prime concern in teaching was salary, and pupils whose first concern as learners was outwitting the teacher. The subject matter was too unrelated, the lesson too diluted, the teacher too indifferent, the classes were too large, and the behavior of those in authority at once hidebound and vacillating.

Fundamentally, there was no meeting of minds between pupils and teachers. The latter taught a perfunctory course laid out on a plan combining pedagogic tradition with current fashion, and adapted, but not too well, to community pressures. The course looked to "liberal education." It included such items, for example, as some plays of Shakespeare, and other "great books," and "liberal" disciplines. The adolescent candidates for the high-school diploma who were required to take this course preferred, however, to read the deliverances of the tabloid press, and discussed them in their local dialects which challenge a Shavian Pygmalion to transform. "Why doesn't Shakespeare write English?" one such candidate complained. The news and ideas most significant to the pupils, their teachers had to ignore as too controversial; their first responsibility was to avoid any subject that might arouse thought and provoke vital difference of opinion. The experiences, events and ideas which most filled the pupils' minds the teachers had to disregard as extracurricular. The author of *Your School, Your Children,* declares that she is "always impressed by the exact knowledge my pupils have of the mysteries of football and baseball, of the talents of the band-leader and crooner." She underlines the event that one of her "least articulate and least promising pupils" could give a "detailed and learned lecture on the art of shining shoes."

If for football and baseball we read *physical education,* for band-leader and crooner, *music,* for shining shoes, *vocation,* the abstract words transvalue the shocking contemporaneity and concreteness of that effective adolescent interest into the universal and necessary disciplines approved by Platonizers to this day. The difference between what a syllabus provides and youth takes is relevancy. Where a subject is irrelevant, it cannot awaken and energize passions, powers and interests, as education must. Like any item of the environment to which response is not willing but compelled, it can be learned by training, by conditioning through instruction, indoctrination and habituation; and it is like to figure in the whole personality as an isolated habit of talking or doing, unorchestrated to its growing, mobile totality. Reflection upon the role of their education in the rank and file of the college graduates in the "liberal arts" will make clear that where those arts survive they do so as but one or more specialties, like parlor tricks. Fundamentally, the consequences of such liberal education are illiberal. They are illiberal because it belittles, to the student, the diverse actualities of life and labor that make up a community. Over against them it sets as measure an arbitrarily selected, artificially supported and authoritatively transmitted cultural syndrome. Excommunicating and cutting off the belittled from all contact with the elect, it undertakes to shut the latter into its own exclusive grammar of assent. Instead of freeing the minds and hearts of youth, it locks them behind the walls of its own snobism.

Under such conditions no true meeting of minds is possible, and if no meeting of minds, no education. If youth minds football and baseball with the passionate absorption which brings knowledge and skill, then these modern sports can very readily be taken for the meaningful center whence the spirit may freely move to all meanings of the culture of the body in every time and clime. If youth spontaneously evinces clear and distinct ideas of the talents of bandleader and crooner, then its interest can move from those absorbing foci of the musical art, to the cultural economy of music everywhere in the world. If a bootblack is aware of his art with its tools and materials, if shoeshine is at the center of his interest, all the arts and sciences that illumine this center can be brought to focus at it with his co-operation and not against his resistance. A transition from shoeshine to Caligula and Roman history becomes an unforced event, while a change of center would have to be a matter of coercion and "discipline" at best foredoomed to a specious success. Any thought or thing, any vocation or technique momentous to a mind may become the base of its liberation by education. Any art or craft, any theme, datum or system of ideas, is an instrument of liberal education when it serves as a road and not as a wall for him who studies it. Whatever be the avowed field and purpose of the study—farming, engineering, business, law, medicine, the ministry, teaching, garbage collecting, archaeology— when it liberates, it is liberal. This is of course the case also with the curriculum of the traditional liberal education. That too sets the student free if and as it succeeds in investing his mind with good will toward, and equipping it with means for, sympathetic understanding and free communication with the works and ways and spirit of peoples other than his own, peoples removed in place or remote in time—peoples different in their speech and their occupations, other in their faith, their works, their ways, like the Greeks and Romans and even the Hebrews, whose language and literature are still the doxologies of orthodox liberal education; peoples like Shakespeare's English or Cervantes' Spanish, or Moliere's French or Dostoevski's Russians or Confucius' Chinese or Hafiz' Persians or Gautama's Hindus. It a student has learned how to understand, to appreciate and freely think such differents, he has been freed from the exclusive provincialism of his land and time; his education has been "liberal" at least with respect to a world past and gone.

To be liberated into the life more abundant of the actual world, however, has so obvious a priority over this other, that the recurrent debate over its dignity and worth argue an inexplicable blindness of spirit in those who deny it. The very past they exalt is a living past only as living men cherish and study and use it, only as they live their lives *now*. Its whole meaning is its present diversification into future consequences. Hence, the imperativeness of relevancy. Hence, any valid measure of the liberating efficacy of a given discipline must be in the skill, the swiftness, the sureness with which it brings people who are different from each other out of their mutual isolation into intercommunication. The measure is in how willingly they learn about each other; how well, understanding, respecting and appreciating each other's differences, they work together; how far, working thus together, each grows more fully and freely himself than he could if he went it alone.

Liberal education, thus, starts from people as they are where they are, with all their diversities of vocation and culture, faith and custom and tradition, knowledge and skill and power. Whether in the local community or in global society, liberal education takes such *nows* not as dwellings for the spirit to rest in but as stations to depart from. That such a posture of the spirit is difficult must by now be clear. The passion which sees the works and ways of one's own communion as the sole true earthly vicar of the Eternal and Universal is endemic among all the peoples of the world; the urge to take the doctrine and discipline of one's own society as the sole fulfillment of God's infinite purposes thrusts inveterate in the will of every man. In all of us there lives a naive absolutism, an infantile imperialism of the spirit, to which what is different cannot be worthy, what changes cannot be real, what is plural cannot be true. Worth, reality and truth must be one and the same always and everywhere, and where they are not, must be conformed to our own uniquely ineffable Unity by every means within our power. The experiences of life, but especially the works and ways of the arts and the sciences, bring home to us how cruelly mistaken is this presumption. Of course, the arts and the sciences have their "tradition," and if unity and universality cannot be attributes of their variety, they can be of that tradition which is presumed to carry each over into the others, and to derive all from one identity. The fact is, however, that tradition is not a persisting identity but an activity of identifying variations, both the spontaneous and the planful, with that from which they are variations and dissents. Tradition is in fact not a repetition of identicals but a process in which new-comings absorb, digest and transform old goings-on. When Protestants challenge Catholic "traditionalism," they invoke the ancient Bible against the latest as well as the earliest pope, and oppose an earlier to a later moment of Christian tradition. When the American colonists challenged British rule, they invoked ancient common law against recent parliamentary legislation, thus opposing an earlier to a later moment of English political tradition. In practice, it is the present interest and desire of the chooser, not the nature of the chosen, which decide what shall be "tradition." In practice, the thing called tradition is something going on *now*, and those who challenge or reject those who invoke it, may as like as not do so by giving life to a part of it that had become as inert and lifeless as the pith of a growing tree.

So with the idea of the liberal education: it is John Dewey and the educational progressives who are defending the living tradition; it is the *soi-disant* traditionalists, with their mortuary cult of *trivium* and *quadrivium* and "humanities" who are laboring to revitalize a moribund past. While the latter cultivate our perennial snobism by exalting one phase of one aspect of our culture and battling to bring all others under its domination, the former labor to orchestrate the diversities presently composing this culture in the democratic way on equal terms. Their fighting faith is in that religion of religions we are accustomed to call democracy. The signature of their faith is their acknowledgment and respect for diversity, their understanding that the unity of human cultures is not an identification but an orchestration, their hope of a federal union of the diverse consisting in their team play and growing more intimate and vigorous through this team play, be it in religion, in business, in government, in letters, in the arts, in the sciences. On every level of union, from the tiniest village to the United Nations, the device of its spirit is *E pluribus unum*. It signalizes one civilization of many cultures.

Literature, the arts and the sciences, have always lived and grown by the rule of union. Despite the uttermost effort of the censor and index-maker, the poets, the painters, the sculptors, the builders, the philosophers and scientists of the world, have always sought and used and cherished each other's works and nourished their own upon their fellows'. If the world of letters has never been to its citizens other than "the republic of letters" so also have the worlds of music, the graphic arts and the sciences of nature and man been republics. Without the co-operative competition and competitive co-operation which informs free trade in things of the spirit as in all other things, art and science and letters starve, they do not flourish. Whether the work be Greek or Roman or Hebrew or Moslem or mediaeval or Renaissance or modern, its singularity has been fed on foreign foods and watered from alien streams. Whatever soil it be a growth of, its nutriment has come to it from other soils. No culture can feed on itself and grow by what it feeds on. So the censor and inquisitor, the maker of iron curtains and indices of forbidden books, the policemen of the arts or the sciences become, where they are successful, the executioners of that which they have been appointed only to isolate. Lacking the fluid team play of the different, the arts become repetitive and sterile, atrophy and die; in the sciences, discovery comes to a standstill in dogma, and science becomes a totalitarian metaphysic or theology. For the arts and the sciences, isolation is murder, and they have ever repudiated isolation.

Men of religion have been less ready to recognize that this is true, also for living faith. Let us recall once more that from the coming of Christianism to power, each diverse denomination or sect or cult has always said to others it differed from: *I am right. You are wrong. When you are in power, you must shelter and defend me, because I am right. When I am in power I shall outlaw you and abolish you because you are wrong.* The Protestant denominations, however, have in the course of generations come closer to the stance of the arts and the sciences. Beginning in almost a war of infallible each against infallible each, they moved first to a hard-bitten tolerance of one another—a certainty in each that the other was wickedly wrong; a resolution in each to suffer the wrongful, not gladly, but without aggression; living, also to let live, but only to let live. From this virtuous tolerance they came, not easily, not unbitterly, to a desire for genuine understanding, hence to free communication, and from free communication to free co-operation on equal terms. Thus, once again, the Federal Council of the Churches of Christ in America is such a stance of a diversity of denominations—Methodist, Presbyterian, Baptist, Congregational, Episcopal, Christian, Quaker and the like—each cherishing its difference from the others, each adding its singularity to the union of the different strengths, and each being in its turn confirmed and increased in its singularity by this equal union, its orchestration with the diverse others. It already has an overseas development. In the schooling of the ministers of the diverse denominations, Union Theological Seminary embodies the educational correlate of the Federal Council of Churches. Among laymen, this trend has taken form in the interfaith movements which in principle reappraise ancient misbelief and heresy into genuine attitudes of the religious conscience, equally entitled to life and liberty and growth, and a fellow-worker on equal terms toward the attainment of these ends for each. In conception, the members of the interfaith movements are one for all and all for one. True, their association is still a limited and closed companionship. Orthodox, Bahais, Mormons,

Christian Scientists, Unitarians, Humanists, agnostics, atheists do not figure among the interfaith fellowships; nor do Buddhists, Mohammedans, Brahmins, Parsees, Sikhs, and others of the multitudinous cults that together utter the supernatural faith of mankind. The interfaith groups are still more or less co-operative groups only of willing Jews and Protestants and reluctant Catholics. It may be that the logic of events is likely to change them from a closed to an open union of the cults, alike on the national and on the global scale.

For the alternative to this change can be only the repudiation of the democratic idea and rule. Between the two world wars devotion to the latter has brought, not without personal hazard, labor and suffering of the devotees, in many walks of life, the religious not the least, a wide-ranging consensus in Cultural Pluralism as the most hopeful working hypothesis for liberal education as the education of free men in a free society. It seems to many the one practical answer to the cultural imperialism of the rival monist Communist, Fascist, and Nazi,—to say nothing of ecclesiastical— totalitarianism, and to their retrospectionist echoes in the United States. Indeed, a historian of the future may find himself intrigued by the observation that the insurgence of these cultural monisms in the political economy of Europe concurred with the resurgence and advocacy of the traditional authoritarian liberal education in the United States and its attack on the American school. The interdenominational, interfaith and intercultural movements were to some degree counterattacks on the monisms as well as new affirmations of the democratic idea. Diplomats, politicians, bankers and businessmen joined scientists, artists, clergymen and teachers in a new awareness, a democratic awareness at last, of the ever-present fact that the differences of neighbor from neighbor called for reciprocal understanding and appreciation of neighbor by neighbor; that understanding and appreciation were the basis of community and the springs of cultural abundance as against monistic cultural scarcity. The American State Department once set up a Division of Cultural Relations, and undertook "planned, educational, intellectual, cultural, artistic exchanges." The church federations organized international conferences. The public schools—set going by the personal initiative and enterprise of a lonely woman idealist, laboring in a New Jersey village school to unite school children of

different origins, faiths and cultures into a class of mutually understanding, reciprocally respectful, and appreciative Americans—now
contemplate such exchanges not between their pupils only, but
parents as well, as the means and ends of neighborly communion.
Schoolmen and lay leaders in Springfield, Massachusetts, put their
heads together to devise the "Springfield, Plan." In New York, a
Bureau of Intercultural Education somehow grew into being, with
the purposes of studying the forms and functions of such communion, its problems and principles; of training men and women
to lead and serve it; of organizing the teaching of it; and of providing the nations's schools with teaching materials and consultants
in its characteristic arts. Its staff have become "trouble shooters"
for intercultural problems, ready to answer the call from wherever
a school conflict presents a hazard to the democratic idea. They
bring to the nation's schools the new meaning of liberal education.

This meaning, it may be said, is now consciously global. One
session of the Princeton University Bicentennial Conference on
"The University and Its World Responsibilities" was given to considering "UNESCO and the Universities." UNESCO stands for
the United Nations Educational, Scientific and Cultural Organization. The speaker was Dr. Howard E. Wilson of the Carnegie
Endowment for International Peace and one of the chieftains of
UNESCO. Dr. Wilson's address, by implication, pointed to the
illiberality of the prevailing liberal, or as he called it "general"
college education.

In emphasizing the international factor in each university program, he said, attention may first be turned to the level of
general education. It is still too commonly true in universities
and colleges throughout the world that the program of studies
by which a man or woman is expected to achieve formal education is relatively provincial. Within the United States, even more
than in many other countries, men and women graduate from
college each year whose horizons do not extend substantially
beyond the United States. The curriculum basis and pattern of
general education needs reinvigoration with more rigorous and
scholarly analysis of cultures other than our own, and with study
of the techniques and procedures of public participation in international action. The introduction—sometimes even the requirement—of college courses in international relations, in the
history of diplomacy, in planetary geography or economics is
not sufficient, important as some of these movements may be.

Certain standard elements in the traditional program of courses need reorientation in the light of international realities. For illustration, in the teaching of United States history, we have interpreted the nation's story in the light of the influence of the frontier as Turner taught us; we have with Beard dealt with industrialism as a conditioning element in American life, and with Schlesinger studied the social influence of urbanization. We seem now on the verge of a fresh analysis of American development giving due emphasis to the international influences and contacts which helped mould American life even during the days of theoretical isolation. In fields additional to American history such a reorientation needs also to be made if the emerging citizen-leader is to be adequately conscious of the conditions and complexities and problems and potentialities of one world.

Such a reform of the liberal education still offered by the colleges and universities postulates a shift of its base from the traditional cultural monism to cultural pluralism. Mr. Wilson concluded his address by indicating UNESCO's realistic acceptance of this pluralism as the point of departure for its works and ways. "UNESCO rests," he said, "upon the assumption that there are, there always will be, and there should be, many differences among the peoples of the world. It presupposes a society based upon cultural pluralism. Each culture has its own premises, its own forms of thought and action, exactly as each university does. The UNESCO belief is that the common ground underlying this wide diversity is sufficiently great that men may, with wisdom, live together in peace. . . . UNESCO seeks to strengthen the common elements in diverse cultures by providing specific opportunities for people of all nations to cooperate together. It believes that there are many possibilities for constructive cooperation immediately practicable in education, science, and culture, and that such possibilities will increase as we succeed in the first steps immediately before us."

The expressions, "common ground," "common elements," are likely to be misleading, however. They hint at ultimacies, irreduceable and unchangeable finalities everywhere and always the same, whereon diversities come to identity and conflicts to peace. The peace and identity have always been there and need only to be uncovered and acknowledged. But this is the traditional metaphysic over again. Such commonalty never was and never can be any less a foundation for war than a foundation for peace. As a rule, co-operation is a free trade of the unlike, competition of the like. Rivalries occur between similar powers wanting identical things, as between two males desiring the same female. The "common grounds" then, the "common elements" must be rather a mode of association, a way of going together, than a set of unchanging doctrines and an inalterable discipline. In the history of free societies this comes about in the form of the consensus of the diverse concerning their ever-diversifying functions. It is a continuous condition of the life together of arts and letters, and is at its height in the method of the sciences. For in these the spirit of man experiences freedom at its purest, and grows in freedom through its experiences. So long as the arts and crafts and sciences are conceived as simply content—these one hundred "best" books, those one hundred "best" pictures, statues, musical compositions, buildings, systems of physics, astronomy, sociology—thought is at a standstill. Culture is a "body" of doctrine and discipline, more or less aesthetic, science is a "body" of knowledge more or less intellectual. Cultural and scientific activity become the reproductions and repetitions characteristic of mimetic artists, musical virtuosos, pulp-wood authors, newspaper critics, laboratory technicians, engineers, production managers and schoolmasters, with their blueprints of order, precision and sequential measurements. But alike in the life of a man of art, a man of science, and of their occupational communities, art and sciences are each an ongoing process which compounds observations with inspirations, imaginative responses to the impact of a problem with challenges and denials of existing solutions and choices between alternative solutions. It is a process of planning, organizing and hazarding trial drafts and experimental tests of a faith, a vision, a hypothesis, whose truth is not guaranteed in advance. When we win insight into what is this process we become aware of the full meaning of the arts and the sciences. We then see that a "body of knowledge" or a body of culture is not a configuration of the universal and eternal, but something continually being surpassed and reshaped, while the acts of surpassing and reshaping become ever surer and ever of greater power. We then see the history of science as the tale of errors discarded and method diversified yet sustained, strengthened and refined. We then see the history of the cultures as the tale of the ever greater, more varied and swifter and smoother intercommunication of the diverse and the diversifying. Their common ground and their common elements are understood as the roads they travel on, not the places they stand on or the possessions they carry. The bonds of their union are here the conditions of their liberty. And this is true whether we speak of the relations of neighbors in a village, workers in an industry, peoples of a country, or nations on the globe.[1] The liberal education is one that frees each and all

---

[1] On December 10, 1948, many months after this book was finished, the General Assembly of the United Nations proclaimed the Universal Declaration of Human Rights "as a common standard of achievement for all peoples and all nations." The latter have now the task to implement it by means of conventions which shall secure its "universal and effective recognition and observance."

By its vote, the General Assembly had affirmed the democratic idea to be the principle of union and program of action common to all mankind. Whether its declaration shall be an assemblage of "glittering generalities" or the fighting faith of an ever-growing company of men and peoples only the event can show. But history is on the side of the fighting faith, as the record since the Democratic Revolution attests. The vote of the Assembly has taken its stand upon the indefeasible yet always disputed fact that mankind is a multitude of individuals each different from the others and united in different societies, different faiths, different cultures having to live together with each other on the common earth. The vote affirms that each, as different, is the equal of the others in his rights to life, liberty and the pursuit of happiness. The thirty articles composing the Declaration specify these more general rights and list them in detail.

They affirm that the power of government, be it sacerdotal, political, economic or cultural, may not in any way abrogate or abolish these rights and must in every way maintain and secure them; that governments are not ends but alterable means of the furtherance of these rights, especially the rights of equal liberty of the different to think, to believe, to worship, to speak, to listen, to write, to read, to marry, to own property, to travel, to be a citizen, to be safe and to be educated as each shall choose and decide.

The universal right to education is specified in the twenty-sixth article, thus:

1. Everyone has the right to education. Education shall be free, at least in the elementary and fundamental stages. Elementary education shall be compulsory. Technical and professional education shall be made generally available and higher education shall be equally accessible to all on the basis of merit.

2. Education shall be directed to the full development of the human personality and to the strengthening of respect for human rights and fundamental freedoms. It shall promote understanding, tolerance and

safely and happily to live and to move and have his personal being in fact or in idea among the others of his choice.

This is what liberal education must mean in the modern world.

---

friendship among all nations and racial or religious groups and shall further the activities of the United Nations for the maintenance of peace.

3. Parents have a prior right to choose the kind of education that shall be given to their children.

Clause 2 states the educational ideal which the suffrage of their delegated spokesmen sets before the peoples of the world. It rejects all cultural imperialisms. It repudiates all spiritual totalitarianisms. It recognizes that education must be the learning of freedom; that freedom is the *sine qua non* of understanding and tolerance and friendship; that these are consequences of free communication; that free communication is consummated in hyphenation and that hyphenation is the life-stream of all civilization. It establishes as international consensus the conclusions reached in this book—namely that the works of education must be the freeing of every man's spirit and education's faith the equal liberty of all men.

INDEX

137, 138, 139, 142, 152 *n.*, 214 *n.*, 216,
220 *n.*, 245, 246, 261
Jesus, diverse images of, 305
Jewell, Frank, quoted, xvii
Justice, Platonic, 164
Justinian, and the Church, 208

Kalergi-Coudenove, Count, 194
"Keeping up with the Joneses," in educa-
tion, 28 *ff.*, 158 *ff.*; among Germans, 160,
290
Knowledge, Francis Bacon on, 294 *ff.*
Kravchenko, v., 206
Kretschmer, 172
Krivitsky, 204
Kultur, 183, 300, 302

Labor, as social ideal, 279, 282; classical
scorn of, 280, 293; a curse of God, 281 *ff.*,
297; paradoxes of dignity of, 283 *ff.*
Lafayette, 71
Learning, 44, 45; modern conceptions of,
55; tasks of psychology of, 61 *ff.*, 129,
155 *n.*; as growing, 156; as impersona-
tion, 159; in discipline of freedom, 278
Leisure, 279, 282, 283, 290
Lenin, V., 202
Leo XIII, 187 *n.*, 188, 191
Lewin, Kurt, 62 *n.*, 63, 268, 273 *n.*
Liberalism, xii; Catholic teaching regard-
ing, 193, 193 *n.*, 194 *n.*; Mussolini on,
195; to be supplanted by Nazism, 195
Liberty, *see* Freedom
Libre examen, the, 134, 150, 151
Life, and schooling, xv *ff.*; College, vs.
classroom, 81
Lippitt, Ronald, 273 *n.*
Literacy, 20
Loisy, Abbé, 190
Lorge, Irving, 169
Loyalty, civic, as loyalty to rights of man,
134
Loyola, St. Ignatius, 202, 258
Luxury, 291, archaeology as, 311

Madison, James, 140, 209, 214 *n.*, 220 *n*,
242, 245
Mann, Horace, 24, 25
Martin, George Madden, 66 *n.*
Marx, Karl, 199
Materialism, Dialectical, 199; Lenin and
Stalin's revisions of, 202
Maturation, 64
Maturity, various standards of, x *ff.*
Mayo, Elton, 262
Mayo, Katherine, 72
McGuffey's Readers, 26
Memory, spans distance between time and
eternity, 54; as learning, 54; as personal
identity and as social history, 104
Michigan, education in, 24 *ff.*
Militia, 246, 253
Mill, John Stuart, quoted, 144; 146, 227
Milton, John, 240, 253
Mind, and body, 151 *ff.*
Miracle, and freedom, xi
Modern errors, syllabus of, 188, 189

Molière, 300
Monopoly, religious, 188, 208, 220 *n.*
Morality, and religion, 220, 227
Morrill Act, 27, 256
Murchison, Carl, 222
Mussolini, 187 *n.*, 188, 195, 196

Nadeau Township School, 267 *ff.*
National Education Association, 40, 50
National Socialism supersedes Marxism,
195, 196
Necessity, and freedom, xi *ff.*; and luxury,
291; garbage collecting as, 311
Negativity, and dialectic, 197
Nelson, Horatio, 71
Neutrality, 247
New School for Social Research, 31
Night life, *see* Culture

Obedience, and freedom, xii
Orchestration, social, 117
Original nature, 259, 261 *ff.*
Original sin, 260, 282
Owen, Robert, 73

Paine, Thomas, 130, 132
Papen, Franz von, 194
Parker, Theodore, quoted, xiii
Pascal, Blaise, 71, 158
Peace, and war, 240; a democratic goal,
242; progress toward international, 246,
247; understanding not necessarily a
means to, 253
Pedagese, in teacher training, 42
Pedagogue, 48
Peoples, in the making of America, 106 *ff.*
Pericles, 241
Personality, xiv *ff.*; how known, 151; and
the body, 153 *ff.*; and culture, 156; psychological explanations of, 157; as passive
effect, 164; as changing, 168; democratic
view of, 169; acquired, 172; and hyphenation, 174 *ff.*, 182; and industry, 262 *ff.*;
of free man, a growth of free communications, 227; and the religious hyphen,
229; and military training, 225 *ff.*; as consumer and producer, 287 *ff.*; generalized
into labor, 289; cultural pluralist, 306
Personality-image, 151 *ff.*, 157, 158, 159,
160
Pestalozzi, 19, 63, 264, 300
Philosophy, defined, ix *ff.*; and education,
153 *ff.*, 157; natural, as knowledge which
is power, 296
Pinkevitch, Albert, 206 *n.*
Pius IX, 211
Pius X, 188, 213
Pius XI, 187 *n.*, 191, 192, 212
Plato, his educational ideal, 9; on children
under democracy, 57; "noble lies" of, 65,
238, 239, 280, 296
Pluralism, religious, 208, 209, 210
Plutarch, 238
President's Advisory Commission on Uni-
versal Military Training, recommenda-
tions of, 254 *ff.*; false premise of, 255